FROMMER'S

COMPREHENSIVE
TRAVEL GUIDE

Berlin
3rd Edition

by Beth Reiber

MACMILLAN • USA

ABOUT THE AUTHOR

Beth Reiber worked for several years in Tokyo as editor of the *Far East Traveler* and for two years in Bremen, Germany, as a freelance travel writer. Now residing in Lawrence, Kansas, she continues to write travel articles and is the author of several Frommer guides: *Japan, Tokyo, Hong Kong, Berlin on $50 a Day, Walking Tours of Berlin, Walking Tours of Tokyo,* and *St. Louis & Kansas City.* She also contributes to *Europe on $50 a Day.*

MACMILLAN TRAVEL

A Prentice Hall Macmillan Company
15 Columbus Circle
New York, NY 10023

ISBN 0-02-860046-0
ISSN 1047-787X

Design by Michele Laseau
Maps by Geografix Inc. and Ortelius Design

Contents

List of Maps

What the Symbols Mean

⭐ **FROMMER'S FAVORITES**—Hotels, restaurants, attractions, and entertainments you should not miss

💲 **SUPER-SPECIAL VALUES**—Really exceptional values

In Hotel & Other Listings

The following symbols refer to the standard amenities available in all rooms:

A/C   air conditioning
MINIBAR   refrigerator stocked with beverages and snacks
TEL   telephone
TV   television

The following abbreviations are used for credit or charge cards:

AE   American Express
CB   Carte Blanche
DC   Diners Club
DISC   Discover
ER   enRoute
EU   Eurocard
MC   MasterCard
V   Visa

Trip Planning with this Guide

Use the following features:

Calendar of Events   To plan for or avoid

Easy-to-Read Maps   Walking tours, city sights, hotel and restaurant locations—all referring to or keyed to the text

Fast Facts   All the essentials at a glance: climate, currency, embassies, emergencies, information, safety, taxes, tipping, and more

Suggested Itineraries   For seeing the city and environs

What Things Cost In   To help you plan your daily budget

What's Special About Checklist   A summary of the city's highlights

OTHER SPECIAL FROMMER FEATURES

Frommer's Smart Traveler Tips   Hints on how to secure the best value for your money

Cool for Kids   Hotels, restaurants, and attractions

Did You Know . . . ?   Offbeat, fun facts

Famous Berliners   The city's greats

Impressions   What others have said

Invitation to the Reader

In researching this book, I have come across many wonderful establishments, the best of which I have included here. However, I'm sure that many of you will also come across other appealing hotels, inns, restaurants, guesthouses, shops, and attractions. Please don't keep them to yourself. Share your experiences, especially if you want to comment on places I have covered in this edition that have changed for the worse. You can address your letters to:

Beth Reiber
Frommer's Berlin, 3rd Edition
c/o Macmillan Travel
15 Columbus Circle
New York, NY 10023

A Disclaimer

Readers are advised that prices fluctuate in the course of time and travel information changes under the impact of the varied and volatile factors that affect the travel industry. The author and publisher cannot be held responsible for the experiences of readers while traveling. Readers are invited to write to the publisher with ideas, comments, and suggestions for future editions.

1

Introducing Berlin

WITHOUT QUESTION, 1989 CAN BE HAILED AS A YEAR THAT USHERED IN A new era. That was when the Communist system began to crumble and the Wall came tumbling down, paving the way for the reunification of the two Germanys. Rarely has there been a revolution of such magnitude without widespread bloodshed and war. But East Germany's revolution of November 9, 1989, not only was completely free of violence—but also it was one of the most joyous revolutions of our time.

The focus of Germany's reunification has been, of course, Berlin, once again capital of a united Germany. For more than 40 years, Berlin was both a symbol and a victim of the Cold War, a divided city buried deep within Communist East Germany, a division made even more poignant after the erection of the Wall. More than 100 miles long and 13 feet high, the Berlin Wall was built in 1961 to stop the mass exodus of East Germans into West Berlin that was draining East Germany of its youngest, best-educated, and brightest citizens. How ironic that in 1989 it was another exodus from East to West that triggered the Wall's sudden demise.

Today, Germany is still wrestling with the challenges posed by reunification, and the euphoria caused by the Wall's collapse has long given way to grim economic and political realities, even disillusionment. Reunification is costing former West Germany more than anyone ever imagined—in former East Germany, factories and businesses have closed and unemployment has skyrocketed.

No city has been more affected by reunification than Berlin. If you visited Berlin before the Wall came down, you know how shockingly different the two sides of the city were. Many of those differences remain. Even though new hotels, restaurants, and shops have opened in the former eastern sector, much of eastern Berlin still seems like the city's poorer cousin, while western Berlin is booming like never before. There may no longer be a physical barrier between the halves, but there is still a psychological one, and Berliners still speak of "East" or "West" Berlin as though they remain two separate entities.

The city has a huge task ahead of it: to integrate two separate systems that had 40 years to develop, each with its own political, social, economic, cultural, and ideological values. Everything—from bus lines to telephone lines—has had to be coordinated or changed. Even Berlin's similar museum systems grew out of collections divided between East and West after the war, so that today Berlin contains two Egyptian museums, two historical museums, two museums of modern art, and two museums of European masterpieces. It also has two city centers, two major opera houses, three airports, and two universities! And that's only the tip of the iceberg.

But history has taught Berlin to adapt quickly, and the city is busily piecing itself back together even as I write this. Visitors from around the globe are flocking to see Berlin without the Wall, making the capital one of the most popular travel destinations in Germany, and the entire city is once again the lively, crowded, and vibrant place it

What's Special About Berlin

Museums

- The Pergamon Museum in East Berlin, with the Pergamon Altar, Market Gate of Miletus, Babylonian Processional Street, and other architectural wonders.
- The Gemäldegalerie in Dahlem, with 20-plus Rembrandts among other masterpieces.
- The Ägyptisches Museum, with the bust of Nefertiti.
- The Neue Nationalgalerie and Nationalgalerie, for outstanding collections of Berliner impressionist and expressionist artists.
- Museum Haus am Checkpoint Charlie, a small but important museum documenting the history of the Wall and nonviolent revolutions around the world.

Nightlife

- Famous opera houses and concert halls, including the Deutsche Oper Berlin and the Philharmonie.
- Cabarets, a Berlin tradition.
- Live-music houses, featuring jazz, rock, folk, and international stars on tour.
- Bars and pubs that stay open all night long.
- Discos and dance halls for all ages.

Shopping

- KaDeWe, the largest department store on the European continent; famous for its food floor.
- Ku'damm, one of Europe's most fashionable streets—great for window-shopping.
- Europa-Center, a large mall with 70 shops, restaurants, and bars.
- More than 100 art galleries.
- Outdoor and indoor markets, a treasure trove for antiques, junk, and crafts.

Festivals

- International Film Festival, held every February.
- Jazz-Fest Berlin in autumn, a colorful mix of avant-garde and classical jazz, with musicians from around the world.
- Weihnachtsmarkt, an annual Christmas market, held around the Ku'damm.

Diversity

- A large ethnic population, including Turks and Greeks.
- Colorful neighborhoods, including Kreuzberg with its Turkish population, working-class Köpenick, and Dahlem with its middle-class homes.
- Restaurants featuring cuisines from around the world: Greek, Turkish, Italian, Japanese, Chinese, Indian, Thai.

used to be. Berlin has always been Germany's least provincial city, liberal, tolerant, and open-minded, with a distinct "live for today" attitude only partly created by years of living with the Wall. No wonder it's always been a magnet for Germans seeking alternative lifestyles, as well as for young Europeans, who generally overlook Germany in favor of the more easygoing atmosphere of Paris, Amsterdam, or Copenhagen or the warm beaches of Greece. Of course, it doesn't hurt that the bars of Berlin stay open all night long. Its nightlife is one of the best in Europe.

But more than anything else, Berlin has inherited a rich cultural legacy. Not only does it have some of the best museums in the world—with treasures such as the bust of Nefertiti and the magnificent Pergamon Altar—but also opera, theater, symphony, jazz, international film premieres, and much, much more. And with the opening up of eastern Europe, it also serves as a perfect gateway to other destinations, especially the eastern half of Germany, Poland, and the Czech Republic.

In short, this is a great time to visit Berlin, as it forges ahead to a new beginning. It gives me indescribable pleasure to write about a Berlin that is whole again, about a Wall that is now history. The wonder of future generations will be that there ever was a Wall at all.

1   Geography & People

Geography

Berlin lies in the geographical center of Europe, about halfway between Moscow and Lisbon. It shares the same latitude with London and Vancouver, the same longitude with Naples. With almost 3.5 million people and a total area of 340 square miles, it is Germany's largest city. In fact, it's larger than New York City and could easily accommodate the cities of Atlanta, Boston, Cleveland, and San Francisco within its boundaries. Western Berlin alone has 60 square miles of woods, lakes, rivers, and parks, which served as an important breathing space for its dwellers during the decades of the Wall. Berlin is 184 miles from Hamburg, 343 miles from Frankfurt, and 363 miles from Munich. After the division of Germany following World War II, Berlin was more than 100 miles inside East Germany, closer to Poland (60 miles) than to West Germany (100 miles).

People

No one could ever accuse the Germans of being too lighthearted or frivolous. Indeed, they rank as among the most reserved people in Europe. They take pleasure in neatness, precision, and the established order of things, and even their language has changed little over the centuries. Instead of creating new words for new concepts or objects, for example, the Germans are more apt to string together words they already know.

There's little doubt that Berliners are German through and through; they are even Prussian on top of that, making them almost more German than the Germans. Still, differences between eastern and western Berliners remain. West Berliners, after decades of living within the confines of the Wall and the uncertainty posed by an encircling hostile regime, developed a distinct "live for today" philosophy about life and were known for being much more bohemian and liberal than their compatriots in other German cities.

Berlin's liberal climate was further enhanced by policies of the West German government. To encourage young West Germans to live in this metropolitan outpost, residents were granted generous housing subsidies and exemption from military service, thereby attracting artists, activists, rebels, and others in search of alternative lifestyles. Because of its isolation, the city identified itself more with Paris and New York than with the much more staid Munich or Hamburg.

Thus, when the Wall came down and the initial jubilation wore off, East Berliners came as something of a shock to the liberal west Berliners. Unmistakable with their sputtering Trabant automobiles and Eastern Bloc clothing, East Germans seemed so serious, so naive, so obedient to authority—so German—and also slightly backward. But West Berlin was no less shocking to East Berliners, with its decadent nightlife, drugs, and unabashed pursuit of capitalism. West Berliners were seen as arrogant and greedy; East Berliners began feeling like second-class citizens and suffered a loss of self-esteem.

It will take time to resolve all the differences, but there's no mistaking the fact that those differences are shrinking daily. Even now, it's not always easy to tell which side of the city a Berliner hails from— and surely the day will come when citizens of eastern and western Berlin are known once again as simply Berliners.

After all, Berliners are bound together by certain characteristics that are thoroughly and unmistakably German. They have what's called *Schnauze,* a Texas-like attitude that says everything in Berlin is bigger and better—a trait they share with the Bavarians. According to one joke that recently made the rounds, a Bavarian boasted that Bavaria was better than Berlin because it contained the Alps. He then smugly asked a Berliner whether Berlin had any mountains that compared.

"No," answered the Berliner calmly, looking his rival squarely in the eyes. "But if we did, you can be sure they'd be higher than yours."

IMPRESSIONS

Take, for instance, the Prussians: they are saints when compared with the French. They have every sort of excellence; they are honest, sober, hardworking, well instructed, brave, good sons, husbands, and fathers and yet . . . all with whom I have been thrown were proud as Scotchmen, cold as New Englanders, and touchy as only Prussians can be.
—Henry Labouchère, 1871

Along with their dry wit and humor, Berliners have a penchant to nickname everything in sight. The Kongresshalle, for example, built as the American contribution in a 1957 architectural competition, is irreverently called the "pregnant oyster," while the new church next to the Gedächtniskirche is known as the "lipstick and powder puff," a large global fountain in front of the Europa-Center is the "wet dumpling," and the Television Tower on Alexanderplatz is the "tele-asparagus."

Another distinct characteristic of Berlin is that it contains the largest non-German population of any German city. One of the first and biggest tides of immigration brought the Huguenots fleeing France in the 17th century, followed by Poles, Silesians, and East Prussians in Imperial times. After World War II, Turkish, Yugoslavian, Greek, and Polish immigrants found homes and ready employment in Berlin. Turks are the largest minority in Berlin, numbering more than 100,000 and living mainly in the western precincts of Kreuzberg, Neukölln, and Wedding. Since the fall of Communism in eastern Europe, Berlin has been a magnet for refugees.

Today, foreign nationals make up more than 10% of Berlin's total residents; 20% of all children under six have parents with foreign passports. Although problems do arise because of differences in customs and cultural backgrounds, occasionally escalating to animosity and violence toward foreign workers and their families, on the whole Berlin enjoys greater racial harmony than many parts of Germany. Decades of isolation have helped forge a sense of community spirit, and years of living with the Wall have bred tolerance and determination.

FAMOUS BERLINERS

Otto von Bismarck   (1815–98) Known as the Iron Chancellor, Bismarck was a brilliant politician who succeeded in uniting all of Germany in 1871 and became the empire's first chancellor. Although he was dismissed from office by Kaiser Wilhelm II in 1890, Bismarck remained a popular figure in Berlin.

Willy Brandt   (1913–92) A prominent and popular member of the Social Democratic Party (SPD), Brandt served as mayor of Berlin from 1957 to 1966, weathering such critical events as the construction of the Wall. In 1969 he became chancellor of West Germany and received the Nobel Peace Prize in 1971; in 1974, however, he stepped down after the uncovering of an espionage ring caused as much uproar in Germany as Watergate did in the United States.

Bertolt Brecht   (1898–1956) One of Germany's best-known playwrights, Brecht came to Berlin in 1920, working with Max Reinhardt at the Deutsches Theater. An ardent Marxist, Brecht wrote epic dramas that scorned the materialistic self-absorption of the upper class and underscored the plight of the poor and the working class. In 1928 he achieved fame with the success of his *Dreigroschenoper (Threepenny Opera)*. Other well-known plays include *Mother Courage and Her Children* and *The Good Woman of Szechuan*. In 1933 Brecht left the city, but after the war he returned to East Berlin, where he founded his own theater, the famous Berliner Ensemble, which continues to stage his works.

Friedrich II, Frederick the Great   (1712–86) The third and most well known king of Prussia, Friedrich at first rebelled at the idea of becoming king and tried to flee to England with an army officer. However, he was caught and punished by his father, known as the strict Soldier King, by being forced to watch the beheading of his friend (who, so the story goes, was also his lover). Friedrich went on to double the size of the Prussian army and build the charming Sanssouci Palace in Potsdam. An advocate of the Enlightenment, he was also a composer and musician.

Walter Gropius   (1883–1969) Born in Berlin, Gropius studied architecture not only there but also in Munich. In 1919 he became director of the Weimar School of Art, which he reorganized into the legendary Bauhaus. From 1928 to 1934 he worked as an architect in Berlin, immigrating in 1934 to England and then in 1937 to the United States, where he worked as a professor at Harvard University until 1952. Among his accomplishments in Berlin are an apartment building he designed in the Hansaviertel as part of a 1957 international competition and the Bauhaus-Archiv, which was built after his death, according to his designs.

Heinrich von Kleist   (1777–1811) Kleist, who served for a time in the Prussian army, wrote a number of short stories and plays, including *Der Zebrochene Krug* (*The Broken Pitcher*) and *Prinz Friedrich von Homburg*. Throughout his life, however, Kleist was plagued with depression and restlessness, causing him to leave and return to Berlin many times. He ended up taking his own life on the shores of Wannsee Lake on the outskirts of Berlin.

Georg Wenzeslaus von Knobelsdorff   (1699–1753) After studying in Italy, Paris, Spain, and Dresden, Knobelsdorff went on to become one of Germany's leading rococo architects. A friend of Frederick the Great, he actualized sketches drawn by Frederick for Schloss Sanssouci in Potsdam, which today remains Knobelsdorff's greatest achievement. He also designed the Deutsche Staatsoper (destroyed by fire in 1843) on Unter den Linden in East Berlin. A noted landscape architect, he laid out the Sanssouci park.

Käthe Kollwitz   (1867–1945) A Berliner, Kollwitz was a gifted graphic artist, painter, and sculptress who sought to capture such emotions as tenderness, despair, grief, and happiness in her studies of common Berliners, particularly those of the working class. See her works at the Käthe-Kollwitz-Museum on Fasanenstrasse near the Ku'damm.

Max Liebermann   (1847–1935) Liebermann, a painter and graphic artist who was born and died in Berlin, is considered the main representative of impressionism in Germany. He was founder and president of the Secession movement, a group of artists concerned with developing their own impressionist style. His works are on display in the Neue Nationalgalerie in Tiergarten and the Alte Nationalgalerie on Museumsinsel.

Adolph von Menzel   (1815–1905) A painter, a graphic artist, a draftsman, and an illustrator, the self-taught Menzel is credited with anticipating impressionism in his paintings of the 1840s and 1850s. He gained fame and popularity in many Berlin circles through his portraits and was known to frequent the city's lively cafes. The Neue Nationalgalerie in Tiergarten contains the world's largest collection of this Berliner artist.

Otto Nagel   (1894–1967) Nagel became one of the main representatives of proletarian art in Germany, with realistic portraits of Berlin's working class figuring importantly in his output. Dating mainly from the 1920s and 1930s, his works are on display at the Otto-Nagel-Haus in East Berlin.

Max Reinhardt   (1873–1943) Reinhardt, one of the legendary names in German theater, is credited with introducing German-language theater to the rest of the world. He served as director of the Deutsches Theater from 1905 to 1920 and again from 1924 to 1932. Reinhardt also founded the renowned Salzburg Festival.

Karl Friedrich Schinkel   (1781–1841) Schinkel was a gifted artist whose talents went beyond architecture—he worked as a landscape painter and stage designer in addition to pursuing a career as an architect, for which he received his training in Berlin. His works include the Neue Wache (New Guardhouse) on Unter den Linden, which today houses a memorial to victims of fascism and militarism, and the Alte Museum on Museumsinsel (Museum Island); the latter resembles a Greek temple. Particularly delightful is his summerhouse behind Schloss Charlottenburg, built in the style of an Italian villa and known today as the Schinkel Pavilion.

Andreas Schlüter   (1660–1714) Schlüter, Berlin's top baroque architect, is credited with giving the city a royal physical presence. Also a sculptor, he was greatly influenced by Michelangelo and Italian baroque sculpture during a trip to Italy in 1696; in fact, Schlüter is best known for his 21 masks of dying warriors in the courtyard of the Arsenal on Unter den Linden (now the Museum of German History) and his equestrian statue of the Great Elector that now sits in the forecourt of Schloss Charlottenburg. As the court architect, he rebuilt the palace (no longer in existence), but fell out of favor when a tower he designed collapsed.

Heinrich Zille   (1858–1929) Zille is known for his sketches and caricatures of turn-of-the-century life in Berlin, including those depicting the poor and working class. Having come from a poor family himself, he had an eye for the absurd and the comic and contributed regularly to satirical journals. Zille's works can be seen at the Berlin Museum in Kreuzberg.

2 History & Politics

MEDIEVAL TOWN TO ROYAL CAPITAL

As ironic as it now seems, Berlin started out as a divided city back in the 12th century, when two settlements were founded on opposite sides of the Spree River. Located about halfway between the fortresses of Spandau and Köpenick, Berlin and Cölln developed as trading towns, spreading along the banks of the Spree in what is now Berlin-Mitte. Convenient stopovers on a much-traveled trade route, Berlin and Cölln cleverly required all traveling tradesman who passed through to offer their merchandise for sale, giving the towns' merchants an opportunity to purchase rye, wool, oak, hides, fur, and other goods and then export them as far afield as Hamburg, Flanders, and even England. Both towns grew and prospered, and although their citizens were not particularly interested in unifying, it eventually became inevitable. In 1307 they merged under the name of Berlin and built a joint town hall. Berlin also joined the powerful Hanseatic League, a protective commercial federation of free towns along the Baltic Sea.

Throughout the next century, Berlin fell under the rule of various dynasties and suffered repeated attacks by robber barons. In desperation, Berlin finally appealed for protection to the Holy Roman Emperor in 1411. To the rescue came Graf (Count) Friedrich von Nürnberg from the Hohenzollern house in Nuremberg, and by 1414 he had defeated the most notorious robber barons of the day. Once he had completed his task, however, Graf Friedrich decided not to leave and instead proclaimed himself the prince elector of Brandenburg, thus taking control of Berlin and surrounding Brandenburg. Although the people of Berlin revolted against the Hohenzollern takeover, their rebellion was easily quashed: In 1470 Berlin lost the freedom it had enjoyed as an independent trading town and became the official residence of the elector of

Dateline

- **1200** Two settlements. Berlin and Cölln, grow up along the Spree River.
- **1237** Cölln, first mentioned in documents.
- **1244** Berlin first mentioned in documents.
- **1307** Berlin and Cölln unite and build a joint town hall.
- **1415** Graf Friedrich von Nürnberg of the house of Hohenzollern becomes Friedrich I, prince elector of Brandenburg.
- **1470** Berlin becomes the official residence of the electors of Brandenburg.
- **1539** Prince Elector Joachim II converts to Protestantism, and the Reformation comes to Berlin.
- **1618–48** The Thirty Years' War reduces Brandenburg's population by half.
- **1640–88** Reign of Prince Elector Friedrich Wilhelm II, known as the Great Elector.
- **1685** The Great Elector invites 6,000 Huguenots from France to settle in Berlin.
- **1701** Prince Elector Friedrich III crowns ➤

Brandenburg. (The German word for "elector," by the way, is *Kurfürst,* which literally means "choosing prince," one who has the right to elect the emperor.)

The Hohenzollerns ruled from Berlin for the next 500 years, during which time this town of merchants evolved into a city of civil servants and government administrators. Setting the social tone were the elector's courtiers and officials, who had an unabashed fondness for lavish festivities and feasts. To curb the wild consumption of alcohol and the loose morals that gradually filtered down from the privileged to the lower classes, the authorities responded in a typically Prussian manner by issuing decrees against drunkenness and disturbing the peace. They even placed restrictions on the types of clothing each social class was allowed to wear. Nevertheless, from 1450 to 1600 the population grew from 6,000 to 12,000. But then came the plague, smallpox, and the destructive Thirty Years' War (1618–48). Fought between Protestants and Catholics, the war destroyed half the city's population. Luckily for Berlin, however, Friedrich Wilhelm II came to power in 1640; one of the city's most able rulers, he gained great popularity after defeating the Swedes in the decisive battle of Fehrbellin in the Thirty Years' War. To this day he is still known as the Great Elector. To bolster the town's economy, in 1685 he invited 6,000 Huguenots—French Protestants, who were forced to flee religious persecution—to settle in Berlin. By 1700 nearly one Berliner in five was of French extraction.

In 1701 the Great Elector's son, Prince Elector Friedrich III, crowned himself the first king of Prussia and became Friedrich I. Up until then, Prussia had been only a duchy under the rule of electors. In 1709 the Prussian king merged Berlin and several surrounding towns into one community, declared Berlin his royal residence, and made it the royal capital of Brandenburg-Prussia.

On the whole, however, Friedrich I was an unpopular and unloved king. Mocked for his vanity, he nevertheless did have the insight to marry the beautiful and intelligent Sophie Charlotte, who was adored by the masses. An ardent advocate of intellectual and spiritual growth, she built a small summer residence where she could entertain some of the great minds of the age. Upon nearing death at age 36, she said she was ready to see what the afterlife had in store. As for her husband, she predicted that her death and subsequent funeral would provide him with another "opportunity to demonstrate his magnificence." She was right: Friedrich enlarged the palace and named it for her. Today Schloss Charlottenburg remains the finest example of baroque architecture in Berlin.

During the 18th century, Berlin became the most important political, economic, and cultural center of the area. The town, which blossomed under the skillful talents of such well-known architects as Andreas Schlüter, Karl Friedrich Schinkel, and Georg Wenzeslaus von Knobelsdorff, grew by leaps and bounds. In a flurry of activity, the royal palace (later destroyed in World War II) was enlarged; the boulevard of Unter den Linden was laid out; the Brandenburger Tor (Brandenburg Gate) and 12 other city gates were built; and such buildings as the Supreme Court (now the Berlin Museum), the Opera, and the Arsenal were completed.

But the man credited with elevating Berlin to one of Europe's premier capitals was Friedrich II, better known as Frederick the Great, who reigned from 1740 to 1786. During his reign he doubled the size of the Prussian army and made Prussia the greatest military power in Europe. An enlightened administrator, he instituted many social reforms and encouraged improvements in industry and encouraged improvements in industry and agriculture. He also built a charming summer residence in nearby Potsdam, Schloss Sanssouci, where he could escape from time to time.

Dateline

- **1920** Greater Berlin is formed and subdivided into 20 precincts.
- **1933** Hitler and the National Socialists come into power; the Third Reich begins.
- **1936** Jesse Owens, an African-American athlete, wins in the 11th Summer Olympics held in Berlin.
- **1939** Hitler invades Poland, beginning World War II.
- **1945** The German army surrenders. Berlin is divided into four zones occupied by the Four Powers.
- **1948** Eleven-month Berlin Blockade. Berlin Airlift supplies West Berlin.
- **1949** Founding of the German Democratic Republic (DDR), with East Berlin as its capital.
- **1961** Construction of the Wall begins on August 13, sealing off the Western Sector.
- **1963** President John F. Kennedy visits Berlin, pledging support of a free West Berlin.
- **1971** Allies sign the Four-Power Agreement on Berlin, confirming political and legal ties between West

➤

Dateline

Berlin and West Germany.

- **1972** West Berliners are allowed to visit East Germany.
- **1987** 750th anniversary of Berlin, celebrated in both parts of the city.
- **1988** Berlin is declared the Cultural City of Europe.
- **1989** Hungary opens its borders to allow East Germans to go to the West. On November 9 the Wall is opened by the East German government. The Wall itself is dismantled.
- **1990** East Germany adopts West German currency and drops all visa requirements for entering East Berlin.
- **1990** Reunification takes place on October 3.
- **1991** Berlin is made capital.

Under Frederick the Great, Berlin became a mecca for the Enlightenment, attracting the philosopher Moses Mendelsohn; the author Gotthold Ephraim Lessing; the publisher Friedrich Nicolai; and the philosopher Voltaire, who came to Potsdam as the king's guest and stayed three years. In 1763 Friedrich took over a failing porcelain company and gave it a production monopoly, banning all foreign imports. The company, the Königliche Porzellan-Manufaktur (KPM), is still well known today. By 1800 Berlin boasted 200,000 inhabitants, making it the third-largest city in Europe after London and Paris.

On October 27, 1806, Napoleon marched into the capital of Prussia, entering triumphantly through the Brandenburger Tor. As part of the spoils from his victory over Prussia, he removed the Quadriga—a chariot drawn by four horses, the symbol of Berlin—from atop the gate and carted it off to Paris. This struck at the very heart of the proud Prussians, who finally managed to rout the French a couple of years later. They recovered their Quadriga, added an Iron Cross and a Prussian Eagle, and replaced it atop the Brandenburger Tor.

In the 1800s, as the tidal wave of the Industrial Revolution swept across Europe, Berlin emerged as a center of trade and industry, producing silk, woolens, porcelain, and machinery. Many of the city's working class, however, found themselves left behind in a wake of increasing poverty and destitution. Although educational reform and abolition of serfdom helped to alleviate the poor person's lot, life for a majority of the people remained a struggle for survival. Peasants flocked into Berlin hoping to find work, and women and children were exploited in dismal factories. The middle class, meanwhile, demanded political power in keeping with their newly acquired social status. Although there were several revolts, notably the March Revolution of 1848, few concessions were gained. By the 1870s, 70,000 out of a population of 826,000 were homeless. Even those with a roof over their heads often lived in gloomy and depressing flats that never saw the light of day. As many as one-tenth of the total population lived in basements; one-third lived in one-room apartments that averaged 4.3 occupants. Berlin had the dubious distinction of being the world's largest tenement city.

FROM CAPITAL OF THE GERMAN REICH TO CAPITAL OF THE THIRD REICH In 1871 Otto von Bismarck, the Prussian chancellor, succeeded in uniting all of Germany with a nationalist policy under the slogan "iron and blood." Berlin became the capital of this new German Empire, attracting even more industry and settlers; by 1906 the city had 2 million inhabitants. After the turn of the century Berlin began to challenge Munich as the country's cultural capital, attracting such artists as Max Liebermann, Lovis Corinth, and Max Slevogt. Ornate apartment dwellings sprang up, sprouting the intricate lines of art nouveau. Max Reinhardt came to Berlin to take over as director of the Deutsches Theater, and Richard Strauss became conductor of the Royal Opera.

In 1920 Berlin incorporated 7 formerly autonomous towns, 59 rural communities, and 27 landed estates to form a Greater Berlin, which was then divided into 20 precincts. This made Berlin the Continent's industrial giant, the nucleus of the North German railway network, and a major commercial, banking, and stock-exchange center. Throughout the golden '20s, Berlin continued to flourish as an avant-garde intellectual and cultural center, and such architectural greats as Walter Gropius and Hans Scharoun left their marks on the city. In 1926 a young playwright named Bertolt Brecht scored a huge success with the premiere of his *Dreigroschenoper (Threepenny Opera)*. Altogether there were 35 theaters, several opera houses, and more than 20 concert halls. Berlin's university gained a reputation as one of the best in the country, and Albert Einstein, who was director of physics at what would later become the Max-Planck Institute, received the Nobel Prize in 1921. As many as 150 daily and weekly newspapers were published in Berlin.

However, underneath the glittering facade, trouble was brewing. The woes of the working class had become increasingly acute, and the general feeling of despair and hopelessness was captured by such artists as Käthe Kollwitz and Heinrich Zille and writer Kurt Tucholsky. Like the rest of Germany, Berlin had suffered hardships during World War I, including a weekly rationing of one egg, 20 grams of butter, and 80 grams of meat per person. Heating fuel, lighting, and clothing were rationed as well. But the end of the war brought little relief, even though the emperor had abdicated and Germany was proclaimed a republic. Parts of the country were sliced off and given to the victors, and Germany was saddled with huge war reparations. In the winter of 1918–19 there were 300,000 people out of work in Berlin alone. To make matters worse, inflation had reached such grotesque proportions that money was virtually worthless: It took barrelfuls just to buy a loaf of bread. When new bank notes were finally issued, one new bank note equaled 1,000 billion of the worthless old paper marks.

In the crisis, sections of the middle class were wiped out, and extremist factions were strengthened. There were struggles between extreme rightists and leftists, often resulting in street fights, brawls, militant strikes, and bloody riots. As Germany began to move toward recovery, the Great Depression hit in 1929. The economic crisis went from bad to worse, with 636,000 unemployed in Berlin by the end of 1932. Many families lost their jobs and their homes; some people committed suicide.

Little wonder that an obscure political party called the National Socialists arose from the ashes of World War I and gained followers with promises of making Germany great again. On January 30, 1933, Adolf Hitler became chancellor of Germany. Hitler had risen to power in Munich, and he knew he was not a popular figure in Berlin—his Nazi party had been consistently defeated in elections here. One of his first moves, therefore, was to rid "Red Berlin" of its leftist majority. First, Berlin's Communist Party headquarters were raided by police on the pretense that the party had planned a coup d'état. Then, on the night of February 27, 1933, the Reichstag building was mysteriously set on fire. Although no one ever proved who set the fire—indeed, some people think it was the Nazis themselves—hundreds of Communists, Social Democrats, trade unionists, and intellectuals were rounded up, imprisoned, tortured, and even murdered.

But the reign of terror had only just begun, and after 20,000 books by German authors were publicly burned in a Berlin square in May 1933, the country's best writers left the country. Scientists soon followed. On November 9, 1938, Berlin was the scene of the so-called Kristallnacht (literally "Crystal Night," the night of broken glass), a wave of terror directed against Jews. The streets were filled with the sound of shattering windows as synagogues and Jewish businesses were ransacked and/or burned to the ground. During the next years, as many as 50,000 Berliners of Jewish faith died in concentration camps. By the time Germany invaded Poland in 1939 and catapulted Europe into another world war, it had rid itself of virtually all opposition.

POSTWAR BERLIN On May 8, 1945, the German army surrendered. Berlin had suffered heavy casualties and was virtually destroyed in World War II. The legacy the "Thousand-Year Reich" left behind was a wasteland of ruin. Of the 245,000 buildings in Berlin before the war, 50,000 were destroyed. As many as 80,000 Berliners had lost their lives. Of the 160,000 Jews who had lived in Berlin before 1933, only 7,247 remained. At first, peace brought little relief. There were food and fuel shortages, and anyone who had anything to sell resorted to the black market. Berliners laden with furs and jewelry headed for farms in the country, trying to barter luxuries for food. Even drinking water had to be brought in from the country. Fuel was so scarce that all the trees were cut down along the streets and in city parks so people wouldn't freeze to death.

Yet soon Berliners were at work clearing away the rubble, too busy trying to survive and create a livable world to worry about what might happen tomorrow. But their fate had been sealed even before the end of the war—the Allies had divided Germany and Berlin into occupation zones to be governed by Great Britain, the United States, the Soviet Union, and, later, France. Although each Allied Power had supreme authority in its own zone in Germany, Berlin was to be ruled jointly. This proved easier said than done, however.

In the summer of 1945 Churchill, Truman, and Stalin converged on Potsdam, where they agreed to disarm and demilitarize Germany. There was never any intention to split the country in half or change Berlin's role as capital. Rather, they agreed that Nazism must be abolished and that local self-government should be set up on a democratic basis. But they had no plans for how things should proceed and differing ideas of what constituted a democracy. And as time went on, political aims and ideological differences between the Soviet and Western powers became more evident.

When elections were held for Berlin's Municipal Assembly in October 1946, the Social Democrats (SPD) won almost half the votes, while the Socialist Unity party, the Soviet-sponsored Communist party, garnered only 19.8%, clearly a rejection by the majority. In 1948 the introduction of the deutsche mark (DM) by the Western Powers delineated a financial separation between their zones and East Germany, strengthening West Berlin's ties with West Germany.

As far as the Soviets were concerned, Berlin, with a growing democratic following, was becoming a dangerous thorn in their side. In retaliation, they introduced their own currency and declared it legal tender throughout all Berlin. They then imposed a road blockade of Berlin. Since food, raw materials, and necessities for 2 million people came from West Germany, the only alternative was to fly in supplies. Gen. Lucius D. Clay, who organized the Berlin Airlift, called the blockade "one of the most brutal attempts in recent history to use mass starvation as a means of applying political pressure."

Although some Berliners did respond to offers of food from the East, the majority preferred to bear hardship rather than come under Soviet influence. On June 26, 1948, the largest airlift in history began, and within weeks 4,000 tons of supplies were being flown into Berlin daily; Tegel Airport was built in only three months. At the peak of the airlift, a plane was landing every one to two minutes, and in April 1949 a record was set when nearly 13,000 tons of supplies were flown in on a single day. During the eleven months the airlift lasted, more than 200,000 flights had brought in 1.7 million tons of supplies.

The Soviets had hoped the blockade would prove the end of Western influence in Berlin, but instead it drew the Western Powers together, formed a bond of friendship between Berliners and the West, and convinced the Western Powers they must remain in Berlin to defend their concept of freedom. Soon thereafter, the Municipal Assembly and the City Council, which had had their seats in the

IMPRESSIONS

All free men, wherever they live, are citizens of Berlin, and therefore, as a free man, I take pride in the words, "Ich bin ein Berliner."
—John F. Kennedy, 1963

eastern sector, moved to the western sector. The Communists responded by appointing their own City Council. The city was now divided, politically and ideologically. From then on, each part of the city followed its own course of development. In 1949 East Berlin became capital of the German Democratic Republic (GDR). In 1952 telephone communications between the two cities were cut off, tram and bus lines were severed, and West Berliners were no longer allowed into the surrounding East German countryside. However, there was still unrestricted movement throughout Berlin, with many East Berliners working in the western sectors. In 1955 West Germany became a member of NATO; East Germany, a member of the Warsaw Pact. The Cold War was on.

And yet hardly anyone could imagine that a divided Germany was anything but temporary. As far as West Germany was concerned, its goal was reunification and the reestablishment of Berlin as capital. An uprising of East German workers on June 17, 1953, which was brutally quashed by Soviet soldiers, only reconfirmed West Germany's commitment.

Meanwhile, Berlin began to grow and prosper. Whereas 300,000 Berliners were unemployed in 1950, the number decreased to 90,000 just seven years later. Since Berliners could travel freely throughout the city, many East Berliners flocked to factories in West Berlin. Housing estates mushroomed, replacing homes that had been destroyed in the war. In 1957 West Berlin hosted a competition that brought 50 leading architects from around the world to design housing for the Hansaviertel (Hansa Quarter). Clearly, West Berlin was recovering much more rapidly than East Germany, and it soon became an attraction for East Germans eager for a look at the new Berlin. Many of them decided to stay, including skilled specialists. In fact, East Germany was losing people to the West in unprecedented numbers: from 1949 to 1961, approximately 3 million East Germans left their country.

In November 1958 Nikita Khrushchev issued the Berlin Ultimatum, demanding that the Western Powers withdraw from West Berlin. Since Berlin was seen as an important player in the "domino theory" of Communist takeovers, the Western Powers refused.

THE WALL   On August 13, 1961, East Germany began erecting a wall between East and West Berlin by tearing up streets and putting up posts and barbed wire. A few days later the wall was reinforced with concrete and brick. Movement between the two Berlins was now forbidden, leaving families and friends separated by what soon became known around the world simply as the Wall. Measuring 13 feet high and approximately 100 miles long, the Wall was backed up by hundreds of guardhouses, 293 sentry towers, patrol dogs, and a vast swath of brightly illuminated no-man's-land. However, that didn't completely stop the East German exodus; approximately 5,000 of them managed to escape to West Berlin, most during the early years, when the Wall was not yet perfected; 78 people lost their lives trying to do so.

For 28 years the Wall stood as a constant reminder of Germany's forced division. Even for visitors, the shock of seeing the Wall for the first time was chilling, a feeling that intensified at border control points such as Checkpoint Charlie. Mirrors were shoved under cars to make sure no one was hiding underneath; travelers on foot were shuttled through doors that clanged shut behind them, as though they were entering a high-security prison. The difference between the two Berlins became more radical over time. West Berlin was a capitalist's dream—intense, aggressive, and chaotic, a whirling blend of traffic, people, neon, and noise. East Berlin, on the other hand, was conservative and subdued, sterile and quiet, with soldiers everywhere. The contrast was like night and day.

In 1971 the Four Powers signed an agreement that confirmed political and legal ties between West Berlin and West Germany. Telephone communications between the two Berlins were restored, and West Berliners were allowed to visit East Germany. For the next 18 years, conditions between East and West improved steadily. However, Westerners traveling into East Germany were required to exchange a minimum amount of Western currency into East German marks, and travel was still complicated and difficult for non-Germans.

In autumn of 1989 Hungary dismantled its borders to the West and allowed East Germans to pass through. This prompted a full-scale exodus, as tens of thousands of East Germans poured into Hungary on their way to the West. Pro-reform demonstrations began throughout East Germany, resulting in the ouster of hard-line East German leader Erich Honecker on October 18. By November 1989 approximately 175,000 East German refugees had fled their homeland, almost 1% of the country's total population. It was clear something had to be done to staunch the flow. But no one dreamed the Wall itself would fall.

On the evening of November 9, 1989, East Germany announced that it was permanently lifting travel restrictions on its citizens, giving them freedom to travel for the first time since the Wall was erected in 1961. That evening 50,000 East Berliners streamed into West Berlin and were welcomed on the other side with embraces and tears. Many Berliners climbed on top of the Wall to dance and celebrate.

A teacher working in West Berlin recalled what it was like in those first heady days of the Wall's opening: "On Friday [November 10] I went to the school where I work, but the director decided to cancel all classes, because history was being made in the streets and the children should see it. So I went to Potsdamer Square, and the whole experience was so emotional, so strange, that I had goosebumps several times that day. We watched the East Berliners come through the opening in the Wall. The first ones seemed very unsure of themselves, as though they still didn't believe they could. They came slowly, with big eyes. Some of them, especially the older ones, wept. It was as if they were being let out of prison after so many years."

FROM 1990 TO THE PRESENT   Soon after the Wall came down, West Germany reiterated its dedication to reunification, and East German elections held on March 18, 1990, signaled the official demise of the Communist regime. Reunification of the two Germanys followed on October 3, 1990. Berlin became Germany's capital, with the seat of government remaining for the time being in Bonn.

As the jubilation of reunification wore off, new problems began to surface, causing fears about the future in both East and West. After all, by March 1990, as many as 500,000 East Germans had settled in the West, entitling them to "adjustment money," household compensation, housing subsidies, and job retraining. In keeping with a policy that had been established years before, any East German coming into West Germany for the first time, even for a day, was entitled to a welcoming token of 100 DM ($59), but the West German government had never dreamed that virtually the entire country would come over to get it. Many West Germans began worrying about the financial burdens of reunification, especially the cost of East German economic development. Many also felt that East Germans expected too much too soon and that if East Germans wanted a more affluent lifestyle, they should have to work hard to achieve it, just as the West Germans had.

East Germans, on the other hand, were concerned about their ability to compete in a capitalist society, the impact of materialism on their youth, the sudden and previously unheard-of influx of drugs, and their treatment economically and socially as second-class citizens. They worried about the loss of the old regime's cradle-to-grave benefits, such as controlled rents, job security, and old-age pensions. Many, especially those who had envisioned reunification as an opportunity to combine the best of socialism and democracy, felt powerless in the wave of new laws and reforms that drowned the very values they thought worth saving. Some went so far as to describe reunification as a hostile takeover.

With the closing of noncompetitive, formerly subsidized enterprises, unemployment skyrocketed. By the end of 1991, unemployment in former East Germany had risen to 11%. Many people are still jobless today, especially East Germany's youths. The problem has been compounded by waves of foreign asylum seekers entering Germany in record numbers (climbing from 57,000 in 1987 to 500,000 in 1992), some of whom have been victims of attacks by right-wing extremists.

Berlin faces the challenge of integrating two systems that have existed side by side for decades. Pitied for years as a victim of the Cold War, it must also deal with ghosts from the past, as neighbors of reunified Germany remember it as capital of the Third Reich.

For the moment, however, Berlin is too self-engrossed with its own problems and challenges to worry much what others think. Investors have flocked to the capital, real estate prices have skyrocketed, and major companies are scrambling to get a piece of the newly created economic pie.

The future will certainly be one of change, especially in eastern Berlin as sorely needed hotels, restaurants, and service-oriented businesses set up shop. By 2000, Bonn is expected to relinquish its role as administrative center, with the government and parliament moving to Berlin. So the story of Berlin, one of the most compelling and riveting of our time, is still being written.

3   Art, Architecture & Cultural Life

Home of the Deutsche Oper and the Staatsoper, the Berlin Philharmonic Orchestra, and more than 80 museums, Berlin is Germany's cultural capital. Visually, however, it's a new city, with little remaining after the destruction of World War II. Its oldest buildings, for example, are actually reconstructions. Thus, even the Nikolaikirche and the Marienkirche, considered the city's oldest structures, have been either rebuilt or renovated. The Berlin Palace, a sumptuous Renaissance residence for the Prussian kings, was deemed by the East German government to be irreparably damaged and was torn down to make way for East Berlin's modern Palace of the Republic.

Fortunately, not all of Berlin is new. Schloss Charlottenburg, built by Friedrich I as the summer residence for Prussian kings, rates as Berlin's most beautiful baroque building. Berlin also boasts fine turn-of-the-century patrician homes with rich art-nouveau stucco facades, projecting balconies, recessed arched windows, sweeping staircases, and high ceilings.

There are also many public buildings from previous centuries, mostly in eastern Berlin. Among these are the 17th-century Arsenal on Unter den Linden, the museums on Museumsinsel, and the Staatsoper built by Georg Wenzeslaus von Knobelsdorff in the mid-1700s (although the original Staatsoper burned in 1843, the present building is a faithful reconstruction of Knobelsdorff's design). From the same period is Berlin's most famous landmark, the Brandenburger Tor (Gate), completed in 1786 as one of 13 city gates that used to mark the entrance to Berlin.

Probably the most well known architect during Berlin's formative architectural era was Karl Friedrich Schinkel (1781–1841), a protomodernist who used Gothic, Byzantine, and Renaissance designs in his creations. His works include the Alte Museum on Museum Island and the delightful Schinkel Pavilion on the grounds of Schloss Charlottenburg.

As for modern architecture, there's the Bauhaus-Archiv by Walter Gropius, a light and airy building housing a museum dedicated to the principles of the Bauhaus school of design; as well as the Hansaviertel (Hansa Quarter), a residential area designed by 50 leading architects from around the world, each of whom was asked to design one building. Among the participants were Alvar Aalto, Walter Gropius, Oscar Niemeyer, and Arne Jacobsen.

And, of course, there's also a lot of empty land waiting for development—notice the snaking scar left from the removal of the

Wall. Potsdamer Platz, once the lively heart of prewar Berlin, became a wasteland of weeds and vacant lots after the Wall went up. Bordered on the west end by Hans Sharoun's impressive Philharmonie with its golden tentlike roof, Potsdamer Platz became the focus of hot debate following the Wall's demise, as different interest groups presented their own plans for development. Some thought it should become a park; others thought it should go to the highest bidder. Today, it's a maze of construction sites as Sony and Daimler-Benz construct new office buildings. More construction is taking place in former East Berlin, especially in Berlin-Mitte along Friedrichstrasse. Plans are in the works to transform Alexanderplatz into a mountain of skyscrapers. The Berlin of tomorrow depends heavily on decisions made by today's city planners.

For the most part, Berlin's artistic heritage lives on in its museums. The city's love affair with museums can be traced back to the 1820s, when construction of a museum complex was begun by Friedrich Wilhelm III, who wished to make his collection of masterpieces available to the viewing public. Located on Museumsinsel (Museum Island) in eastern Berlin, the complex grew through the next century, as German archeologists searched the world for treasures from Egypt, Persia, and Greece. Today, Berlin is home of the famous bust of Nefertiti, the incredible Pergamon Altar, and the breathtaking Gate of Ishtar. It boasts not only a wide array of art museums but also history museums, collections of applied arts, and special-interest museums. Luckily for tourists, most are concentrated in four areas of Berlin—Dahlem, Tiergarten, Charlottenburg, and Museumsinsel.

Of course, it would be wrong to assume that all Berlin's treasures originated someplace else, for the city was home to a great many artists during the past century. One of the earliest to gain fame was Adolph von Menzel (1815–1905), a largely self-taught painter who became known for his portraits. A man who sought company in Berlin's many coffeehouses, he is considered a forerunner of the impressionists. He was followed by a group of artists who in 1892 founded the Secession movement, headed by Max Liebermann, which was concerned with developing its own stylistic approach to impressionism. Liebermann, Lovis Corinth, and Max Slevogt are considered the foremost German impressionists.

But the real shot in the arm for Berlin's artistic circles was the new generation of painters who flocked to Berlin after the turn of the century. Foremost among them was a group that came from Dresden during 1910 and 1911, known as Die Brücke (The Bridge). What they found was the fastest-growing city in Europe, with villas, tenements, and factories springing forth at an amazing tempo. Many of the new crop of artists viewed this industrial giant as something of a nightmare, a place that inspired fear, longing, unrest, and expectation of impending doom. Rather than simply imitating nature or photographing people, these painters felt their work should reflect inner feelings and conflicts. Thus was born German expressionism. Ernst Ludwig Kirchner, Emil Nolde, Max Pechstein, and Oskar

Kokoschka were important artists of the time, as were Käthe Kollwitz and Heinrich Zille, both Berliners dedicated to portraying the city's growing army of the poor.

Berlin's artists are richly represented in the city's many museums, including the Brücke-Museum in Dahlem, with works of Die Brücke artists; the Käthe-Kollwitz-Museum near the Ku'damm; and the Neue Nationalgalerie (New National Gallery), in the Tiergarten museum complex. The Neue Nationalgalerie, in particular, has an outstanding collection of works by Berlin's artists, including Menzel, Max Beckmann, Corinth, Kokoschka, and Kirchner. Another great museum for Berliner art is the Alte Nationalgalerie (National Gallery) on Museumsinsel in eastern Berlin, with works by Liebermann, Slevogt, Kirchner, Nolde, Kokoschka, and Kollwitz. In addition, works by contemporary artists of Berlin are shown regularly in special exhibitions in the Neue Nationalgalerie and the Berlinische Galerie.

As for the rest of Berlin's cultural scene, it boasts a rich tradition of the stage. Much of Germany's theatrical history stems from Berlin, for it was here that playwrights Gerhart Hauptmann and Bertolt Brecht, as well as Henrik Ibsen and August Strindberg, made their first major breakthroughs. Max Reinhardt, recognized as the man who introduced German theater to the world, was director of Berlin's Deutsches Theater from 1905 to 1920 and again from 1924 to 1932 (he was also the mastermind behind the world-famous Salzburg Festival). In the 1920s Berlin had approximately 35 theaters, several opera houses, and more than 20 concert halls.

Today, Berlin is still famous for its theater, including the Schaubühne (probably the city's best dramatic theater), and the Berliner Ensemble, the theatrical legacy of Bertolt Brecht. Berlin also boasts no fewer than three opera houses of international acclaim and is home to the renowned Berlin Philharmonic Orchestra. It also has cabaret, as well as a number of concert halls and live music houses that are regular stopovers for the big names in music entertainment. Berlin's International Film Festival is now one of the most important film festivals in the industry. Add to that the hundreds of bars that stay open until dawn, and it's little wonder Berlin has a reputation as the city that never sleeps. Since there's so much to do and see, who would want to?

4 Food & Drink

German food means pork, pork, and yet more pork. Surely the Germans have invented more ways to serve pork than any other people—from simple pork sausages with a dab of mustard to pig's knuckle with Sauerkraut and potatoes. Berlin's KaDeWe department store, famous for its massive food floor, features 1,000 kinds of sausage—most, you guessed it, made of pork.

Portions in German restaurants are huge, consisting of an entree plus a couple of side dishes (usually Sauerkraut or potatoes) heaped onto the plate, not to mention the almost obligatory rounds of beer.

Simply add to this a soup or dessert and a beverage to have a complete meal.

As you've probably figured out, German food is not a weight-reducing cuisine, but few seem to worry about calories in Germany—witness the coffee shops packed at 4pm, the unofficial coffee break around the country, when everyone downs cups of coffee and mountains of tortes and cakes as though it were his or her last meal.

Dining Customs

Germans customarily eat their biggest meal at midday. Except in the more expensive restaurants, where customers are seated by the management, diners are expected to seat themselves. It's perfectly acceptable to take any available seat, even if the rest of the table is occupied, but it's polite to ask first whether the seat is indeed free. Although it's increasingly rare, in some restaurants, especially those in eastern Berlin, you may be expected to check your coat or jacket with the coat clerk at the *Garderobe* and to give a small tip of a mark (60¢).

As for dining etiquette, Germans use a fork and knife for almost everything, including eating french fries, sandwiches, pizza, chicken, and other foods that Americans are more likely to eat with their fingers. Historically, it wasn't until 1846 that forks were produced for the masses; before that, Germans ate with their fingers, too. Fifteenth-century etiquette called for using three fingers to pick up meat from plates but frowned on stuffing food into one's mouth with both hands or keeping one's hands resting on plates for too long. By the way, some restaurants in Berlin specialize in medieval dining, where guests are required to feast the old-fashioned way using their fingers.

Everywhere else, however, you'll observe Germans holding their fork in their left hand and keeping the knife in their right. Once you've mastered this technique, you'll find it makes a lot more sense than switching your fork from hand to hand every time you want to cut that piece of pork.

If you're taking a breather from your meal and don't want the waiter to clear your plate, lay your fork and knife down in the same position they're held by Germans, that is, with your fork on the left side of the plate and your knife on the right. Placing your knife and fork side by side on the plate is a signal to the waiter that you've finished your meal. When you get up to leave, it's considered good etiquette to say good-bye to the other diners at your table, even if you haven't exchanged a word with them during the entire meal.

Drinking also has its rules. Never take a sip until your host raises his or her glass. Quite often you'll bash your beer mugs or clink your wineglasses together before taking your first sip. This custom grew out of a superstition that the devil could enter the body of a person who was drinking—the clashing together of glasses was meant to create a colossal noise and scare the devil away.

The Cuisine

BREAKFAST The typical German breakfast consists of bread or rolls topped with marmalade, cheese, or—you guessed it—sausage. Unlike in America, where sandwiches are stuffed with as many ingredients as they can hold, in Germany it's customary to place only a single ingredient upon each roll or slice of bread. If it's a slice of bread, a German is apt to eat it with a knife and fork, the fork turned upside down. Along with the bread is a soft-boiled egg in an eggcup. If it's a buffet breakfast in a hotel, other items may include cereals such as *Muesli* (a grain cereal similar to granola) and cornflakes, fruit, juices, and coffee. German coffee is much stronger than the American equivalent—and there's rarely a bottomless cup in Germany, though some hotels give extra servings to guests during breakfast. In higher-class hotels, breakfast buffets will also include scrambled eggs, bacon, and hash brown potatoes. At the other extreme is a continental breakfast, consisting simply of coffee or tea and rolls with marmalade.

If your hotel doesn't serve breakfast, you have a choice of many famous coffeehouses, most of them up and down the Ku'damm. An alternative is one of the many breakfast cafes, which are open not only early in the morning but much of the night as well—to serve the needs of hungry night hawks, most of them young people.

LUNCH & DINNER For lunch or dinner, your choice of venue ranges from expensive restaurants serving continental cuisine (a mixture of German, French, and Italian ingredients and dishes) to the neighborhood *Gaststätte,* simple German restaurants that often serve as the local pubs as well. Traditionally, most Germans eat their big meal of the day at lunch.

In a German restaurant, start your meal with a hearty bowl of soup—which may end up being all you can consume. One of my favorites is *Linsensuppe* (lentil soup, often with pieces of sausage). *Leberknödelsuppe* (a dumpling soup made with beef liver, onions, and garlic) and *Kartoffelsuppe* (potato soup) are other common choices. *Gulaschsuppe,* borrowed from Hungary, is a spicy soup featuring beef, paprika, and potatoes. Appetizers include *Hackepeter* (raw minced meat or steak tartare) and *Soleier* (pickled eggs). Breads, which are delicious in Germany, are almost endless in variety—from rye or Pumpernickel to various kinds of hard rolls called *Brötchen.*

For the main dish, one of Berlin's best-known specialties is *Eisbein* (pig's knuckle), usually served with *Sauerkraut* and potatoes or puréed peas. *Kasseler Rippenspeer* is smoked pork chops, created long ago by a butcher in Berlin named Kassel. A *Boulette,* introduced by the French Huguenots, is a type of cold meatball served with mustard. Other pork items you might find on a German menu include *Schweinebraten* (pot-roasted pork) and *Spanferkel* (suckling pig). If you come across a *Schweinshaxen,* it's grilled knuckle of pork. A *Schlachteplatte* (roughly translated, it means a butcher's platter) is only for the adventuresome, consisting as it does of fresh blood sausage, *Leberwurst* (liverwurst), pig's kidneys, and boiled pork.

As for those *Würste,* or sausages, you'll encounter them on almost every menu, as well as at stand-up food stalls, where they're served with a hard roll and mustard. Every region of Germany has its own specialties. In Berlin it's *Bockwurst,* a superlong boiled sausage often served with *Erbsensuppe* (split-pea soup). Another favorite is *Bratwurst* from Nürnberg, often prepared with beer, and the *Wiener.* A *Currywurst* is a sausage served with a curry-flavored sauce.

If you want something other than pork, choices readily available may include *Sauerbraten* (marinated beef in a thick sauce), *Schnitzel* (breaded veal cutlet), *Brathering* (grilled herring), *Brathuhn* (roast chicken), *Aal grün* (boiled eel in a dill sauce), and *gebratene kalbsleber Berliner Art* (sautéed veal liver with onions and apples). Other main courses include *Tafelspitz* (boiled beef with vegetables), *Leberkäs* (a type of German meat loaf, common to southern Germany), and *Sülze* (jellied meat). The vegetarian, in almost any restaurant, can order a *Gemüseplatte,* or dish of assorted vegetables.

In addition to traditional German fare, Berlin boasts an astounding assortment of international cuisine, thanks, in part, to the Wall. In order to attract businesses to preunification Berlin, the West German government offered generous subsidies that induced immigrants from Turkey, Greece, Italy, Asia, and other countries to open up shop. With time, Berliners have grown more and more appreciative of and sophisticated about international cuisine. With the largest Turkish population of any city outside Istanbul, Berlin is especially known for its Turkish restaurants in all price categories. These range from *Imbisse* (stand-up food stalls) found all over town offering *dönerkebab* (pita bread filled with grilled lamb, lettuce, and garlic sauce) to restaurants serving everything from lamb in a spicy sauce to shish kebab, often with entertainment provided by a belly dancer. Italian eateries—particularly those specializing in inexpensive pizzas—seem to be on every street corner. Beware, however, that if you order a *pepperoni pizza,* you'll get one with hot jalapeño peppers; order a *salami* pizza if you want an American-style pepperoni pizza. Other international cuisines readily found in Berlin include Indian; Chinese; Greek; French; Middle Eastern; Kosher; and, the latest craze, Mexican.

DRINKS   Germany is known for its wines and beers, both in plentiful supply in Berlin. The city, however, is not a wine-producing region. Frederick the Great tried it at his summer residence at Potsdam—but the rows of grape vines at Schloss Sanssouci are all that remain of his efforts. Berlin does, however, offer wines from other German regions, including the Rhine region (Rheingau, Rheinhesse, and Rheinpfalz), Baden-Württemberg, and Franken. Wines range from the Riesling to Sekt (a sparkling wine), from dry *(Trocken)* to sweet *(Süss).* Unless you know your German wines or simply want to experiment, ask your sommelier or waiter for a recommendation.

As for beer, Berlin's most famous brew is called *Berliner Weisse,* a draft wheat beer served with a shot of raspberry or green woodruff syrup and usually drunk in summer. Strangely enough, Berliners rarely drink the stuff, so those who order it are immediately recognized as tourists. If you simply order *ein Bier,* you'll get either a draft beer *(vom Fass)* or bottled beer *(eine Flasche).* An Export is slightly stronger but is still considered light; a Bock beer is dark and rich. A Pils or Pilsener is light and slightly bitter. One of my favorites is *Hefeweizen,* a wheat beer.

Although it's considered safe, Germans don't drink their tap water, preferring bottled water. A *Mineralwasser* is bottled mineral water, usually carbonated; if you don't like the bubbly stuff, add the words "*ohne Kohlensäure.*"

5   Recommended Books & Films

Books

POLITICS, CULTURE & HISTORY In *Before the Deluge: A Portrait of Berlin in the 1920s* (HarperCollins, 1986), Friedrich Otto captures the intellectual life of Berlin in the 1920s, when it was the third-largest city in the world and was home to such well-known people as Marlene Dietrich, Albert Einstein, Greta Garbo, Bertolt Brecht, Walter Gropius, Wassily Kandinsky, and Paul Klee. *Bertolt Brecht's Berlin* (Anchor Press/Doubleday, 1975), by Wolf von Eckardt and Sander L. Gilman, covers the years of the Weimar Republic, from 1918 to 1933, describing everything from Berlin's nightlife and the underworld to the media and architecture, along with the personalities that influenced each. It contains more than 280 photographs.

John Willett's *Weimar Years: A Culture Cut Short* (Abbeville Press, 1983) also reflects on the politics and culture of the ill-fated German republic.

Norman Geb's *The Berlin Wall: Kennedy, Khrushchev, and a Showdown in the Heart of Europe* (Times Books, 1988) explains Berlin's pivotal role in the Cold War. *Living with the Wall: West Berlin 1961–1985* (Duke Publishing Co., 1985) is Richard and Anna Merritt's description of Berlin as a divided city during the decades of the Wall.

Similarly, Peter Wyden's *Wall—The Inside Story of Divided Berlin* (Simon & Schuster, 1989) is a documentation of the Wall based on eyewitness accounts and interviews with intelligence agents and government officials. Wyden's account is a gripping human drama complete with stories of people who escaped East Germany, those who died in the attempt, and families ripped apart by Berlin's division.

Events leading up to and following the fall of the Wall are chronicled by Ken Smith in *Berlin: Coming in from the Cold* (Penguin, 1990), which provides an insider's view of what it was like to be in Berlin before and during those joyous days of celebration.

Those celebrations are also vividly captured in *The Wall Came Tumbling Down: The Berlin Wall and the Fall of Communism* (Arch Cape Press, 1990) by Jerry Bornstein. With an introduction by Willy

Brandt and more than 100 photographs, it's a pictorial presentation of those heady days in 1989 that saw the beginning of the end of a divided Germany.

For a history of Berlin from the reigns of the Great Elector and Frederick the Great through the rise of Bismarck to both world wars and the 1945 fall of the city, try Alexander Reissner's *Berlin 1675–1945: The Rise and Fall of a Metropolis* (Oswald Wolff, London, 1984).

Berlin Diary: The Journal of a Foreign Correspondent 1934–1941 (Little, Brown, 1988) is a personal narrative by well-known correspondent William L. Shirer, who went on to write one of the definitive books on Nazi Germany, *The Rise and Fall of the Third Reich* (Simon & Schuster, 1960).

Ann and John Tusa's *The Berlin Airlift* (Atheneum, 1988) recreates the most massive airlift ever undertaken—11 months in 1948, when more than 200,000 flights brought 1.7 million tons of supplies to the people of Berlin.

Berlin's very recent history is captured in John Borneman's thought-provoking *After the Wall: East Meets West in the New Berlin* (Basic Books, 1991). Borneman addresses the realities of reunified Berlin, especially the disorientation and disillusionment experienced by former East Berliners who had hoped East Germany would survive as a new type of democracy but instead watched its disintegration as it became absorbed by the materialistic West. Also by Borneman is *Belonging in the Two Berlins: Kin, State, Nation* (Cambridge University Press, 1992), which examines the social, economic, and political life of today's Berliners.

We Were the People: Voices from East Germany's Revolutionary Autumn of 1989 (Duke Publishing Co., 1992) by Dirk Philipsen is an oral history of dissidents in former East Germany who dared petition and demonstrate against a monolithic police state, contributing to its demise; most of these former East Germans also express bitter disappointment with the results of reunification.

FICTION   Having lived in Berlin from 1929 to 1933, Christopher Isherwood wrote about the people he met in the two novels contained in *The Berlin Stories* (New Directions, 1954). The more famous is *Goodbye to Berlin,* a fictionalized account of the last days of the Weimar Republic and the rise of the Nazis, which was the source for the stage play and movie *Cabaret.*

A more recent depiction of life in Berlin is provided by Ian Walker in his colorful *Zoo Station: Adventures in East and West Berlin* (Atlantic Monthly Press, 1987), which explores the alternative and underground cultural life of former divided Berlin.

Films

One of the first impressionistic documentaries, *Berlin, Symphony of a Great City* (1927) offers a look at life in old Berlin.

The tragic story of an elderly professor who is seduced by a sultry cabaret singer is the subject of *Der Blaue Engel* (*The Blue Angel*)

(1930), filmed at Babelsberg Studios outside Berlin. The film catapulted Marlene Dietrich to international stardom and captured the atmosphere of 1920s Berlin.

Berlin Express (1948), a documentary-style espionage thriller, uses actual footage of bombed-out Berlin and stars Merle Oberon and Paul Lukas.

Bob Fosse's award-winning musical *Cabaret* (1972) is set in 1931 Berlin. Starring Liza Minnelli, Michael York, and Joel Grey, it's based on John van Druten's stage play (which was based on Christopher Isherwood's Berlin stories).

Acclaimed German director Rainer Werner Fassbinder depicts a working-class man's life in Berlin from 1927 to 1978 in his mammoth film *Berlin Alexanderplatz* (1980).

Wim Wender's *Wings of Desire* (1989), with Peter Falk and Bruno Ganz, takes place in contemporary Berlin and depicts the dilemma of angels who can observe but not help humanity.

2

Planning a Trip to Berlin

Much of the anxiety associated with travel comes from not knowing what to expect. This chapter will help you prepare for your trip to Berlin, but don't stop here. Reading through the other chapters before leaving home will also provide useful information and will give you an idea of what Berlin is like and what you might like to see or do. Just learning that Berlin has many lakes great for swimming, for example, may prompt you to pack your swimsuit; on the other hand, learning that there are many nude beaches may prompt you to leave your suit at home.

1 Information, Entry Requirements & Money

Sources of Information

The **German National Tourist Office (GNTO)** publishes a wealth of colorful free items available to travelers, including a map of Germany, a general-information brochure about travel in Germany, a brochure on Berlin itself, and one on the city's hotels.

If you'd like information and literature before leaving home, contact one of the GNTO offices:

United States: GNTO, 122 E. 42nd St., 52nd floor, New York, NY 10168 (☎ **212/661-7200**); GNTO, 11766 Wilshire Blvd., Suite 750, Los Angeles, CA 90025 (☎ **310/575-9799**).

Canada: GNTO, Office National Allemand du Tourisme, 175 Bloor St. E., North Tower, Suite 604, Toronto, Ontario M4W 3R8 (☎ **416/968-1570**).

United Kingdom: GNTO, Nightingale House, 65 Curzon St., London W1Y 7PE (☎ **071/495-3990**).

Australia: GNTO, Lufthansa House, 9th floor, 143 Macquarie St., Sydney 2000 (☎ **012/367-3890**).

Additional information is available in the United States by calling the **Berlin Desk** in New York at **212/705-1371.** Call toll free **800/248-9539** to request the free Berlin Travel Kit, which contains a hotel brochure, a program of current exhibits and happenings, and other information; it will be sent in seven to ten days.

Entry Requirements

DOCUMENTS   Citizens of the United States, Canada, Australia, and New Zealand need only a valid passport for entry into Germany and stays of up to three months. Visitors from the United Kingdom need only an identity card.

Students should be sure to bring an International Student Identification Card, as well as an I.D. from their university showing current student status, to qualify for discounts to Berlin's museums. If you plan to rent a car, be sure to bring a valid driver's license (a U.S. license is fine).

CUSTOMS • For U.S. Travelers   If you are a citizen of a country outside Europe, you can bring duty-free into Germany 400 cigarettes or 100 cigars or 500 grams of tobacco, 1 liter of spirits, and 2 liters of wine. If you are an American or a Canadian residing in Europe, however, your allowance is only half that given above for tobacco products. You are also allowed a reasonable amount of perfume and coffee for your own personal use. You may bring into Germany gifts totaling 620 DM ($365), including a maximum of 155 DM ($91) gifts from non–European Union countries.

Since customs regulations may change, it would be wise to confirm German customs requirements before departing.

• **For U.K. Travelers**   On January 1, 1993, the borders between European countries were relaxed as the European markets united. When you're traveling within the European Union (EU), this will have a big impact on what you can buy and take home for personal use.

If you buy your goods in any duty-free shop or from a non-EU country, then the old rules still apply—you're allowed to bring home 200 cigarettes and 2 liters of table wine, plus 1 liter of spirits or 2 liters of fortified wine. If you don't want the fortified wine, you can take an extra 2 liters of table wine. The perfume allowance is 60 milliliters, and you can take home £36 worth of other assorted goodies. You must declare any goods in excess of these allowances.

If you're shopping in an EU country, on the other hand, you're allowed to buy your wine, spirits, or cigarettes in an ordinary shop and bring home *almost* as much as you like. U.K. Customs and Excise does set theoretical limits: 10 liters of spirits, plus 110 liters of beer, 20 liters of fortified wine, 90 liters of ordinary wine (no more than 60 liters of this can be sparkling wine), 800 cigarettes, 400 cigarillos, 200 cigars, and 1 kilo of tobacco. But remember that this applies only to goods bought in ordinary shops of EU countries. If you buy in duty-free shops or in non-EU countries, these lenient new rules don't apply.

You cannot buy goods and take them with you to sell to others. This is a criminal offense in the United Kingdom, and customs officers claim to be looking out for those making repeated trips or those laden down with goods.

Money

CASH & CURRENCY   The basic unit of currency in Germany is the **deutsche mark (DM).** One DM equals 100 pfennigs. Coins come in denominations of 1, 2, 5, 10, and 50 pfennigs, and 1, 2, and 5 DM. Bills are issued in denominations of 5, 10, 20, 50, 100, 200, 500, and 1,000 DM.

Although rates fluctuate continually, all conversions in this book are based on a rate of 1.70 DM to U.S. $1 (then rounded to the nearest nickel). At press time, the pound sterling exchanged at the rate of £1 to 2.50 DM. However, keep in mind that the currency conversion rate may change by the time you arrive in Germany, so plan your budget accordingly. In addition, because of skyrocketing real estate prices due to reunification, prices for accommodations have

The German Mark

For U.S. Readers   At this writing \$1 = approximately 1.70 DM (or 1 DM = 59¢), and this was the rate of exchange used to calculate the dollar values given in this chapter (rounded to the nearest nickel).

For U.K. Readers   At this writing £1 = approximately 2.50 DM (or 1 DM = 40 p), and this was the rate of exchange used to calculate the pound values in the table below.

Note   The rates given here fluctuate from time to time and may not be the same when you travel to Germany. Therefore this table should be used only as a guide:

DM	U.S.\$	U.K.£	DM	U.S.\$	U.K.£
1	.59	.40	45	26.55	18.00
2	1.18	.80	50	29.50	20.00
3	1.77	1.20	60	35.40	24.00
4	2.36	1.60	70	41.30	28.00
5	2.95	2.00	80	47.20	32.00
6	3.54	2.40	90	53.10	36.00
7	4.13	2.80	100	59.00	40.00
8	4.72	3.20	120	70.80	48.00
9	5.30	3.60	150	88.50	60.00
10	5.90	4.00	200	118.00	80.00
15	8.85	6.00	250	147.50	100.00
20	11.80	8.00	300	177.00	120.00
25	14.75	10.00	350	206.50	140.00
30	17.70	12.00	400	236.00	160.00
35	20.65	14.00	450	265.50	180.00
40	23.60	16.00	500	295.00	200.00

climbed in the past few years, a trend that is likely to continue. Prices given in this book, therefore, should be used only as a guideline.

TRAVELER'S CHECKS   Instead of traveling with large amounts of cash, be sure to convert most of your money to traveler's checks. Traveler's checks issued in U.S. dollars and other foreign currencies can be exchanged only in banks, major hotels, some large department stores, and the American Express office. If you plan to spend all your time in Germany, you may wish to purchase traveler's checks in German marks. Be aware, however, that they are not accepted as cash at stores or restaurants and must therefore be cashed at banks or exchange offices. Generally, traveler's checks bring a better rate of exchange than cash.

In any case, buy traveler's checks in both small and large denominations (you are usually charged a commission fee for each transaction, not on the total number of checks cashed at any one time). Similarly, be sure to include large and small denominations in the cash

What Things Cost in Berlin	U.S. $
Taxi from Tegel Airport to Bahnhof Zoo train station	17.70
Underground from Kurfürstendamm to Dahlem	2.05
Local telephone call	.18
Deluxe double room (at Bristol Hotel Kempinski)	277.00
Moderate double room (at Berlin Mark Hotel)	159.30
Budget double room (at Pension Cortiná)	53.10
Deluxe lunch for one, without wine (at Fioretto)	47.00
Moderate lunch for one, without wine (at Dorfgasthaus)	20.00
Budget lunch for one (at Rogacki)	8.50
Deluxe dinner for one, without wine (at Rockendorf's)	130.00
Moderate dinner for one, without wine (at Hardtke)	18.00
Budget dinner for one, without wine (at Athener Grill)	6.00
Half liter of beer	3.50
Glass of wine	3.00
Coca-Cola in a restaurant	1.80
Cup of coffee	1.75
Roll of 100 ASA slide film, 36 exposures	4.50
Admission to Dahlem Gemäldegalerie	2.35
Movie ticket	5.90
Opera ticket	7.05

you bring. I always carry at least $10 worth of $1 bills when I travel, for tips and small favors upon arrival. I also include several $10 and $20 bills, just in case I need to exchange a small amount of money at the end of my trip.

CREDIT & CHARGE CARDS   As for credit and charge cards, American Express, Diners Club, MasterCard (the same as EuroCard in Europe), and Visa are the ones most readily accepted (and JCB, of course, in case you happen to have a Japanese credit card). All major hotels and many shops and restaurants accept plastic, particularly in western Berlin. In eastern Berlin, however, credit cards are accepted only in places frequented by international tourists, such as hotel restaurants. In addition, smaller establishments in both east and west are not equipped to deal with credit cards. You'll therefore want to carry a certain amount of cash, which you should keep secure in a money belt. Take only what you need for the day—keep the rest of your cash and traveler's checks in your hotel's safety-deposit box. Cash can be obtained from credit cards at major banks in Berlin.

2 When to Go—Climate, Holidays & Events

Berlin is a tourist destination throughout the year. In fact, now that it's become one of the hottest destinations in Europe, it can be as lively and crowded in February as in August.

Climate

Berlin is at about the same latitude as Vancouver and enjoys the changes of the four seasons. Its summers are generally mild and even pleasantly cool, which accounts for the fact that very few hotels and establishments bother with air conditioning. Spring and autumn can be glorious—my favorite time of year is October. Winters, on the other hand, can be quite severe, though not as bad as those in the northern regions of the United States. Though it rarely snows, the wind can be icy and it often rains. On the other hand, it sometimes warms up in February; I've seen it snow in April. In other words, be prepared for all kinds of weather, since temperatures and the amount of rainfall seem to vary from year to year. However, the following averages may help you plan your trip.

Berlin's Average Daytime Temperature & Rainfall

	Jan	Feb	Mar	Apr	May	June	July	Aug	Sept	Oct	Nov	Dec
Temp. (°F)	30	32	40	48	53	60	64	62	56	49	40	34
(°C)	-1	0	4	9	12	16	18	17	13	9	4	1
Rainfall (in.)	2.2	1.6	1.2	1.6	2.3	2.9	3.2	2.7	2.2	1.6	2.4	1.9

Holidays

There are a few official and religious holidays to keep in mind. Some museums and restaurants are closed on certain holidays; most museums, for example, are closed on New Year's Day and Christmas. To avoid disappointment, be sure to telephone in advance if you wish to visit a certain establishment on a holiday.

Holidays in Berlin are New Year's (January 1); Good Friday; Easter Sunday and Monday; Ascension Day; Whitsunday and Monday; Labor Day (May 1); German Reunification Day (October 3); Day of Prayer and Repentance (third Wednesday in November), and Christmas (both December 25 and 26).

A few museums are closed on Maundy Thursday (the Thursday before Easter).

Berlin Calendar of Events

If you're lucky, your trip may coincide with one of Berlin's cultural events. But if you do arrive during any of the major events described below, it's a good idea to reserve a hotel room in advance. For other events, including sporting events, art exhibits, or other onetime happenings, contact the German National Tourist Office nearest you.

In Berlin, the organization in charge of arranging all major festivals is the **Berliner Festspiele GmbH,** Budapester Strasse 48–50 (☎ **030/25 48 90** or **25 489-250**). The **Verkehrsamt Berlin** (tourist office), located in the Europa-Center on Budapester Strasse (☎ **030/262 6031**), is another invaluable source of information.

February

★ International Film Festival

The calendar year starts off with a bang with this festival, known locally as the Berlinale, which attracts stars, directors, movie critics, and film lovers from all over the world. Established back in 1951, it lasts almost two weeks and usually features about 700 films from some 20 countries at the main showings, all open to the public. In addition, there are other movies shown around the clock under such headings as "International Forum of Young Filmmakers" and "New German Movies."
Where: Various theaters. **When:** Last half of February. **How:** Tickets, which run from about 10 DM to 25 DM ($5.90 to $14.75), can be purchased at the box offices or at a special booth set up on the first floor of the Europa-Center, open daily from 11:30am to 6:30pm. The best showings sell out quickly, but something is always available.

May

- **Theatertreffen,** or "Theater Meeting," is a festival featuring German-language productions from throughout the German-speaking world, including Austria and Switzerland. You have to understand the language, therefore, to appreciate the various offerings. If you do and you love theater, you'll be in heaven.

June–July

- **Serenade Concerts** in Charlottenburg Palace. Call Verkehrsamt Berlin (☎ **262 60 31**) for information.

September

★ Berliner Festwochen

The Berlin Festival Weeks, one of the biggest events of the year, recognizes excellence in all fields of the arts. Included are symphonic, operatic, and theatrical performances.
Where: Various theaters. **When:** End of August through September. **How:** Ticket cost depends on the venue, and may be purchased at the box offices.

October–November

★ Jazz-Fest Berlin

A colorful mix of avant-garde and classical jazz musicians from around the world. There's everything from blues and swing to bebop, cool jazz, and free jazz.
Where: Philharmonie, Delphi, and Musikinstrumenten Museum. **When:** End of October or early November.

How: Tickets costing from 10 DM ($5.90) to 45 DM ($26.55) may be purchased at the box office.

December

- **Weihnachtsmarkt,** from the Gedächtniskirche to Wittenbergplatz. This is the largest, most popular, and most convenient of the several traditional Christmas markets held around the city. Open daily from 11am to 9pm, it features more than 150 stalls selling cookies, candy, mulled wine, Christmas ornaments, and more. (Other Christmas markets include those in the Spandau Altstadt, in Karl-Liebnecht-Platz, and on Alexanderplatz. December 1 to Christmas Eve.)

3   Health & Insurance

HEALTH   No shots or inoculations are required for entry into Germany. If you need special medications, however, it's a good idea to bring them with you. Otherwise, German pharmacies are well equipped with their own brands of medicine, whether it's cough syrup or aspirin. If a pharmacy cannot fill your American prescription, it will give you a German substitution.

INSURANCE   Medical and hospital services are not free in Germany, so ask your insurance company before leaving home if you are covered for medical emergencies or treatment abroad. If not, you may want to take out a short-term traveler's medical policy before leaving. If an emergency arises during your stay in Berlin, consult "Fast Facts: Berlin" in Chapter 3 for emergency telephone numbers.

You may also want to take extra precautions with your possessions. Is your camera or video equipment insured everywhere in the world through your home insurance? Is your home insured against theft or loss if you're gone longer than a month (some insurance companies will not cover loss for homes unoccupied longer than a specified amount of time)? If you are not adequately covered, you may wish to purchase an extra policy to cover losses.

For U.K. Travelers   Most big travel agents offer their own insurance and will probably try to sell their package when you book a holiday. Think before you sign. Britain's Consumer Association recommends you insist on seeing the policy and read the fine print before buying travel insurance. You should also shop around for better deals. Try **Columbus Travel Insurance Ltd.** (☎ **071/375-0011**) or, for students, **Campus Travel** (☎ **071/730-3402**). If you're unsure about who can give you the best deal, contact the **Association of British Insurers,** 51 Gresham St., London EC2V 7HQ (☎ **071/600-3333**).

4   What to Pack

Since Germans are known throughout the world for the quality and quantity of their goods and since they import just about everything else, you can probably find anything you might need in Berlin during your stay. Thus, pack as lightly as possible—if you shop, you'll probably end up leaving with a lot more than you came with.

Berlin has a moderate continental climate (warm in summer and cold in winter), so bring appropriate clothing. Also be prepared for unusual temperature changes—it can sometimes become quite cool on a summer's evening. Dress is generally fairly casual, but if you're going to the theater or opera, you'll want to pack one dressy outfit. Try to get mileage out of your wardrobe by packing clothes you can mix and match.

If you're staying in youth hostels, you'll want to bring your own towel and maybe your own sleeping bag or sheets (sheets are available at youth hostels for an extra charge). If you're staying in a pension with a shared bathroom down the hall, you may want to pack a light robe. Throughout the year it's imperative to have a folding umbrella, and be sure to bring good walking shoes (ones already broken in). I also never travel without my Swiss army knife and a travel alarm clock (in cheaper pensions, you won't have a phone in your room for wakeup calls).

5 Tips for the Disabled, Seniors, Singles, Families & Students

FOR THE DISABLED   There are many organizations in Berlin for the disabled. For information, including where to rent wheelchairs and which hotels are best equipped for the disabled, contact **Landesamt für Zentral Soziale Aufgaben,** Landesversorgungsamt, Sächsische Strasse 28–30 (☎ **030/867 61 14** or **867 63 71**). More assistance for the disabled, including advice and wheelchair rental, is available through **Service-Ring-Berlin** (☎ **859 40 10** or **938 92 41-0**). Free wheelchair use is offered by **Verband Geburts & anderer Behinderter;** call **341 17 97** and leave a message.

On a personal note, a few years ago, I broke my leg skiing and then spent a week in Berlin on crutches. I found Berliners extremely polite and helpful, holding doors open for me and offering me their seat on buses and trains (special handicapped seats are marked on buses, subways, and trains). But the biggest obstacle is probably stairs. Some of the larger subway and train stations have elevators and escalators (indicated on the free map available from transportation authorities), but most do not. In addition, most inexpensive pensions are located on upper floors of multistory buildings, many without elevators or bathrooms large enough to accommodate a wheelchair. When making your hotel reservation, make sure the hotel is equipped to handle your needs.

FOR SENIORS   Museums sometimes offer discounts of up to 50% for senior citizens—even though such discounts may not be posted. Men must be 65, women 60. Carry your passport with you at all times as proof of your age.

FOR SINGLES   Although it doesn't seem fair, single travelers usually pay more than half the price of a double room. Expensive hotels may even charge the same price for single or double occupancy. If you're alone, look for hotels that offer single rates; some even have a few single rooms, usually the smallest on the premises.

Women traveling alone to Berlin may want to contact **Fraueninfothek Berlin,** located in eastern Berlin not far from Alexanderplatz at Dircksenstrasse 47 (☎ **282 39 80**). An organization managed by women for women, it can provide general information about Berlin, help find accommodations, and provide more information about women's groups and meetings.

FOR FAMILIES   I took my son to Berlin when he was six months old and found the city easily accessible for a stroller. Buses have marked doors for strollers, as well as a special area near the door where strollers can be parked and secured. Major subway stations have escalators or elevators. Children younger than 6 travel for free on public transportation; those younger than 14 travel at a discounted rate.

Restaurants are a bit more problematic—except in those that cater especially to families, high chairs are virtually nonexistent and children's menus a rarity. Children would be out of place at Berlin's better restaurants; no-smoking sections are few and far between. If you have a young child, you may find yourself eating at McDonald's more often than you ever thought possible.

Berlin has many attractions that appeal to children, including a wonderful zoo and several museums (see "Cool for Kids" in Chapter 6). Children usually pay half fare for attractions that charge admission; admission is usually free for children younger than 3.

FOR STUDENTS   Most museums in Berlin offer student discounts. In addition, some theaters and opera houses (including the Deutsche Oper Berlin) offer unsold tickets to students for up to 50% off.

A student's key to cheaper prices is the **International Student Identity Card (ISIC),** available to all students enrolled full- or part-time in a degree program. Another benefit of the card is that it gives all holders access to a worldwide traveler's assistance hotline, a toll-free service for use in medical, financial, and legal emergencies. Valid for one year, the card is available from the Council on International Educational Exchange (CIEE), 205 E. 42nd St., New York, NY 10017 (☎ **212/661-1414**). Applications must include a $16 registration fee, one passport-size photo, and proof of current student status (an official letter from the school, a school transcript, or a registrar's receipt). Allow three weeks when applying for the card by mail.

6   Getting There

For most readers of this book, a trip to Berlin is likely to begin with a plane trip across the ocean to the European continent. Berlin itself is easily accessible by plane, train, or car. Below are some pointers to get you headed in the right direction.

BY PLANE   Airlines that fly between North America and Germany include **Lufthansa,** the German national airline (☎ toll free **800/645-3800**); **American** (☎ toll free **800/433-7300**); **Continental** (☎ toll free **800/231-0856**); **Delta** (☎ toll free **800/241-4141**); **TWA** (☎ toll free **800/892-4141**); **United** (☎ toll free **800/241-6522**); and **USAir** (☎ toll free **800/622-1015**). Contact your travel agent or specific carriers for current information.

To get a head start on your travel adventure, however, it seems only fitting to fly Germany's own Lufthansa, known throughout the world for its punctuality, dependability, and high-quality service. It operates the most frequent flights from the United States and Canada to Germany, with more than 115 weekly flights from 17 North American gateways, and it also flies to the greatest number of cities in Germany. Of course, Lufthansa also offers the most flights to Berlin from all major cities in Germany and elsewhere.

Transatlantic Airfares   Researching airfares from North America to Germany can be difficult and time-consuming, since the cheapest fares vary depending on the season and even the day of week you travel. In addition, airlines sometimes lower prices at the last minute to fill empty seats or offer special promotional fares—valid at certain times of year—that may include car-rental options. It pays to invest time shopping around.

While first- and business-class fares are the same year-round, cheaper tickets vary with the season. The most expensive time to fly is during peak season, usually June through September. The lowest fares are available during winter, usually November through March (with the exception of December 12 to 24). During the shoulder season, usually April, May, and October, fares vary from high to low. In addition, during all seasons there are different rates for weekday and weekend flights.

APEX (Advance-Purchase Excursion)   You can cut the cost of your flight to Germany by purchasing your nonrefundable ticket in advance and complying with certain restrictions. These are known as APEX (advance-purchase excursion) fares, and the restrictions may vary with the airline but always require an advance purchase and minimum and maximum stays. Lufthansa's nonrefundable APEX fares require reservations be made at least 21 days prior to departure. Payment and ticketing must be completed within 72 hours of reservation or 21 days prior to departure, whichever comes first. There is a minimum 7-day stay and a maximum 1-month stay. Rates on all nonrefundable APEX fares vary according to the season, with peak season in effect from June through September. Round-trip weekday (Monday through Thursday) flights are approximately $60 cheaper than weekend flights. At press time, Lufthansa's nonrefundable APEX fares ranged from as low as $568 round trip from New York to Berlin on a weekday in winter to a high of $828 for the same flight in summer.

For those who wish to stay in Germany a little longer than a month, Lufthansa also offers a **Special APEX fare** for just $100 more than the prices quoted above; it allows a maximum 2-month stay, requires only a 14-day advance purchase, permits no stopovers, and carries a cancellation penalty.

Economy Fares   In addition to its APEX fares, Lufthansa offers some other options for budget travel that allow for greater flexibility. If you are unable to plan your trip and purchase your ticket in advance or wish to stay fewer than seven days or longer than two months, you may, for example, want to take advantage of Lufthansa's **Instant Purchase (PEX) fare.** You cannot return prior to the first Sunday after departure, and stays are good for up to six months. At press time, PEX fares ranged from as low as $768 round trip from New York to Berlin on a weekday in winter to a high of $1,028 for the same flight in summer. One stopover is permitted for an additional charge of $50, and there's a $150 cancellation fee.

Lufthansa also offers an **Excursion fare** that requires no advance purchase, carries no cancellation penalty, has no minimum stay, and is valid for stays up to one year. This fare permits one free stopover and an additional one at an extra $50 charge. At press time, the round-trip fare was $1,268 from New York to Berlin. In contrast, Lufthansa's regular economy round-trip ticket, which carries no restrictions and allows one free stopover en route, costs $2,536 from New York to Berlin year-round.

Lufthansa's **Youth fare,** available to those from 12 to 24, is a good value for students going to Germany for a year's study, since its round-trip ticket allows for a maximum one-year stay. It has a 72-hour advance purchase requirement, allows no stopovers, and requires the return reservation be left open but made 72 hours before flying. At press time, the one-way weekday fare from New York to Berlin was $284 in low season and $414 in peak season.

First- & Business-Class Fares   If you wish to fly in style, you'll want to take advantage of luxuries provided to first- and business-class passengers. In Lufthansa's new **Airbus 340,** seat configurations guarantee you either an aisle or a window seat, and for the ultimate in comfort, the aircraft's first-class sleeper seats each have an integral footrest and lumbar support and recline to 60 degrees; in business class, seats recline to 28 degrees. In addition to travel kits and deluxe meals, passengers on A340s and Boeing 747s receive the luxury of personal video screens, with a choice of eight programs ranging from feature films to news broadcasts. Fares for first and business class are the same year-round and allow an unlimited number of stopovers. At press time, the round-trip business-class fare from New York to Berlin was $2,906, while first class was $5,180. Remember, however, that fares are subject to change without notice. Be sure to contact your travel agent or the airlines for current information.

Other Options   Certainly the best strategy for securing the lowest airfare is to shop around. Consult the travel section of major newspapers since they often carry advertisements for cheap fares. You may,

Frommer's Smart Traveler: Airfares

1. Shop all the airlines that fly to your destination.

2. Keep calling the airlines since the availability of cheap seats changes daily. As the departure date nears, you might be able to obtain a seat at a great discount because an airline would rather sell a seat than have it empty.

3. Read the advertisements of newspaper travel sections—they often offer special deals and packages.

4. You can also save money by buying your ticket as early as possible—the cheapest fares, such as APEX (advance-purchase excursion), usually require 30 days' advance purchase.

5. Ask whether there's a difference in price if you fly on a weekday—weekday flights are often $60 cheaper round trip than weekend flights.

6. Travel off-season if you're trying to save money since APEX and economy tickets often cost less if it's the off-season.

for example, find bargains offered by so-called **"bucket shops"** that sell discounted tickets at reductions of about 20% to 30%. Tickets are usually restrictive, valid only for a particular date or flight, nontransferable, and nonrefundable.

Another option is a charter flight, which may offer a combination package that includes such land transportation as a rental car and hotel accommodation. One reputable charter company is **Condor,** a Lufthansa subsidiary, which is located in Chicago and sells tickets to tour operators throughout the country.

Finally, be sure to ask airlines for any **special packages** being offered. Lufthansa, for example, offers a city package for Berlin that includes round-trip airfare from New York, three nights' accommodation, a daily breakfast, taxes, and service charges. At press time, the fare ranged from $749 to $899 per person, depending on the hotel (a choice of six hotels is available) and based on double occupancy. Lufthansa also offers a fly/drive package that includes round-trip airfare and a rental car for seven days as well as a fly/rail package that includes five days of unlimited rail travel in Germany within a one-month period. Contact Lufthansa or your travel agent for more information on special packages.

Airfares from the United Kingdom   There are no hard and fast rules about where to get the best deals for European flights, but there are strategies that may help you save money.

First, check daily papers for advertisements of companies offering cheap flights. London's *Evening Standard* has a daily travel section, and the Sunday editions of almost any newspaper will run many ads. Highly recommended companies include

Trailfinders (☎ 071/938-3366 or 937-5400), **Benz Travel** (☎ 071/439-4181), and **Platinum Travel** (☎ 071/937-5122).

In London, around Victoria and Earl Court are many **"bucket shops"** that offer cheap fares. Make sure the company you deal with is a member of the IATA, ABTA, or ATOL. These umbrella organizations will help you out if anything goes wrong.

Finally, **CEEFAX**, a British television information service included on many home and hotel TVs, runs details of package holidays and flights to Europe and beyond. Just switch to your CEEFAX channel and you'll find a listings menu that includes travel information.

BY TRAIN It's easy to get to Berlin by rail because there are good connections from Frankfurt, Hamburg and other major cities. The trip from Frankfurt to Berlin takes about seven hours, and at press time it cost 152 DM ($89.70) for second class and 218 DM ($128.60) for first class one way. From Hamburg, with the trip taking about three hours, the one-way second- and first-class fares were 49 DM ($28.90) and 74 DM ($43.65), respectively.

Other first- and second-class fares are 393 DM ($231.85) and 285 DM ($168.15) from London; and 335 DM ($197.65) and 223.50 DM ($131.85) from Paris.

Rail Passes for U.S. Travelers If you plan to travel extensively throughout Europe, you should consider buying a **Eurailpass.** Good for travel through 17 European countries, it must be purchased before entering Europe. A number of options are available, including passes good for unlimited travel from 15 days to 3 months, as well as Flexipasses good for any 5, 10, or 15 days of travel within 2 months. All these passes are for first class only, though **Eurail Youthpasses** for second class are available to travelers from 12 to 25. Children 4 to 11 pay half the adult fare, while those under 4 travel free.

In addition to saving money, a plus of a rail pass is that you don't have to stand in line each time to buy a ticket. At press time, a 5-day first-class Flexipass cost $348, while a 15-day Flexipass cost $740; a Eurailpass with 15 consecutive days of unlimited travel cost $498. For more information on these and other fares, contact a travel agent.

If you plan to travel exclusively in Germany, you may wish to purchase a **GermanRailpass,** which must also be purchased before entering Europe and offers a variety of options for travel within Germany. A particularly good deal is the Flexipass, available first or second class for any 5, 10, or 15 days of travel within a 1-month period. At press time, a 5-day Flexipass cost $260 for first class, $178 for second class, and only $138 for travelers under 26. For more information on the GermanRailpass, contact your travel agency.

Rail Passes for U.K. Travelers Many different rail passes are available in the United Kingdom for travel in Britain and Europe. Stop in at the **International Rail Centre,** Victoria Station, London SW1V 1JY (☎ 071/834-2345), or **Wasteels,** 121 Wilton Rd., London SW1V 1JZ (☎ 071/834-7066). Staff members can help you find the best option for the trip you're planning.

If you're younger than 26, there are several rail ticket options for U.K. residents, including the **InterRail card** (similar to the Eurailpass) and **Eurotrain tickets** (single tickets sold to final destinations that allow stopovers en route).

BY BUS   Daily bus service is available between Berlin and a number of German cities, including Frankfurt, Hamburg, and Munich. Buses are modern coaches, equipped with Pullman seats and toilets. Tickets are slightly cheaper than train fares and can be purchased at all DER travel agencies. A one-way trip from Frankfurt to Berlin costs 99 DM ($58.40) and takes slightly less than 11 hours. The 9-hour trip from Munich to Berlin costs 123 DM ($72.55). Discounts are available for those younger than 26.

BY CAR   Traffic can be the main obstacle to car travel. Germans are keen on exploring new territories in their reunified country, and congestion in eastern Germany is further compounded by poor road maintenance (look out for those ruts and potholes). How long it takes you to drive to Berlin will therefore depend on the roads you select, traffic, and how fast you drive. Berlin is 343 miles from Frankfurt, 184 miles from Hamburg, and 363 miles from Munich. Although there is no speed limit on Autobahns in western Germany, eastern Germany still imposes a 100-kph (62-mph) speed limit and enforces it with radar. In addition, do not drink and drive because penalties are severe and fines high. Keep alcoholic beverages in the trunk to be on the safe side.

By Car & Ferry from the United Kingdom   Ferry/drive reservations can be made with any good travel agent. There are many options and routes, so it's advisable to shop around for the best deals.

Brittany Ferries is the United Kingdom's largest ferry/drive company, sailing from the south coast of England to five destinations in France and Spain. **Stena Sealink Lines** runs ferries from Dover to Calais, Southampton to Cherbourg, Newhaven to Dieppe, and Harwich to the Hook of Holland. **P&O Ferries** sails from Portsmouth to Cherbourg and Le Havre in France; from Dover to Calais and Ostend; and from Felixstowe to Zeebrugge, Belgium. Finally, **Scandinavian Sea Ways** allows you to travel farther afield, including to Germany.

To Europe from the United Kingdom Via the Channel Tunnel   The 31-mile Channel Tunnel, popularly called the "Chunnel," is set to open for passenger service by the autumn of 1994, reducing the travel time from Folkestone to Calais, France, to 30 minutes. Traveling directly from London to Paris and Brussels, the trains can accommodate more than 700 persons in first and second class. Since you can travel via the the tunnel on a train from London's Waterloo Station, you don't need a car to take advantage of the service. If you do take a car, it will be stowed away on the shuttle trains, for you to drive off at the destination. No prices or schedules are yet fixed as we go to press, but you can get up-to-the-minute information by calling **0302/270-111.**

3

Getting to Know Berlin

THIS CHAPTER WILL ANSWER ANY QUESTIONS YOU MIGHT HAVE UPON ARRIVAL in Berlin and during your stay as well as furnish you with practical information—from how to get to your hotel from the airport to numbers to call during an emergency. Note that information about Berlin's airports, train stations, and other transportation centers may change.

1   Orientation

Arriving

BY PLANE

TEGEL AIRPORT   Located only 5 miles northwest of the city center, Tegel Airport (☎ **41 01-1**) is the major airport for flights from the rest of Germany, western Europe, and North America. It's rather small as international airports go, consisting of one main hall and a circular-shaped passenger terminal. One of the first things you'll want to do upon arrival is stop at the Berlin information counter, located in the main terminal. Pick up a map of the city and available brochures. If you don't yet have a hotel reservation, the tourist office here will book one for you for a 5-DM ($2.95) fee. It's open daily from 8am to 11pm.

Other facilities at the airport include banks for money exchange; luggage storage; a post office from which you can make international calls; a first-aid station; a police station; car-rental firms; a restaurant; and shops selling film, newspapers, souvenirs, and travel necessities.

Getting Into Town   The best and least expensive way to get into town is on **city bus no. 109,** which departs about every 10 to 15 minutes from just outside the arrival hall. The fare is 3.50 DM ($2.05) one way, and the trip to the city center takes approximately half an hour. The bus travels along the Kurfürstendamm, where most of Berlin's hotels are concentrated, all the way to Bahnhof Zoologischer Garten (Berlin's main train station); some continue on to Budapester Strasse. Ask someone at the airport tourist information counter which stop is most convenient to your hotel. Once inside the bus, you'll find each stop clearly displayed on a panel at the front.

The easiest and quickest way to get into town, of course, is by **taxi,** which is not as prohibitively expensive as in many other major cities. It costs approximately 30 DM ($17.70) one way to the city center, and there are always plenty of taxis waiting to take you to your destination.

SCHÖNEFELD AIRPORT   Formerly East Berlin's major airport, Schönefeld Airport (☎ **60 91-0**), is located a couple miles south of Berlin and serves intercontinental flights from Asia and eastern Europe, including Moscow, St. Petersburg, Singapore, Tel Aviv, and Warsaw.

Getting Into Town   The Berlin-Schönefeld S-Bahn station of the **public rail system** is about a five-minute walk from the airport. From there, S-Bahn 9 (usually abbreviated to S-9) travels through Alexanderplatz to Bahnhof Zoologischer Garten, Savignyplatz, and Charlottenburg stations in the city center. S-45 serves southwestern Berlin. If you don't want to walk the five minutes to the S-Bahn station, an alternative is to board bus no. 171 from Schönefeld Airport for the short ride to Rudow, where you can then board the U-Bahn 7 for a ride into the city (note that the U-7 does not go to the city center; to reach the Kurfürstendamm or Bahnhof Zoologischer Garten, transfer to U-9 at Berliner Strasse). Regardless of the transportation method you choose, both routes cost 3.50 DM ($2.05) one way. A taxi to the city center will set you back about 55 DM ($32.45).

BERLIN-TEMPLEHOF AIRPORT   Western Berlin's oldest airport, Templehof Airport (☎ **69 51-0**), was brought back to civilian use after the Wall fell and Berlin found itself unable to handle increased flights to the new capital. Serving flights from both European and German cities, it is located just a few miles south of the city center.

Getting Into Town   The U-Bahn 6 **subway line** connects the airport's station, Platz der Luftbrücke, with Friedrichstrasse station, where you can easily transfer to S-Bahn lines to the rest of the city. The fare is 3.50 DM ($2.05).

Bus no. 119 travels directly from the airport to the Kurfürstendamm, where most of Berlin's hotels are located. The fare is 3.50 DM ($2.05). The trip by taxi runs about 25 DM ($14.75).

BY TRAIN

If you're arriving by train from western Europe, you'll probably end up at **Bahnhof Zoologischer Garten,** Berlin's main train station, popularly called Bahnhof Zoo. It's located in the center of town, not far from the Kurfürstendamm with its hotels and nightlife. An underground and bus system connects the train station to the rest of the city. Bus no. 109, for example, travels along the Ku'damm and continues to Tegel Airport; bus no. 100 travels to Alexanderplatz in eastern Berlin. Your first stop at Bahnhof Zoo should be the tourist information counter, open daily from 8am to 11pm. In addition to picking up maps and brochures, you can have your hotel reservation made here for a 5-DM ($2.95) fee. Both a post office and a money-exchange office are located in the train station. For information on train schedules, call **194 19** or stop by the information office in the station.

Formerly eastern Berlin's major train stations, the **Berlin Hauptbahnhof** (once called Ostbahnhof) and **Berlin-Lichtenberg stations** now serve trains from both eastern and western Europe. Berlin-Lichtenberg serves trains from Copenhagen, Budapest, Vienna, Prague, Munich, Moscow, and Warsaw, while Berlin Hauptbahnhof serves trains from Leipzig, Munich, Warsaw, Prague, and Dresden. Note that some trains also stop at Bahnhof Zoologischer Garten in addition to both these train stations, so decide beforehand where you want to get off (Bahnhof Zoo is closer to most of Berlin's hotels). Note also that train schedules and services to both these stations may change in the future. At any rate, both the Hauptbahnhof and Berlin-Lichtenberg stations are connected to the S-Bahn 5 and S-Bahn 7, with direct service to Alexanderplatz and Bahnhof Zoo.

BY BUS

Since Berlin is easily accessible from most European cities by rail and plane, it's unlikely you'll arrive by bus. However, there are some 30 omnibus lines that connect Berlin daily with some of Germany's major cities, including Frankfurt, Hamburg, and Munich, as well as smaller towns not accessible by rail. In any case, if you travel by bus, you'll arrive at the Zentraler Omnibusbahnhof (Central Bus Station), located near the Radio Tower at Messedamm. From there you can board a taxi or a city bus for your hotel; the nearest subway station is Kaiserdamm U-Bahn station. If you need omnibus information, dial 301 80 28 in Berlin.

Tourist Information

There are several branches of **Verkehrsamt Berlin,** Berlin's tourist information office, ready to serve you. The main one, conveniently located in the Europa-Center with its entrance on Budapester Strasse (☎ **030/262 60 31**), is just a couple minutes' walk from both Bahnhof Zoo and the Ku'damm. In addition to stocking maps and brochures about the city, the tourist office will book a hotel room for you for a 5-DM ($2.95) fee. It's open Monday through Saturday from 8am to 10:30pm and Sunday from 9am to 9pm.

In eastern Berlin, you'll find a convenient tourist office in the Hauptbahnhof train station (☎ **030/279 52 09**). Open daily from 8am to 8pm, it's the best source of information regarding museums, sightseeing, and restaurants in eastern Berlin.

Other tourist offices are located at Tegel Airport (☎ **030/ 41 01-31 45**) and Bahnhof Zoo (☎ **030/313 90 63**). Both are open daily from 8am to 11pm and will also book your hotel room.

For information in English on the latest cultural events in Berlin, your best bet is *Checkpoint Berlin,* a monthly entertainment magazine available at selected newsstands for 3 DM ($1.75). In addition to telling what's being performed when and where, it carries articles of interest to visitors, including restaurant reviews, information on art exhibitions and shopping, film reviews, and news items about Berlin.

Although not as detailed or current, another source of information in English is a pamphlet called *Berlin Turns On,* available free at the tourist office. It gives a six-month overview of what's happening in Berlin in the way of concerts, opera and theater, sports, and festivals and special events. Specifics—such as times, venues, and prices—are not given, but at least you can get an idea of what's going on before looking or inquiring elsewhere. Also available at the tourist office and at magazine kiosks for 2.80 DM ($1.65) is *Berlin Programm,* an excellent monthly publication published only in

German but valuable for its listings of plays, operas, concerts, train and plane schedules to and from Berlin, museum opening hours, and much other useful information. Even if you can't read German, you should be able to figure out what's being performed where.

If you do read German, you'll probably want to pick up a copy of either *tip* or *zitty*, two German city magazines that alternate weekly with information on fringe theater, film, rock, and folk music, and all that's happening on the alternative scene; *zitty* costs 3.30 DM ($1.95), *tip* costs 3.70 DM ($2.15).

City Layout

The layout of Berlin is markedly different from what it was just a few years ago, when former West Berlin fanned westward from Brandenburger Tor and former East Berlin was everything east of Brandenburger Tor. Now that there is no Wall slicing the city in half, roads that had been severed are being reconnected, and new buildings, grass, and trees are covering the scars left from the Wall's removal. But even though there is no longer a physical barrier between East and West, there is still a psychological one. The Wall may be gone, but for most Germans and Berliners, there is still an East and a West Berlin. Berlin is now composed of 23 precincts, each with its own town hall and shopping area. Of these, the most important for visitors are Charlottenburg in western Berlin and Berlin-Mitte in eastern Berlin. Charlottenburg contains the famous Kurfürstendamm boulevard, most of the city's hotels, the main train station (Bahnhof Zoo), the Europa-Center shopping-and-restaurant complex, many museums, and Schloss Charlottenburg (Charlottenburg Palace). Berlin-Mitte, so named because it was once the middle of Berlin and was where the city originated 800 years ago, contains Museumsinsel (Museum Island), with a number of outstanding collections; a famous boulevard, Unter den Linden; a replica of old Berlin called the *Nikolaiviertel;* and Alexanderplatz, the heart of former East Berlin. If you want, you can walk from Charlottenburg to Berlin-Mitte in less than two hours, a pretty stroll that takes you through the Tiergarten, the largest park in the city.

Running diagonally through the city is the Spree River. From the Grosser Müggelsee at the southeast end of Berlin, it runs through Köpenick, where it picks up the Dahme River; through eastern Berlin, where it's joined by the Panke River; past the Reichstag building and the Tiergarten; and on to Spandau, where it empties into the Havel River. It was on the banks of the Spree River, halfway between Köpenick and Spandau in Berlin-Mitte, that the two settlements called Berlin and Cölln sprang up centuries ago, growing and merging and eventually becoming the city we know today.

MAIN STREETS & SQUARES

The most famous street in western Berlin is the **Kurfürstendamm,** affectionately called the **Ku'damm.** About 2.5 miles long, it starts at the Kaiser-Wilhelm Gedächtniskirche (Kaiser Wilhelm Memorial Church), a ruined structure that has been left standing as a

Berlin Orientation

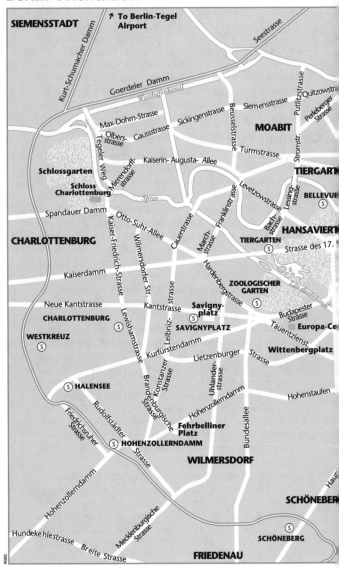

permanent reminder of the horrors of war. This is at the eastern end of the boulevard, and it's here you'll find Bahnhof Zoo (Berlin's main train station); a large park called the Tiergarten; and the Europa-Center, a 22-story building with shops, an observation platform, and Verkehrsamt Berlin (the tourist information office). From the Europa-Center, **Tauentzienstrasse** leads straight to

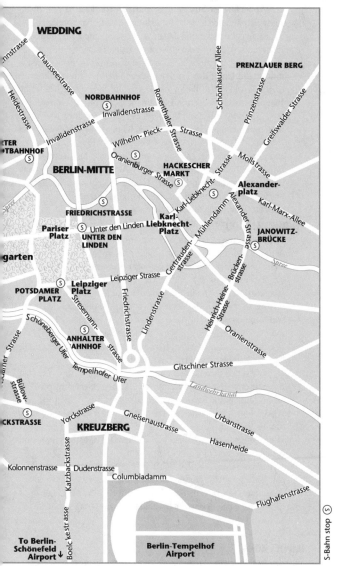

Wittenbergplatz, the location of KaDeWe, the largest department store on the European continent.

From the Gedächtniskirche, the Ku'damm stretches toward the west and is lined with many of the city's smartest boutiques, as well as many of its hotels. Just a five-minute walk north of the Ku'damm, off Knesebeckstrasse, is a square called **Savignyplatz,** noted for its bars and restaurants.

Wilmersdorfer Strasse, a pedestrian street located west of Savignyplatz and north of the Ku'damm, near a U-Bahn station of the same name, boasts several department stores, numerous shops, and restaurants. This is where most of the natives shop.

Berlin's other famous boulevard—and historically much more significant—is **Unter den Linden** in eastern Berlin. This was the heart of pre–World War II Berlin, its most fashionable and liveliest street. Its most readily recognized landmark is the Brandenburger Tor (Brandenburg Gate), and buildings along the tree-lined street have been painstakingly restored. Unter den Linden leads to Museumsinsel (Museum Island), which boasts the outstanding Pergamon Museum and a number of other great museums. Only a five-minute walk away is the modern center of eastern Berlin—**Alexanderplatz,** with its tall Fernsehturm (Television Tower). Nearby is the Nikolaiviertel (Nikolai Quarter), a reconstructed neighborhood of shops, bars, and restaurants built to resemble old Berlin.

FINDING AN ADDRESS

Although some of Berlin's streets are numbered with the evens on one side and the odds on the other, many are numbered consecutively up one side of the street and back down the other. The numbering system of the Ku'damm, for example, begins at the Gedächtniskirche and increases on the same side of the street all the way to the end of the boulevard, then jumps to the other side of the street and continues all the way back. Thus, Ku'damm 11, site of the Tschibo coffee shop, is across the street from Ku'damm 231, the Wertheim department store. It's a bit complicated at first, but numbers for each block are posted on street signs.

For a bit of German, you might be interested in knowing that *Strasse* means "street" and *Platz* means "square." Generally speaking, streets south of the Ku'damm are named after important towns and regions—such as Augsburger Strasse, Nürnberger Strasse, and Pariser Strasse. Streets north of the Ku'damm are more likely to be named after famous Germans—such as Kantstrasse, Goethestrasse, and Schillerstrasse.

Keep in mind, too, that floors are numbered as they are in Britain, starting with the ground floor (called *Erdgeschoss,* or "earth floor," in German and thus marked *E* on elevators). The next floor up is therefore the first floor (which would be the American second floor), and so on.

IMPRESSIONS

The two principles of Berlin architecture appear to me to be these. On the housetops, wherever there is a convenient place, put up the figure of a man; he is best placed standing on one leg. Wherever there is room on the ground, put either a circular group of busts on pedestals . . . or else the colossal figure of a man killing, about to kill, or having killed a beast . . . a dragon is the correct thing, but if that is beyond the artist, he may content himself with a lion or a pig.
—Lewis Carroll, 1867

When you're searching for an address, it helps to know that new ZIP codes for all of Germany were introduced in 1993 to unify the country under one postal system. Berlin now has five-digit ZIP codes similar to those in the United States; the codes vary according to the precinct and appear before the city's name.

Be aware, too, that some street and station names have been changed, particularly those named after former Communist party leaders who have fallen out of favor. Some have reverted back to their original names before Berlin was divided following the war. Most notably, these include Marx-Engels-Platz station (now Hackescher Markt), Platz der Akademie (now Gendarmenmarkt), and Marx-Engels-Forum (now Rathausstrasse), all in Berlin-Mitte.

MAPS

Unless the situation changes, the free map issued by the Berlin tourist office is flimsy and is not adequate for an in-depth study of the city. Luckily, many hotels have free maps that help supplement the tourist-office map. In addition, *Berlin Turns On,* a free publication available from the tourist office, contains a map of central Berlin. Both *Checkpoint Berlin* and *Berlin Programm,* two monthly publications, also contain maps of Berlin's city center.

If you're planning to spend more than several days in Berlin or simply want a more detailed map of the city, you'll find many maps of greater Berlin for sale at bookstores. Both Falk and Euro City put out folding city maps complete with an index of street names. Less unwieldy is Rand McNally's "City Flash," which is smaller and waterproof and shows only central Berlin (Dahlem and Spandau, for example, are not on the map). Good places to look for maps are **Kiepert,** located at the corner of Knesebeckstrasse and Hardenbergstrasse, less than a 10-minute walk from Bahnhof Zoo, and the **Europa Presse Center,** a magazine-and-newspaper store in the Europa-Center.

For a map of Berlin's transportation system, stop by the **BVG kiosk** in front of Bahnhof Zoo, where for 3 DM ($1.75) you can purchase a detailed map showing all bus, tram, S- and U-Bahn lines. More information on BVG is given below under "Getting Around."

Neighborhoods in Brief

Charlottenburg   This is western Berlin's most important precinct, named after Sophie Charlotte, wife of Prussia's Friedrich I. Here is where you'll find **Schloss Charlottenburg** (Charlottenburg Palace), built for Sophie Charlotte, with a cluster of fine museums nearby, including the **Ägyptisches Museum** (Egyptian Museum), with its famous bust of Nefertiti, and the **Bröhan Museum,** with its art nouveau collection. The majority of Berlin's hotels are in Charlottenburg, along with **Bahnhof Zoo** (the main train station), the **Ku'damm,** the **Europa-Center,** and such well-known theaters as the **Deutsche Oper** and **Theater des Westens.** Charlottenburg is huge, stretching from the Tiergarten all the way to the Havel River in the west.

Savignyplatz   Actually a part of Charlottenburg and just a five-minute walk north of the Ku'damm, Savignyplatz is a pleasant square lined with restaurants and bars boasting outdoor seating. It's a great place to relax over a beer. Radiating out from Savignyplatz (or only a few minutes' walk away) are a number of other streets important for all you nightlife bloodhounds, including Kantstrasse, Schlüterstrasse, and Bleibtreustrasse.

Tiergarten   Tiergarten, which literally means "animal garden," refers to both the **Tiergarten Park** and a precinct of the same name. Sandwiched in between Charlottenburg and Berlin-Mitte, it also encompasses a residential district called **Hansaviertel** (Hansa Quarter); the **Zoologischer Garten** (Berlin Zoo); the **Reichstag** (Parliament); the **Bauhaus-Archiv;** the **Philharmonie** (home of the famous Berlin Philharmonic Orchestra); and such museums as the **Neue Nationalgalerie** (New National Gallery), the **Kunstgewerbe Museum** (Museum of Applied Arts), and the **Musikinstrumenten Museum** (Museum of Musical Instruments). By the end of the century, several museums now in Dahlem will move to new homes in this museum district, making it the center for European art in western Berlin.

Hansaviertel   Stretching along the northern edge of Tiergarten park, the Hansaviertel is a residential district of housing projects, from one-family dwellings to apartment buildings. Each building was designed by a different architect as the result of an international gathering in 1957 of 50 leading architects, including Alvar Aalto, Walter Gropius, and Le Corbusier.

Dahlem   Once its own village and now a part of Zehlendorf precinct, Dahlem is home of western Berlin's Free University (formed after World War II, when the division of Berlin gave the city's only university to the Eastern Sector), the Max-Planck Institute, and, most important for visitors, a number of fine museums. These include the world-renowned **Gemäldegalerie** (Picture Gallery), with its European masterpieces from the 13th to the 18th century; the **Skulpturengalerie** (Sculpture Gallery); the **Museum für Volkerkunde** (Ethnological Museum); the **Museum für Deutsche Volkskunde** (Museum of German Ethnology); the **Museum für Indische Kunst** (Museum of Indian Art); and the **Museum für Ostasiatische Kunst** (Museum of Far Eastern Art). After the Gemäldegalerie and the Skulpturengalerie move to new headquarters in the Tiergarten museum district by the end of the decade, Dahlem will serve as the city's showcase of non-European art.

Spandau   Located on the western edge of the city at the juncture of the Spree and Havel Rivers, Spandau is older than Berlin itself, albeit by only five years. An independent city until swallowed up by Greater Berlin in 1920, Spandau still has its own flavor and character, including an **Altstadt** (old town) and an Italian-style **citadel** dating from the 16th century. Known also for its Christmas market in December, its shops (in the Alstadt), its woods and water recreation, it's a popular destination for both Berliners and visitors alike.

Kreuzberg   Once one of the poorest districts of Berlin, with a high concentration of immigrants, students, and others drawn by the low rents, Kreuzberg has become almost hip and is the scene of much of Berlin's counterculture. It is western Berlin's most densely populated precinct, with as many as 30% of its inhabitants from Turkey, Greece, and former Yugoslavia. About 65% of its apartments were built around the turn of the century. Known for its nightlife, Kreuzberg is also home to the **Berlin Museum,** depicting the fascinating history of the city (presently closed for renovation); the **Martin-Gropius-Bau,** with its gallery of modern art; and the **Museum Haus am Checkpoint Charlie,** which documents the history of the Wall and of nonviolent revolutions around the world.

Berlin-Mitte   Once the cultural and political heart of Berlin, Berlin-Mitte fell on the eastern side of the Wall after the city's division. It was here that Berlin originated back in the 13th century, when two settlements called Berlin and Cölin sprang up on opposite banks of the river. Included in the precinct, known as the First Precinct, is **Museumsinsel** (Museum Island), the restored **Nikolaiviertel** (Nikolai Quarter), and the boulevard **Unter den Linden.** Unfortunately, both the war and the postwar years took their toll on Berlin's historic district. What wasn't destroyed in the fighting was largely destroyed later under Communist rule, including Berlin's former royal palace, which had been the home of the Prussian monarchy for centuries; the ancient buildings on Fischerinsel, which were replaced by high-rises; and the old Acadamy of Architecture designed by Schinkel. Fortunately, those along Unter den Linden have been painstakingly restored.

Museumsinsel   Located in the middle of the Spree River, this is Berlin's oldest museum complex. Begun in the 1820s and falling under the jurisdiction of East Berlin after the war, this amazing collection of museums includes the outstanding **Pergamon Museum** with its architectural treasures.

Alexanderplatz   Originally serving as a market for oxen, Alexanderplatz was once one of Berlin's most important and liveliest squares, bounded on one side by the Rathaus (town hall). After much of Alexanderplatz was destroyed during World War II, however, the Communists rebuilt it in typical eastern block fashion—large, sterile, and nondescript. Nonetheless, it served as the heart of the East German capital, dominated by a soaring Television Tower. There's also a large S-Bahn and U-Bahn station here. The Rathaus is one of the few old buildings remaining from prewar Berlin, built in 1930 and now serving once again as the home of Berlin's central government.

Nikolaiviertel   Just southwest of Alexanderplatz and bounded on the other side by the Spree River, the Nikolaiviertel is a re-created neighborhood of old Berlin as it might have looked centuries ago. It's named after the **Nikolaikirche** (St. Nicholas's Church), Berlin's oldest church, which rises from the middle of the quarter. Grouped around the church are copies of buildings that used to exist and have been faithfully reconstructed down to the minutest historical details. In the Nikolaiviertel are approximately 30 town houses with 788 apartments (some with ceilings as high as 12 feet), as well as a number of restaurants, pubs, and shops.

Köpenick   Located at the southeast end of the city, Köpenick has a history stretching back to the 9th century and still has a much more provincial atmosphere than the inner city. An important industrial area, it is home primarily to the working class. It's a pleasant place for a stroll and boasts the 17th-century Köpenick Palace, now housing East Berlin's **Kunstgewerbe Museum** (Museum of Applied Arts).

---

2 Getting Around

Once in Berlin, you can find out about departures of trains, buses, and planes by picking up a copy of *Berlin Programm,* available for 2.80 DM ($1.65) from any Berlin tourist information office. Printed monthly, it contains an abbreviated schedule for both arrivals and departures of trains, buses, and planes in Berlin. Berlin is served by three airports and three train stations, the most important of which are Tegel Airport and Bahnhof Zoologischer Garten.

BY PUBLIC TRANSPORTATION   Berlin has an excellent public transportation network, including buses, trams (in eastern Berlin only), the U-Bahn (underground), and the S-Bahn (overhead inner-city railway). All are run by Berlin's **BVG** (☎ **752 70 20**), the largest public transportation department in Germany. You can ride farther for less money in Berlin than anywhere else in Germany. In fact, even trips to and throughout Potsdam are included in the transportation network and cost no more than the normal ticket price.

If you have any questions regarding public transportation throughout Berlin, drop by the BVG information booth located in front of Bahnhof Zoo on Hardenbergplatz. It's open daily from 8am to 8pm; in addition to giving information, it sells various tickets outlined below, including the 24-hour ticket, the Sammelkarte, and the 7-day pass. It gives out free maps of Berlin's subway and S-Bahn network and also sells a map for 3 DM ($1.75) outlining all bus, tram, and S- and U-Bahn routes throughout Berlin.

IMPRESSIONS

> *The Wall is a kind of masterpiece of the squalid, the cruel, and the hideous, the most naked assertion one could find anywhere that life was not intended to be anything but nasty, brutish, and short.*
> —Goronwy Rees, 1964

> *I love Germany so much I am glad there are two of them.*
> —François Mauriac, quoted by Roger Berthoud, 1978

One of the best things about Berlin's public transportation system is that the same ticket can be used throughout Greater Berlin for every branch of it—including the S-Bahn, the U-Bahn, and the buses. Furthermore, you can use the same ticket to transfer from one line to another, whether it's from bus to subway or vice versa. But even better is the fact that your ticket is good for up to two hours, allowing transfers, round trips, or even interruptions of your trip (you could, for example, go to Spandau for an hour or so and then return with the same ticket, as long as your entire trip is completed in two hours).

A single ticket, good for travel anywhere in Berlin, costs 3.50 DM ($2.05) for adults and 2.30 DM ($1.35) for children. If you're traveling only a short distance (six stops by bus or three stops by subway), you can purchase a **Kurzstreckenkarte** for 2.30 DM ($1.35) for adults and 1.80 DM ($1.05) for children. However, if you plan on traveling frequently by bus or subway, you're much better off buying a **Sammelkarte,** a card with four tickets at discounted rates. A normal Sammelkarte good for four rides costs 12 DM ($7.10); a Sammelkarte with four short-distance tickets costs 7.80 DM ($4.60). You can also buy a 24-hour ticket, which costs 13 DM ($7.65) for adults and 6.50 DM ($3.85) for children. And if you're going to be in Berlin for at least a week, of excellent value is the seven-day pass for 35 DM ($20.65), valid for any seven consecutive days you wish to travel. Note that it's sold only at the BVG information booth (see above).

At press time, a different tariff applied for travel exclusively within eastern Berlin, with slightly cheaper prices on single tickets, a Kurzstreckenkarte, and Sammelkarte. These were 3.10 DM ($1.80), 2 DM ($1.20), and 10.50 DM ($6.20), respectively. The problem, of course, is that you must know which stations are in former East Berlin. In addition, keep in mind that the tariffs are subject to change. If in doubt, stop by BVG.

You can purchase tickets from automatic machines at all S- and U-Bahn stations, from bus drivers, and even at some machines located at bus stops. You can also purchase tickets from the BVG kiosk in front of Bahnhof Zoo and at larger stations—such as Zoologischer Garten at Bahnhof Zoo—that have staffed ticket windows. Since most automatic machines are in German only and can be quite confusing, you may be best off heading for the BVG kiosk or a staffed ticket window to buy a Sammelkarte, a 24-hour ticket, or a weekly pass.

By U-Bahn & S-Bahn   The fastest and easiest way to get around Berlin, especially during rush hour, is by underground **(U-Bahn)** or inner-city rail system **(S-Bahn).** Trains run every 5 or 10 minutes from about 4am until midnight or 1am, except on Saturday night, when they run about an hour later. Two subway lines, the U-1 (the major east-west axis) and U-9 (the north-south axis), run all night on Friday and Saturday nights, with departures from Bahnhof Zoo approximately every half an hour. Some stations have ticket windows

The U-Bahn & the S-Bahn

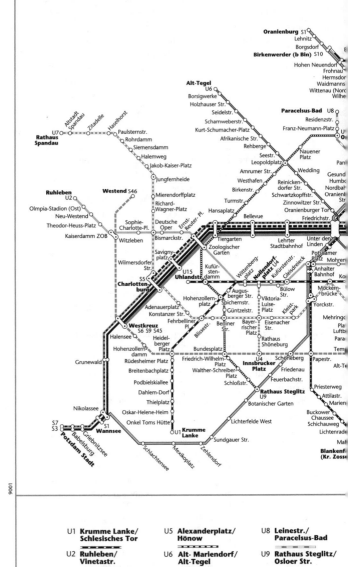

U1 **Krumme Lanke/**
Schlesisches Tor

U2 **Ruhleben/**
Vinetastr.

U4 **Innsbrucker Platz/**
Nollendorf-platz

U5 **Alexanderplatz/**
Hönow

U6 **Alt- Mariendorf/**
Alt-Tegel

U7 **Rudlow/**
Rathaus Spandau

U8 **Leinestr./**
Paracelsus-Bad

U9 **Rathaus Steglitz/**
Osloer Str.

U15 **Uhlandstr./**
Schelesisches

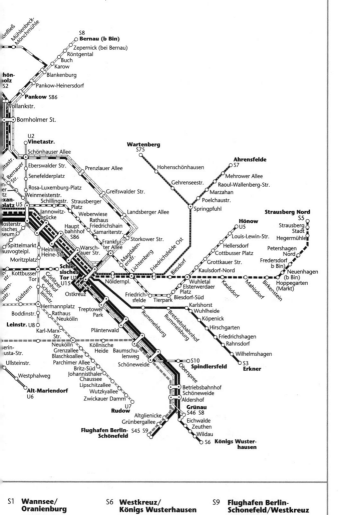

S1 **Wannsee/**
Oranienburg

S2 **Blankenfelde**
(Kr. Zossen)/
Schönholz

S3 **Potsdam Stadt/**
Erkner

S5 **Charlottenburg/**
Strausberg Nord

S6 **Westkreuz/**
Königs Wusterhausen

S7 **Potsdam Stadt/**
Ahrenfelde

S86 **Hauptbahnhof/**
Pankow

S8 **Bernau (b Bin)/**
Grünau

S9 **Flughafen Berlin-**
Schonefeld/Westkreuz

S10 **Birkenwerder (b Bin)/**
Spindlerfeld

S45 **Westkreuz/Flughafen**
Berlin-Schonefeld/

S46 **Westend/Grünau**

S75 **Warschawer Str./**
Wartenberg

where you can purchase a single ticket or Sammelkarte; most, however, have only automatic vending machines for tickets. In any case, you must validate your ticket yourself at one of the little red boxes before boarding the train. This is on the honor system—and if you're caught without a ticket you'll be charged with a 60-DM ($35.40) fine.

To board the U-Bahn or S-Bahn line bound for your destination, you have to know that line's final stop. If, for example, you're in Bahnhof Zoologischer Garten and you wish to board the U-2 to Nollendorfplatz, you have to know that Nollendorfplatz is in the direction of Vinetastrasse because you won't find Nollendorfplatz mentioned on any signs. If instead you board the U-2 going toward Ruhleben, you'll end up headed in the wrong direction. Refer to the subway map in this book or the map in all stations to determine the direction you need to go. It's not complicated, but Berlin has yet to figure out that everything would be a lot easier if directional signs included a list of stations along the way in addition to the final stop.

By Bus   With more than 170 routes, buses in Berlin carry more passengers than any other mode of transport. They are easy to use, and many are double-deckers, affording great views of the city. Some of the newer buses even have lighted panels at the front clearly displaying the next stop. In any case, a list of all stops is posted in each bus as well as at bus stops. One of my favorite lines is bus no. 100, which runs around the clock from Bahnhof Zoo to Alexanderplatz, passing the Reichstag Building and Brandenburger Tor and traveling the length of Unter den Linden along the way. It's a great way to travel to eastern Berlin's most important sites, since you can see much more on a bus than via S-Bahn. You may also wish to take advantage of the buses that run along the Ku'damm (nos. 109, 119, and 129). If you have any questions regarding which bus to take or where a bus stop is located, drop by the BVG booth in front of the Bahnhof Zoo.

You can purchase a ticket from the bus driver or use your Sammelkarte (described above). If you're transferring, simply show the bus driver your ticket. Apart from the normal day services, there are also special Nachtbusse (night buses, marked with an *N* before their number) that run the entire night, most from Bahnnof Zoo. You can pick up a brochure with their routes and schedules from the BVG booth in front of the Bahnhof Zoo. In summer, there are special excursion buses marked with a triangle that make fast and convenient runs from Theodor-Heuss-Platz to recreation areas at Grünewald, from Wannsee station to Pfaueninsel, and from Nikolassee station to Wannsee Beach.

BY TAXI   If you need a taxi, you can find one at the many taxi stands in the city, or you can telephone one of several taxi companies: 6902, 26 10 26, 69 10 01, 21 01 01, or 21 02 02. The meter starts at 3.80 DM ($2.25), plus 1.93 DM ($1.15) per kilometer. Fares from 11pm to 6am, Sundays and holidays are 2.13 DM ($1.25) per kilometer. Luggage costs 1 DM to 2 DM (60¢ to $1.20) extra.

BY CAR   You don't need a car for trips within Berlin. Public transportation is excellent, traffic jams are horrendous, and being burdened with a car means having to find a parking space. However, you may wish to rent a car for forays to the outskirts of town or such destinations as Potsdam. If you plan to stay overnight in eastern Germany, you should book your hotel room in advance.

You'll find driving in the outskirts of Berlin no more complicated than elsewhere in Germany. Driving is on the right side of the road, and standard international road signs are used. Be sure to obey the speed limit, which is 100 kph (60 mph) on the expressways outside Berlin.

Rentals   If you wish to rent a car, you'll need a valid driver's license (your U.S. license is fine) or an international driver's license. Third-party insurance is compulsory in Germany. Foreign visitors, with the exception of most European drivers, must either present their international insurance certificate (Green Card) or take out third-party insurance.

There are several well-known car-rental agencies in Berlin. **Avis** has a counter at Tegel Airport (☎ **030/410 13 148**), as well as an office near Bahnhof Zoo at Budapester Strasse 43 (☎ **030/261 18 81**). The latter office is open Monday through Friday from 7am to 6pm and Saturday from 8am to 1pm. Prices here start at 185 DM ($109.15) for one day in an Opel Corsa, including 15% sales tax and unlimited mileage.

Hertz, another big name, also has a counter at Tegel Airport (☎ **030/410 13 315**) and at Budapester Strasse 39 (☎ **030/261 10 53**). The downtown office is open Monday through Friday from 7am to 6:30pm and Saturday from 8am to 2pm. Its rates for an Opel Corsa or a Ford Fiesta start at 185 DM ($109.15) for one day, including 15% sales tax and unlimited mileage.

Keep in mind, however, that there are often special promotions with cheaper prices than those given above, including weekend and weekly rates. It pays to shop around.

Parking   If you've driven to Berlin, try to stay at a hotel that offers parking space. Otherwise, there are many parking garages in the inner city open day and night. These include **Parkhaus am Zoo,** Budapester Strasse 38; **Parkhaus Europa-Center,** Nürnberger Strasse 5–7; **Parkhaus Los-Angeles-Platz,** Augsburger Strasse 30; and **Parkhaus Metropol,** Joachimstaler Strasse 14–19. All four, which charge approximately 2 DM ($1.20) per hour, are located within a few minutes' walk of the Ku'damm, Gedächtniskirche, Europa-Center, and Bahnhof Zoo.

BY BICYCLE   You'll probably want to forgo the experience of riding a bicycle in the center of Berlin's traffic-clogged streets, but it is a fast and pleasant way to see other parts of the city. It's important to know that you're allowed to take bicycles onto certain compartments of both the U-Bahn and S-Bahn for an extra 2.30 DM ($1.35). Note, however, that bicycles are forbidden on the U-Bahn and S-Bahn during rush hours: Monday through Friday before 9am and again in the afternoon between 2 and 5:30pm. At any rate, you may wish to rent a bicycle, take the subway to the outskirts, then begin your ride from there.

Berlin by Bike, Möckernstrasse 92 (☎ **216 91 77**), is located in Kreuzberg near the Yorkstrassse S-Bahn and Möckernbrücke U-Bahn stations. From the Ku'damm, you can also reach the shop by taking bus no. 119. Rental prices for standard bikes are 15 DM ($8.85) for one day, 50 DM ($29.50) for three days, and 85 DM ($50.15) for one week. Mountain bikes start at 20 DM ($11.80) for one day, rising to 110 DM ($64.90) for one week. Racers and tandems are also available. Students receive a 15% discount. The staff gives advice on sightseeing, dispenses a free map with recommended routes, and even organizes bike tours of Berlin. Shop hours are Monday through Friday from 10am to 6pm and Saturday from 10am to 2pm.

Fast Facts: Berlin

This section is designed to make your stay in Berlin as problem-free as possible. However, keep in mind that the information below may have changed by the time you arrive. The concierge at your hotel may be able to help you if problems arise; another invaluable source is the Berlin tourist information office in the Europa-Center (☎ **262 60 31**).

American Express   The most convenient office is located in the center of town, just off the Ku'damm at Uhlandstrasse 173–174 (☎ **8845 880**). It's open Monday through Friday from 9am to 5:30pm and Saturday from 9am to noon.

There's another American Express in eastern Berlin, located at Friedrichstrasse 172 (☎ **23 84 102**), near the Französische U-Bahn station. Open Monday through Friday from 9am to 5:30pm and Saturday from 9am to noon, it has a 24-hour automatic-teller machine (for which, of course, you need a PIN number).

Area Code   The telephone area code for Berlin is 030 if you're calling from within Germany, 30 if you're calling from outside Germany. The country code for Germany is 49 if you're calling from the United States, 0049 if you're calling from most European countries.

Auto Rentals   See "Getting Around" earlier in this chapter for information on car-rental agencies and prices.

Babysitters   Most major hotels in Berlin can arrange babysitting services.

Bookstores   Kiepert is a well-known bookstore within a 10-minute walk of Bahnhof Zoo, near the Technical University at the corner of Knesebeckstrasse and Hardenbergstrasse (☎ **311 00 9**). Stocking maps and travel books in English (including books and maps of Berlin), it's open Monday through Friday from 9am to 6:30pm and

Saturday from 9am to 2pm. The nearest U-Bahn station is Ernst-Reuter-Platz.

Even more extensive are the books offered by the **British Book Shop,** Mauerstrasse 83–84 (☎ **238 46 80**), located just a couple minutes' walk from the Museum Haus am Checkpoint Charlie and near the Kochstrasse or Stadtmitte U-Bahn stations. It stocks English-language books on all subjects, including fiction, travel, and books on Berlin. It's open Monday through Friday from 9am to 6:30pm and Saturday from 9am to 2pm (to 4pm the first Saturday of the month).

Business Hours   Downtown **businesses and shops** are open Monday through Friday from 9 or 10am to 6 or 6:30pm and Saturday from 9am to 2pm. On the first Saturday of the month (called *langer Samstag*), shops remain open until 4pm in summer and 6pm in winter. In addition, most shops remain open on Thursday until 8:30pm.

Banks are open Monday through Friday from 9am to 1 or 3pm, with slightly longer hours one or two days of the week depending on the bank.

Climate   See "When to Go" in Chapter 2.

Currency   See "Information, Entry Requirements, and Money" in Chapter 2.

Currency Exchange   You can exchange money at any bank, at exchange bureaus (called *Wechsels tuben*), or at the American Express offices (see listings above). There's an exchange counter at **Tegel Airport,** open daily from 8am to 10pm. You can also exchange money at the **Wertheim** and **KaDeWe department stores,** at major hotels, and at major post offices, but the best exchange rates are offered by banks.

If you need to exchange money outside banking hours, your best bet is the **Deutsche Verkehrs-Kredit-Bank** (☎ **881 71 17**), an exchange office at Bahnhof Zoo. It's open Monday through Saturday from 7:30am to 10pm and Sunday and holidays from 8am to 7pm. You can also receive a cash advance for Diners Club, MasterCard, and Visa credit cards at the Deutsche Verkehrs-Kredit-Bank and at major banks, for which you'll need your passport. International credit cards are also accepted at various automatic-teller machines (ATMs) throughout Berlin.

Dentists/Doctors   Some first-class hotels offer medical facilities or an in-house doctor. In addition, the Berlin tourist office in the Europa-Center has a list of English-speaking doctors and dentists in Berlin. If you need a doctor in the middle of the night or in an emergency, call **31 00 31**. For an emergency-dentist, call **011 41**.

Documents Required   See "Information, Entry Requirements, and Money" in Chapter 2.

Driving Rules   See "Getting Around" earlier in this chapter.

Drugstores   Called *Apotheken* in Germany, drugstores have normal business hours just like any other shops. However, there are always a few that stay open at night and during weekends and holidays, and all drugstores post a list of those that are open. Otherwise, to find out which pharmacies are open at night in western Berlin, call 011 41. *Note:* Drugstores in Germany are pharmacies only. Stores selling cosmetics and sundries are called *Drogeries.*

Electricity   Berlin's electrical current is 220 volts AC, 50 cycles, which is much different from the American current of 110 volts, 60 cycles. In addition, plugs are different from those in the United States. You'll therefore need an adapter if you're bringing a hairdryer, electric razor, or other electrical appliance. The major hotels will probably have adapters you can use. Otherwise, you can purchase one at an electrical shop or a department store in Berlin.

Embassies/Consulates   The **U.S. Consulate** is in Dahlem at Clayallee 170 (☎ **832 40 87**). For Americans who have lost their passports, it's open Monday through Friday from 8:30 to noon; its visa section (☎ **819 74 54**) is open Monday through Friday from 8:30 to 10:30am.

The **Canadian Consulate,** located in Berlin-Mitte at Friedrichstrasse 95 (☎ **261 11 61**), is open Monday through Friday from 1:30 to 3pm, with extra morning hours for visa matters. Call first to make sure the department you need is open.

The **Australian Consulate** is at Markgrafenstrasse 46 in Berlin-Mitte (☎ **392 21 09**), open Monday through Friday from 9am to noon and 2 to 4pm. The **U.K. Consulate,** Uhlandstrasse 7–8 (☎ **309 52 93** or **309 52 92**), is open Monday through Friday from 9am to noon and 2 to 4pm (visa section, only in the morning).

Emergencies   Throughout Berlin, the emergency number for police is **110;** for fires and ambulances, it's **112.** For an emergency doctor, dial **31 00 31.**

Eyeglasses   If you need a pair of eyeglasses, you'll find most shops in the area of the Ku'damm and Tauentzienstrasse. One of these is **Apollo Optik,** Kurfürstendamm 40–41 (☎ **882 52 58**), open Monday through Friday from 9:30am to 6:30pm (Thursday to 8pm) and Saturday from 9am to 2pm (to 4pm first Saturday of the month in summer, 6pm in winter). It's best to carry your prescription with you from home.

Hairdressers/Barbers   Many first-class hotels have beauty salons and barbershops, which may be your best bet for an English-speaking stylist.

Holidays   See "When to Go" in Chapter 2.

Hospitals   If you need emergency hospital treatment, the ambulance service will deliver you to the one best suited to your case. If you need a doctor in an emergency, telephone 31 00 31. Otherwise, if you wish to check into a hospital and it's not urgent, contact your consulate for recommendations.

Information See "Information, Entry Requirements, and Money" in Chapter 2.

Language Useful phrases in German and menu translations are listed in the Appendix. In addition, the "Food and Drink" section in Chapter 1 has descriptions of German cuisine that might appear on menus. If you wish to learn German in more depth, there are countless phrase books and language books on the market, including *German for Travellers* published by Berlitz.

Note: The German alphabet contains a special character called ess-tset and written **ß.** It represents a double *s.* You'll probably see this character in street signs—for example, in Voßstraße (Vossstrasse, Voss Street) and Schloßtraße (Schlossstrasse, Schloss Street).

Laundry/Dry Cleaning All upper-bracket and most medium-price hotels offer laundry and/or dry cleaning services, with same-day services available weekdays. If not, ask the staff where the most conveniently located Laundromat is. Otherwise, there's a **Wasch Center** near the center of town at Leibnizstrasse 72 (on the corner of Kantstrasse) and another at Uhlandstrasse 53 (between Pariser Strasse and Düsseldorfer Strasse). Hours for both locations are daily from 6am to 10:30pm. A wash cycle with detergent is 6 DM ($3.55), 1 DM (60¢) for a spin, and 1 DM (60¢) for each 10 minutes' use of a dryer.

Libraries The **Amerika-Gedenkbibliothek,** Blücherplatz 1 in Kreuzberg (☎ **6905-0**), was founded to commemorate the 1948 blockade and Berlin airlift. Located near the Hallesches Tor U-Bahn station, it's open Monday from 4 to 7pm and Tuesday through Saturday from 11am to 7pm. In addition, the **Amerika-Haus,** located at Hardenbergstrasse 20 (☎ **31 10 99 10**), next to Bahnhof Zoo, houses a small library and is open Monday, Wednesday, and Friday from 11:30am to 5:30pm and Tuesday and Thursday from 11:30am to 8pm. In both cases, out-of-town visitors may read books only inside the library.

Liquor Laws Compared to U.S. liquor laws, Germany's seem rather liberal. As in many European countries, drinking beer or wine with a meal is so much a part of the culture that even teenagers may receive a glass at home. The minimum drinking age is 16 if accompanied by parents, 18 if alone. However, laws against drunk driving in Germany are strictly enforced and respected. Don't drink more than one beer if you intend to drive.

Lost Property **Berlin's general-property office** is at Platz der Luftbrücke (☎ **699-0**). For property lost on public transportation services, check the **BVG lost-and-found** at Lorenzweg 5 (☎ **751 80 21**).

Luggage Storage There's luggage storage at both Tegel Airport and the main train station, Bahnhof Zoologischer Garten (Bahnhof Zoo), where you'll also find lockers.

Mail   Mailboxes are yellow in Germany; for out-of-town delivery, use the ANDERE RICHTUNG slot. Airmail letters to North America cost 3 DM ($1.75) for the first 20 grams, while postcards cost 1.05 DM (65¢).

The **post office** in Bahnhof Zoo is open Monday through Friday from 6am to midnight and Saturday and Sunday from 8am to midnight for mail, telephone calls, and telegrams. You can have your mail sent here in care of Hauptpostlagernd, Postamt 120 Bahnhof Zoo, D-1000 Berlin 12 (☎ **313 97 99** for inquiries). You can also have your mail sent to you via the **American Express office,** Kurfürstendamm 11 (☎ **882 75 75**), a service that is free if you have American Express traveler's checks or credit card. Otherwise, the service costs a steep 2 DM ($1.20) *per inquiry.*

If you want to mail a package, you'll have to go to one of the city's larger post offices. Two that are conveniently located are at Goethestrasse 2–3 and at Marburger Strasse 12–13, which is near the Europa-Center. Both have regular post-office hours, which are Monday through Friday from 8am to 6pm and Saturday from 8am to 1pm. Both sell cardboard boxes, complete with string and tape, which come in five sizes ranging in price from 2.90 to 5.50 DM ($1.70 to $3.25).

Maps   See "Orientation" earlier in this chapter.

Newspapers/Magazines   *Checkpoint Berlin,* an English-language city magazine, is published monthly with listings of current concerts, exhibits, restaurant reviews, news items, and other information of interest to visitors. There are no English-language newspapers published in Berlin, but you can pick up such English-language newspapers and magazines as the *International Herald Tribune, USA Today, Time,* and *Newsweek* at a newsstand called **Europa Presse Center,** located on the ground floor of the Europa-Center (☎ **216 30 03**); it's open daily from 9am to 11pm.

Photographic Needs   Film, batteries, and other photographic necessities are available at the **Wertheim** and **KaDeWe department stores,** described in Chapter 8. In addition, **Photo Huber** is conveniently located in the Europa-Center (☎ **262 46 66**) and provides color print development in one hour. It's open Monday through Friday from 9am to 6:30pm and Saturday from 10am to 2pm (to 6pm on the first Saturday of the month in summer, 4pm in winter).

Police   The emergency number for police throughout Berlin is **110.**

Radio/TV   For radio programs in English, tune in 90.2 FM (87.6 on cable) for the BBC. As for television, many medium- and all upper-bracket hotels offer cable TV with CNN news broadcasts from the United States; a sports channel in English; the Super Channel, with programs from the United Kingdom; and MTV, a music channel. Many also offer in-room pay-per-view video selections.

Restrooms   If you ask for the "bathroom" in Germany, your host is going to think it mighty strange that you wish to take a bath in his home or restaurant. A restroom in Germany is called a *Toilette* and is often labeled *WC* in public places. Women's toilets are often marked with an *F* for *Frauen* or *D* for *Damen,* while men's are identified with an *H* for *Herren* or *M* for *Männer.*

In the center of Berlin there are public facilities at Wittenbergplatz and near the Europa-Center on Tauentzienstrasse. Other places to look for facilities include fast-food outlets, department stores, hotels, restaurants, and pubs. If there's an attendant, it's customary to tip 30 to 50 pfennigs (20¢ to 30¢).

Safety   Berlin is a relatively safe city, particularly in places frequented by tourists, such as the Ku'damm. However, as in any unfamiliar city, it's wise to stay alert and be aware of your immediate surroundings, because every society has its criminals. Wear a moneybelt and don't sling your camera or purse over your shoulder, particularly at night or in crowded places; wear the strap diagonally across your body. This will minimize the possibility of becoming the victim of a crime. Keep your valuables in a safety-deposit box at your hotel.

There's no denying that Germany has recently seen a number of violent acts committed against minorities by right-wing extremists. Although Berlin has not suffered as much from such acts as have other parts of the country, it would be wise to avoid the outskirts of former East Berlin (an area of little tourist interest) if this is a concern.

Shoe Repairs   For quick service on shoe repairs, head for **Wertheim department store,** 231 Kurfürstendamm, or either **Karstadt** or **Hertie department store,** both on Wilmersdorfer Strasse, where you'll find a Mister Minit counter specializing in repairs.

Taxes   A 15% government tax is included in the price of restaurants, hotels, and goods in Germany. On many goods, however, tourists can obtain a refund of the value-added tax (VAT)—see Chapter 8 for information on how to obtain a refund. There is no airport departure tax.

Taxis   See "Getting Around" earlier in this chapter.

Telephone   Berlin's telephone system is not much different from that in the United States when it comes to a dial tone or a busy tone, but it does differ in the amount of telephone digits. Some telephone numbers have four digits, others may have seven or eight. Area codes in Germany are often enclosed in parentheses—such as (030) for Berlin—and the rest of the digits are simply grouped into twos or threes. Thus, a seven-digit number in Berlin would be written (030) 881 47 68. If you come across a number with a dash, the number following the dash is the extension number, which you can reach directly simply by dialing the entire number.

Local telephone calls from public telephone booths, which are yellow or gray and pink in Berlin, cost 30 pfennigs (20¢) for the first three minutes and allow you to telephone throughout Berlin. Note, however, that public phones in some restaurants and other establishments cost 50 pfennigs for the first three minutes. To make sure you don't get cut off in the middle of a conversation, insert some extra

10-pfennig coins—unused coins will be returned to you at the end of the call.

If you want to make an international call, look for phone booths with the white-and-green INTERNATIONAL sign and make sure you have a handful of change. Otherwise, you can purchase a telephone card, available at post offices. They come in values of 12 DM ($7.10) and 50 DM ($29.50). Simply insert them face-up into the telephone slot. Telephone cards are becoming so popular in Germany that many public telephones no longer accept coins. The 12-DM card gives you approximately 40 minutes of local telephone calls; the 50-DM card is useful for long-distance calls.

Easiest, however, is to make long-distance calls from a post office, where you can also send telegrams. The main post office at Bahnhof Zoo (Berlin's main train station) is open until midnight. It costs 9.66 DM ($5.70) to make a three-minute long-distance call to the United States. Try to avoid making calls from your hotel room— a surcharge added to the bill may double or even triple the rate. Toll-free access codes are **0130 0010** for AT&T, **0130 0012** for MCI, and **0130 0013** for Sprint.

If you need information on a telephone number in Berlin or Germany, dial **011 88** for information.

Time   Berlin is 6 hours ahead of Eastern Standard Time in New York, 7 hours ahead of Chicago, and 9 hours ahead of Los Angeles. Berlin operates on Central European Time—except that it's officially 6 minutes and 22 seconds behind Central European Time. Don't ask me why. Germany goes on and off Daylight Saving Time at slightly different dates than the United States, with the result that Berlin is 7 hours ahead of New York for short periods in spring and fall. Since this can affect rail timetables, make sure you double-check if you're traveling during spring or fall.

Tipping   Since a service charge is usually included in hotel and restaurant bills, you are not obliged to tip. However, it is customary to round off restaurant bills to the nearest mark, which you give directly to the waiter or waitress rather than leave on the table. If your bill is 14 DM, therefore, say "15 DM" if you hand her a 20-DM note and you'll receive 5 DM in change. If a meal costs more than 20 DM ($11.80), most Germans will add a 10% tip. For taxi drivers, it's customary to round off to the nearest mark. Tip hairdressers or barbers 10%. Porters receive 2 DM ($1.20) per bag.

Water   Although the water is technically safe to drink in Berlin, take your cue from the Germans, who almost never drink their tap water. Instead, they ask for bottled water, either carbonated or noncarbonated.

3 Networks & Resources

If you need more information than what's given above, contact the tourist information office or telephone one of the organizations below for advice on where to turn.

FOR STUDENTS   Berlin's oldest university, now called Humboldt University, was founded in 1810 and suffered the fate of the divided city after World War II. Most departments and institutes of the university were located in the Soviet zone, and when some students were suspended for political reasons in 1948, teachers and students founded the Free University in West Berlin. Also in western Berlin is the University of Technology, located near Bahnhof Zoo. Today, with a student population of well over 100,000, Berlin is Germany's largest "university city." As in most German cities, there are student cafeterias with budget-priced meals (see Chapter 4). Most museums offer student discounts, and some theaters (such as the renowned Schiller-Theater) offer unused tickets to students at a 50% reduction on the night of the performance.

For discounts, you'll need an International Student Card to prove you're a bona fide student. It's easiest to apply for the card at your own university (see "For Students" in Section 5 of Chapter 2), but if you've arrived in Berlin without one and can show proof of current student status, you can obtain one at **ARTU,** Hardenbergstrasse 9 (☎ **31 04 66**). A travel agency, it's located in the district of the University of Technology, not far from Bahnhof Zoo, and also offers discounted plane fares around the world. It's open Monday through Friday from 10am to 6pm (Wednesday from 11am to 6pm) and Saturday from 10am to 1pm.

FOR GAY MEN & LESBIANS   Berlin has a very active alternative scene, with many different organizations for gay men and women. **Kommunikations- und Beratungszentrum für Homosexuelle Männer und Frauen,** a center of communication and counseling for both gay men and lesbians, is located at Kulmer Strasse 20 in Schöneberg. Call **215 90 90** for Shwulenberatung (counseling for gay men) and **215 20 00** for Lesbenberatung (counseling for lesbians). For nightlife information, see "Gay and Lesbian Bars" under "The Bar Scene" in Chapter 9.

FOR WOMEN   Fraueninfothek Berlin, located in eastern Berlin at Dircksenstrasse 47 (☎ **282 3980**), near Alexanderplatz or Hackescher Markt S-bahn station, is a women's information center run by and for women. The center's staff provides sightseeing information, makes hotel reservations, recommends counseling centers, and even gives advice on transportation routes and tips about restaurants and bars. Office hours are Monday through Friday from 10am to 6pm.

As for establishments that cater to women only, **Artemisia,** Brandenburgische Strasse 18, W-1000 Berlin (☎ **030/87 89 05**), is a bright and cheery hotel geared toward the needs of female travelers (see Chapter 4), while the cafe **Extra Dry,** Pariser Strasse 3 (☎ **885 22 06**), sells snacks and nonalcoholic beverages in a comfortable, friendly, and pleasant atmosphere (see Chapter 9 under "The Bar Scene").

4

Berlin Accommodations

Aѕ in most major cities, your biggest daily expense in Berlin will be for accommodations. These range from deluxe hotels to modestly priced pensions, with a great many choices in between. What's more, unlike most big cities, Berlin boasts a wealth of accommodations smack in its center, clustered along or near its main boulevard, the Kurfürstendamm, called the Ku'damm for short. Even budget-range accommodations abound near the Ku'damm, but if you opt for a hotel removed from the hustle and bustle of the city center, you're never more than a short bus or subway ride from Bahnhof Zoologischer Garten (Bahnhof Zoo), Berlin's main train station.

As for eastern Berlin, it has not yet developed a tourist-oriented sector, though that is slowly changing. Presently there are only a few upper-range hotels, and most of Berlin's best restaurants and nightlife entertainments remain in the west. However, business or your own interests may lead you to eastern Berlin, so I've included a few choices. Hopefully, there will be many more choices in the future, particularly in the medium- and budget-range hotels.

All rates given below include the 15% government tax and the service charge. In addition, note that many hotels, from budget to expensive, include a continental or buffet-style breakfast in their rates. Many visitors report they eat so much for breakfast that it tides them over until an early dinner, thus saving on lunch. If you thrive on breakfast, therefore, it would make sense to pay slightly more for a room that includes a full breakfast in its rates than to opt for one that doesn't.

Hot showers, even those in cheaper pensions (where the shower is down the hall), are also included in all room rates. The rates are much higher for rooms with private showers and toilets (a toilet is usually referred to as a WC, or water closet). If you're on a budget, therefore, you can save lots of money by taking a room without private facilities. If you do desire your own shower and WC, note that some hotels charge more for a bathtub than for a shower (bathtubs are somewhat of a rarity in Berlin's hotels and are considered a luxury). And remember, a "bathroom" in Germany refers to a room containing a bathtub or shower (usually a room separate from the WC).

Another thing to keep in mind: Some hotels charge more for a twin-bedded room (a room with two beds), while others charge more for a double room (a room with one full- or king-size bed). Most hotels, however, charge the same for both a double room and a twin-bedded room. I've referred to both twins and doubles simply as doubles, meaning the price for two persons. Finally, few hotels outside the expensive category have air conditioning—except for an occasional two weeks in August, it rarely gets hot enough to warrant it.

The rates given below for each accommodation are those charged throughout the year. For upper- and moderate-price hotels, these rates usually vary according to the season, with more charged during *Messen* (international conferences and conventions) and in the main tourist season from spring through autumn. Since rates can vary as much as 100 DM ($59) throughout the year, be sure to ask for the exact rate

Frommer's Smart Traveler: Hotels

Value-Conscious Travelers Should Take Advantage of the Following:

1. Lodging in the heart of town in all price categories, near the Ku'damm, Bahnhof Zoo, the Europa-Center, shops, restaurants, and bars.

2. Rooms without private bathrooms or showers, which are much cheaper.

3. Rooms on upper floors of inexpensive pensions without elevators, which are sometimes cheaper than rooms near the ground floor.

4. Winter discounts, offered primarily by expensive and moderately priced hotels but also by a few inexpensive hotels.

5. Weekend rates.

6. Accommodations that include breakfast in the price.

7. Youth hotels and hostels, open throughout the year.

Questions to Ask If You're on a Budget

1. Is breakfast included in the price? Is it buffet style, allowing you to eat as much as you want?

2. Are prices different for a double or a twin-bedded room? Some hotels charge more for a double, others for a twin, though most charge the same for both.

3. How much is the surcharge on local and long-distance telephone calls? You may pay almost twice as much for a call from your room than you would from a public telephone.

4. Is there parking space at the hotel, and if so, what is the charge per day? Some hotels outside the city center offer free parking.

when making your reservation and inquire whether you can be given a discount for off-season or weekend stays or if you're paying more because of a *Messe*. In any case, remember that rates given below reflect both high- and low-season rates; the lowest rates for each single or double are therefore usually available only off-season, though some hotels offer cheaper-priced rooms with fewer amenities year-round.

In contrast, note that most inexpensively priced and budget hotels keep the same rates year-round, regardless of the season.

Keep in mind, too, that while every effort was made to be as accurate as possible, rates may change during the lifetime of this book—which means they may go up. In fact, Berlin has become such a hot destination and land prices have risen so dramatically since reunification that some hotels and pensions have responded by doubling their rates. To avoid misunderstanding or embarrassment when it comes time to pay the bill, be sure to ask the rate when making your reservations.

The hotels below are divided into five price categories. The very expensive hotels charge more than 400 DM ($236) for two persons but provide first-rate accommodations and a wide range of services, which may include free use of a health club and swimming pool, a concierge to help you with any problems that may arise, cocktail lounges or bars, and fine restaurants. Hotels in the next category, expensive, charge 300 DM to 400 DM ($177 to $236) for two persons and also offer comfortable rooms with usual amenities like private bathrooms, cable TVs offering programs in English or in-house videos, minibars, radios, and telephones. However, don't expect the same roominess or facilities you'd find in a hotel of comparable price, say, in the midwestern United States. However, prices often include breakfast, and some hotels in this category have pools guests can use for free. In addition, some hotels have outfitted all their rooms with hairdryers, room safes, and "trouser pressers," a contraption that irons pants or skirts. You may also encounter a free shoeshine machine, which has a rotating brush.

Moderately priced hotels, charging from 200 DM to 300 DM ($118 to $177) for a double, offer rooms with private showers and WCs and other amenities, which may include minibars. Inexpensive lodgings, ranging from 100 DM to 200 DM ($59 to $118) for a double room, offer accommodations with or without private showers and WCs. They are usually smaller hotels and pensions. Although a pension usually has fewer rooms and lower prices than a hotel, sometimes there is only a fine line between the two. Finally, budget accommodations include pensions that charge less than 100 DM ($59) for a double room, as well as rock-bottom youth hotels and hostels.

Note that in Germany floors are counted beginning with the ground floor (which would be the American first floor) and go up to the first floor (the American second floor) and beyond. Directions are given for each establishment listed below, including instructions from Tegel Airport or Bahnhof Zoologischer Garten (Bahnhof Zoo), as well as the nearest U-Bahn or S-Bahn station where relevant.

It's always a good idea to reserve a room in advance to avoid disappointment or time wasted searching for a room. In addition, rooms become scarce during the International Film Festival (end of February) and the Berlin Festival (running from the end of August to October), as well as during the frequent international conferences, fairs, and conventions (Messen) held in Berlin. And since reunification, Berlin has become a popular destination for visitors from around the world. Even winters, once slow periods for tourism in Berlin, are bustling with life.

Remember: If the recommendations below are full, the tourist office (☎ **262 60 31**) will find a room for you for a 5-DM ($2.95) fee.

1 Very Expensive

On or Near the Ku'damm ─────────────

Bristol Hotel Kempinski, Kurfürstendamm 27, 10719 Berlin.
☎ **030/88 43 40,** or toll free **800/426-3135** in the U.S.
Fax 030/883 60 75. 315 rms, 44 suites. MINIBAR TV TEL
Bus: 109 from Tegel Airport to Uhlandstrasse.
U-Bahn: Kurfürstendamm.

Rates: 380–510 DM ($224–$300) single; 470–580 DM ($277–$342)
double; 650–820 DM ($383.50–$483.80) junior suite; from 930 DM
($548.70) suite. Extra bed 50 DM ($29.50). Children under 12 stay free
in parents' room. Buffet breakfast 30 DM ($17.70). AE, DC, MC, V.
Parking: 30 DM ($17.70).

A member of the Leading Hotels of the World, the Kempinski is
considered by many to be the top hotel in Berlin. Certainly it's the
best known. Although the present building dates from 1952 and has
been renovated several times since then, its name stretches back before World War II, when the original Hotel Bristol was located on
Unter den Linden and was regarded as one of Germany's foremost
establishments. Today the hotel still exudes an old-world elegance,
with antiques, chandeliers, and elaborate tapestries in the lobby. It
occupies a prime spot on the Ku'damm, only a five-minute walk from
Bahnhof Zoo; in fact, its restaurant Kempinski Eck is a favorite place
for people-watching, with tables on the sidewalk in summer.

All rooms are luxuriously appointed, complete with soundproof
windows, remote-control TVs with cable stations, hairdryers, magnifying makeup mirrors in the bathrooms, and vanity stools. Room
styles vary, from those with modern furnishings to those with antiques or Chinese decor.

Dining/Entertainment: Both the Kempinski and the Kempinski
Eck offer dining in a relaxed atmosphere with a view of the Ku'damm.
For a more elegant atmosphere, the Kempinski Grill & Hummer Bar
excels in lobster and international cuisine and has long been consid-
ered a Berlin institution. After dinner, guests can retire to the Bristol
Bar for a drink and dancing.

Services: Same-day laundry and dry cleaning, 24-hour room service, limousine service, babysitting.

Facilities: Indoor pool, sauna, massage, solarium, fitness room,
business center, beauty parlor and barbershop, house doctor, newsstand, counter for theater tickets, no-smoking rooms.

★ **Grand Hotel Esplanade,** Lützowufer 15, 10785 Berlin.
☎ **030/26 10 11,** or toll free **800/223-5652** in the U.S.
Fax 030/265 11 71. 369 rms, 33 suites. A/C MINIBAR TV TEL
Bus: 109 from Tegel Airport to Budapester Strasse.
U-Bahn: Nollendorfplatz.

Rates: 420–515 DM ($247.80–$303.85) single; 470–570 DM
($277.30–$336.30) double; 700 DM ($413) penthouse; from 1,050 DM

($619.50) suite. Extra bed 50 DM ($29.50). Children under 12 stay free in parents' room. Buffet breakfast 29 DM ($17.10) extra. AE, DC, MC, V. **Parking:** 25 DM ($14.75).

Privately owned by a Berliner, the Esplanade opened in 1988 and quickly established itself as one of the best hotels in the city. Its lobby is modern and simple yet pleasant and refined, with gray-speckled marble floor and walls, black-leather chairs, and a rug the color of the Caribbean Sea. As much as 1.8 million DM ($1.12 million) was spent on artwork alone. The hotel stands beside a canal, across from the Bauhaus-Archive (featuring the works of Walter Gropius and other famous designers) and about a 15-minute walk from the Ku'damm.

Rooms are bright and cheerful, with white walls, beautifully crafted ash-wood furniture, soundproofing, and queen-size beds fitted with down quilts. Both the radios and the cable TVs with in-house pay videos are operated by remote control, and the bathrooms have magnifying makeup mirrors and hairdryers. Penthouse rooms are larger and have their own terraces.

Dining/Entertainment: Harry's New York Bar is one of the best and best-known bars in Berlin, good for a cocktail either before or after dinner in the adjoining Gourmet-Restaurant Harlekin. Buffet breakfast is served in the cheerful Orangerie, while Berlin specialties and beer are dished out in the Eck-Kneipe.

Services: 24-hour room service, same-day laundry, shoeshine machines on each floor, in-house doctor and nurse, babysitting, limousine service.

Facilities: Indoor pool, whirlpool, sauna, solarium, massage, hair salon, boutique, 30 no-smoking rooms.

Inter-Continental Berlin, Budapester Strasse 2, 10787 Berlin.
☎ **030/260 20,** or toll free **800/327-0200** in the U.S. Fax 030/260 280 760. 511 rms, 33 suites. A/C MINIBAR TV TEL
Bus: 109 from Tegel Airport to Budapester Strasse.
U-Bahn: Bahnhof Zoologischer Garten.
Rates: 370–480 DM ($218.30–$283.20) single, 580 DM ($342.20) in peak season; 425–540 DM ($250.75–$318.60) double, 645 DM ($380.55) in peak season; from 700 DM ($413) suite. Extra bed 55 DM ($32.45). Buffet breakfast 29 DM ($17.10) extra. AE, DC, MC, V. **Parking:** 25 DM ($14.75).

Americans should feel at home at this branch of the international chain, Berlin's largest hotel. Its modern and very spacious marble lobby features palm trees, huge flower arrangements, and Asian-influenced furniture; be sure to take a look at its glass-pyramid entryway, which pre-dates those at the Louvre in Paris. The Inter-Continental has a good location near the zoo and the Tiergarten and is only a five-minute walk from the Europa-Center and the Ku'damm. Rooms, many with views of the zoo or the Gedächtniskirche, were recently updated and enlarged and are outfitted with the usual cable TVs, soundproof windows, and first-class amenities.

Western Berlin Accommodations

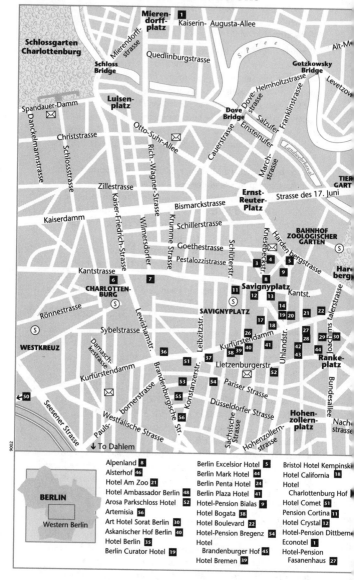

Alpenland **8**	Berlin Excelsior Hotel **5**	Bristol Hotel Kempinski
Alsterhof **46**	Berlin Mark Hotel **44**	Hotel California **18**
Hotel Am Zoo **21**	Berlin Penta Hotel **24**	Hotel
Hotel Ambassador Berlin **48**	Berlin Plaza Hotel **41**	Charlottenburg Hof
Arosa Parkschloss Hotel **52**	Hotel-Pension Bialas **9**	Hotel Comet **51**
Artemisia **56**	Hotel Bogata **38**	Pension Cortina **11**
Art Hotel Sorat Berlin **30**	Hotel Boulevard **22**	Hotel Crystal **12**
Askanischer Hof Berlin **40**	Hotel-Pension Bregenz **54**	Hotel-Pension Dittberne
Hotel Berlin **35**	Hotel	Econotel **1**
Berlin Curator Hotel **19**	Brandenburger Hof **45**	Hotel-Pension
	Hotel Bremen **39**	Fasanenhaus **27**

Dining/Entertainment: Zum Hugenotten is the hotel's finest restaurant and serves traditional international cuisine; the L.A. Café is its breakfast and snack restaurant; and Marlene, named after Berlin's most famous daughter, is the place to go for a late-night drink.

Services: 24-hour room service, same-day laundry, valet, babysitting.

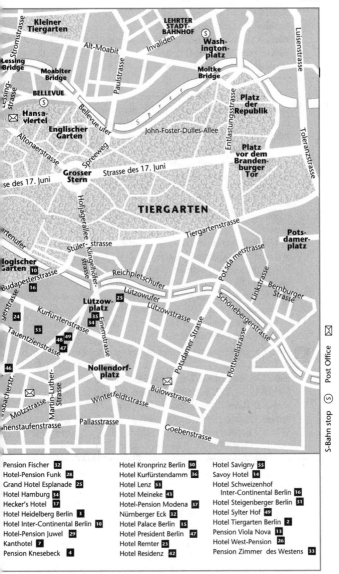

0.5 mi
0 ⊟⊟⊟⊟⊟ 0.8 km

⊠ Post Office

Ⓢ S-Bahn stop

Pension Fischer **32**
Hotel-Pension Funk **28**
Grand Hotel Esplanade **25**
Hotel Hamburg **34**
Hecker's Hotel **17**
Hotel Heidelberg Berlin **3**
Hotel Inter-Continental Berlin **10**
Hotel-Pension Juwel **29**
Kanthotel **7**
Pension Knesebeck **4**

Hotel Kronprinz Berlin **50**
Hotel Kurfürstendamm **36**
Hotel Lenz **53**
Hotel Meineke **43**
Hotel-Pension Modena **37**
Nürnberger Eck **32**
Hotel Palace Berlin **15**
Hotel President Berlin **47**
Hotel Remter **23**
Hotel Residenz **42**

Hotel Savigny **55**
Savoy Hotel **14**
Hotel Schweizenhof
  Inter-Continental Berlin **16**
Hotel Steigenberger Berlin **31**
Hotel Sylter Hof **49**
Hotel Tiergarten Berlin **2**
Pension Viola Nova **13**
Hotel West-Pension **26**
Pension Zimmer des Westens **33**

Facilities: Indoor pool, sauna, shopping arcade, business center, beauty salon and barbershop, newsstand, rental bicycles, no-smoking floor, rooftop helipad.

Hotel Palace Berlin, Europa-Center, 10789 Berlin. ☎ **030/25 02-0.** Fax 030/262 65 77. 322 rms, 16 suites. A/C MINIBAR TV TEL

Bus: 109 from Tegel Airport to Budapester Strasse.
U-Bahn: Bahnhof Zoologischer Garten or Kurfürstendamm.
Rates: 320–490 DM ($188.80–$289) single; 400–550 DM ($236–$324) double; from 700 DM ($413) suite. Extra bed 70 DM ($41.30). Buffet breakfast 26 DM ($15.35) extra. AE, DC, MC, V.

You can't get much closer to the Europa-Center than this—the Palace Berlin is right inside the huge complex with its casino and many shops and restaurants. It enjoys an international clientele and has a comfortable, personable lobby filled with plants and fresh flowers. Hotel guests have free use of the Thermen, a large health spa with sauna and pool in the Europa-Center.

Guests receive credit-card-size electronic "keys" to their rooms. The rooms are soundproof and offer trouser pressers, radios, hairdryers, and remote-control cable TVs. The more expensive rooms, located in the newer Casino Wing, offer marble bathrooms with telephones and magnifying makeup mirrors and separate tubs and showers.

Dining/Entertainment: One restaurant, specializing in French and international dishes, is located inside the hotel; there are also a lounge and a bar. In addition, the Palace operates two informal restaurants in the Europa-Center: Tiffany's, with its "outdoor" terrace dining, and Alt-Nürnberg, serving Bavarian and Berlin specialties.

Services: 24-hour room service, same-day laundry, shoeshine.

Facilities: Free use of Thermen pool and sauna in Europa-Center, no-smoking rooms.

$ Hotel Schweizerhof Inter-Continental Berlin,
Budapester Strasse 21–31, 10787 Berlin. ☎ **030/269 60,** or toll free **800/327-0200** in the U.S. Fax 030/269 69 00. 420 rms, 10 suites. MINIBAR TV TEL **Bus:** 109 from Tegel Airport to Budapester Strasse. **U-Bahn:** Bahnhof Zoologischer Garten.
Rates: 325–490 DM ($191.75–$289) single; 380–545 DM ($224–$321.55) double; from 650 DM ($383.50) suite. Extra bed 50 DM ($29.50). Children under 12 stay free in parents' room. Buffet breakfast 29 DM ($17.10) extra. AE, DC, MC, V. **Parking:** 24 DM ($14.15).

Established by a Swiss firm that prides itself on providing only the best in Swiss hospitality, the Schweizerhof belongs to the Inter-Continental group and is practically across the street from the Inter-Continental Berlin. To live up to its Swiss name, the hotel displays lots of natural wood in its decor and offers native specialties in its Grill Restaurant. Its pool is one of Berlin's largest. Some rooms have air conditioning. All around, it's one of the best values in its category.

Rooms are nice and pleasant, with radios and cable TVs (with video programs). The deluxe rooms in the newer west wing even have balconies overlooking the zoo.

Dining/Entertainment: A breakfast buffet, offering everything from rye bread and Muesli to eggs and smoked ham, is served in the Alter Markt, a restaurant designed to look like a marketplace. The

Grill Restaurant serves not only Swiss and German specialties but also international dishes and a changing four-course menu. There are also two bars.

Services: 24-hour room service, complimentary shoeshine, same-day laundry and dry cleaning, in-house nurse.

Facilities: Large indoor pool, sauna, solarium, whirlpool, massage, fitness center, Japanese boutique, rental bicycles, no-smoking floor.

$ **Hotel Steigenberger Berlin,** Los-Angeles-Platz 1, 10789 Berlin. ☎ **030/212 70,** or toll free **800/223-5652** in the U.S. Fax 030/212 71 17. 366 rms, 11 suites. AC MINIBAR TV TEL
Bus: 109 from Tegel Airport to Tauentzienstrasse.
U-Bahn: Kurfürstendamm.
Rates: 315–435 DM ($185.85–$256.65) single, up to 490 DM ($289) single during Messen; 370–500 DM ($218.30–$295) double, up to 585 DM ($345.15) during Messen; from 820 DM ($483.80) suite. Extra bed 65 DM ($38.35). Children under 12 stay free in parents' room. Buffet breakfast 26 DM ($15.35) extra. AE, DC, MC, V. **Parking:** 20 DM ($11.80).

This hotel, with a great location on a quiet square near the Gedächtniskirche and the Europa-Center, about a five-minute walk from Bahnhof Zoo, boasts excellent service and a well-trained, efficient staff. It's been a favorite haunt of visiting businesspeople and journalists ever since it opened in 1981, not only for its location but also for its facilities. If you want to be close to the hustle and bustle of the Ku'damm but without the accompanying noise, this is a good choice.

Rooms are virtually the same throughout and boast the same amenities, including two sinks and magnifying makeup mirrors in the bathrooms, hairdryers, TVs with cable and pay videos, radios, safes, and soundproof windows that can also be opened. The more expensive rooms in each category are slightly larger in size.

Dining/Entertainment: The hotel's finest restaurant is the Park Restaurant, which offers classic international dishes, nouvelle cuisine that changes with the seasons, and more than 400 wines and spirits. The Berliner Stube is decorated in the tradition of old Berlin, with solid-oak tables and period engravings of the city, and offers hearty German fare. The Café Charlotte exudes the atmosphere of a Viennese coffeehouse, with various coffees, cakes, and tarts, as well as international newspapers. The Cocktail Bar has a happy hour daily except Monday from 5 to 7pm, and there's music in the Piano Bar from 5pm.

Services: 24-hour room service, complimentary shoeshine, house doctor, babysitting, same-day laundry.

Facilities: Indoor pool, sauna, massage, solarium, shopping arcade, hairdresser, newsstand, no-smoking floor, rooms for the disabled.

Berlin-Mitte (Eastern Berlin) ——————————————

★ **Maritim Grand Hotel,** Friedrichstrasse 158–164, 10117 Berlin. ☎ **030/232 70,** Fax 030/2327 33 62. 312 rms, 34 suites.

A/C MINIBAR TV TEL **S-Bahn:** Friedrichstrasse.
U-Bahn: Französische Strasse.
Rates: 390–590 DM ($230–$348) single; 520–720 DM ($306.80–$424.80) double; from 800 DM ($472) junior suite; from 990 DM ($584.10) regular suite. Extra bed 80 DM ($47.20). Children under 12 stay free in parents' room. Buffet breakfast 28 DM ($16.50). AE, DC, MC, V.

This would be a luxury hotel no matter where in the world it was. Constructed by a Japanese firm and opened in 1987, it is so cleverly designed it looks as if it's been here forever. From its mock turn-of-the-century facade to its atrium lobby with a sweeping staircase (Scarlett O'Hara would have killed for this one), the hotel has a grand, elegant, yet cozy ambience. It has one of the best locations in the city, right off Unter den Linden, and even boasts its own lovely roof garden, where guests can sit and relax in the summer. There are plants throughout the hotel, as well as exotic orchids.

Even the rooms are what you'd expect in a first-class establishment, along with a few extras—such as bathroom scales and phones, magnifying makeup mirrors, hairdryers, TVs with videos, and bathrobes. The regular suites are decorated in various styles, including a Japanese apartment complete with futon, tatami, and beautifully papered walls. In short, this is one of Berlin's finest hotels, East or West.

Dining/Entertainment: Unsurprisingly, this hotel offers some of the best dining in the city. Le Grand Restaurant Silhouette, decorated in art nouveau style and with a different place setting of exquisite china for each table, offers superbly prepared courses served by an attentive staff. Zur Goldenen Gans looks like a house in the countryside and features roast goose and Thuringian potato dumplings. Stammhaus Kindl is the place to go for a foaming mug of beer; Pfauenauge is a classy cocktail bar.

Services: 24-hour room service, limousine service, hotel doctor, same-day laundry, babysitting.

Facilities: Indoor pool, whirlpool, massage, sauna, hairdresser, beautician, no-smoking floor, two rooms for the disabled.

---

2 Expensive

On or Near the Ku'damm

Hotel Ambassador Berlin, Bayreuther Strasse 42–43, 10787 Berlin. ☎ **030/2190 2-0,** or toll free **800/223-6764** in the U.S. Fax 030/219 02380. 191 rms, 8 suites. MINIBAR TV TEL **Bus:** 109 from Tegel Airport to Budapester Strasse. **U-Bahn:** Wittenbergplatz.
Rates (including buffet breakfast): 270–320 DM ($159.30–$188.80) single; 340–380 DM ($200.60–$224.20) double; from 480 DM ($283.20) suite. Extra bed 65 DM ($38.35). Children under 12 stay free in parents' room. AE, DC, MC, V. **Parking:** 15 DM ($8.85).

Located near Wittenbergplatz with its famous KaDeWe department store, this hotel has a simple lobby but a lot of extras, including comfortable rooms and a heated pool with sunning area on the roof. Rooms all have soundproof windows and radios.

Dining/Entertainment: Schöneberger Krug dishes out international food and typical German meals. Drinks are served in the Bar Ambassador.

Services: Room service (6:30am–11pm), same-day laundry, valet, babysitting.

Facilities: Indoor pool, solarium, Finnish sauna, massage, no-smoking floor.

Hotel am Zoo, Kurfürstendamm 25, 10719 Berlin.
☎ **030/88 43 70.** Fax 030/884 37 714. 135 rms, 1 suite. MINIBAR TV TEL **Bus:** 109 from Tegel Airport to Joachimstaler Strasse.
U-Bahn: Kurfürstendamm.

Rates (including buffet breakfast): 195–300 DM ($115.05–$177) single; 345–420 DM ($203.50–$247.80) double; from 510 DM ($300) suite. Extra bed 59 DM ($34.80). Children under 7 cost an extra 28 DM ($16.50) in parents' room. AE, DC, MC, V. **Parking:** 8 DM ($4.70).

Right on the Ku'damm and only a five-minute walk from the Bahnhof Zoo train station, this older hotel has undergone such extensive renovation that it's modern in every sense of the word. Its lobby has a glass facade that looks out onto Berlin's famous boulevard, and rooms are soundproof with light-proof curtains so guests can get a good night's sleep. A fourth of the rooms face the Ku'damm; the rest face toward the back and are quieter. All have safes, radios, and hairdryers. First opened in 1911, the Hotel am Zoo has been family-run ever since. Guests can enjoy drinks at the hotel's bar.

Services: Room service (for drinks and snacks only to 11pm), shoeshine machines, laundry and dry cleaning.

Arosa Parkschloss Hotel, Lietzenburger Strasse 79–81, 10719 Berlin. ☎ **030/88 00 50.** Fax 030/882 45 79. 81 rms. MINIBAR TV TEL **Bus:** 109 from Tegel Airport to Uhlandstrasse. **U-Bahn:** Uhlandstrasse.

Rates: 235–345 DM ($138.65–$203.55) single; 360–480 DM ($212.40–$283.30) double. Extra bed ($47.20). Children under 12 stay

IMPRESSIONS

An air of silence and dejection reigns in the streets, where at noonday scarcely any passengers are seen except soldiers.
—Sir N. W. Wraxall, 1779

It is distressing to see the multitude of soldiers here—to think of the nation's vitality going to feed 300,000 puppets in uniform. In the streets one's legs are in constant danger from officers' swords.
—George Eliot, 1854

free in parents' room. Buffet breakfast 17 DM ($10) extra. AE, DC, MC, V. **Parking:** 15 DM ($8.85).

Just a few minutes' walk south of the Ku'damm, the Arosa Parkschloss has undergone extensive renovation in its lobby, including the addition of a fireplace. Its owners are a young couple with plans to turn this small and personable hotel into one of the best in the city. With a staff that's efficient and courteous, it's one of the few hotels to boast both an outdoor pool and outdoor dining.

Rooms are tastefully decorated in muted floral prints and modern furniture, and all come with hairdryers, radios, and cable TVs. One of the best features of this hotel is its facilities for babies, from infant bathtubs to nursing tables, cribs, and high chairs.

Dining/Entertainment: The hotel restaurant offers international cuisine and outdoor seating.

Services: Room service (6:30am–midnight), same-day laundry, babysitting.

Facilities: Outdoor pool.

⭐ **Berlin Curator Hotel,** Grolmanstrasse 41–43, 10623 Berlin. ☎ **030/884 26-0.** Fax 030/884 26 500. 100 rms. MINIBAR TV TEL **Bus:** 109 from Tegel Airport to Uhlandstrasse. **U-Bahn:** Uhlandstrasse. **S-Bahn:** Savignyplatz.

Rates (including buffet breakfast): 240–260 DM ($141.60–$153.40) single; 300–350 DM ($177–$206.50) double; 380–550 DM ($224.20–$324.50) apartment. Extra bed 60 DM ($35.40). Children under 12 35 DM ($20.65) extra. AE, DC, MC, V. **Parking:** 16 DM ($9.45).

This modern brick hotel, located on a side street that connects the Ku'damm with Savignyplatz, opened in 1989 to accommodate the growing number of business travelers making trips to the capital. Rooms are modern and spotless, with such added features as large desks, bathroom phones, clock-radios, safes, and remote-control cable TVs. Some rooms even have terraces at no extra charge. In summer, breakfast is available on an outdoor terrace.

Dining/Entertainment: The Curator features a bar as well as a restaurant.

Services: Room service (6:30am–10pm), same-day laundry.

Facilities: Sauna complex with a sun terrace and solarium (fee charged).

Berlin Excelsior Hotel, Hardenbergstrasse 14, 10623 Berlin. ☎ **030/3155-0** or **3155-22** (reservations). Fax 030/3155-1002. 315 rms, 3 suites. A/C MINIBAR TV TEL **Bus:** 109 from Tegel Airport to Bahnhof Zoologischer Garten.

Rates (including buffet breakfast): 269–355 DM ($158.70–$209.45) single; 325–400 DM ($191.75–$236) double; from 820 DM ($483.80) suite. Extra bed 50 DM ($29.50). Children 2 and under stay free in parents' room. AE, DC, MC, V. **Parking:** 20 DM ($11.80).

The Excelsior, near the train station and the university and about a five-minute walk north of the Ku'damm, appeals to many of the city's international business guests because of its location, meeting rooms, simple and no-nonsense guest rooms, and dining facilities. Although the front of the hotel faces a busy street, rooms are soundproof. All come with hairdryers, cable TVs, safes, and radios. Some rooms have small balconies, and doubles have large desks. The penthouse suites on the top floor are especially roomy, with huge windows overlooking the city.

Dining/Entertainment: The Rum Corner, just off the lobby, offers cocktails other than just those with rum. Diners have a choice between the casualness of the Store House Grill, built in the style of a Mississippi warehouse and offering steaks, fish, and a salad bar, and the more formal Restaurant Peacock, serving international cuisine.

Services: Same-day laundry, babysitting, shoeshine machine.

Facilities: No-smoking floor.

Berlin Penta Hotel, Nürnberger Strasse 65, 10787 Berlin.
☎ **030/21 00 70,** or toll free **800/225-3456** in the U.S. and Canada. Fax 030/213 20 09. 415 rms, 10 suites. A/C MINIBAR TV TEL **Bus:** 109 from Tegel Airport to Budapester Strasse.
U-Bahn: Wittenbergplatz or Kurfürstendamm.
Rates: 290–410 DM ($171.10–$241.90) single; 350–470 DM ($206.50–$277.30) double; from 650 DM ($383.50) suite. Extra bed 50 DM ($29.50). Buffet breakfast 27 DM ($15.95) extra. AE, DC, MC, V. **Parking:** 25 DM ($14.75).

Conveniently situated right across the street from the Europa-Center complex, this hotel is just a short walk from the Ku'damm, the Gedächtniskirche, the KaDeWe department store, and Bahnhof Zoo. A chain hotel, it has all the expected modern conveniences and facilities, from restaurants and bars to a pool and comfortable rooms. Each room is soundproof and comes equipped with combination bath/shower, hairdryer, radio, and cable TV with pay video, with bedside control panels for both the TV and radio.

Dining/Entertainment: The Globetrotter is the hotel's primary restaurant, serving breakfast and international meals. The Pinte Bierstube, with a rustic atmosphere typical of old Berlin bars, serves draft beer and German snacks, while the Senator features live piano music.

Services: Room service (noon–10pm), babysitting, same-day laundry.

Facilities: Indoor pool, sauna, solarium, massage, fitness center, boutique, no-smoking floors, rooms for the disabled.

★ **Hotel Brandenburger Hof,** Eislebener Strasse 14, 10789 Berlin. ☎ **030/214 05-0.** Fax 030/214 05 100. 87 rms. MINIBAR $ TV TEL **Bus:** 109 from Tegel Airport to Joachimstaler Strasse.
U-Bahn: Kurfürstendamm or Augsburger Strasse.
Rates (including buffet breakfast): 290–400 DM ($171.10–$236) single; 340–465 DM ($200.60–$274.35) double. Extra bed 90 DM ($53.10). AE, DC, MC, V. **Parking:** 18 DM ($10.60).

This classy hotel combines the best of two worlds with its turn-of-the-century elegance and modern-day comforts. Located on a quiet side street a short walk from the Ku'damm, Europa-Center, and KaDeWe department store, it's a small and personable hotel boasting a two-storied lobby with pillars supporting a stucco ceiling. Even more impressive is its winter garden, a greenhouse where hotel guests eat breakfast with a view of a Japanese-style garden.

The white-walled guest rooms feature the latest in furniture design and come with cable TVs with pay movies, radios (there's even a radio speaker in the bathroom), and hairdryers. The most expensive doubles are spacious and are outfitted with either bay windows or small balconies. With an eye toward the environment and conservation, guests are advised to hang up towels that do not need to be replaced daily—used ones are to be thrown on the floor. Instead of pens, rooms come with pencils and pencil sharpers. All in all, a great place to stay.

Dining/Entertainment: The hotel's restaurant serves nouvelle German food.

Services: Room service (7am–midnight), same-day laundry, babysitting.

Hotel Bremen, Bleibtreustrasse 25, 10707 Berlin. ☎ **030/881 40 76.** Fax 030/882 46 85. 48 rms, 5 suites. MINIBAR TV TEL **Bus:** 109 from Tegel Airport or Bahnhof Zoologischer Garten to Bleibtreustrasse.

Rates (including buffet breakfast): 270–300 DM ($159.30–$117) single; 340–370 DM ($200–$218.30) double; from 370 DM ($218.30) suite. Children under 12 stay free in parents' room. AE, DC, MC, V.

Located just off the Ku'damm, this quarter-century-old hotel was completely renovated in 1989, from its new marbled lobby to its pleasant breakfast room on the fifth floor. The latter, cheerfully decorated in peach and blue, has large windows overlooking turn-of-the-century facades across the street—a good way to start the day in Berlin. Rooms, decorated in soft pastels of mauve and sky blue, have the modern conveniences of remote-control cable TVs with pay videos, radios, magnifying makeup mirrors, trouser pressers, and hairdryers. A good choice if you prefer a smaller hotel. The lobby bar is open round the clock.

Services: Room service (7:30am–10:30pm), same-day laundry and dry cleaning, babysitting, shoeshine machine.

Hecker's Hotel, Grolmanstrasse 35, 10623 Berlin. ☎ **030/88 900.** Fax 030/889 02 60. 73 rms. MINIBAR TV TEL **Bus:** 109 from Tegel Airport to Uhlandstrasse. **U-Bahn:** Uhlandstrasse.

Rates: 260–280 DM ($153.40–$165.20) single; 310–330 DM ($182.90–$194.70) double. Extra bed 60 DM ($35.40). Children under 12 stay free in parents' room. Buffet breakfast 15 DM ($8.85) extra. AE, DC, MC, V. **Parking:** 10 DM ($5.90).

A well-known family-owned establishment that has undergone extensive renovation, Hecker's calls itself Berlin's "small, private hotel." It has a good location between the Ku'damm and an interesting square called Savignyplatz. Rooms are large and feature walk-in closets, double doors to block out corridor noise, king-size beds, remote-control cable TVs, hairdryers, safes, and radios.

Dining/Entertainment: The hotel contains a restaurant, a coffeeshop, and a bar.

Services: Room service (7am–midnight), complimentary English newspaper, complimentary shoe shine, same-day laundry, free bottle of mineral water.

Hotel President Berlin, An der Urania 16–18, 10787 Berlin.

☎ **030/21 90 30,** or toll free **800/223-9868** in the U.S. Fax 030/ 214 12 00. 242, 11 suites. MINIBAR TV TEL **Bus:** 109, 119, or 129 to An der Urania. **U-Bahn:** Wittenbergplatz.

Rates (including buffet breakfast): 280–325 DM ($165–$191.75) single, 325–355 DM ($191.75–$209) single in Park Consul Club; 325–390 DM ($191.75–$230) double, 390–410 DM ($230–$241.90) double in Park Consul Club; from 490 DM ($289) suite. Extra bed 50 DM ($29.50). Children under 14 stay free in parents' room. AE, DC, MC, V. **Parking:** 15 DM ($8.85).

Although it doesn't look like much from the outside and is easily overlooked, this small hotel is pleasant and personable on the inside and has recently renovated and upgraded its facilities. It stands about halfway between the Europa-Center and Nollendorfplatz, about a five-minute walk from both. For the security-conscious, it has added such extras as peepholes in the doors and electronic credit-card-size room keys. All accommodations come with hairdryers, cable TVs with in-house videos, and radios; most rooms have air conditioning.

Adopting the concept of a hotel-within-a-hotel, the Park Consul Club offers 54 rooms served by a private elevator activated by electronic card and the extra benefit of a special lounge complete with happy-hour drinks. Rooms here are very pleasant, each featuring modern furniture and original artwork and such extra facilities as two telephones, a vanity area, a safe, a trouser presser, a makeup mirror, and a bathroom scale.

Dining/Entertainment: As its name suggests, Die Saison offers seasonal dishes, as well as a salad buffet. There's one hotel bar, the President.

Services: Room service, shoeshine machine, same-day laundry, babysitting, complimentary newspaper.

Facilities: Fitness room, sauna, steam bath, solarium, rooftop sun terrace, no-smoking floor (Consul Club only).

★ **Savoy Hotel,** Fasanenstrasse 9–10, 10623 Berlin.

☎ **030/311 03-0,** or toll free **800/223-5652** in the U.S. Fax 030/ 311 0 33 33. 116 rms, 14 suites. MINIBAR TV TEL **Bus:** 109 from Tegel Airport to Hardenbergstrasse. **U-Bahn:** Bahnhof Zoologischer Garten or Kurfürstendamm.

Rates: 280–345 DM ($165–$203.55) single; 365–430 DM ($215.35–253.70) double; from 570 DM ($336.30) suite. Extra bed 80 DM ($47.20). Children under 12 stay free in parents' room. Buffet breakfast 28 DM ($16.50) extra. AE, DC, MC, V.

An old-timer by Berlin standards, this is one of my favorite hotels in the city, and judging by the people who have stayed here, my opinion is shared by others. The late conductor Herbert von Karajan was a regular guest for 25 years; Benny Goodman and Maria Callas also stayed at the Savoy (it is close to the Theater des Westens and Deutsche Oper). When it first opened more than 60 years ago, it was an instant sensation because each room had its own private bathroom, a novel idea for the time. As one of the few buildings left standing after World War II, it served as British headquarters until 1955. Now, having recently been lovingly restored, this family-owned establishment is once again a great hotel. From its masculine Times Bar to the roof garden overlooking the city, the Savoy is a great choice in this category.

The lobby is small and unassuming, with the emphasis on the rooms above. Each of these is slightly different, but all have trouser pressers; radios; remote-control cable TVs with free English video movies; and bathrooms with their own telephones, hairdryers, and bidets. Some doubles even have small kitchenettes, complete with hot plates, refrigerators, and utensils. The most expensive rooms are on the sixth floor, called the Belle Etage, where TVs also serve as computers and fresh fruit and flowers are supplied daily. Rooms on the sixth floor also have air conditioning.

Dining/Entertainment: The Times Bar, cozy and wood-paneled, is stocked with international newspapers. A sumptuous buffet breakfast, which includes everything from salmon to exotic fruits like kiwi, is served in the Belle Epoque, where there's even outdoor seating in a small garden. It's also open for lunch and dinner, when the emphasis is on modern, health-conscious cuisine.

Services: Complimentary shoeshine, babysitting, room service (6am–midnight), same-day laundry, limousine service.

Facilities: Fitness club, sauna, solarium, no-smoking rooms.

Hotel Sylter Hof, Kurfürstenstrassee 116, 10787 Berlin.
☎ **030/21 200.** Fax 030/214 28 26 or 030/214 16 48 (reservations). 158 rms, 32 suites. MINIBAR TV TEL **Bus:** 109 from Tegel Airport to Budapester Strasse. **U-Bahn:** Wittenbergplatz.
Rates: 215 DM ($126.85) single; 325 DM ($191.75) double; from 330 DM ($194.70) junior suite; from 410 DM ($241.18) regular suite. Extra bed 50 DM ($29.50). Buffet breakfast 26 DM ($15.34) extra. AE, DC, MC, V. **Parking:** 15 DM ($8.85).

Built in 1966 but renovated since then, the small and comfortable Sylter Hof has a cozy lobby that looks as if it could be someone's living room. Rooms are small but adequate, with radios, alarm clocks, and cable TVs with pay videos. The majority of rooms are singles; the 49 double rooms have bidets. The hotel is about a seven-minute walk from the Ku'damm.

Dining/Entertainment: The Friesenstube serves German and international choices. There's a small bar for relaxation just off the reception area, and an American-style coffee shop that specializes in breakfasts.

Services: Room service (6am–10:30pm), shoeshine machines, same-day laundry.

Berlin-Mitte (Eastern Berlin)

Forum Hotel Berlin, Alexanderplatz, 10178 Berlin. ☎ **030/23 89-0,** or toll free **800/327 0200** in the U.S. and Canada.
Fax 030/23 89-43 05. 945 rms and suites. MINIBAR TV TEL
S- and **U-Bahn:** Alexanderplatz.
Rates (including buffet breakfast): 260–295 DM ($153.40–$174) single; 335 DM ($197.65) double; from 500 DM ($295) suite. Children under 12 stay free in parents' room. AE, DC, MC, V. **Parking:** 18 DM ($10.60).

Built under the Communist regime and recently renovated as a member of the Inter-Continental chain, this 37-story structure hasn't quite rid itself of the dullness and sterility characteristic of socialist architecture. Located in the heart of eastern Berlin, however, it does offer something most other hotels don't—unparalleled views from rooms on higher floors (request a room facing the Television Tower and western Berlin). The lobby is a bit noisy, perhaps because it's uncarpeted and rather bare. Rooms are simple but pleasant, containing TVs with pay videos, windows that open, trouser pressers, and small bathrooms.

Dining/Entertainment: The top-floor restaurant offers continental cuisine and great views of the city, while casual dining is offered in an old-style bar/cafeteria. Also on the top floor is a casino.

Services: Room service, laundry.

Facilities: Fitness room, sauna, three no-smoking floors, two rooms for the disabled.

Maritim Hotel Metropol, Friedrichstrasse 150–153, 10117 Berlin.
☎ **030/23875.** Fax 030/2387-4209. Telex 114141. 380 rms, 19 suites. A/C MINIBAR TV TEL **S-Bahn:** Friedrichstrasse.
Rates: 330–465 DM ($194.70–$274.35) single; 350–500 DM ($206.50–$295) double; from 570 DM ($336.30) suite. Extra bed 60 DM ($35.40). Breakfast 30 DM ($17.70) extra. AE, DC, MC, V.

A two-minute walk from the S-Bahn and the famous Unter den Linden, this older hotel is being completely renovated, with completion slated for April 1995 (I'd bet, however, it won't be completed on time). In any case, rooms already completed feature large working desks with good lighting, satellite TVs, radios, safes, and fax capabilities. Bathrooms, in marble and granite, have hairdryers, makeup mirrors, and telephones.

Dining/Entertainment: The hotel's main restaurant serves international and local cuisine; there are also a casual coffee shop and a bistro serving French and Italian snacks.

Services: Room service (7am–midnight), same-day laundry.

Facilities: Indoor pool, sauna, solarium, fitness room, no-smoking rooms.

Radisson Plaza Hotel Berlin, Karl-Liebknecht-Strasse 5, 10178
Berlin. ☎ **030/23 82-8** or **23 82 75 12** (reservations), or toll free
800/333-3333 in the U.S. and Canada. Fax 030/23 82 75 90.
600 rms and suites. A/C MINIBAR TV TEL **S-Bahn:** Alexanderplatz
or Hackescher Markt.

Rates: 275–570 DM ($162.25–$336.30) single; 330–570 DM
($194.70–$336.30) double; from 825 DM ($486.75) suite. Extra bed
50 DM ($29.50). Children under 14 stay free in parents' room. Buffet
breakfast 27 DM ($15.95) extra. AE, DC, MC, V. **Parking:** 18 DM
($10.60).

The Radisson group took over this existing hotel in 1993 and is
making it one of the top hotels in eastern Berlin. Occupying a prime
spot near Alexanderplatz, Unter den Linden, and Museumsinsel, it
offers comfortable rooms outfitted with bay windows that can open,
satellite TVs with pay videos, radios, alarm clocks, and hairdryers.

Dining/Entertainment: The restaurant T.G.I. Fridays offers what
may be the widest selection of American food and cocktails in Berlin. There are also a coffee shop, a restaurant serving German and
international food, and a bar.

Services: 24-hour room service, same-day laundry, babysitting.

Facilities: Indoor pool, fitness room, sauna, solarium, massage,
gift shop, hairdresser, car rental, travel agent, no-smoking floor.

On the Lietzensee

⭐ **Hotel Seehof Berlin,** Lietzensee Ufer 11, 14057 Berlin.
☎ **030/32 00 20.** Fax 030/230 02 251. 77 rms (most with bath),
1 suite. MINIBAR TV TEL **Bus:** 149 from Bahnhof Zoo.

Rates: 150–165 DM ($88.50–$97) single with toilet only, 215–290 DM
($126.85–$171.10) single with bath; 350–460 DM (206.50–$271)
double with bath; from 470 DM ($277.30) suite. Extra bed 60 DM
($35.40). Buffet breakfast 24 DM ($14.15). AE, DC, MC, V.

Idyllically situated on the bank of a picturesque lake with willow trees
and a park, this hotel is as close as you can get to resortlike accommodations in the heart of the city. It's in a peaceful and quiet residential area of Charlottenburg, just a 10-minute walk from the
Internationales Congress-Centrum (ICC) and the Funkturm (Radio Tower). There's a jogging path around the lake, and the hotel
pool is surrounded by glass walls that can be pushed open in summer. Guests can dine outside on a terrace beside the lake, where there's
also a bar.

As for the rooms, all doubles overlook the lake, but some singles
with bathtub face the street and are the same price as the lakeside
singles with showers, so be sure to specify which you prefer—I'd ask
for one with a lake view. Rooms on the second floor have small balconies. Amenities include hairdryers, magnifying makeup mirrors,
cable TVs with pay videos, and radios.

Dining/Entertainment: Au Lac, serving a different international
menu every day, features evening piano music; guests can dine either outdoors on a terrace overlooking the lake or indoors in a

romantic, candlelit ambience. For drinks, there are both an outdoor terrace bar and an indoor bar with a rustic, open-beamed ceiling.

Services: Room service (6:30am–midnight), same-day laundry, babysitting.

Facilities: Pool, sauna, solarium.

3   Moderate

On or Near the Ku'damm

Alsterhof, Augsburger Strasse 5, 10789 Berlin. ☎ **030/212 420.** Fax 030/218 39 49. 199 rms. MINIBAR TV TEL **Bus:** 109 from Tegel Airport to Joachimstaler Strasse. **U-Bahn:** Augsburger Strasse.

Rates (including buffet breakfast): 215–315 DM ($126.85–$185.85) single; 290–360 DM ($171.10–$212.40) double. Extra bed 50 DM ($29.50). Children under 14 stay free in parents' room. AE, DC, MC, V. **Parking:** 20 DM ($11.80).

About a four-minute walk south of the Europa-Center, this small place first opened more than 25 years ago and recently added a 60-room addition. The older rooms tend to be undersize, but rooms in the addition are larger. A number of facilities make the Alsterhof worthwhile, including an indoor pool. Rooms all have hairdryers, radios, trouser pressers, and cable TVs with pay movies. The most expensive doubles boast terraces.

Dining/Entertainment: The hotel contains a German restaurant and a bar.

Services: Room service (6am–11pm), same-day laundry.

Facilities: Indoor pool, sauna, solarium, massage.

★ **Art Hotel Sorat Berlin,** Joachimstaler Strasse 29, 10719 Berlin. ☎ **030/88 44 70.** Fax 030/88 44 77 00. 75 rms. MINIBAR TV TEL **Bus:** 109 from Tegel to Joachimstaler Strasse. **U-Bahn:** Kurfürstendamm.

Rates: 250–270 DM ($147.50–$159.30) single; 290–310 DM ($171.10–$182.90) double. Buffet breakfast 25 DM ($14.75) extra. AE, DC, MC, V. **Parking:** 15 DM ($8.85).

This small, moderately priced hotel is proof that good taste and fine design do not have to be sacrificed when it comes to price, making one wonder why more hotels aren't as smartly decorated. Nothing in the hotel is mundane—chairs are by Arne Jacobsen, barstools by Philippe Starck and Javier Mariscal, the breakfast-lounge carpet is by David Hockney, and artwork in each room is by Berlin artist Wolf Vostell; even the newspaper stand in the lobby makes a design statement. Rooms are sleek and up-to-date, with everything from the telephone to the hangers selected with an eye toward the avant-garde. Available in different sizes for slightly different prices, rooms feature cable TVs, radios, and hairdryers. The breakfast buffet, with seating available on an outdoor terrace, offers smoked salmon and champagne in addition to the usual eggs and cereals. Just a few minutes' walk from the Ku'damm and Gedächtniskirche, this hotel is a winner.

Services: Room service (6:30am–midnight), laundry, babysitting, complimentary newspaper.

★ **Askanischer Hof Berlin,** Kurfürstendamm 53, 10707 Berlin.
☎ **030/881 80 33** or **881 80 34.** Fax 030/881 72 06. 16 rms.
MINIBAR TV TEL **Bus:** 109 to Olivaerplatz.

Rates (including buffet breakfast): 210–230 DM ($123.90–135.70) single; 250–280 DM ($147.50–$165.20) double. Extra bed 50 DM ($29.50). AE, DC, MC, V.

Right on the Ku'damm about 10-minute walk from the Europa-Center, this first-floor hotel serviced by an elevator is a great choice for travelers who like small, personable, old-fashioned accommodations. Opened in 1925 and typical in architecture of Berlin's turn-of-the-century patrician homes, it features photographs of artists and theatrical performers who have stayed here through the decades. No two rooms are alike, though all offer the comforts of cable TVs, radios, bathroom scales, hairdryers, safes, makeup mirrors, and fax capabilities. Seven rooms face the Ku'damm, and two even have so-called winter gardens (glass-enclosed rooms). Rooms are furnished in a variety of styles, from Jugendstil to modern. Same-day laundry service is offered. All in all, this is a good choice if you want to wake up in the morning knowing you're in Berlin.

Hotel Berlin, Lützowplatz 17, 10785 Berlin. ☎ **030/260 50.**
Fax 030/260 52 716. 670 rms, 21 suites. TV TEL **Bus:** 109 from Tegel Airport or Bahnhof Zoologischer Garten to Schillstrasse.
U-Bahn: Nollendorfplatz.

Rates: 240–330 DM ($141.60–$194.70) single; 270–360 DM ($159.30–$212.40) double; 360 DM ($212.40) family room; from 450 DM ($265.50) suite. Buffet breakfast 25 DM ($14.75) extra. AE, DC, MC, V. **Parking:** 10 DM ($5.90).

One of Berlin's largest establishments, this hotel consists of three parts—an older wing built three decades ago but recently renovated and offering modern and spacious rooms at reasonable prices, a newer modern wing built in 1987, and a third wing that added 200 rooms in 1994. All rooms come with hairdryers, radios, remote-control cable TVs, two telephones, and magnifying makeup mirrors in roomy tiled bathrooms. Family rooms feature a double bed and two single beds, with lots of room to spread out and play.

Dining/Entertainment: The hotel's casual restaurant features a children's menu. The Globe restaurant/piano bar serves international and German food, including a lunch buffet. The Patio Restaurant offers outdoor dining, complete with a fountain.

Services: Room service (6am–midnight), same-day laundry, babysitting, free continental breakfast for early risers.

Facilities: Beauty salon and barbershop; fitness center with sauna, solarium, steam bath, and training machines (fee charged); no-smoking floor.

Frommer's Cool for Kids: Hotels

Arosa Parkschloss Hotel   (see p. 79) This hotel offers a lot of services for babies, including infant bathtubs, nursing tables, and high chairs.

Hotel Berlin   (see p. 88) Spacious family rooms with a double bed and two single beds, a family package rate, and a children's menu make this a good place to take the kids.

Pension Cortina   (see p. 104) This inexpensive pension offers two large family rooms that sleep up to five or six persons.

Econtel   (see p. 95) In addition to having economically priced family rooms, the Econtel also boasts special facilities for the little ones, including cribs, bottle warmers, and surprise diversions and games.

Berlin Mark Hotel, Meinekestrasse 18, 10719 Berlin.
☎ **030/88 00 20** or **880 02 802**. Fax 030/880 02 804. 217 rms.
TV TEL Bus: 109 from Tegel Airport to Kurfürstendamm/ Joachimstaler Strasse. **U-Bahn:** Kurfürstendamm or Uhlandstrasse.
Rates (including buffet breakfast): 200 DM ($118) economy standard single, 240–295 DM ($141.60–$174) single in "comfort" rm; 265 DM ($156.35) economy standard double, 325–345 DM ($191.75–$203.55) double in "comfort" rm; Children under 12 stay free in parents' room. AE, DC, MC, V.

This conveniently located hotel, on the corner of Lietzenburger Strasse and Meinekestrasse just a few minutes' walk south of the Ku'damm and Gedächtriskirche, offers two types of accommodations: 27 economy standard rooms, which can be rented to single or two travelers, and which come only with bathrooms, TVs, and telephones; and 190 "comfort" rooms, which come with such extra perks as remote-control cable TVs, minibars, and radios. The Bistro restaurant, complete with a bar and an outdoor terrace, offers an Italian buffet, snacks, and desserts.

Berlin Plaza Hotel, Knesebeckstrasse 63, 10719 Berlin.
☎ **030/88 41 30** or **884 13 444** (reservations).
Fax 030/884 13 754. 131 rms. MINIBAR TV TEL
Bus: 109 to Bleibtreustrasse. **U-Bahn:** Uhlandstrasse.
Rates (including buffet breakfast): 245–285 DM ($144.55–$168) single; 290–370 DM ($171.10–$218.30) double; Extra bed 50 DM ($29.50). AE, DC, MC, V. **Parking:** 20 DM ($11.80).

With a good location just off the Ku'damm and friendly personnel, this older hotel recently underwent renovation. It features a modern marble lobby and a pleasant hot-pink breakfast room with white curtains; its clean rooms are decorated in white and plum and come with cable TVs, radios, and safes. No-smoking rooms are available.

The hotel's restaurant, which has a summer terrace, serves specialties of Berlin, as well as beer and wine. There's also a bar.

Hotel Boulevard, Kurfürstendamm 12, 10719 Berlin.

☎ **030/88 42 50.** Fax 030/884 25 450. 57 rms. MINIBAR TV TEL **Bus:** 109 from Tegel Airport to Joachimstaler Strasse. **U-Bahn:** Kurfürstendamm.

Rates: 215–270 DM ($126.85–$159.30) single; 280–380 DM ($465.20–$224.20) double. Extra bed 60 DM ($35.40). Buffet breakfast 22 DM ($13) extra. AE, DC, MC, V.

Just a stone's throw from the Gedächtniskirche and a few minutes' walk from Bahnhof Zoo, the Boulevard is a good choice in this category, especially if you like a modern, crisp interior and plenty of sunshine. Reception is up on the sixth floor, a sleek and spacious area with marble floors, plants, and wide windows overlooking the rooftops on the other side of the Ku'damm. Especially grand is the large outdoor terrace off the lobby, where you can enjoy breakfast in the morning or simply relax with a coffee or an evening drink, observing life on the busy boulevard below. Rooms are modern, with hairdryers, safes, and radios; those facing the Ku'damm are outfitted with soundproof double-pane windows. Room service is available from 6:30am to 10pm, and same-day laundry service is provided. The hotel has a pleasant bar, as well as a cafe. All in all, a great place to stay.

Hotel Comet, Kurfürstendamm 175, 10707 Berlin.

☎ **030/882 70 21.** Fax 030/882 57 07. 30 rms. MINIBAR TV TEL **Bus:** 109 from Tegel Airport or Bahnhof Zoo to Olivaer Platz. **U-Bahn:** Adenauerplatz.

Rates (including buffet breakfast): 180 DM ($106.20) single; 220–265 DM ($129.80–$156.35) double. Extra bed 35 DM ($20.65). AE, DC, MC, V. **Parking:** 20 DM ($11.80).

The entryway of this hotel's building is rather weird—with its cold, silver surface, it looks more like the entrance to a space ship or a bank vault than a hotel. Even the hotel's name is a bit odd. However, the hotel itself, located on the third floor and reached via elevator, is surprisingly old world, with tall ceilings and a large tank of exotic fish awaiting guests in the reception room and comfortable lobby. Each guest room is slightly different, but all have radio alarm clocks, cable TVs, hairdryers, and safes.

Hotel Hamburg, Landgrafenstrasse 4, 10787 Berlin.

☎ **030/26 477-0.** Fax 030/262 93 94. 240 rms. MINIBAR TV TEL **Bus:** 109 from Tegel Airport or Bahnhof Zoologischer Garten to Kurfürstenstrasse. **U-Bahn:** Wittenbergplatz.

Rates (including buffet breakfast): 250–275 DM ($147.50–$162.25) single; 265–295 DM ($156.35–$174) twin; 320–340 DM ($188.80–$200) double. Crib 16 DM ($9.45). AE, DC, MC, V. **Parking:** 12 DM ($7.10).

Just off the busy Kurfürstenstrasse (not to be confused with the Kurfürstendamm, about a seven-minute walk away) on a quiet side street, this simple hotel is more than 25 years old but has been reno-vated. Rooms have the basic comforts of remote-control cable TVs, hairdryers, and radios. There is a restaurant/bar; services include same-day laundry, babysitting, and room service from 7am to 10pm. No-smoking rooms are available.

Kanthotel, Kantstrasse 111, 10627 Berlin. ☎ **030/32 30 26.**
Fax 030/324 09 52. 55 rms. MINIBAR TV TEL **Bus:** 109 from Tegel Airport or Bahnhof Zoologischer Garten to Wilmersdorfer Strasse. **U-Bahn:** Wilmersdorfer Strasse.

Rates (including buffet breakfast): 229 DM ($135.10) single; 260 DM ($153.40) double. Extra bed 60 DM ($35.40). AE, DC, MC, V. **Parking:** 17 DM ($10).

About a six-minute walk north of the Ku'damm, this simple, basic place is convenient to the Wilmersdorfer Strasse pedestrian shopping lane with its many department stores and boutiques. Built in 1981, the hotel offers clean rooms with soundproof windows, TVs (with pay videos), and radios. In summer, breakfast is served on an out-door terrace.

⭐ **Hotel Kronprinz Berlin,** Kronprinzendamm 1, 10711 Berlin.
☎ **030/89 60 30.** Fax 030/893 12 15. 66 rms. MINIBAR TV TEL **Bus:** 109 from Tegel Airport to Adenauerplatz, then 119 or 129 to Hallensee, from Bahnhof Zoologischer Garten, 119 or 129 to Hallensee. **S-Bahn:** Hallensee.

Rates (including buffet breakfast): 200–270 DM ($118–$159.30) single; 270–330 DM ($159.30–$195) double. Extra bed 45 DM ($26.55). Children under 12 stay free in parents' room. AE, DC, MC, V.

The Kronprinz, with a lovely facade dating from 1894, stands on the far western edge of the Ku'damm, more than a 30-minute walk from the Gedächtniskirche but it is easily connected to the city cen-ter in less than 10 minutes by bus no. 119 or 129 (each of which travels up and down the Ku'damm). The hotel's interior is modern and renovated. Rooms vary in size (and therefore rates) but are out-fitted with the same amenities of cable TVs, hairdryers, and radios. At day's end, guests tend to gather in the cozy bar for a bit of cama-raderie and conversation. In summer there's an outdoor beer garden.

Hotel Kurfürstendamm, Kurfürstendamm 68, 10707 Berlin.
☎ **030/88 46 30.** Fax 030/882 55 28. 30 rms, 4 apts.
MINIBAR TV TEL **Bus:** 109 from Tegel Airport or Bahnhof Zoologischer Garten to Adenauerplatz. **U-Bahn:** Adenauerplatz.

Rates (including buffet breakfast): 195 DM ($115.05) single; 290 DM ($171.10) double; from 336 DM ($198.25) apartment. AE, DC, MC, V. **Parking:** 15 DM ($8.85).

True to its name, this modern hotel is on the Ku'damm, at its west end, about a 20-minute walk from the Gedächtniskirche and the Europa-Center. Recently renovated from top to bottom, it looks a bit out of place amid facades dating from earlier decades and its rooms are a bit unimaginative, but its prices are reasonable. Especially good are the four two-room apartments, two of which even have their own terraces. Rooms, equipped with radios and safes, face either the busy Ku'damm or the quieter back side of the hotel; specify which you prefer when making your reservation.

Hotel Lenz, Xantener Strasse 8, 10707 Berlin. ☎ **030/881 51 58** or **884 86-0.** Fax 030/881 55 17. 28 rms. TV TEL **Bus:** 109 from Tegel Airport or Bahnhof Zoologischer Garten to Adenauerplatz. **U-Bahn:** Adenauerplatz.

> **Rates** (including continental breakfast): 190–220 DM ($112.10–$130) single; 220–280 DM ($130–$165.20) double; 345 DM ($203.55) triple. AE, DC, MC, V.

A family-owned hotel, the Lenz is on a quiet residential street not far from Olivaer Platz. The building dates from 1916, reflected in the fact that each room and each floor is different. Some rooms are decorated with antique furniture; others have balconies. Some repeat guests get so attached to certain rooms they request them over and over. All rooms have safes, cable TVs, and hairdryers. There's an elevator (activated by a key that each guest receives), and corridors are all nicely wallpapered. A pleasant place to stay.

Hotel Meineke, Meinekestrasse 10, 10719 Berlin. ☎ **030/88 28 11.** Fax 030/882 57 16. 68 rms. TV TEL **Bus:** 109 from Tegel Airport to Uhlandstrasse. **U-Bahn:** Uhlandstrasse.

> **Rates** (including continental breakfast): 240–260 DM ($141.60–$153.40) single; 130–160 DM ($76.70–$94.40) double. Extra bed 60 DM ($35.40). AE, DC, MC, V.

About a 10-minute walk from Bahnhof Zoo south of the Ku'damm, this hotel has its reception area up on the first floor, with rooms spread over several floors serviced by an ancient elevator (proof the Meineke has been around since the beginning of the century). Rooms are fairly large, and some that face the front have small balconies (but more traffic noise). The majority of rooms face the back courtyard, where there's no view but it's much quieter. Essentially, this is a place to lay your head with just the basics. There's also a bar.

Hotel Remter, Marburger Strasse 17, 10789 Berlin. ☎ **030/218 60 61.** Fax 030/213 86 12. 34 rms. TV TEL **Bus:** 109 from Tegel Airport to Budapester Strasse. **U-Bahn:** Kurfürstendamm.

> **Rates** (including buffet breakfast): 180–200 DM ($106.20–$118) single; 220–270 DM ($129.80–$159.30) double. AE, DC, MC, V.

Though the tiny Remter has a great location almost in front of the Europa-Center, it is off on a side street with much less traffic. Catering mostly to businesspeople, it has a small reception area up on the first floor and offers rooms with hairdryers, radios, and safes. Approximately half the rooms face the back of the hotel. Each room is slightly different and is available with either a shower or a bathtub.

Hotel Residenz, Meinekestrasse 9, 10719 Berlin. ☎ **030/88 44 30.** Fax 030/882 47 26. 67 rms, 4 apts, 9 suites. MINIBAR TV TEL **Bus:** 109 from Tegel Airport to Uhlandstrasse. **U-Bahn:** Uhlandstrasse or Kurfürstenstrasse.

Rates: 215 DM ($126.85) single; 290 DM ($171.10) double; 340 DM ($200.60) apartment; Suite rate upon request. Extra bed 55 DM ($32.45). Buffet breakfast 22 DM ($13) extra. AE, DC, MC, V.

About a 10-minute walk south of Bahnhof Zoo and only a few minutes from the Ku'damm, the Residenz was built around the turn of the century and boasts an elegant facade and a very ornate art nouveau entryway. Because they were once part of private apartments, rooms vary in size but are all the same price. Most have high stucco ceilings, and some have balconies; those facing the back are quieter. Apartments consist of large double rooms with kitchenettes, while suites have bedrooms, living rooms, and kitchens. There is a good French restaurant called Grand Cru, plus a bar. Services include same-day laundry, babysitting, and room service from 7am to midnight.

Berlin-Mitte (Eastern Berlin)

$ **Berlin Hilton,** Mohrenstrasse 30, 10117 Berlin. ☎ **030/23 820,** or toll free **800/HILTONS** in the U.S. Fax 030/2382 42 69. 502 rms, 30 suites. A/C MINIBAR TV TEL **U-Bahn:** Stadtmitte.

Rates 215–370 DM ($127–$218) single in Krone-Wing, 355–525 DM ($209–$309) standard single; 260–400 DM ($153–$236) double in Krone-Wing, 410–575 DM ($242–$339) standard double; from 650 DM ($383.50) suite. Extra bed 50 DM ($29.50). Children under 14 stay free in parents' room. Buffet breakfast 30 DM ($17.70) extra. AE, DC, MC, V. **Parking:** 20 DM ($11.80).

Hilton was one of the first western enterprises to move into eastern Berlin after the Wall came down, taking over an existing first-class hotel within walking distance of the famous Unter den Linden and located across from the historic Gendarmenmarkt square. Its bright and airy lobby features a two-story atrium filled with plants, while facilities rival those of any first-class hotel in the city.

Standard rooms, including no-smoking rooms, are constructed around an inner courtyard—choose one facing the courtyard for tranquillity, one facing outside for a view. They offer all the amenities you'd expect from a first-rate hotel, including remote-control cable TVs with pay videos and that also display messages; radios; soundproof windows that can be opened; and hairdryers.

A recent addition, the Krone-Wing boasts almost 200 rooms that are as large as the older, standard rooms and offer almost the same amenities; however, they are more simply decorated. Staying in one of these rooms is a real bargain, since guests are entitled to use all hotel facilities.

Dining/Entertainment: There are seven restaurants and bars, from La Coupole with gourmet dining to the Dominus wine cellar with hearty regional fare. There's also a disco.

Services: 24-hour room service, same-day laundry, babysitting, house doctor, shoeshine machines, complimentary newspapers.

Facilities: Business center, beauty salon, pool, sauna, solarium, fitness room, massage, squash hall, bowling alley, no-smoking rooms, two rooms for the disabled.

Moderate

⭐ **Charlottenhof**, Charlottenstrasse 52, 10117 Berlin.
☎ **030/23 80 6-0.** Fax 030/23 806-100. 86 rms and apartments.
TV TEL **U-Bahn:** Französische Strasse. **Bus:** 100 from Bahnhof Zoo
to Französische Strasse.

Rates (including buffet breakfast): 205–250 DM ($121–$147.50) single;
230–270 DM ($135.70–$159.30). double; 350–430 DM ($206.50–
$253.70) apartment. Extra bed 50 DM ($29.50). AE, DC, MC, V.

This small hotel, housed in a classical-style building, would be my
choice for a moderately priced room in the heart of eastern Berlin. It
has a great location near the famous Unter den Linden, across from
the historic Gendarmenmarkt and the French Cathedral. Rooms on
the fifth floor have balconies, with views of historic buildings. Otherwise, rooms are fairly basic and a bit worn down but comfortable
enough, with radios, toilets, and showers. Most of the rooms are twins
(there are only ten singles), and apartments consist of two separate
sleeping rooms and a living room. Breakfast is served in a two-story-
high room reminiscent of another era; the fifth floor has an outdoor
terrace with tables and chairs. **Note:** With the fluctuation of owner-
ship in eastern Berlin, this place may no longer exist by the time you
read this. On the other hand, it may be undergoing renovation. Call
first.

Hotel Unter den Linden, Unter den Linden 14, 10117 Berlin.
☎ **030/220 03 238 11-0.** Fax 030/238 11 100 or 391 95 07.
320 rms. TV TEL **S-Bahn:** Friedrichstrasse. **Bus:** 100 from
Bahnhof Zoo to Friedrichstrasse.

Rates (including breakfast): 200–230 DM ($118–$135.70) single; 280–
300 DM ($165.20–$177) double. AE, DC, MC, V.

This rather nondescript hotel has a very envied location—on the
corner of Unter den Linden and Friedrichstrasse. Rooms are small
(they remind me of those in a Japanese business hotel) and are com-
prised of older, unrenovated rooms and updated rooms with
tiled bathrooms at slightly higher rates. Although windows are
double-paned, rooms that face the busy intersection can be noisy.
Most of the rooms have minibars. The hotel contains restaurant, a
bar, and an outdoor summer cafe.

Near Güntzelstrasse Station

Queens Hotel, Güntzelstrasse 14, 10717 Berlin. ☎ **030/87 02 41.**
Fax 030/861 93 26. 109 rms. MINIBAR TV TEL **U-Bahn:** U-9 from
Bahnhof Zoologischer Garten to Güntzelstrasse.

Rates: 215–280 DM ($126.85–$165.20) single; 260–280 DM
($153.40–$165.20) double. Extra bed 50 DM ($29.50). Buffet break-
fast 21 DM ($12.40). AE, DC, MC, V. **Parking:** Free.

The Queens is located south of the city center near Güntzelstrasse
station, with direct U-9 subway service to the Kurfürstendamm (two
stops) and Bahnhof Zoo (three stops). If you like walking, you can
stroll to the Ku'damm in about 20 minutes. Member of an English
chain of hotels with an English-speaking staff, the Queens is a

modern place with rooms similar to those you'd find anywhere in the world, all containing TVs with pay videos, radios, alarm clocks, and trouser pressers; no-smoking rooms are available. There's also a bar, and laundry service is provided.

Near Schloss Charlottenburg

Econtel, Sömmeringstrasse 24, 10589 Berlin. ☎ **030/346 81-0.** Fax 030/344 70 34, 205 rms (all with shower and toilet). TV TEL **Bus:** 109 from Tegel Airport to Jakob-Kaiser-Platz, then U-Bahn 7 to Mierendorffplatz.

Rates (including buffet breakfast): Economy rooms 200 DM ($118) single; 225 DM ($132.75) double. Tourist-class rooms, 226 DM ($133.35) single; 250 DM ($147.50) double; 270 DM ($159.30) triple; 405 DM ($239) quad. Business Class and Lady Class rooms 236 DM ($139.25) single, 260 DM ($153.40) double. No credit cards. **Parking:** 10 DM ($5.90).

With accommodations especially designed for families and young travelers, as well as female travelers and businesspeople, this economy hotel tries to appeal to everyone. Each of its economy rooms sleeps one or two persons and offers just the basics of shower and toilet, cable TV, radio-alarm clock, and room safe. The tourist-class rooms, perfect for families, are outfitted with bunkbeds that sleep up to four and provide special facilities for babies and children, including cribs, bottle warmers, children's toilets, baby tubs, and surprise diversions for little ones. The Lady Class rooms feature sofas, magnifying makeup mirrors, hairdryers, typewriters on request, and a few other amenities, while the Business Class rooms offer desks, sofas, minibars, trouser pressers, and typewriters on request. All accommodations have radios and safes; 10 have minibars; and 8 have small balconies. There are also no-smoking rooms. The Econtel's modern lobby is pleasant, with a high ceiling, plants, and a wall of glass, and there's a hotel bar.

Hotel Riehmers Hofgarten, Yorckstrasse 83, 10965 Berlin. ☎ **030/78 10 11.** Fax 030/78 66 059. 21 rms. MINIBAR TV TEL **Bus:** 119 from the Ku'damm to Mehringdamm. **U-Bahn:** U-7 to Mehringdamm.

Rates (including breakfast): 220–260 DM ($129.80–$153.40) single; 260–300 DM ($153.40–$177) double. AE, DC, MC, V. **Parking:** 16 DM ($9.45).

This hotel occupies part of what was once a huge apartment complex built for the upper class in the 1880s. Constructed of red sandstone, the elegant structure still houses apartments in the back courtyard. The hotel itself has a great facade, but the interior is ordinary, its rooms outfitted with nondescript modern furniture, cable TVs, radios, safes, hairdryers, and trouser pressers. As a nice personal touch, breakfast is served à la carte and allows guests to order cereal, yogurt, juices, and eggs cooked several styles. Another plus is that the hotel is in the heart of Kreuzberg, an area full of bars and restaurants.

Spandau

Hotel Achat, Heidereuterstrasse 37/38, 13597 Berlin.
☎ **030/330 72-0.** Fax 030/330 72-455. 70 rms. MINIBAR TV
TEL **Bus:** 145 from Bahnhof Zoo to Heiderreuterstrasse stop, then a
three-minute walk.
Rates (including buffet breakfast): 175–240 DM ($103.25–$141.60)
single; 240–300 DM ($141.60–$177) double. Extra bed 40 DM ($23.60).
AE, DC, MC, V. **Parking:** Free.

Opened in 1993, this modern hotel in Spandau features a light and
airy reception area and double-bedded rooms, each with hairdryer,
cable TV with pay video, room safe, and trouser presser. In fine
weather, breakfast is served on an outdoor terrace. However, since
it's a 40-minute bus ride from Bahnhof Zoo, try this place only if
the others are full. Facilities include a bar, a sauna, and no-smoking
rooms.

4 Inexpensive

On or Near the Ku'damm

Alpenland, Carmerstrasse 8, 10623 Berlin. ☎ **030/312 39 70** or
312 48 98. Fax 030/313 84 44. 47 rms (10 with shower, 33 with
shower and toilet). TEL **Bus:** 109 from Tegel Airport to
Uhlandstrasse. **S-Bahn:** Savignyplatz.
Rates (including continental breakfast): 85 DM ($50.15) single with-
out shower or toilet, 105 DM ($61.95) single with shower, 130 DM
($76.70) single with shower and toilet; 120 DM ($70.80) double without shower or toilet, 175 DM ($103.25) double with shower, 210 DM
($123.90) double with shower and toilet. Extra bed 60 DM
($35.40). MC, V.

North of the Ku'damm near Savignyplatz, which has a number of
trendy bars and restaurants, the Alpenland is an older hotel that has
been somewhat modernized. Catering mostly to group travelers, it
offers accommodations spread on four floors; there is no elevator.
With high ceilings and outfitted with safes and Scandinavian-style
wooden furniture, rooms face either the front or the back of the
hotel—those facing the back are quieter but the view is not as interesting. Its one restaurant serves German food. The Alpenland is less
than a 10-minute walk from Bahnhof Zoo.

★ **Artemisia**, Brandenburgische Strasse 18, 10707 Berlin.
☎ **030/87 89 05.** Fax 030/861 86 53. 8 rms (6 with shower and
toilet). TEL **Bus:** 109 from Tegel Airport or Bahnhof Zoologischer
Garten to Adenauerplatz. **U-Bahn:** Konstanzer.
Rates (including buffet breakfast): 119 DM ($70.20) single without
shower or toilet, 75–205 DM ($103.25–$121) single with shower and
toilet; 195 DM ($115.05) double without shower or toilet, 240 DM
($141.60) double without shower and toilet; from 250 DM ($147.50)
suite. Children under 8 stay free in parents' room. AE, DC, MC, V.

This is a wonderful pension—*for women only*. Opened in 1989, it is a modern, spotless, cheerful, and thoughtfully planned establishment that gives much attention to the needs of female travelers. Reception is up on the fourth floor (reached by elevator), and there's a sunny breakfast room, as well as a rooftop terrace and winter garden (perfect for writing those postcards). Also on the premises are a small library and a hotel bar with a fireplace. The walls of the corridor serve as a changing art gallery. Rooms are beautifully done, with a mixture of antiques and sleek modern furniture. Each accommodation is dedicated to a famous "forgotten" woman (such as the composer Fanny Mendelssohn-Hensel, who lived in her brother's shadow) and contains a few items in memory of her, as well as a hairdryer, full-length mirror, and desk. The suite is actually two separate rooms, with two beds in each and a shared bathroom. Boys up to 14 years of age can stay here with their mothers. The only disadvantage to this place is its limited number of rooms—I wish it were much larger. Highly recommended.

Hotel-Pension Bialas, Carmerstrasse 16, 10623 Berlin.
☎ **030/312 50 25** or **312 50 26.** Telex 186506. 40 rms (10 with shower and toilet, 2 with toilet).

Rates (including continental breakfast): 90 DM ($53.10) single without shower or toilet, 100 DM ($59) single with toilet, 110 DM ($64.90) single with shower and toilet; 120–130 DM ($70.80–$76.70) double without shower or toilet, 165 DM ($97.35) double with shower and toilet. Extra bed 40–50 DM ($23.60–$29.50). No credit cards.

The no-frills Bialas, a cross between a hotel and a pension, is located on a quiet street off Savignyplatz, less than a 10-minute walk from the Ku'damm. Its reception area is up on the first floor of an older building, with rooms spread over several floors. The rooms on the fifth floor are quite a hike, since there is no elevator. Two of the rooms have telephones.

★ **Hotel Bogota**, Schlüterstrasse 45, 10707 Berlin.
$ ☎ **030/881 50 01.** Fax 030/883 58 87. 130 rms (12 with shower, 65 with shower and toilet). TEL **Bus:** 109 from Tegel Airport or Bahnhof Zoologischer Garten to Bleibtreustrasse stop.
U-Bahn: Adenauerplatz.

Rates (including continental breakfast): 75 DM ($44.25) single without shower or toilet, 105 DM ($61.95) single with shower, 135 DM ($79.65) single with shower and toilet; 120 DM ($70.80) double without shower or toilet, 160 DM ($94.40) double with shower, 195 DM ($115.05) double with shower and toilet; 160 DM ($94.40) triple without shower or toilet, 200 DM ($118) triple with shower, 240 DM ($141.60) triple with shower and toilet. AE, DC, MC, V.

If you like older hotels, you'll like the Bogota, an old-fashioned establishment with character. The building itself is a century old and features high ceilings; a stairway that wraps itself around an ancient elevator, which nevertheless is one of the more "modern" additions to the hotel; and lobbies on each floor reminiscent of another era. No two rooms are alike, and there's a cozy TV room where you can spend a relaxing evening. The hotel is just off the Ku'damm, not far from Olivaer Platz.

Hotel-Pension Bregenz, Bregenzer Strasse 5, 10707 Berlin.

☎ **030/881 43 07.** Fax 030/882 40 09. 22 rms (5 with shower, 10 with shower and toilet). MINIBAR TV TEL **Bus:** 109 from Tegel Airport or Bahnhof Zoologischer Garten to Leibnizstrasse. **U-Bahn:** Adenauerplatz.

Rates (including continental breakfast): 75–80 DM ($44.25–$47.20) single without shower or toilet, 105–135 DM ($61.95–$79.65) single with both shower and toilet; 110–120 DM ($64.90–$70.80) double without shower or toilet, 140–150 DM ($82.60–$88.50) double with shower, 170–185 DM ($100–$109.15) double with shower and toilet. Extra person 35 DM ($20.65). MC.

This family-run pension, on a quiet residential street just a few minutes' walk south of Olivaer Platz and the Ku'damm, is located on the fourth floor (yes, there is an elevator). Each room is different, but all are clean and roomy and have double doors separating them from the corridor, which helps cut down on noise. The staff will make bookings for the theater and for sightseeing tours, and there's a coffee vending machine.

Hotel California, Kurfürstendamm 35, 10719 Berlin.

☎ **030/88 30 11.** Fax 030/88 30 16. 40 rms (all with shower and toilet). MINIBAR TV TEL **Bus:** 109 from Tegel Airport to Uhlandstrasse. **U-Bahn:** Uhlandstrasse.

Rates: 160–190 DM ($94.40–$112.10) single; 190–215 DM ($112.10–$126.85) double. Extra bed 40–50 DM ($23.60–$29.50). Buffet breakfast 18 DM ($10.60). AE, DC, MC, V.

Right on the Ku'Damm, with a reception area on the third floor (reached by elevator), the California is a modern, simple, and pleasant place to stay. It was recently renovated from top to bottom, and rooms all have tall ceilings, safes, makeup mirrors, hairdryers, and cable TVs. There are vending machines selling drinks, but there's also a bar, plus a solarium that costs 5 DM ($2.95) for 10 minutes.

★ Hotel-Pension Dittberner, Wielandstrasse 26, 10707 Berlin.

☎ **030/881 64 85** or **882 39 63.** Fax 030/885 40 46. 22 rms (13 with shower, 7 with shower and toilet). TEL **Bus:** 109 from Tegel Airport or Bahnhof Zoologischer Garten to Leibnizstrasse. **U-Bahn:** Adenauerplatz.

Rates (including continental breakfast): 80–90 DM ($47.20–$53.10) single without shower or toilet, 100 DM ($59) single with shower, 135–175 DM ($79.65–$103.25) single with shower and toilet; 125–140 DM ($73.75–$82.60) double without shower or toilet, 155–175 DM ($91.45–$103.25) double with shower, 175–220 DM ($103.25–$129.80) double with shower and toilet. No credit cards.

The 35-year-old Dittberner is beautifully decorated, with a Japanese screen, antiques, and artwork in the lobby; woodblock prints and posters in the corridors; and thickly upholstered chairs, white tablecloths, and fresh flowers in the breakfast room. The pension is situated on the third floor of an older building (guests receive a special key for the elevator) above an exclusive gallery. In fact, the best room is the one that overlooks a small courtyard containing the gallery's sculpture garden. Little wonder that guests return again and again, including a number of artists. TVs can be provided. The Dittberner is found just off the Ku'damm, near Olivaer Platz.

Hotel-Pension Fasanenhaus, Fasanenstrasse 73, 10719 Berlin. ☎ **030/881 67 13.** Fax 030/882 39 47. 25 rms (4 with shower, 15 with shower and toilet). **Bus:** 109 from Tegel Airport to Uhlandstrasse. **U-Bahn:** Uhlandstrasse and Kurfürstendamm.

Rates (including continental breakfast): 80 DM ($47.20) single without shower or toilet, 90–110 DM ($53.10–$64.90) single with shower, 110–140 DM ($64.90–$82.60) single with shower and toilet; 110–140 DM ($64.90–$82.60) double, 120–175 DM ($70.80–$103.25) double with shower, 155–200 DM ($91.45–$118) double with shower and toilet. Extra bed 45 DM ($26.55). No credit cards.

This delightful pension has a great location not far from the very expensive Bristol Hotel Kempinski and the Käthe-Kollwitz-Museum, about a seven-minute walk from Bahnhof Zoo. On a fashionable street lined with many older buildings, the Fasanenhaus is reached via an incredibly ornate entry stairway. The very pleasant breakfast room with exposed ceiling beams adjoins a living room with a TV and large French doors that open onto a balcony with potted plants. Rooms are large, with high ceilings typical of Berlin's older buildings. The wide price ranges above reflect the seasons with the higher prices charged during peak season.

Hotel-Pension Funk, Fasanenstrasse 69, 10719 Berlin. ☎ **030/882 71 93.** Fax 030/88 333 29. 15 rms (11 with shower, 1 with shower and toilet). TEL **Bus:** 109 to Uhlandstrasse. **U-Bahn:** Uhlandstrasse and Kurfürstendamm.

Rates (including buffet breakfast): 70–85 DM ($41.30–$50.15) single without shower, 85–90 DM ($50.15–$53.10) single with shower; 110–120 DM ($64.90–$70.80) double without shower or toilet, 125–135 DM ($73.75–$79.65) double with shower, 150–160 DM ($88.50–$94.40) double with shower and toilet. No credit cards.

Walk up the sweeping white-marbled staircase to reach this first-floor pension, once the home of silent-film star Asta Nielsen. Clean, orderly, and nicely decorated with French provincial reproduction furniture and flowered wallpaper in its high-ceilinged rooms, it is convenient to the Europa-Center, Gedächtniskirche, and Bahnhof Zoo.

Hotel Heidelberg Berlin, Knesebeckstrasse 15, 10623 Berlin. ☎ **030/31 01 03** or **31 08 53.** Fax 030/313 58 70. 40 rms (all with shower or tub and toilet). TEL **Bus:** 109 from Tegel Airport to Bahnhof Zoologischer Garten.

Rates (including continental breakfast): 110–175 DM ($64.90–$103.25) single; 175–215 DM ($103.25–$126.85) double. Extra person 35 DM ($20.65). AE, DC, MC, V. **Parking:** 12 DM (87.10).

Standing north of Savignyplatz about a 10-minute walk from the Ku'damm or Bahnhof Zoo, this casual establishment caters primarily to youth groups but also takes in individual travelers. Its reception desk is located in its ground-floor cafe, which dispenses coffee, drinks, and snacks in addition to room keys. Breakfast is served any time. An elevator delivers guests to the rooms above, all of which have safes and are clean and bright (white walls). In addition, all but those on the first floor have small balconies. TVs are available. The price ranges above reflect the seasons.

Hotel-Pension Juwel, Meinekestrasse 26, 10719 Berlin.

☎ **030/882 71 41.** Fax 030/885 14 15. 22 rms (15 with shower, 3 with shower and toilet). TEL **Bus:** 109 from Tegel Airport to Uhlandstrasse. **U-Bahn:** Uhlandstrasse or Kurfürstendamm.

Rates (including continental breakfast): 105 DM ($61.95) single without shower or toilet, 115–125 DM ($67.85–$73.75) single with shower; 150–160 DM ($88.50–$94.40) double without shower or toilet, 175–185 DM ($103.25–$109.15) double with shower, 195–205 DM ($115.05–$121) double with shower and toilet. Extra bed 30 DM ($17.70). No credit cards.

With a great location just off the Ku'damm, not far from the Café Kranzler (one of Berlin's most famous coffeehouses) and Hard Rock Café, this unpretentious small pension occupies part of a turn-of-the-century building. Once the home of a Jewish merchant and his family; the pension boasts tall ceilings (some decorated with stucco); stark white walls; and temporary exhibitions of Berlin artists, including paintings, ceramics, and sculpture. Since all but two rooms face a back street, the location is very quiet. Some of the singles, however, are quite small.

Pension Knesebeck, Knesebeckstrasse 86, 10623 Berlin.

☎ **030/31 72 55.** Fax 030/313 9507. 15 rms (none with bath). **Bus:** 109 from Tegel Airport to Bahnhof Zoologischer Garten, then a seven-minute walk. **S-Bahn:** Savignyplatz.

Rates: 85–90 DM ($50.15–$53.10) single; 130 DM ($76.70) double; 160 DM ($94.40) family room. AE, MC, V.

Owned by English-speaking and friendly Jutta Jorende, this older pension has some modern twists, including artistic light fixtures in the breakfast room and flowers and plants that make the place more livable and pleasant. Ten rooms face an inner courtyard, making them very quiet, and there's a large family room with four beds. Two of the rooms have telephones, and TVs are available. The place is less than a 10-minute walk north of the Ku'damm, past Savignyplatz.

Hotel-Pension Modena, Wielandstrasse 26, 10707 Berlin.

☎ **030/88 57 01-0.** Fax 030/881 52 94. 21 rms (9 with shower, 5 with shower and toilet). **Bus:** 109 from Tegel Airport or Bahnhof Zoologischer Garten to Leibnizstrasse. **U-Bahn:** Adenauerplatz.

Rates (including continental breakfast): 70–75 DM ($41.30–$44.25) single without shower or toilet, 85–90 DM single with shower, 105–115

DM ($61.95–$67.85) single with shower and toilet; 120–130 DM ($70.80–$76.70) double without shower or toilet, 140–155 DM ($82.60–$91.45) double with shower, 160–175 DM ($94.40–$103.25) double with shower and toilet. Extra person 50 DM ($29.50). No credit cards.

On the second floor of a lovely building dating from the turn of the century, the Modena is located off the west end of the Ku'damm near Olivaer Platz. A good choice in terms of price and location, it's managed by Frau Kreutz, who keeps the rooms spotlessly clean. She'll give you a key to operate the old-fashioned elevator, an ancient-looking box still common in old buildings all over Berlin.

Nürnberger Eck, Nürnberger Strasse 24a, 10789 Berlin.

☎ **030/218 53 71.** Fax 214 15 40. 8 rms (none with bath).
Bus: 109 from Tegel Airport to Joachimstaler Strasse.
U-Bahn: Augsburger Strasse.
Rates: 65–75 DM ($35.40–$44.25) single; 110–120 DM ($64.90–$70.80) double; 140–155 DM ($82.60–$91.45) triple. Breakfast 10 DM ($5.90) extra. No credit cards.

This old-fashioned first-floor pension looks as if it could have been used as a set for *Cabaret*—a look that the owners have consciously cultivated. Rooms are very nice, with comfortable old-style furniture, stucco ceilings, and massive doors. Fresh flowers decorate the hallway.

Hotel Savigny, Brandenburgische Strasse 21, 10707 Berlin.

☎ **030/88 13 01.** Fax 030/882 55 19. 58 rms (3 with shower, 31 with shower and toilet). TEL **Bus:** 109 from Tegel Airport or Bahnhof Zoologischer Garten to Adenauerplatz.
U-Bahn: Adenauerplatz.
Rates (including breakfast): 75 DM ($44.25) single without shower or toilet, 120 DM ($70.80) single with shower and toilet; 140 DM ($82.60) double without shower or toilet, 155 DM ($91.45) double with shower, 185 DM ($109.15) double with shower and toilet. Extra bed 39 DM ($23). MC.

This unpretentious hotel dates from before World War II and has an old-fashioned atmosphere. Rooms are small with just the basics, although some of the most expensive doubles with bathroom are huge and are furnished with antiques. It's located just south of the Ku'damm and Adenauerplatz.

Pension Viola Nova, Kantstrasse 146, 10623 Berlin.

☎ **030/31 64 57.** Fax 030/312 33 14. 15 rms (2 with shower, 4 with shower and toilet). TEL **S-Bahn:** Savignyplatz. **Bus:** 109 from Tegel Airport to Uhlandstrasse, or 149 from Bahnhof Zoo to Savignyplatz (two stops).
Rates (including continental breakfast): 90–100 DM ($53.10–$59) single without shower or toilet, 120–130 DM ($70.80–$76.70) single with shower, 140–155 DM ($82.60–$91.45) single with shower and toilet; 110–120 DM ($64.90–$70.80) double without shower or toilet,

140–155 DM ($82.60–$91.45) double with shower, 160–175 DM ($94.40–$103.25) double with shower and toilet; 150–165 DM ($88.50–$97.35) triple without shower or toilet, 170–180 DM ($100–$106.20) triple with shower, 180–200 DM ($106.20–$188) triple with shower and toilet; 180–200 DM ($106.20–$118) quad without shower or toilet, 200–220 DM ($118–$129.80) quad with shower. AD, DC, MC, V.

Located just east of Savignyplatz, about a 5-minute walk from the Ku'damm and a 10-minute walk from Bahnhof Zoo, this updated pension has a cheerful breakfast room and reception area on the ground floor overlooking Kantstrasse. It offers bright and modern accommodations, with sleek black furniture, modern lighting, and tall stucco ceilings. TVs are provided in some rooms and are available for rent in others. All in all, this is a good place to stay.

Hotel West-Pension, Kurfüstendamm 48–49. 10707 Berlin. ☎ **030/881 80 57** or **881 80 58.** Fax 030/881 38 92. 33 rms (8 with shower, 15 with shower and toilet). TEL **Bus:** 109 from Tegel Airport or Bahnhof Zoologischer Garten to Bleibtreustrasse. **U-Bahn:** Uhlandstrasse.

Rates: 75–80 DM ($44.25–$47.20) single without shower or toilet, 90 DM ($53.10) single with shower, 100 DM ($59) single with shower and toilet; 120 DM ($70.80) double without shower or toilet, 140 DM ($82.60) double with shower, 165–220 DM ($97.35–$129.80) double with shower and toilet. Extra bed 30 DM ($17.70). Buffet breakfast 12 DM ($7.10) extra. MC, V.

This second-floor pension, located right on the Ku'damm, dates from the 1920s and has an old-world feel to it. In addition to its pleasant breakfast room with its high stucco ceiling, it has a comfortable bar for guests. Some rooms have antique furnishings; others have modern. Some of the double rooms with shower and toilet face the Ku'damm; the rest face toward the back. Since a variety of rooms is available, be specific in what you want when making your reservation.

North of the Tiergarten

Hotel Les Nations, Zinzendorfstrasse 6, 10555 Berlin. ☎ **030/392 20 26.** Fax 030/392 50 10. 42 rms (6 with shower, 16 with shower and toilet). TEL **Bus:** 245 from Bahnhof Zoologischer Garten to Alt Moabit. **U-Bahn:** U-9 from Bahnhof Zoologischer Garten to Turmstrasse station (2 stops), then a 10-minute walk.

Rates (including continental breakfast): 80–85 DM ($47.20–$50.15) single without shower or toilet, 100–110 DM ($59–$64.90) single with shower, 130–140 DM ($76.70–$82.60) single with shower and toilet; 140–150 DM ($82.60–88.50) double without shower or toilet, 150–165 DM ($88.50–$97.35) double with shower, 195–215 DM ($115.05–$126.85) double with shower and toilet. AE, DC, MC, V. **Parking:** 7.50 DM ($4.40).

Easily and quickly connected to Bahnhof Zoo and the Ku'damm via a direct subway line, this small, comfortable hotel offers clean, pleasant rooms that have recently been renovated with new furniture, carpeting, and wallpaper. Some of the rooms have TVs. Those rooms facing the front that have private bathrooms also have small balconies. Proprietor Frau Hilde Meier speaks English, as does her front-desk staff, and there's a small hotel bar.

★ **Hotel Tiergarten Berlin,** Alt-Moabit 89, 10559 Berlin.
$ ☎ **030/391 30 04.** Fax 030/393 86 92. 40 rms (all with shower and toilet). MINIBAR TV TEL **U-Bahn:** U-9 to Turmstrasse.

Rates (including buffet breakfast): 165–180 DM ($97.35–$106.20) single; 195–215 DM ($115.05–$126.85) double. Extra person 35 DM ($20.65). Children under 10 stay free in parents' room. AE, DC, MC, V.

This intimate hotel has all the makings of a first-rate establishment: a polite and efficient staff; a beautiful building with a facade dating from 1890; and a breakfast room that still retains its turn-of-the-century charm and elegance, with great buffet breakfasts to match. All rooms are different in size, furnishings, and atmosphere—one room, for example, is wood-paneled while another has a detailed stucco ceiling. All rooms are large, high-ceilinged, and airy, containing cable TVs with pay videos, radios, and alarm clocks; half the rooms also have hairdryers and makeup mirrors. The reception area and hotel bar are on the ground floor; rooms up above are serviced by the elevator. This is a fine little hotel, the kind you'd come back to again and again.

5   Budget

On or Near the Ku'damm

$ **Hotel Charlottenburg Hof,** Stuttgarter Platz 14, 10627 Berlin.
☎ **030/324 48 19.** Fax 030/323 37 23. 45 rms (38 with shower and toilet). TV TEL **Bus:** 109 from Tegel Airport or Bahnhof Zoo to Bahnhof Charlottenburg. **U-Bahn:** Charlottenburg.

Rates: 70–80 DM ($41.30–$47.20) single without shower or toilet, 90–120 DM ($53.10–$70.80) single with shower and toilet; 90–110 DM ($53.10–$64.90) double without shower or toilet, 110–150 DM ($64.90–$88.50) double with shower and toilet. Extra bed 40–45 DM ($23.60–$26.55). No credit cards.

A great choice in terms of price, facilities, and location, this is one of Berlin's finest budget hotels. Rooms are bright and cheerful, with white walls, colorful pictures, modern furniture, safes, alarm clocks, and cable TVs. The staff is young and friendly. Facilities include a laundry room and drink vending machine. Although breakfast is not included in the price, you'll probably want to go to the adjoining Café Voltaire (open 24 hours) with its large windows, plants, and artwork, where continental breakfast costs a low 5 DM ($2.95). The hotel is located two S-Bahn stops from Bahnhof Zoo and a five-minute walk north of the Ku'damm.

Pension Cortina, Kantstrasse 140, 10623 Berlin. ☎ **030/313 90 59.**
Fax 030/312 73 96. 21 rms (5 with shower). **Bus:** 109 from Tegel
Airport to Schlüterstrasse. **S-Bahn:** Savignyplatz.

Rates (including continental breakfast): 65–70 DM ($35.40–$41.30)
single without shower; 90–100 DM ($53.10–$59) double without
shower, 110–130 DM ($64.90–$76.70) double with shower; 120–130
DM ($70.80–$76.70) triple without shower, 150–165 DM ($88.50–
$97.35) triple with shower. Extra bed 40–50 DM ($23.60–$29.50). No
credit cards.

Owned by a native Berliner and her Italian husband for 30 years,
the Cortina is in a century-old building. The breakfast room has been
pleasantly remodeled in bright, cheerful colors, and most of the rooms
are large, all slightly different in size and shape. Some rooms have
telephones. Two family-size rooms that sleep up to five or six people
even have small balconies with flowers. Reception is up on the first
floor. The location is great, just west of Savignyplatz about a five-
minute walk from the Ku'damm.

Hotel Crystal, Kantstrasse 144, 10623 Berlin. ☎ **030/312 90 47**
or **312 90 48.** Fax 030/312 64 65. 33 rms (7 with shower, 21
with shower and toilet). TEL **Bus:** 109 from Tegel Airport to
Bleibtreustrasse; or 149 from Bahnhof Zoologischer Garten to
Savignyplatz (three stops). **S-Bahn:** Savignyplatz.

Rates (including continental breakfast): 70–75 DM ($41.30–$44.25)
single without shower, 80–90 DM ($47.20–$53.10) single with shower,
90–130 DM ($53.10–$76.70) single with shower and toilet; 90–100 DM
($53.10–$59) double without shower or toilet; 110–120 DM ($64.90–
$70.80) twins with shower; 120–130 DM ($70.80–$76.70) double with
shower, 130–150 DM ($76.70–$88.50) double with shower and
toilet; 190 DM ($112.10) triple with shower and toilet. AE, MC, V.
Parking: Free.

This is a typical older hotel, the kind that was plentiful throughout
Germany just a decade ago but is slowly dying out in the era of ram-
pant renovation. The building dates from the early 1900s and boasts
a striking facade to match, but the interior seems more like a relic
from the 1950s—old-fashioned, comfortable, and endearingly German. Owners John and Dorothee Schwarzrock (John is an American) are real characters: entertaining, friendly, outgoing, and happy
to see American guests. Rooms, supplied with just the basics, are
spotlessly clean, and TVs are available. All employees speak English,
and there's a small bar off the lobby for guests. The Crystal's rooms
with bath are among the cheapest in the city center. The location is
also convenient, just west of Savignyplatz, about a five-minute walk
north of the Ku'damm.

$ **Pension Fischer,** Nürnberger Strasse 24a, 10789 Berlin.
☎ **030/218 68 08.** Fax 030/213 42 25. 10 rms (8 with shower).
Bus: 109 from Tegel Airport to Joachimstaler Strasse.
U-Bahn: Augsburger Strasse.

Rates: 45–50 DM ($26.55–$29.50) single without shower, 60–65 DM ($35.40–$38.35) single with shower; 80–85 DM ($47.20–$50.15) double without shower, 90–100 DM ($53.10–$59) double with shower. Extra person 40 DM ($23.60) Breakfast 7–9 DM ($4.15–$5.30) extra. No credit cards.

With a great location within walking distance of the Ku'damm, Gedächtniskirche, Europa-Center, and KaDeWe department store, this second-floor pension is a pleasant place to stay. Accommodations are clean, high-ceilinged, and airy—with large windows letting in plenty of sunshine—and they have old-fashioned tiled heaters of the sort that once heated all German homes. Some rooms face a quiet inner courtyard. The breakfast room is especially nice and cozy with plants, flowers, and a TV. An automatic machine dispenses cups of coffee or hot chocolate, and there's a refrigerator for guests' use.

Pension Zimmer des Westens, Tauentzienstrasse 5, 10789 Berlin.
☎ **030/214-11 30.** 8 rms (1 with shower, 1 with shower and toilet). **U-Bahn:** Wittenbergplatz.
Rates (including continental breakfast): 70–75 DM ($41.30–$44.25) single with shower, 85–90 DM ($50.15–$53.10) single with shower and toilet; 95–105 DM ($56.05–$61.95) double without shower or toilet. Extra bed 40 DM ($23.60). No credit cards.

You couldn't ask for a better location than this—right between the Europa-Center and Wittenbergplatz in the heart of western Berlin. Even though it's on a busy thoroughfare, this modestly priced pension is tucked away in an inner courtyard, up three flights of rickety stairs (no elevator). The pension itself is pleasant, clean, and quiet. Only the single rooms have a shower or bathroom. All in all, a good value.

Near Güntzelstrasse Station ─────────────

★ **Pension München,** Güntzelstrasse 62, 10717 Berlin.
$ ☎ **030/857 912-0.** Fax 030/853 27 44. 8 rms (4 with shower and toilet). TEL **U-Bahn:** U-9 from Bahnhof Zoologischer Garten to Güntzelstrasse (3 stops).
Rates: 58–60 DM ($34.20–$35.40) single without shower and toilet; 85–95 DM ($50.15–$56.05) double without shower and toilet, 130–140 DM ($76.70–$82.60) double with shower and toilet. Extra bed 35 DM ($20.65). Breakfast 9 DM ($5.30) extra. No credit cards. **Parking:** 12 DM ($7.10).

The third-floor Pension München, reached by elevator, is only two subway stops from the Ku'damm or less than a 30-minute walk. You can tell immediately upon entering that this place belongs to an artist—the original artwork by Berlin artist on the walls, the vases of flowers, the aesthetic way everything is arranged. Frau Renate Prasse, the charming proprietress, is in fact a sculptress (her work decorates the corridor), and she rents rooms that are bright, white, and spotless. Two rooms have balconies; some have TVs. You'll like this place.

Kreuzberg

Pension Kreuzberg, Grossbeerenstrasse 64, 10963 Berlin.
☎ **030/251 13 62.** 13 rms (none with bath). **Bus:** 119 from Kurfürstendamm to Grossbeerenstrasse; 109 from Tegel Airport to Adenauerplatz, then 119 to Grossbeerenstrasse. **U-Bahn:** Mehringdamm.

Rates (including buffet breakfast): 60–65 DM ($35.40–$38.35) single; 90–100 DM ($53.10–$59) double; 120–135 DM ($70.80–$79.65) triple; 160–180 DM ($94.40–$106.20) quad. MC, V.

A pension for more than 50 years and located on the second floor of an older building that still shows traces of grander days (there is no elevator), the Kreuzberg was recently renovated and has a bright and airy breakfast room complete with plants and artwork. The tall-ceilinged guest rooms are each comfortably furnished with a wardrobe, table, and chairs. It caters largely to young backpackers.

$ Hotel Transit, Hagelberger Strasse 53–54, 10965 Berlin.
☎ **030/785 50 51.** Fax 030/785 96 19. 49 rms (all with shower). **Bus:** 119 from Ku'damm to Mehringdamm; 109 from Tegel Airport to Adenauerplatz, then 119 to Mehringdamm. **U-Bahn:** U-9 from Bahnhof Zoologischer Garten to Berliner Strasse, then U-7 to Mehringdamm.

Rates (including buffet breakfast): 70–75 DM ($41.30–$44.25) single; 95–105 DM ($56.05–$61.95) double; 130 DM ($76.70) triple; 165 DM ($97.35) quad; 30 DM ($17.70) per person in 6-bed dormitory. AE, MC, V.

Attracting a large international clientele of young travelers, the Transit opened in 1987 in a converted former tobacco factory. Its entryway is in an inner courtyard of the old brick building; reception, up on the fourth floor, is reached via elevator. Rooms throughout are painted a stark white, with high ceilings, modern black furniture, and new fixtures. The buffet in the airy breakfast room offers unlimited coffee or tea, and there is a bar with a big-screen cable TV, plus a laundry room. Guests often use breakfast as an opportunity to exchange travel advice and tips. This hotel is great for the price.

Near Rathaus Schöneberg

Studenten-Hotel Berlin, Meininger Strasse 10, 10823 Berlin.
☎ **030/784 67 20** or **784 67 30.** Fax 030/788 1522. 50 rms (none with bath). **Bus:** 146 from Bahnhof Zoologischer Garten to JFK Platz. **U-Bahn:** Schöneberg.

Rates (including continental breakfast): 85 DM ($50.15) double; 36 DM ($21.24) per person for bed in multibed rm. No credit cards.

This simple establishment is located near John F. Kennedy Platz and Rathaus Schöneberg. Despite its designation as a student hotel, it also welcomes nonstudents and guests of any age, and there's no curfew.

In a building that resembles a student dormitory, it offers 20 double rooms and rooms with four or five beds. There's a game room with a pool table, soccer game, and pinball machine.

Youth Hostels & Hotels

Technically, a youth-hostel card is required for stays at Berlin's youth hostels, but nonmembers can circumvent this by paying an extra 6 DM ($3.55) per night for a "guest" card. After six nights, this guest card automatically qualifies as a youth-hostel card. There's no age limit, but, "seniors," those 27 and older, pay a slightly higher rate. Keep in mind that curfew at these youth hostels is at midnight.

Jugendgästehaus am Wannsee, Badeweg 1, 14129 Berlin.
☎ **030/803 20 34.** Fax 030/803 59 08. 264 beds. **S-Bahn:** S-3 or S-7 to Nikolassee.

Rates per person (including breakfast and sheets): 28 DM ($16.50) for juniors 26 and younger; 35 DM ($20.65) for seniors 27 and older. Lunch or dinner 8.50 DM ($5) extra. No credit cards.

This is Berlin's newest and most modern youth hostel, a handsome brick building with red trim. It's located close to Wannsee, a lake popular for swimming and boating in summer, with bathing facilities nearby. Rooms have four beds each, with showers per every two rooms. A good place to stay in summer if you're in need of a relaxing environment.

Jugendgästehaus am Zoo, Hardenbergstrasse 9a, 10623 Berlin.
☎ **030/312 94 10.** 17 rms (none with bath).

Rates: 50–55 DM ($29.50–$32.45) single; 90–100 DM ($53.10–$59) double; 35 DM ($20.65) per person in dormitory rm. No credit cards.

It's easy to miss this no-frills budget establishment appealing to young backpackers and school groups—only a small sign outside advertises its existence, and the building itself looks a bit run-down and neglected but is under renovation. However, take the elevator up to the fourth floor (that is, if the elevator is working) and you'll find a youth hotel with all the normal facilities. No youth-hostel card is required. Rooms have just the basics: beds and sinks. There's an age limit of 27, but any age is welcome if there's room for 5 DM ($2.95) extra per night. Note, however, that no reservations are accepted for the two single or five double rooms, so call when you get to town and inquire whether they're available. Otherwise, there are also more economically priced larger dormitory-style accommodations with four to eight beds per room. Facilities include a bar, which is open from 9:30pm to an astonishing 6am. Near the university and the Mensa student cafeteria.

Jugendgästehaus Berlin, Kluckstrasse 3, 10785 Berlin.
☎ **030/261 10 97.** 364 beds. **Bus:** 129 from Bahnhof Zoologischer Garten to Kluckstrasse. **U-Bahn:** Kurfürstenstrasse.

Rates per person (including breakfast and sheets): 28 DM ($16.50) for juniors 26 and younger; 35 DM ($20.65) for seniors 27 and older. No credit cards.

This modern building houses the most popular youth hostel in the city, primarily because it is the most conveniently located. In fact, it's so popular that you should write at least a month in advance to reserve a room. All rooms are dormitory style, with four to six beds per room, and everyone gets a locker with a key.

Jugendherberge Ernst Reuter, Hermsdorfer Damm 48–50, 13467 Berlin. ☎ **030/404 16 10.** 110 beds. **Directions:** From Tegel Airport, bus 128 to Kurt Schumacher Platz, then U-Bahn 6 to Tegel stop, then bus 125 to Jugendherberge stop; from Bahnhof Zoologischer Garten, U-9 to Leopoldplatz, then U-6 to Tegel station, then bus 125 to Jugendherberge stop.

Rates per person (including breakfast and sheets): 23 DM ($13.55) for juniors 26 and younger; 28 DM ($16.50) for seniors 27 and older. Dinner 8.50 DM ($5) extra. No credit cards.

The disadvantage to staying here is that it's on the far outskirts of Berlin, at least 35 minutes from the city center (longer if connections are bad and you have to wait for the bus). However, it's surrounded by woods in a peaceful part of town and offers table tennis and a TV lounge. All rooms have eight beds.

5

Berlin Dining

IT'S TOUGH BEING IN A CITY WHERE THERE IS SO MUCH CHOICE.
Pork knuckles with Sauerkraut? Vegetable curry? Sushi? Pizza?
Nouvelle cuisine? Altogether there are an estimated 6,000 pubs and
restaurants in Berlin, and the number seems to increase almost daily.
I wouldn't be surprised to hear that Berlin boasts more international
restaurants than any other city in Germany; certainly it offers more
ethnic diversity in dining than many cities with twice its population.

One reason, of course, is Berlin's large foreign population and
many international visitors. But even young Germans are more likely
to go out for Greek or Italian food than for their own heavier cuisine. During the four years I lived in Germany, my German friends
and I rarely went out to German restaurants, primarily because we
ate German food at home. According to a recent survey, only half
the Germans surveyed said they preferred their own cuisine. And in
Berlin, ethnic restaurants are often among the city's cheapest.

That's not to say there aren't excellent German restaurants in
Berlin in all price categories. Many in the medium-price and budget
range are worth visiting for both the food and the experience since
they are often boisterous, lively establishments, good places to mix
with the locals and to strike up a conversation. Germans are not
known for their reticence, especially in their neighborhood pub/res-
taurant—and especially after they've downed a few beers.

The vast majority of Berlin's restaurants are found on and around
the Ku'damm, including Savignyplatz, Wilmersdorfer Strasse, and
the Europa-Center. This is where you'll find the greatest concentration of German Gaststätten (neighborhood restaurant/pubs), as well
as ethnic restaurants serving international cuisine. In addition to the
many take-out establishments here, there are a number of Imbisse,
stand-up food stalls serving everything from sausages and french fries
to dönerkebab.

To make your dining selections easier, all restaurants below are
arranged by location, including those on or within a 10-minute walk
of the Ku'damm, those on or near Wilmersdorfer Strasse, those in
eastern Berlin, and those in Dahlem.

As a gauge for what a meal will cost, including appetizer or soup,
main course, a glass of wine or beer, and dessert, expect to spend more
than 150 DM ($88.50) per person in the very expensive restaurants,
85 to 150 DM ($50 to $88.50) in the expensive ones, 40 to 85 DM
($24–$50) in those that are moderately priced, 20 to 40 DM ($12
to $24) in inexpensive establishments, and less than 20 DM ($12)
in the budget restaurants. As you can see, dining is very reasonable
in Berlin, in all price categories. If you opt for the less expensive items
on the menu and cut out appetizers and desserts, you can even dine
at the expensive restaurants for as little as 50 DM ($29), especially
since main courses served in German restaurants almost always include one or two side dishes. Thus, even if you're on a budget, don't
automatically assume that the more pricey places are beyond your
means. Be sure to check out the expensive category for restaurants
that also have moderately priced entrees.

Keep in mind that most Germans take their big meal of the day at lunch, which in most restaurants is served from about 11:30am to 2pm. Some restaurants offer lunch specials or a lunch menu during this time, at prices cheaper than those charged for their dinners. The most popular dinner hours are from 7 or 8 to 10pm. Some of the more expensive places close during the afternoon, while others are open only at night. The vast majority of restaurants, however, are open throughout the day. Thus, to avoid waiting for a table, try to eat in the off-hours.

Reservations are a necessity for most of the expensive restaurants, especially for dinner. In addition, some of the more reasonably priced establishments are so popular you'll never get a table unless you reserve one. I've indicated restaurants that require or recommend reservations.

As for dining etiquette, except for the more expensive restaurants, where you'll be seated by the management, it's considered perfectly fine to seat yourself wherever there's an empty place, even if the rest of the table is occupied. But simply sitting down would be rude, so ask first whether the seat is free and whether your fellow diners object. In some restaurants it's customary, and sometimes compulsory, to give your coat or jacket to the coat clerk at the *Garderobe*, for which the clerk expects a small tip of a mark or so ($60¢).

For waiters and waitresses, you should also leave a small tip, even though tax and service charge are included in all restaurant bills. For meals costing less than 20 DM ($12), simply round off to the nearest mark or two. For meals costing more than 20 DM, most Germans will add a 10% tip. Unlike in the United States, where tips are left on the table, in Germany tips are indicated to the server before change is given back. If your bill is 14 DM and you want to give your waiter a 1-DM tip, say "15 DM" when you hand her your 20-DM bill. If she doesn't understand English (or your high school German), simply hand back the 1 DM.

And by the way, in eastern Berlin you may need to take at least 30 pfennigs with you on a trip to the restaurant's bathroom, to pay the woman in charge of the toilets. Some of the larger, tourist-oriented establishments in western Berlin also charge for use of their public facilities, though this is becoming increasingly rare.

In addition to the restaurants listed in this chapter, check the nightlife chapter for pubs and other places that serve food in addition to wine and beer.

1   On or Near the Ku'damm

Very Expensive

⭐ **Bamberger Reiter,** Regensburger Strasse 7. ☎ **218 42 82.**
Cuisine: INTERNATIONAL. **Reservations:** Recommended. **U-Bahn:** Spichernstrasse.

Prices: Appetizers and soups 20–60 DM ($11.80–$35.40); main courses 55–65 DM ($32.45–$38.35). AE, DC, V.
Open: Dinner only, Tues–Sat 6–10pm. **Closed:** First two weeks Jan.

Located on the corner of Bamberger and Regensburger, about a 10-minute walk south of the Ku'damm or one stop away by subway, this well-known restaurant is a Berlin institution—indeed, some people claim its owner, Franz Raneburger, is the best chef in town. An intimate dining establishment with a rustic but refined atmosphere, it's decorated like a nobleman's hunting lodge, boasting elaborate flower arrangements, the rosy glow of candles, and efficient and friendly service.

The small menu changes daily, with past dishes ranging from lobster salad and cream of asparagus soup to mussels with lobster ravioli, filet of veal with shiitake mushrooms, and medallions of deer with mushrooms. There are also two fixed-price menus: 160 DM ($94.40) for six courses and 200 DM ($118) for seven courses. You can't go wrong here.

Expensive

Anselmo, Damaschkestrasse 17. ☎ 323 30 94.

Cuisine: ITALIAN. **Reservations:** Recommended for dinner. **U-Bahn:** Adenauerplatz.
Prices: Pasta 16–25 DM ($9.45–$14.75); main courses 36–60 DM ($21.25–$35.40). AE.
Open: Tues–Sun noon–midnight.

Anselmo was one of the first restaurants in Berlin to offer Italian cuisine in a stylish, elegant atmosphere. Although other great Italian restaurants have come onto the scene, this small and exclusive establishment still pulls in a faithful clientele, as well as curious newcomers—drawn, perhaps, to the flamboyance that has become Anselmo's trademark. The dining area has an aura of ultramodern chic, with white leather–and–chrome furniture, shocking-pink walls, white tables with fresh flowers (orchids during my last visit), palm and ficus trees, tanks of bubbling water, and sophisticated lighting. Or you may prefer a table on the outdoor terrace (open in summer only, to 10pm). In any case, Anselmo is located near the far western end of the Ku'damm, off Lehniner Platz. If you're coming from the area near the Gedächtniskirche, you'll probably want to take a taxi; otherwise, it's about a 20-minute walk.

For starters, you might try the day's ravioli, lasagne, or spicy noodles, or perhaps some homemade rigatoni with gorgonzola. Main courses on the Italian-German-English menu include salmon in mustard sauce, breast of duck with marsala, and lamb cutlet with garlic and rosemary. There's a bar where you can wait for your table or have an after-dinner drink. You'll want to dress up in your best for this place, if only to keep the waiter from looking you up and down.

Daitokai, in the Europa-Center. ☎ **261 80 90.**

> **Cuisine:** JAPANESE. **Reservations:** Not required. **U-Bahn:** Kurfür-stendamm or Wittenbergplatz.
>
> **Prices:** Main courses 40–55 DM ($23.60–$32.45); fixed-price lunches 20–50 DM ($11.80–$29.50); fixed-price dinners 60–100 DM ($35.40–$59). AE, DC, MC, V.
>
> **Open:** Lunch daily noon–2:30pm; dinner daily 6–10:30pm.

On the second floor of the Europa-Center, this Japanese teppanyaki restaurant specializes in grilled steaks, seafood, and vegetables. Traditionally decorated with slatted-wood screens, a pond with vermilion carp, and lanterns, the large dining area contains several long tables, each outfitted with a grill where the chef prepares your meal before your eyes. A waitress in kimono takes your order for drinks—ask for Japanese beer (brands include Sapporo and Kirin) or saké. If you're familiar with the many Benihana restaurants in the United States, you'll feel at home here.

The most economical time to come is for lunch, when a variety of set meals is available, including teriyaki chicken, grilled salmon, sukiyaki (paper-thin beef simmered with a stock of vegetables), and a platter of mixed seafood cooked on the grill. All set lunches come with soup, salad, and rice. Dinner is much more expensive but offers a wider variety, from grilled giant shrimp or salmon to grilled steaks. The service, of course, is the best, for which the Japanese are legendary.

 Fioretto, Carmerstrasse 2. ☎ **312 31 15.**

> **Cuisine:** ITALIAN. **Reservations:** Recommended. **S-Bahn:** Savignyplatz or Bahnhof Zoologischer Garten.
>
> **Prices:** Pasta 15–30 DM ($8.85–$17.70); main courses 26–50 DM ($15.35–$29.50). AE, V.
>
> **Open:** Dinner only, Mon–Sat 7pm–1am.

This restaurant is extraordinary for several reasons. For one thing, the chef is a woman, a rarity indeed in most expensive restaurants around the world. In addition, chef Doris Burneleit hails from eastside Berlin and succeeded in creating a name for herself at her original restaurant in the working-class precinct of Köpenick even before the Wall fell. Unable to procure many of the usual ingredients for Italian cookery and not allowed to travel to Italy, she pored over every Italian cookbook she could get her hands on and then improvised her own dishes.

The result is a refreshingly innovative combination of seasonal dishes, now served in her new location in western Berlin. Decorated in soothing white with a huge bouquet of flowers in the entryway, this small, upscale restaurant offers a different menu every two weeks, always with approximately six choices in pasta and eight meat and fish entrees. Pasta selections have included homemade ravioli filled with ricotta and fresh spinach in walnut butter and freshly grated parmesan cheese; and fettucini made with four different herbs, Sicilian tomatoes, and cheese. Entrees may include lamb or seafood choices, such as fish wrapped in foil with potatoes, tomatoes, and herbs and opened steaming at your table. Highly recommended.

Mario, Leibnizstrasse 43. ☎ **324 35 16.**

> **Cuisine:** ITALIAN. **Reservations:** Recommended. **S-Bahn:** Savignyplatz.
> **Prices:** Appetizers and pastas 20–25 DM ($11.80–$14.75); main courses 40–50 DM ($23.60–$29.50) AE.
> **Open:** Lunch Sun–Fri noon–3pm; dinner daily 6:30–11pm.

This modern, uncluttered Italian *ristorante* is decorated with abstract art. The emphasis here is clearly on the food, as shown by the faithful and well-heeled clientele and the fact that many consider this the best Italian restaurant in town.

Most customers eschew the standard menu, which is small and insufficient, and instead go for one of the chef's many daily specials. Every day brings an array of at least 10 appetizers; five homemade pasta dishes; and almost two dozen selections of fish, veal, scampi, and other main courses. Whatever you order, you won't be disappointed.

Paris Bar, Kantstrasse 152. ☎ **313 80 52.**

> **Cuisine:** FRENCH. **Reservations:** Recommended. **S-Bahn and U-Bahn:** Uhlandstrasse or Bahnhof Zoologischer Garten.
> **Prices:** Soups and appetizers 10–17 DM ($5.90–$10); main courses 35–50 DM ($20.65–$29.50).
> **Open:** Daily noon–1am.

Established by two Frenchmen after World War II, this place looks and feels like a typical *bistro*—crowded, tables close together, and noisy, with contemporary posters on the walls. (Despite its name, it's primarily a restaurant.) Even a casual glance around this seemingly informal eatery, however, reveals that most of its customers are smartly dressed, looking like the business types, journalists, film people, and upscale artists they are. This is clearly one of Berlin's top places to see and be seen, a place for the successfully established and those who wish they were. With a French staff, it's been at this location for 40 years—between the Gedächtniskirche and Savignyplatz, near the Theater des Westens.

The menu offers traditional French cuisine, including steak and fish. There are also daily specials, as well as a good selection of desserts. And, of course, the choice of French wines is what you'd expect in a restaurant like this.

Moderate

Astir's, Grolmanstrasse 56. ☎ **313 63 20.**

> **Cuisine:** FRENCH. **Reservations:** Recommended. **S-Bahn:** Savignyplatz.
> **Prices:** Salads, soups, and appetizers 10–23 DM ($5.90–$13.55); main courses 20–34 DM ($11.80–$20). AE, DC, MC, V.
> **Open:** Summer, Mon–Sat noon–1am, Sun 6pm–1am; winter, daily 6pm–1am.

Frommer's Smart Traveler: Restaurants

Value-Conscious Travelers Should Take Advantage of the Following:

1. Daily specials offered by many restaurants. These specials are not on the regular menu and usually include a main course and side dishes.

2. Fixed-price lunches, generally available from about 11am to 2pm, which include an appetizer or soup, main course, and dessert—at prices much cheaper than those found on the dinner menu.

3. Inexpensive entrees, such as Würste or stews, offered by some of the more expensive restaurants, where even budget travelers can dine in style.

4. Berlin's wide variety of ethnic cuisine at very reasonable prices. There are many restaurants serving Chinese, Turkish, Greek, Indian, and Italian food.

5. Restaurants and food counters in department stores, an especially good value in Berlin.

6. Berlin's stand-up food stalls (called **Imbisse**), selling Würste, Turkish specialties, french fries, and other fast foods.

7. Coffee-shop chains such as Tschibo, with coffee costing 1.95 DM ($1.15) per cup.

Questions to Ask If You're on a Budget

1. Is there an extra charge for each piece of bread consumed? Many restaurants charge extra every time you reach for the basket in the middle of your table.

2. Does the entree come with side dishes? If so, it may be all you want to order, unless you have a voracious appetite.

3. Is there a special of the day or a fixed-price lunch not listed on the regular menu? It's especially important to ask about specials if you're reading from an English menu, since specials of the day are often printed only in German.

Located northwest of Savignyplatz, this cheerful Parisian-style bistro serves dependably good food under the keen supervision of proprietress Bettina Laurer, who also speaks excellent English. Casually decorated with a black-and-white-tile floor, checkered tablecloths, and posters and artwork lining the golden-yellow walls, it offers the additional advantage of sidewalk dining in summer. You might wish to start with a port or sherry; the wine list is extensive, offering French, Italian, and California varieties. Lamb dishes are Astir's specialties, including lamb in thyme-mustard crust and grilled lamb cutlets, both served with potatoes and green beans. Other main courses on the interesting menu include mussels accompanied by spinach in puff

Western Berlin Dining

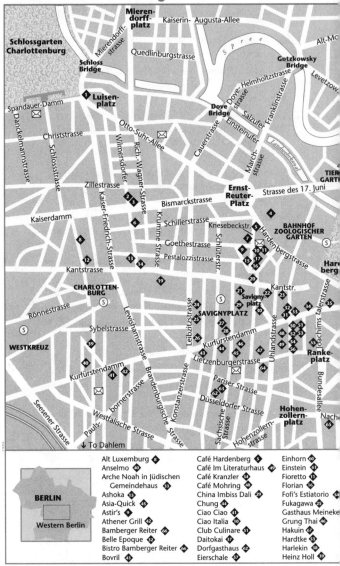

Alt Luxemburg ⬥	Café Hardenberg ⬥	Einhorn ⬥
Anselmo ⬥	Café Im Literaturhaus ⬥	Einstein ⬥
Arche Noah in Jüdischen	Café Kranzler ⬥	Fioretto ⬥
Gemeindehaus ⬥	Café Mohring ⬥	Florian ⬥
Ashoka ⬥	China Imbiss Dali ⬥	Fofi's Estiatorio ⬥
Asia-Quick ⬥	Chung ⬥	Fukagawa ⬥
Astir's ⬥	Ciao Ciao ⬥	Gasthaus Meineke ⬥
Athener Grill ⬥	Ciao Italia ⬥	Grung Thai ⬥
Bamberger Reiter ⬥	Club Culinare ⬥	Hakuin ⬥
Belle Epoque ⬥	Daitokai ⬥	Hardtke ⬥
Bistro Bamberger Reiter ⬥	Dorfgasthaus ⬥	Harlekin ⬥
Bovril ⬥	Eierschale ⬥	Heinz Holl ⬥

BERLIN

Western Berlin

pastry with hollandaise, boeuf bourguignon, and duck breast in sherry-and-honey sauce. Opened in 1990, the restaurant is on its way to becoming a well-established and well-deserved favorite.

$ **Bistro Bamberger Reiter,** Regensburger Strasse 7.
☎ 213 67 33.

Cuisine: INTERNATIONAL. **Reservations:** Recommended. **U-Bahn:** Spichernstrasse.

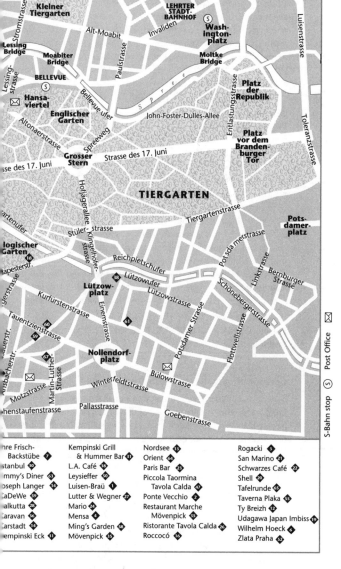

N

0 ___ 0.5 mi
___ 0.8 km

Kleiner Tiergarten

LEHRTER STADT-BAHNHOF

Alt-Moabit

Invaliden

Washington-platz

Stromstrasse

Lessing Bridge

Moabiter Bridge

Paulstrasse

Moltke Bridge

Lessing-strasse

BELLEVUE

Hansa-viertel

Englischer Garten

Bellevue ufer

Spreeweg

John-Foster-Dulles-Allee

Spree

Platz der Republik

Entlastungsstrasse

Platz vor dem Brandenburger Tor

Toleranzstrasse

Altonaerstrasse

Grosser Stern

Strasse des 17. Juni

sse des 17. Juni

Hofjägerallee

TIERGARTEN

Tiergartenstrasse

Pots-damer-platz

artenufer

Stüler- strasse

Klingelhöfer-strasse

logischer Garten

apeststr.

Reichpietschufer

Lützowufer

38

Lützowstrasse

Pots da metstrasse

Linkstrasse

Bernburger Strasse

Schöneberger strasse

gerstrasse

Kurfürstenstrasse

Lützow-platz

Einemstrasse

51

Flottwellstrasse

Tauentzienstrasse

aderstr.

60

59

Martin-Luther-Strasse

Nollendorf-platz

Potsdamer Strasse

Winterfeldtstrasse

Bülowstrasse

nsbacherstr.

67

Motzstrasse

Pallasstrasse

Goebenstrasse

henstaufenstrasse

S-Bahn stop   S   Post Office   ⊠

hre Frisch-Backstübe **7**	Kempinski Grill & Hummer Bar **51**	Nordsee **18**	Rogacki **9**
stanbul **50**	L.A. Café **12**	Orient **54**	San Marino **53**
mmy's Diner **63**	Leysieffer **30**	Paris Bar **31**	Schwarzes Café **22**
oseph Langer **14**	Luisen-Bräu **1**	Piccola Taormina Tavola Calda **47**	Shell **20**
KaDeWe **59**	Lutter & Wegner **27**	Ponte Vecchio **2**	Tafelrunde **65**
alkutta **28**	Mario **24**	Restaurant Marche Mövenpick **43**	Taverna Plaka **55**
Caravan **46**	Mensa **4**	Ristorante Tavola Calda **26**	Ty Breizh **12**
Carstadt **49**	Ming's Garden **58**	Roccocó **16**	Udagawa Japan Imbiss **19**
empinski Eck **41**	Mövenpick **48**		Wilhelm Hoeck **6**
			Zlata Praha **42**

Prices: Appetizers and soups 17–26 DM ($10–$15.35); main courses 30–36 DM ($17.70–$21.25); fixed-price dinners 70–85 DM ($41.30–$50.15). No credit cards.

Open: Tues–Sat 6pm–1am (last order 11pm).

Next door to its famous and more expensive namesake, this bistro is the place of choice for those who want an excellent meal at affordable prices. Consisting simply of a one-room dining hall with tables crowded together, it is popular for the chef's experiments in nouvelle cuisine, as well as for tried-and-true traditional fare. The menu changes daily, with dishes ranging from fresh fish from the nearby Havel, to turkey breast saltimbocca, to deer served with cooked red cabbage and wild mushrooms. Reasonably priced three- and five-course fixed-price dinners are also available.

Bovril, Kurfürstendamm 184. ☎ **881 84 61.**

> **Cuisine:** CONTINENTAL. **Reservations:** Recommended for dinner.
> **U-Bahn:** Adenauerplatz.
> **Prices:** Appetizers and soups 12–18 DM ($7.10–$10.60); main courses 29–40 DM ($7.10–$23.60); fixed-price lunch 25–28 DM ($14.75–$16.50). AE, DC, MC, V.
> **Open:** Mon–Sat noon–2am (last order 12:30am).

A pleasant restaurant on the Ku'damm just north of Olivaer Platz, Bovril provides a healthy mix of old and new in its decor. The facade gives a hint of art nouveau, while the interior features lamps, ceiling fans, red-plastic sofas that look very 1950s, and contemporary murals. In summer, tables are spread outside along the boulevard. The handwritten menu changes daily, with lunch served to 4pm and dinner available from 6pm on. A la carte selections may range from fettuccine or Wiener Schnitzel to beefsteak and rack of lamb. An especially good value are the two- and three-course lunch menus.

Florian, Grolmanstrasse 52. ☎ **313 91 84.**

> **Cuisine:** GERMAN/CONTINENTAL. **Reservations:** Required. **S-Bahn:** Savignyplatz.
> **Prices:** Appetizers 16–20 DM ($9.45–$11.80); main courses 23–35 DM. No credit cards.
> **Open:** Dinner only, daily 6pm–3am (last order 1am).

Serving a changing menu of mainly German-Fränkisch, but also French and other European-inspired dishes, Florian (just north of Savignyplatz) cultivates a devil-may-care atmosphere. No effort has been wasted in decorating the dining room—simply white-clothed tables on a wooden floor with nary a piece of artwork on the painfully bare walls. Florian is so devoid of worldly pretense that it's "in"; in fact, it seems as if everyone is trying to get into the place.

The changing daily menu, handwritten in a hurry, may offer such appetizers as salmon with horseradish on iceberg lettuce, an Italian minced-meat casserole with tomato sauce and parmesan, or goose-liver pâté. Main courses might include roast beef in béarnaise sauce with roast potatoes; chicken fricassee with mushrooms, buttered rice, and salad; and roast lamb with herbs and potato casserole. I'd tell you more, but I have trouble deciphering that handwritten menu (which, by the way, is in German). Check it out for yourself.

★ **Fofi's Estiatorio,** Fasanenstrasse 70. ☎ **881 87 85.**

> **Cuisine:** GREEK. **Reservations:** Required. **U-Bahn:** Uhlandstrasse.
> $ **Prices:** Appetizers and salads 10–25 DM ($5.90–$14.75); main courses 28–44 DM ($16.50–$25.95). No credit cards.
> **Open:** Dinner only, daily 6pm–3am (last order 12:30am).

This very popular restaurant has all the right ingredients for success—good location (a stone's throw from the Ku'damm), dependably good food, interesting interior, sidewalk tables, and a mothering Greek owner named Fofi who greets strangers as warmly as she does her many regulars. The walls are covered with abstract and modern art, and the background music is likely to be easygoing jazz. In summer, try for an outdoor table.

The menu lists the usual national Greek dishes, including such appetizers as bean salad, dolmades (meat and rice rolled in grape leaves), keftedes (fried meatballs), and Greek salad. Entrees range from grilled scampi and moussaka (casserole of eggplant and minced meat) to souvlaki, kebab, and lamb. There's also a changing menu with international dishes, as well as an abundant supply of Greek wines and spirits. If you're a devoted fan of Greek cuisine, you owe it to yourself to eat here. The sign on the facade says Estiatorio, but everyone calls it Fofi's.

Fukagawa, Leibnizstrasse 43. ☎ **324 35 16.**

Cuisine: JAPANESE. **Reservations:** Recommended. **S-Bahn:** Savignyplatz.

Prices: Sushi à la carte 4.50–9 DM ($2.65–$5.30) a piece; mixed sushi plates 25–40 DM ($14.75–$23.60). No credit cards.

Open: Dinner only, Mon–Sat 6–11pm.

There are millions of places like this all over Japan—a minuscule room with only three tables and a sushi bar, where a knife-wielding chef deftly prepares slices of tender raw fish—but sushi is still relatively new to Germany. Enter through the door and you'll be greeted by shouts of "*Irashaimase!*" ("Welcome!"), followed by a steaming hot towel (cold in summer) and tea brought to you by the Japanese waitress.

If you've never had sushi before, I recommend you start with my favorite, maguro (tuna). It tastes like very rare beef, not fishy at all. You might also like to try ika (squid) or whatever catches your fancy behind the refrigerated display case. Saké, of course, nicely complements sushi, but Sapporo or Kirin Japanese beer is equally good.

Hakuin, Martin-Luther-Strasse 1. ☎ **218 20 27.**

Cuisine: VEGETARIAN. **Reservations:** Recommended for dinner. **U-Bahn:** Wittenbergplatz.

Prices: Soups, appetizers, and salads 9–17 DM ($5.30–$10); main courses 20–36 DM ($11.80–$21.25). No credit cards.

Open: Lunch Sun and holidays noon–3pm; dinner Fri–Wed 6–11:30pm.

Don't let the restaurant's mundane facade on the busy corner of Tauentzienstrasse and Martin-Luther-Strasse deter you from eating here. Enter through the mock–temple gate entrance and you'll find yourself in an oasis of greenery, complemented by the soothing sounds of running water and instrumental music, exquisite flower arrangements, and colorful carp swimming lazily in the indoor pond. Named after a famous Zen Buddhist Japanese master, the restaurant specializes in Asian-influenced vegetarian cuisine, with an English menu. You might start with a clear Japanese soup or an Indian soup made with red lentils, coconut milk, and coriander. The main dishes, all of which include side dishes, range from grilled tofu medallions and stuffed eggplant to hot ragoût of tofu and exotic vegetables in coconut milk with fried fruits and tempura. For those who are tired of pork or eschew meat altogether, this place is a godsend.

Heinz Holl, Damaschkestrasse 26. ☎ **323 14 04.**

Cuisine: GERMAN/CONTINENTAL. **Reservations:** Required. **U-Bahn:** Adenauerplatz.
Prices: Appetizers and soups 9–25 DM ($5.30–$14.75); main courses 25–40 DM ($14.75–$23.60). AE, MC.
Open: Mon–Sat 7pm–1am. **Closed:** Holidays.

A Berlin institution, this place is so small, cozy, and personable that being here is like being part of an intimate social gathering. Named after its owner and located here for over a quarter of a century, the restaurant continues to draw a devoted clientele, among them personalities from Berlin's social circles.

Although the ambience gets high marks, the food is even better. This is a good place to try Sülze (jellied meat, served with potatoes and rémoulade), Kohlroulade (stuffed cabbage rolls), Wiener Schnitzel, Tafelspitz (boiled beef with vegetables), beef Stroganoff, or Argentinian steak. Don't neglect the daily specials, however, which may include fresh fish and other items in season. There's a bar where you can sip a pre-dinner cocktail or an after-dinner drink.

★ **Lutter & Wegner**, Schlüterstrasse 55. ☎ **881 34 40.**

Cuisine: GERMAN/CONTINENTAL. **Reservations:** Required. **S-Bahn:** Savignyplatz.
Prices: Appetizers and soups 10–25 DM ($5.90–$14.75); main courses 35–40 DM ($20.65–$23.60). AE, DC, MC, V.
Open: Dinner only, daily 6:30pm–3am (last order 11:30pm).

A combination wine bar and restaurant, Lutter & Wegner has been around since 1811, when it first opened as a wine cellar in eastern Berlin. Moving to West Berlin after World War II, it still has that incomparable old-world style. It's simple and unpretentious, yet refined and civilized, with dark-paneled wainscoting, white tablecloths, candles, and pleasant background music. Catering to a professional and artistic crowd, it also has a small bar where you can come simply for a drink.

The often-changing handwritten menu always offers daily specials, which may include Tafelspitz; Spanferkel; fish; or noodle casserole with cheese, mushrooms, and leeks. The salads, among the cheapest items available, are so huge they're meals in themselves. Since this is a wine bar, indulge in one of its selections from Franken, the Rhine area, Baden, the Mosel Valley, or France. A glass starts at about 8 DM ($4.70).

Ming's Garden, Tauentzienstrasse 16 (entrance on Marburger Strasse). ☎ **211 87 28.**

Cuisine: CHINESE. **U-Bahn:** Kurfürstendamm or Wittenbergplatz.

Prices: Soups and appetizers 9–20 DM ($5.30–$11.80); main courses 22–40 DM ($13–$23.60); fixed-price lunches 13–20 DM ($7.65–$11.80). AE, DC, MC, V.
Open: Daily noon–11:30pm.

Enter this upscale Chinese restaurant, located across from the Europa-Center, by walking over a small pond filled with goldfish into an ornately decorated dining hall with pink tablecloths and flowers on each table. It's a popular place for a business lunch, when a choice of 13 various main courses includes a soup, spring roll, or a salad. It's available Monday to Saturday to 3pm. The regular menu includes a wide selection of seafood, poultry, beef, rice, noodles, and vegetable dishes, including king prawns, lemon-flavored chicken, Szechuan-style duck, and Peking duck.

$ Ristorante Tavola Calda, Leibnizstrasse 45. ☎ **324 10 48.**
Cuisine: ITALIAN. **Reservations:** Required. **S-Bahn:** Savignyplatz.
Prices: Pastas and pizzas 13–18 DM ($7.65–$10.60); main courses 30–38 DM ($17.70–$22.40). No credit cards.
Open: Mon–Sat noon–midnight.

A tiny one-room restaurant with a marble floor, clinical white walls, abstract art, and pink tablecloths, Tavola Calda is another favorite of lovers of Italian cuisine—giving the more expensive Mario down the street stiff competition. Evenings are romantic, despite the fact that tables are close together. The place is trendy without being clichéd.

The pasta and pizza are especially good, and at such moderate prices you can dine here quite reasonably. If you opt for one of the higher-priced lamb, beef, saltimbocca, or scampi dishes, however, you're in for a special treat, since all are wonderfully prepared and presented.

Tafelrunde, Nachodstrasse 21. ☎ **211 21 41.**
Cuisine: GERMAN. **Reservations:** Required. **U-Bahn:** Spichernstrasse.
Prices: Fixed-price dinner 70.50 DM ($41.60). No credit cards.
Open: Dinner only, daily 6pm–midnight.

Dining as it was in the Middle Ages—that's the theme of the Tafelrunde (Round Table). Diners are given only a special knife, just as in the good old days, and are expected to eat with their fingers. Bibs are passed out just in case. The simple dining halls, in the spirit of the times, have only long wooden tables and chairs and an atmosphere enhanced by medieval music and candles, although the building itself is modern. It's about a 10-minute walk south of the Ku'damm or only one stop away by U-Bahn.

Only one fixed meal is served, changing several times a month and centering on different themes, with entertainment provided by the staff. Usually a seven-course meal, it starts with a drink from a cow's horn, loaves of bread, soup, and appetizers. These are followed by a main course such as Spiessbraten (shish kebab) or Spanferkel (suckling pig), a surprise dish, and cheese and fruit.

Zlata Praha, Meinekestrasse 4. ☎ 881 97 50.

> **Cuisine:** CZECHOSLOVAKIAN/HUNGARIAN. **Reservations:** Recommended for dinner. **U-Bahn:** Uhlandstrasse or Kurfürstendamm.
> **Prices:** Appetizers and soups 7–18 DM ($4.15–$10.60); main courses 20–40 DM ($11.80–$23.60). AE, DC, MC, V.
> **Open:** Mon–Sat noon–11:30pm.

Zlata Praha specializes primarily in food from Prague but offers dishes from Hungary and Austria as well. It is decorated in a hushed drawing-room style, with red-velvet chairs, dark furnishings, white tablecloths, and candles and fresh flowers on each table; portraits of noblemen and noblewomen adorning the walls conjure up the time when the Austro-Hungarian Empire still ruled much of eastern Europe. The atmosphere is subdued and would be almost solemn if it weren't for the many customers who seem to know one another and become livelier with each round of Czech beer or spirits.

Most dishes are prepared with a liberal dose of paprika (red pepper)—from paprika chicken with homemade noodles to paprika Schnitzel. Also available are stuffed cabbage in bacon-paprika cream with potatoes; Hungarian paprika veal cutlet; beef Stroganoff; and turkey breast filled with bacon, paprika, and onions in a gypsy sauce. Portions are generous.

Inexpensive

Arche Noah in Jüdischen Gemeindehaus, Fasanenstrasse 79. ☎ 884 20 339.

> **Cuisine:** KOSHER. **U-Bahn:** Uhlandstrasse.
> **Prices:** Fixed-price meals 22–24 DM ($13–$14.15); Sabbath fixed-price meals 35–50 DM ($20.65–$29.50); Tues buffet 38 DM ($22.40). AE, MC, V.
> **Open:** Lunch Sun–Fri 11:30am–3:30pm, Sat 11:30am–2:30pm; dinner daily 6:30–11pm. **Closed:** Sat evening Apr–Oct.

This simple dining hall up on the first floor of the Jewish Community House one of the few places in town for kosher foods, offers a daily menu of Jewish, Oriental, European, and Israeli specialties. There are about three different daily fixed-price meals that include soup, dessert, and a main course that may consist of Gulasch, roast veal, or lamb chops. There's a Tuesday evening buffet with an elaborate spread of warm and cold Jewish specialties; Sabbath fixed-price meals must be ordered by 2pm Friday.

Chung, Kurfürstendamm 190. ☎ 882 15 55.

> **Cuisine:** CHINESE. **U-Bahn:** Uhlandstrasse or Adenauerplatz.
> **Prices:** Appetizers 5–16 DM ($2.95–$9.45); main courses 15–30 DM ($8.85–$17.70); fixed-price lunches 11–15 DM ($6.50–$8.85). AE, MC, V.
> **Open:** Daily 11:30am–midnight (last order 11pm).

Occupying a prime spot on the Ku'damm, with a glass-enclosed dining room that extends right over the sidewalk, this ornately decorated restaurant features Chinese lanterns hanging from the ceiling and an obliging staff. The best deals are the special fixed-price lunches, available only Monday through Friday until 3pm (excluding holidays), which consist of a choice of soup or spring roll, along with almost two dozen entree choices. An English menu offers a seemingly endless list of main dishes, including beef with seasonal vegetables, fish filet Cantonese style with pork and mushrooms, pork with bamboo shoots and mushrooms, chicken Shanghai style, fried noodles with prawns, and roast duck.

Ciao Ciao, Kurfürstendamm 156. ☎ 892 36 12.

Cuisine: ITALIAN. **Reservations:** Recommended for dinner. **U-Bahn:** Adenauerplatz.
Prices: Appetizers and soups 8–26 DM ($4.70–$15.34); pizza and pasta 13–26 DM ($7.65–$15.34); main courses 26–40 DM ($15.34–$23.60). MC, V.
Open: Sun–Thurs noon–2am, Fri–Sat noon–3am.

An informal Italian restaurant standing on the far west end of the Ku'damm past Adenauerplatz, Ciao Ciao makes a lively place to dine, with an animated Italian staff and plenty to watch if you can get a seat outside in summer. While the food is not always up to par, given the prices, the atmosphere is so good that few people seem to mind. To be on the safe side, order the carpaccio and one of the dozen choices of pizza or pasta, the latter including cannelloni, tagliatelle, tortellini, and rigatoni. Scampi is served half a dozen ways.

★ **Dorfgasthaus**, Sächsische Strasse 7. ☎ 881 92 39.

Cuisine: SOUTHERN GERMAN. **Directions:** A five-minute walk south of the Ku'damm, south of Bleibtreustrasse.
Prices: Soups and salads 7–15 DM ($4.15–$8.85); main courses 14–33 DM ($8.25–$19.45). AE, DC, MC, V.
Open: Mon–Sat 4pm–1am, Sun 11am–1am.

Decorated in old-Berlin style with a wood-plank floor, antique light fixtures, and an unusually long bar dominating one wall, Dorfgasthaus nevertheless possesses an aura of trendiness. Whereas many Gaststätten seem to survive primarily on a clientele of older customers, this one also draws in the younger generation, who come for a hearty dose of Swabian ravioli soup, Schnitzel, steak, and Sauerbraten. The Riesen-Grillteller is a pork-lover's delight, with pork medallions, two other cuts of pork, lamb, meatballs, french fries, and a mixed salad. You'll need to go on a diet after you've eaten this meal.

Gasthaus Meineke, Meinekestrasse 10. ☎ 882 31 58.

Cuisine: GERMAN. **U-Bahn:** Uhlandstrasse or Kurfürstendamm.
Prices: Appetizers 6.50–16 DM ($3.55–$9.45); main courses 12–30 DM ($7.10–$17.70). No credit cards.
Open: Daily noon–1am.

Although less than a decade old, this Gaststätte was cleverly designed to look like an old Berliner pub, with a wooden floor, dark-paneled wainscoting, and wooden benches built into private niches in the front-room wall. The place serves as both a bar and a restaurant, dishing out hearty helpings of homemade Leberwurst, Kasseler Rippenspeer with bread and butter, Brathering, Berliner Boulette,

Bauernsalat (farmer's salad), Leberkäs, Sülze, Eisbein, Schnitzel, Forelle (trout), and Rumpsteak. Like everyone else around you, order a beer to wash it all down. Gasthaus Meineke is located just a few minutes' walk south of the Ku'damm, near Lietzenburger Strasse.

Grung Thai, Ku'damm Passage, Kurfürstendamm 202. ☎ **881 53 50.**

Cuisine: THAI. **U-Bahn:** Uhlandstrasse.
Prices: Appetizers and soups 5–13 DM ($2.95–$7.65); main courses 17–30 DM ($10–$17.70). AE, DC, MC, V.
Open: Mon–Fri 6pm–3am, Sat–Sun noon–3am.

Located in a small mall at the corner of the Ku'damm and Knesebeckstrasse, Grung Thai strives to provide the right atmosphere with elephant statues and other Thai artifacts, plus live music every evening (except Monday) starting at 9pm. There are more than 100 items on the menu, including my favorites: chicken soup with coconut milk and lemon grass, Thai noodles with seafood, and a spicy beef salad. There are also curries; salads; and fish, pork, and beef dishes. Wash it all down with Singha beer, Thai's national drink. After midnight you must enter the restaurant through the passage on Knesebeckstrasse.

★ **Hardtke,** Meinekestrasse 27 A & B. ☎ **881 98 27.**

Cuisine: GERMAN. **U-Bahn:** Uhlandstrasse.
$ **Prices:** Appetizers and soups 6.50–23 DM ($3.85–$13.55); main courses 14–30 DM ($8.25–$17.70). No credit cards.
Open: Daily 10am–1am (last order 11:30pm).

Just a minute's walk from the Ku'damm, this popular restaurant has been dishing out hearty Teutonic fare for over 40 years. Many visiting natives make a point of eating here at least once, and on any given evening the place is usually packed with middle-aged and retired German men and women. Because this restaurant has its own butcher shop, its meat has the reputation of being especially fresh, and its homemade sausages are excellent. The dining area is divided into two separate halls (hence the A and B addresses). Both have the rustic appearance of a typical Gaststätte and both offer the same menu, including Berliner Eisbein with vegetables, Sauerkraut, and potatoes; Brathering with potatoes; Sauerbraten or Schweinebraten with red cabbage and potato dumplings; and Schnitzel. You could easily spend 30 DM ($17.70) on a great meal, or dine on sausages for 11.50 DM ($6.80) (available only to 6pm). Try the fresh blood-and-liver sausage, the gigantic Bockwurst with potato salad, the Bratwurst with potatoes and Sauerkraut, or the Wurst platter. All around, this is one of the best places in town for a typical German meal.

Istanbul, Knesebeckstrasse 77. ☎ **883 27 77.**

Cuisine: TURKISH. **S-Bahn:** Savignyplatz.
Prices: Soups and salads 7.50–10.50 DM ($4.40–$6.20); appetizers 10.50–13 DM ($6.20–$7.65); main courses 14–33 DM ($8.25–$19.45). AE, DC, MC, V.
Open: Daily noon–midnight.

One of Berlin's oldest Turkish restaurants, this family-run establishment remains firmly entrenched as one of the best—quite a feat considering Berlin's abundance of Turkish dining spots. Try to get a seat in the back room, which is decorated in mosque style. On Fridays and Saturdays, a belly dancer entertains after 9:30pm. You might wish to start your meal with a Turkish apéritif called Raki, which is sun-ripened raisins flavored with anise. For an appetizer, try yaprak dolmast (vine leaves stuffed with rice, pine nuts, currants, and herbs) or hummus (chick peas with garlic). Main courses range from so-called Turkish pizza (flat bread with chopped meat) to dönerkebab (veal grilled on a rotating spit and served with rice), shish kebab (skewered meat and vegetables), and a wide variety of lamb dishes. If you've never had the pleasure of sampling Turkish cuisine, this is a good place to do so.

Kalkutta, Bleibtreustrasse 17. ☎ 883 62 93.

Cuisine: INDIAN. **S-Bahn:** Savignyplatz.
Prices: Main courses 16–28 DM ($9.45–$16.50); buffet lunch 16 DM ($9.45). AE, MC, V.
Open: Daily noon–midnight.

Just off the Ku'damm, amid the many bars of Bleibtreustrasse, this tiny unpretentious restaurant offers great Indian curries, a generous use of spices giving them an extra pizzazz. Berlin's first Indian restaurant, it is also the only Indian restaurant in Berlin licensed to operate an original clay oven imported from India, which it uses for its breads and excellently prepared grilled foods and tandoori.

With painted wall murals and the obligatory Indian background music, the place attracts a young clientele, most of them well-traveled and many of whom have been to India. Dinner offers a wide assortment of tandoori, vegetable curries, and fish, as well as pork, chicken, beef, and veal dishes. Lunch is more economical, with an all-you-can-eat buffet offered Monday to Friday from noon to 3pm.

Restaurant Marche Mövenpick, Kurfürstendamm 14–15.
☎ 882 75 79 or 882 75 78.

Cuisine: INTERNATIONAL. **U-Bahn:** Kurfürstendamm.
Prices: Main courses 8–15 DM ($4.70–$8.85). AE, V.
Open: Daily 8am–midnight.

This cafeteria, run by the Swiss-owned Mövenpick chain of restaurants, is a great choice for casual dining on the Ku'damm. It imitates the neighborhood market, with various stands and counters offering fresh meals—most prepared in front of each customer. A raw vegetable stand offers a salad bar with half a dozen prepared salads, while the grill stand offers a selection of changing meat dishes ranging from fish to chicken. Other counters specialize in soups, pasta, daily specials, breads, desserts, and freshly squeezed fruit and vegetable juices. Vegetarians will appreciate the interesting salad buffet. Diners have a choice of several dining areas, including no-smoking and sidewalk seating. Depending on the meal you assemble, expect to spend from 15 to 25 DM ($8.85 to $14.75).

Mövenpick, in the Europa-Center. ☎ **262 70 77.**

Cuisine: INTERNATIONAL. **U-Bahn:** Kurfürstendamm or Wittenbergplatz.
Prices: Main courses 11.50–30 DM ($6.50–$17.70). AE, DC, MC, V.
Open: Sun–Thurs 8am–midnight, Fri–Sat 8am–1am.

This huge branch of Mövenpick, a Swiss chain of restaurants, is on the second floor of the Europa-Center and is divided into various sections serving different kinds of food. The Backstube, for example, specializes in pizza and quiche and offers seating on a terrace overlooking the inner atrium of the Europa-Center. The more upscale Le Caveau, a wine cellar with more than 100 different vintages from around the world, offers a changing menu that might include shrimp, roast hare, or turkey breast, with most entrees here costing 25 to 33 DM ($14.75 to $19.45). And the largest dining area, called Café des Artistes, offers herring, smoked salmon, pasta dishes, curries, steak, fish, and pork cutlets, as well as a self-service salad bar. One trip through the salad bar with a small plate costs 9 DM ($5.30); a large plate costs 14 DM ($8.25). In summer, there's outdoor seating with views of the Gedächtniskirche at Mövenpick's ground-floor coffeehouse, which sells snacks and desserts.

Roccoco, Knesebeckstrasse 92. ☎ **313 93 15.**

Cuisine: ITALIAN. **S-Bahn:** Savignyplatz. **U-Bahn:** Ernst-Reuter-Platz.
Rates: Soup, salad, and antipasto 8–20 DM ($4.70–$11.80); pasta 15–20 ($8.85–$11.80); main courses 26–33 DM ($15.35–22.40). MC, V.
Open: Daily noon–midnight.

This simple and pleasant Italian restaurant, located north of Savignyplatz, draws in a young and artsy clientele, especially in fine weather, when tables and chairs are placed along the sidewalk. Specializing in Neapolitan cuisine, it is popular for its Wednesday and Friday fish menu, when fresh fish is flown in from the Mediterranean. The regular menu includes spaghetti, macaroni, linguine, tagliatelle, meat, and fish dishes, but an especially good value is the two-course fixed-price lunch for 15 DM ($8.85), served until 4pm.

San Marino, Savignyplatz 12. ☎ **313 60 86.**

Cuisine: ITALIAN. **S-Bahn:** Savignyplatz.
Prices: Pizzas and pasta 8–18 DM ($4.70–$10.60); main courses 18–35 DM ($10.60–$20.65). AE, MC, V.
Open: Daily 11am–1am.

Similar to the many other trattorias in Berlin, San Marino has the advantage of an ideal location right on Savignyplatz, just a few minutes' walk north of the Ku'damm. In summer you can dine outside on the square, with a pleasant view of grass and trees, and afterward go for a drink in one of the many bars in the neighborhood. In winter you dine indoors in a pleasant atmosphere with candles and flowers on each table. Although there are steaks and seafood on the menu, all you need order is one of the personal-size pizzas or pasta dishes, most priced at less than 15 DM ($8.85). It would be hard, however, to resist a couple of glasses of Lambrusco or Chianti as well.

Shell, Knesebeckstrasse 22. ☎ **312 83 10.**

Cuisine: INTERNATIONAL/VEGETARIAN. **S-Bahn:** Savignyplatz.
Prices: Soups and salads 8–22 DM ($4.70–$13); main courses 18–34 DM ($10.60–$20) AE, MC, V.
Open: Mon–Sat 9am–midnight, Sun 10am–midnight.

Shell occupies what was once a corner gas station (hence its cheeky name and yellow shell banner) and now dispenses beer instead of petrol. A simple and pleasant restaurant on Savignyplatz, it has a curved facade with huge windows that benefit the several indoor palm trees and cacti. Popular with the many young residents of the area, Shell features international dishes, many of them light or vegetarian. The main menu, available throughout the day and evening, lists such diverse selections as risotto with black rice, cashews, crab, and vegetables; tofu with sweet chili, vegetables, sprouts, and noodles; a vegetable plate with hollandaise, potatoes, and salad; salmon and pork chops. In addition, there's also a lunch menu, available until 6pm, with prices of daily specials running less than 22 DM ($13). My only complaint is that service tends to be slow—come here only if you have time, or, if you prefer, for a cup of coffee or a beer.

Taverna Plaka, Joachimstaler Strasse 14. ☎ **883 15 57.**

Cuisine: GREEK. **U-Bahn:** Kurfürstendamm.
Prices: Appetizers and salads 7–15 DM ($4.15–$8.85); main courses 15–30 DM ($8.85–$17.70). No credit cards.
Open: Mon–Fri 4pm–1am, Sat–Sun and holidays noon–1am.

This first-floor Greek restaurant, just off the Ku'damm, is decorated in cheerful Mykonos white and blue, with flowers and candles on each table. The Greek waiters are friendly and accommodating, the recorded music is mainly Greek instrumental, and the food is good no matter what you order or how much you spend. There are the usual moussaka, fish, souvlaki, and gyros on the menu, but if you're on a budget, order the Mesedes Plaka for 11 DM ($6.50). Although it's an appetizer plate, it's plentiful—dolmades (stuffed grape leaves), eggplant salad, feta cheese, and a sampling of other Greek delicacies— and the waiter didn't blink twice when that's all I ordered. An alternative is the huge Greek salad (called choriatiki). A fun place to dine.

Budget

Ashoka, Grolmanstrasse 51. ☎ **313 20 66.**

Cuisine: INDIAN. **S-Bahn:** Savignyplatz.
Prices: 5–13 DM ($2.95–$7.65). No credit cards.
Open: Daily 10am–midnight.

Just north of Savignyplatz, this tiny hole-in-the-wall has an open kitchen that takes up half the restaurant, plus outdoor seating in summer. Popular with students living in the area, it offers more than a dozen vegetarian dishes alone, along with half a dozen meat choices and a daily fixed menu. For an appetizer, try the pakoras, a kind of biscuit with cauliflower and other vegetables, with a dash of chutney. The vegetarian Gemüseplatte Benares (vegetable platter) for 11 DM ($6.50) is a great bargain.

Asia-Quick, Lietzenburger Strasse 96. ☎ **882 15 33.**
   Cuisine: CHINESE. **U-Bahn:** Uhlandstrasse.
   Prices: 10–16 DM ($5.90–$9.45). No credit cards.
   Open: Mon–Fri 11:30am–3am, Sat 4pm–3am.

About a two-minute walk south of the Ku'damm near Bleib-treustrasse, Asia-Quick is a simple and pleasant place for Chinese fast food. Decorated in bright red and white, it offers soups and appetizers for less than 5 DM ($2.95), while most of the main dishes are less than 12 DM ($7.10). Its meat dishes come in three styles: chop suey (with soy sauce), sweet-and-sour, and Szechuan (spicy). Meats to choose from include fish, pork, beef, and chicken; there are also rice, noodle, and vegetarian dishes. As in many restaurants throughout Asia, there is even a TV in the corner. You can either eat here or order take-out.

$ **Athener Grill,** Kurfürstendamm 156. ☎ **892 10 39.**
   Cuisine: GREEK/ITALIAN. **U-Bahn:** Adenauerplatz.
   Prices: 3.50–15 DM ($2.05–$8.85). AE, DC, MC, V.
   Open: Sun–Thurs 11am–4am, Fri–Sat 11am–5am.

A good choice if you can't decide whether you want Greek or Italian—or if you want both. An imaginatively done cafeteria, it's located at the far western end of the Ku'damm, past Adenauerplatz (look for a modern brick building). The menu is written on the wall. After deciding what you want, pay the cashier and then hand your ticket to the cook at the appropriate counter. Counters are divided into various specialties, with Greek food at one counter, pizza at another, wine at yet another. You'll find fish, spaghetti, moussaka, souvlaki, gyros, ice cream, and salads, to mention a few of the dishes available. The Greek and Italian wines start at 3.20 DM ($1.90) per glass, certainly one of the cheapest prices in town.

China Imbiss Dalí, Savignyplatz S-Bahn-Bogen 604. ☎ **312 64 23.**
   Cuisine: CHINESE. **S-Bahn:** Savignyplatz.
   Prices: Soups and appetizers 3.50–6.50 DM ($2.05–$3.55); main courses 9–15 DM ($5.30–$8.85). No credit cards.
   Open: Daily noon–11pm.

Savignyplatz Bogen is a string of establishments located under the S-Bahn tracks between Savignyplatz and Bleibtreustrasse. China Imbiss Dalí, just off Bleibtreustrasse, is a simply decorated Chinese restaurant offering rice and noodle dishes, as well as hearty portions of pork, beef, duck, chicken, fish, and vegetable dishes. There's an English menu, and candles on each table make for slightly more intimate dining than what is usually offered at fast-food Chinese restaurants.

$ **Ciao Italia,** Goethestrasse 84. ☎ **313 76 67.**
   Cuisine: ITALIAN. **U-Bahn:** Ernst-Reuter-Platz. **S-Bahn:** Savignyplatz.
   Prices: 8–15 DM ($4.70–$8.85); fixed-price lunch 20 DM ($11.80). No credit cards.
   Open: Mon–Sat noon–midnight.

It would be easy to walk right by this tiny place and never know it harbored a counter with a variety of pasta dishes, along with a few tables and chairs where you can eat your goodies. That's because it actually is a shop, with walls unceremoniously lined with packages of noodles and bottles of wine. There's hardly room for diners, but people in the know come here for some of the cheapest and best pasta in town, which may range from tortellini and ravioli to rigatoni and lasagne. After selecting a pasta at the counter, diners can then choose one of four sauces: tomato, mushroom, gorgonzola, or meat. There are also olives for sale, and wine by the glass. Because this place is so small, try to eat during the off-hours. Ciao Italia is at the corner of Goethe and Knesebeck Streets, about a three-minute walk north of Savignyplatz or an eight-minute walk north of the Ku'damm.

Club Culinare, in Wertheim department store, Kurfürstendamm 231. ☎ 88 20 61.

Cuisine: GERMAN/SNACKS. **U-Bahn:** Kurfürstendamm.
Prices: 7–20 DM ($4.15, $11.80). No credit cards.
Open: Mon–Wed and Fri 9am–6pm. Thurs 9am–8pm, Sat 9am–1:30pm (to 5:30pm first Sat of the month in winter, 3:30pm in summer).

Most German department stores have grocery departments in their basements, and Wertheim is no exception. Unusual, however, are its several sit-down counters, where various types of snacks and meals are sold. Simply walk around until you find a counter offering the food that's most tempting to you. Among the choices are salads (several dozen kinds), stews, pasta, potato pancakes, grilled chicken, desserts, and beer and wine. There's also a large selection of fresh breads and cheeses.

★ **Café Hardenberg,** Hardenbergstrasse 10. ☎ 312 26 44.
Cuisine: GERMAN/INTERNATIONAL. **U-Bahn:** Ernst-Reuter-Platz.
Prices: 8–14 DM ($4.70–$8.25). No credit cards.
Open: Daily 9am–midnight.

Less than a 10-minute walk from Bahnhof Zoo, and across the street from the Technical University, this popular cafe is always packed with students and people who work nearby. Decorated with museum posters and plants, it serves as a coffeehouse, a restaurant, and, in the evening, a bar. In summer, there are tables and chairs outside. Classical music is played through the sound system until 4pm, when music of the 20th century takes over. It's a good place for a meal, since portions are hearty and the menu includes an interesting range of dishes that change daily. Your choice can range from spaghetti or a huge Greek salad to an omelet, dolmades, pork chops, or chili con carne.

$ **Einhorn,** Wittenbergplatz 5–6. ☎ 218 63 47.
Cuisine: VEGETARIAN. **U-Bahn:** Wittenbergplatz.
Prices: 7–11 DM ($4.15–$6.50). No credit cards.
Open: Mon–Fri 10am–6pm, Sat 10am–2pm.

At the north end of Wittenbergplatz opposite KaDeWe, this natural-foods shop offers changing daily specials of ready-made vegetarian dishes, which in the past have included curried risotto with vegetables, spinach cannelloni, vegetarian lasagne, stews, salads, spinach casserole, and vegetarian moussaka. There are tempting fruit juices as well. You can eat at the stand-up counter or take your purchase outside and sit on one of the benches lining the square.

There's another branch located at Mommsenstrasse 2 (☎ 881 42 41), a minute's walk north of the Ku'damm near Knesebeckstrasse, with the same hours.

Ihre Frisch-Backstübe, Knesebeckstrasse 12. ☎ 319 07 10.

Cuisine: GERMAN. **U-Bahn:** Ernst-Reuter-Platz.
Prices: 4.50–10 DM ($2.65–$5.90). No credit cards.
Open: Mon–Sat 6am–6:30pm, Sun 1–5pm.

Located on the corner of Goethe and Knesebeck Streets, this bakery also has a self-service counter serving good take-out or eat-in food. There are several varieties of breads and cakes, of course, as well as pizza by the slice, sandwiches, and a changing menu of warm dishes, which may range from smoked pork chops to Leberkäs and Sauerkraut. The dining area is cheerful.

Jimmy's Diner, Pariser Strasse 41. ☎ 882 31 41.

Cuisine: AMERICAN/MEXICAN. **Directions:** A five-minute walk south of the Ku'damm, on the corner of Sächsische Strasse and Pariser Strasse.
Prices: 8.50–22 DM ($5–$13). No credit cards.
Open: Sun–Thurs noon–3am, Fri–Sat noon–6am.

Just like back home—that is, if your town still has a 1950s-style diner. This remake has booths with bright-red plastic furniture, lots of chrome, and old advertisements on the walls. Drive-in speakers dangle above the window. Popular with young Berliners who were probably born in the 1970s, it has an eclectic menu, from corn on the cob or "Aunt Mary's chicken salad" to huge quarter pounders, sandwiches, spareribs, spaghetti, salads, tacos, enchiladas, and chili con carne, most under 12 DM ($7.10). It even sells Mexican beers. Interspersed with funny sayings, the menu is good for a few laughs. The music ranges from Mexican to country, along with hits from the 1950s and '60s. A bit of unreality in the heart of Berlin—and for the homesick, much cheaper and quicker than a ticket home. Also, good for a hamburger fix, if that's what you need–they're huge and are served with french fries and coleslaw.

★ KaDeWe, Wittenbergplatz. ☎ 212 10 or 24 01 71.

Cuisine: INTERNATIONAL. **U-Bahn:** Wittenbergplatz.
Prices: 4–20 DM ($2.35–$11.80). No credit cards.
Open: Mon–Fri 9am–6pm (to 8pm on Thurs), Sat 9am–1pm (to 5:30pm first Sat of the month in winter, 3:30pm in summer.).

KaDeWe is the popular name for Kaufhaus des Westens, the largest department store on the European continent. Its top attraction, believe it or not, is the huge food emporium on the sixth floor, which has to be seen to be believed—row after row of gourmet foods, including exotic teas and coffees, spices, jams, sweets, vegetables, fruit, and an amazing array of sausages and cuts of pork. In the middle of all these sections are sit-down counters, each specializing in a different type of food. One counter sells pasta dishes, another Asian cuisine, while others sell grilled chicken, salads, oysters, and more. One counter is devoted to the potato alone, which you can order baked or fried in a number of styles. There are also a wine bar and a coffee bar.

Karavan, Kurfürstendamm 11. ☎ **881 50 05.**

> **Cuisine:** TURKISH. **U-Bahn:** Kurfürstendamm or Bahnhof Zoologischer Garten.
> **Prices:** 4–9 DM ($2.35–$5.30). No credit cards.
> **Open:** Daily 8am–1am.

Because of its large Turkish population, Berlin boasts a number of Turkish restaurants and stand-up food stalls. This simple place, on a square just across the plaza from the Gedächtniskirche, is a cross between the two—tiny and very informal, with a few stools for sitting at the counter. Better yet, order your food take-out and eat it on one of the public benches around the Gedächtniskirche, a prime spot for people-watching. I especially recommend the Turkish pizza, which has a thick, soft crust and a thin spread of minced meat and spices. There are also daily set menus for less than 10 DM ($5.90), as well as dönerkebab, Turkish sandwiches, and salads. Since all the food is visible behind the glass counter, simply point at what looks best. A good and convenient place to sample this ethnic food at very inexpensive prices.

Another branch nearby is Meister Snack, located under the eaves of the Bilka department store on the corner of Joachimstaler Strasse and Kantstrasse. It offers the same Turkish food.

$ Mensa, Technische Universität, Hardenbergstrasse 34. ☎ **3140.**

> **Cuisine:** GERMAN. **U-Bahn:** Ernst-Reuter-Platz.
> **Prices:** main courses 3.40–5 DM ($2–$82.95). No credit cards.
> **Open:** Mon–Fri 11:15am–2:30pm.

A student cafeteria of the Technical University, the Mensa has on the top floor a self-service restaurant that will serve fixed-price meals to students and nonstudents alike. Simply walk through the ground floor of the Mensa and then follow the signs for *Restaurant* to the right and up the stairs. Pick up a tray and choose from one of the changing daily main courses that may range from Gulasch stew or curried rice to turkey breast or a vegetarian ragoût. Side dishes of rice, potatoes, or salad cost less than 2 DM ($1.20). Although the dining area has that unmistakable cafeteria look and feel to it, this is one of the cheapest places in Berlin for a complete meal. It's located about a 10-minute walk from Bahnhof Zoo and is open year-round.

Orient, Lietzenburgerstrasse 77. ☎ **881 24 60.**

> **Cuisine:** MIDDLE EASTERN. **U-Bahn:** Uhlandstrasse.
> **Prices:** Sandwiches 4–6.50 DM ($2.35–$3.85), platters 12–24 DM ($7.10–$14.15). No credit cards.
> **Open:** Daily 11am–4am.

Specializing in Middle Eastern and Mediterranean dishes, the Orient stands on the corner of Lietzenburgerstrasse and Uhlandstrasse. It offers take-out food, but you may want to sit in its simple one-room dining area—bright, white, and newly remodeled—where you'll be serenaded by recorded music. There are several dozen items on the simple menu, most priced under 15 DM ($8.85) and served with side dishes, including falafel, gyros, kebabs, tabbouleh (cracked wheat–and–parsley salad), maali (a vegetarian dish of cauliflower, potatoes, and eggplant), and more than a dozen sandwiches. There are also daily specials, which are displayed behind the take-out counter.

Piccola Taormina Tavola Calda, Uhlandstrasse 29.
☎ **881 47 10.**
Cuisine: ITALIAN. **U-Bahn:** Uhlandstrasse.
Prices: 5.50–15 DM ($3.25–$8.85). No credit cards.
Open: Sun–Thurs 10am–2am, Fri–Sat 10am–3am.

Just a glance inside should convince you this is one of the most popular self-service Italian restaurants in town. The cheap prices attract hungry customers throughout the day and night, especially the pizza by the slice for 2 DM ($1.20). But the menu on the wall lists other choices as well, including more than 25 kinds of personal-size pizzas; omelets; risotto dishes; beefsteak; and such pasta as spaghetti, ravioli, lasagne, and cannelloni. Wine and beer are also available. Order at the counter and the cooks—all Italian—will have your order ready in a flash. There's plenty of dining space in the rear rooms, or you can order take-out.

2 Near Wilmersdorfer Strasse & Bahnhof Charlottenburg

Expensive

⭐ **Alt Luxemburg**, Windscheidstrasse 31. ☎ **323 87 30.**
Cuisine: NOUVELLE CONTINENTAL. **Reservations:** Required.
U-Bahn: Wilmersdorfer Strasse. **S-Bahn:** Bahnhof Charlottenburg.
Prices: Soups and appetizers 17–37 DM ($10–$21.85); main courses 40–53 DM ($23.60–$31.25). AE, DC, V.
Open: Dinner only, Tues–Sat 7pm–1am (last order 11pm).

The Alt Luxemburg, which seats only 35, is considered one of Berlin's top gourmet restaurants because of chef/owner Karl Wannemacher's imaginative dishes. Beautifully decorated in a style reminiscent of the 1800s, with elaborate antique chandeliers, fine pink tablecloths, and mirrors, it makes the perfect place for a romantic tête-à-tête. The service is impeccable yet unobtrusive.

The menu changes with the seasons and according to what's fresh and available. Though the unusual combinations of international spices and foods are at first surprising, they go together so perfectly

Frommer's Cool for Kids: Restaurants

Jimmy's Diner   (see p. 130) Is your teenager bugging you for a hamburger or some "real" food? Head for this 1950s-style diner, which offers hamburgers, sandwiches, chicken, spaghetti, and Mexican food. The diner's clientele, mainly Berlin teenagers striving for just the right look in punk, leather, or '50s clothing, will keep you all entertained as you dine.

Piccola Taormina Tavola Calda   (see p. 132) This is one of the cheapest places in town for pizza, which you can order take-out by the slice or eat at one of the simple wooden tables. You'll also find spaghetti, lasagne, and risotto dishes.

Zitadelle   (see p. 145) Older kids love the drama of this place—a medieval setting in a 700-year-old fortress in Spandau, where customers even eat with their fingers. Expensive, but an evening you won't forget.

T.G.I. Fridays   (see p. 139) This American chain, newly opened in eastern Berlin, offers a children's menu as well as a varied regular menu with selections ranging from fajitas and fettucine Alfredo to blackened Cajun chicken, burgers, and sandwiches.

you'll wonder why you've never had them that way before. Starters have included goose liver with grapes and curried cream of chicken soup with Japanese shiitake mushrooms. Past entrees have included lobster lasagne, beef filet with pesto, rack of lamb with thyme, and pigeon with truffle sauce. In any case, you're in for a culinary treat, and there's a wide range of wines to complement your meal.

Ponte Vecchio, Spielhagenstrasse 3. ☎ **342 19 99.**

Cuisine: ITALIAN. **Reservations:** Recommended. **U-Bahn:** Bismarckstrasse.
Prices: Appetizers and salads 17–26 DM ($10–$15.35); pasta 14–18 DM ($8.25–$10.60); main courses 31–40 DM ($18.30–$23.60). DC.
Open: Dinner only, Wed–Mon 6:30–11pm.

The light-orange facade of this small and unpretentious eatery belies the delights inside, for Ponte Vecchio ranks as one of the best gourmet Italian restaurants in town. The simple yet pleasant dining room caters to a clientele more interested in what touches their palates then what's on the walls.

The cuisine takes its cues from Tuscany, with only the freshest of ingredients used. For an appetizer, you might try the carpaccio with mozzarella and tomatoes or the seafood with basil. There's always a fresh fish of the day, as well as lamb and veal dishes, or perhaps you'll opt for homemade noodles with rabbit sauce or gnocchi with ricotta-and-tomato sauce. The selection of Italian wines is varied and perfect for the dishes on hand.

Inexpensive

Ty Breizh, Kantstrasse 75. ☎ **323 99 32.**

Cuisine: FRENCH. **U-Bahn:** Wilmersdorfer Strasse. **S-Bahn:** Bahnhof Charlottenburg.
Prices: Soups and salads 6.50–10 DM ($3.85–$5.90); main courses 9–27 DM ($5.30–$15.95). No credit cards.
Open: Dinner Mon–Fri 5pm–2am, Sat 6pm–2am.

One of the cheapest places in town for French food, the slightly rustic and oddly decorated Ty Breizh looks more like a bar or campus pizza parlor than a restaurant specializing in dishes from Brittany. Owner Patrick Mattei also serves as chef, and if he has time, he even sings chansons and hand decorates customers' bills. He has created an appetizer of mushrooms with shrimp and cheese that's wonderful. Other dishes include a casserole of eggplant, paprika, onions, and tomatoes; beef cooked in a rich Burgundy sauce with onions, carrots, and butter noodles; omelets; quiches; seafood; and crêpes. The fish soup is especially recommended. Mussels and oysters are available in winter.

Budget

 Wilhelm Hoeck, Wilmersdorfer Strasse 149. ☎ **341 31 10.**
Cuisine: GERMAN. **U-Bahn:** Bismarckstrasse.
Prices: Soups and salads 2.60–5 DM ($1.55–$3.10); main courses 9–15 DM ($5.30–$8.85). No credit cards.
Open: Mon–Sat 11am–11pm.

If you're hungry and want a traditional German meal at modest prices, head for this well-known establishment north of Bismarckstrasse. You'll find two doors at this address—the door on the left leads to the simple family-style restaurant; the one on the right leads to the bar, first opened in 1892. The bar has more character, but the restaurant isn't as smoky. Both offer the same menu of home-cooked foods "from Grandmother's kitchen," including Sülze (jellied meat) with potatoes, Bratwurst (sausage) with Sauerkraut and potatoes, Schnitzel, Eisbein with kraut, pureed peas and potatoes, and Boulette. There are also daily specials written on the chalkboard outside (in German only). Most platters are priced under 15 DM ($8.85).

Joseph Langer, Wilmersdorfer Strasse 118. ☎ **31 67 80.**
Cuisine: GERMAN. **U-Bahn:** Wilmersdorfer Strasse.
Prices: 2–10 DM ($1.20–$5.90). No credit cards.
Open: Mon–Fri 9am–6:30pm, Sat 8:30am–2pm (to 6pm first Sat of the month in winter, 4pm in summer).

Joseph Langer is a butcher shop that also sells simple and inexpensive meals, specializing, of course, in its own meats. You can order take-out or eat standing up at one of the chest-high tables. The cheapest item on the menu is Weisswurst (a Munich sausage) for 1.60 DM (95¢), and other offerings include Leberkäs, Gulasch with noodles, Schnitzel, Kasselerbraten, Boulette, various sausages, and potato salad.

Karstadt, Wilmersdorfer Strasse 109–111. ☎ **31 891.**

> **Cuisine:** GERMAN. **U-Bahn:** Wilmersdorfer Strasse.
> **Prices:** 10–15 DM ($5.90–$8.85). No credit cards.
> **Open:** Mon–Fri 9am–6pm (Thurs to 8pm), Sat 9am–1:30pm (to 5:30pm first Sat of the month in winter, 3:30pm in summer).

Located on Berlin's best-known pedestrian shopping lane, this department store contains a fourth-floor cafeteria that offers several counters with various types of food, including one devoted solely to vegetables (for those of you who miss your veggies, this is a true gift). Another counter offers German specials ranging from fish and Sauerbraten to Schnitzel and duck, while another features daily pasta specials. There are also a dessert counter and a beverage bar. And, wonder of wonders, there's even a no-smoking section.

Nordsee, Wilmersdorfer Strasse 58. ☎ **323 10 44.**

> **Cuisine:** SEAFOOD. **U-Bahn:** Wilmersdorfer Strasse.
> **Prices:** 6.50–11 DM ($3.85–$6.50). No credit cards.
> **Open:** Mon–Fri 9am–7pm (Thurs to 8:30pm), Sat 9am–3pm (to 6:30pm first Sat of the month).

Nordsee is a chain of fast-food fish restaurants that originated in northern Germany. They've made ordering easy, with the menu illustrated on the wall behind the cashier—simply go through the cafeteria line and order one of the dozen choices available, such as fried haddock, herring, fish sticks, or fish soup. There's also take-out service, including all kinds of fish sandwiches starting at around 2.20 DM ($1.30).

$ Rogacki, Wilmersdorfer Strasse 145–146. ☎ **341 40 91.**

> **Cuisine:** GERMAN. **U-Bahn:** Bismarckstrasse.
> **Prices:** 5–15 DM ($2.95–$8.85). No credit cards.
> **Open:** Mon–Fri 9am–6pm, Sat 8am–2pm.

Another butcher shop that sells ready-to-eat meals that can be eaten at chest-high tables, Rogacki devotes most of its considerable space to retail, with glass cases displaying all kinds of meats, Würste, fish, cheeses, breads, and more. Walk toward the back of the shop, where the self-service counter offers a great variety of dishes at prices that must surely be among the lowest in Berlin. No wonder the place has been around for more than 60 years and is still going strong. Entrees may include pig's knuckle, fish, grilled chicken, Wurst, salads, stews. And there are changing daily menus. Located about a seven-minute walk north of the pedestrian shopping section of Wilmersdorfer Strasse, between Bismarckstrasse and Zillestrasse, Rogacki has a picture of a purple fish on its facade.

$ Udagawa Japan Imbiss, Kantstrasse 118. ☎ **312 30 14.**

> **Cuisine:** JAPANESE. **U-Bahn:** Wilmersdorfer Strasse.
> **Prices:** 7–30 DM ($4.15–$17.70); fixed-price lunches 15–20 DM ($8.85–$11.80). No credit cards.
> **Open:** Wed–Mon 12:30pm–midnight.

This tiny self-service restaurant offers Japanese food at reasonable prices, with most dishes ranging from 10 to 20 DM ($5.90 to

$11.80). An informal place with only a few counters and tables, it offers a wide selection, including sashimi, sushi, noodles, tempura (deep-fried foods), teriyaki chicken, and nabe (stews). A complete fixed-price meal of tempura or sashimi (called teishoku) is available for about 30 DM ($17.70); there are also fixed-price lunches served until 3pm. Great food, great prices.

3 Berlin-Mitte (Eastern Berlin)

Expensive

Restaurant Ephraim-Palais, Spreeufer 1, Nikolaiviertel.
☎ **242 51 08** or **242 51 53.**
Cuisine: FRENCH. **Reservations:** Required. **U-Bahn:** Klosterstrasse or Alexanderplatz.
Prices: Appetizers 16–20 DM ($9.45–$11.80); main courses 34–40 DM ($20.05–$23.60). AE, DC, MC, V.
Open: Daily noon–midnight. **Closed:** Mon in winter.

Situated in the Nikolaiviertel (Nikolai Quarter) of eastern Berlin just off Alexanderplatz near the Rathaus, this very fine restaurant is decorated like a palace. In fact, it's an exact replica of Ephraim-Palais, built for a man named Veitel Ephraim who worked as court jeweler to Frederick II. Rococo inside and out, with an ornate facade and shimmering chandeliers in dining halls that resemble a nobleman's drawing rooms, it recalls an atmosphere of yesterday, with waiters dressed in black coats and ties. A classy place, so dress accordingly. The English menu changes often but always includes selections of fish and seasonal specials, as well as traditional dishes like grilled sirloin steak, lamb, and veal. Fixed-price meals start at 60 DM ($35.40).

Restaurant Königin Luise, in the Opernpalais, Unter den Linden 5.
☎ **200 22 69.**
Cuisine: GERMAN. **S-Bahn:** Friedrichstrasse. **Bus:** 100 to Staatsoper stop.
Prices: Appetizers and soups 12–24 DM ($7.10–$14.15); main courses 37–45 DM ($21.85–$26.55). AE, MC, V.
Open: Dinner only, Tues–Sat 5:30pm–midnight.

The Opernpalais, located on one of Berlin's most famous boulevards, is one of the city's most famous establishments. Occupying part of a palace built in 1733, destroyed in World War II, and recently renovated at a great cost, it contains several eating and drinking establishments. On the first floor is its premier restaurant, the Königin Luise, very elegant with chandeliers, elaborate stucco ceilings, and faux marble walls. Offering a view of Unter den Linden, it serves a variety of German and continental dishes, from trout and salmon to duck, veal, lamb, and steak, as well as a four-course meal for 80 DM ($47.20).

On the ground floor of Opernpalais is a classy cocktail bar; Operncafé is a coffeehouse, famous for its breakfast buffet and tortes. In the basement is a fish restaurant.

Eastern Berlin Dining

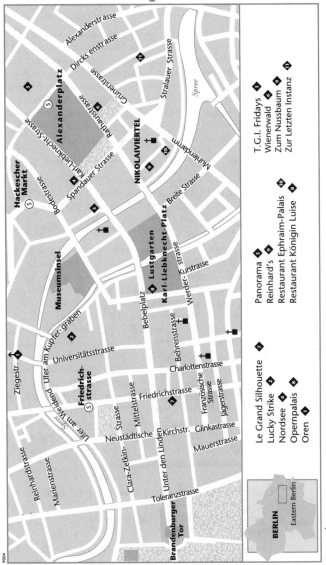

T.G.I. Fridays 3
Wienerwald 6
Zum Nussbaum 9
Zur Letzten Instanz 11

Restaurant Ephraim-Palais 10
Restaurant Königin Luise 6

Panorama 5
Reinhard's 6
Le Grand Silhouette 7
Lucky Strike 2
Nordsee 4
Opernpalais 8
Oren 1

Church ✝ ■   S-Bahn stop Ⓢ

BERLIN
Eastern Berlin

Moderate

Reinhard's, Poststrasse 28, Nikolaiviertel. ☎ **242 52 95.**

    Cuisine: INTERNATIONAL. **Reservations:** Recommended. **U-Bahn or S-Bahn:** Alexanderplatz or Klosterstrasse.

    Prices: Soups and salads 8–21 DM ($4.70–$12.40); main courses 20–37 DM ($11.80–$21.85). AE, DC, MC, V.

Open: Daily 9am–midnight.

Located in the restored Nikolai Quarter not far from Alexanderplatz, this large and lively American-style bistro is popular with Berlin's business set; it consists of a bar and a dining area decorated with photos and posters of famous film stars of yesterday. The music, barely audible over the continual buzz of conversation, tends to be hits of the 1940s and '50s. The menu includes well-known dishes from various countries—such as roast beef with potatoes and rémoulade, tagliatelle with salmon, Tafelspitz, pork medallions, duck breast, spareribs, pepper steak, Norwegian salmon, and rack of lamb.

Inexpensive

Lucky Strike, Georgenstrasse, S-Bahnbögen 177–180. ☎ **3084 8822.**
   Cuisine: AMERICAN. **S-Bahn:** Friedrichstrasse.
   Prices: Breakfast and lunch 7.50–16 DM ($4.40–$9.45); dinner main courses 17–40 DM ($10–$23.60). AE, DC, MC, V.
   Open: Daily 10am–2am.

At last—there are now restaurants within convenient walking distance to all those museums on Museumsinsel. As it happens, the two closest serve American food (also see T.G.I. Fridays below). Located under the arches of the elevated S-Bahn tracks just a couple of minutes' walk from the Pergamon Museum, Lucky Strike is an American-owned New Orleans–style restaurant/music club; it's decorated like an American diner (even the diner chairs and bar are original, imported from the United States). The recorded music is jazz, and an adjoining room serves as a jazz disco on weekends. Breakfast and lunch are served from 10am to 6pm, with a dozen offerings of breakfast specials ranging from scrambled eggs to eggs Florentine and blueberry pancakes; lunch dishes include gumbo, sandwiches, chili con carne, and hamburgers. Dinner, served from 6pm, is more expensive, though sandwiches and gumbo are available for less than 20 DM ($11.80). Other dinner entrees include roasted game hen, stewed rabbit with corn fritters, red snapper, beef tenderloin medallions, barbecued spareribs, and steaks.

★ **Oren,** Oranienburger Strasse 28. ☎ **282 82 28.**
   Cuisine: KOSHER/VEGETARIAN. **S-Bahn:** Oranienburger Strasse.
$ **Prices:** Soups, salads, and appetizers 8–15 DM ($4.70–$8.85); main courses 12–24 DM ($7.10–$14.15). No credit cards.
   Open: Daily 10am–midnight.

This is one of my favorite restaurants in eastern Berlin—great food, low prices, and good atmosphere. Only a six-minute walk north of Museumsinsel, its's located in Berlin's former Jewish district, next to a towering gold-domed synagogue currently under renovation. Oren is smartly decorated in the fashion of a 1920s Berlin coffeehouse, with white walls, tall ceilings, palm trees, candles, and black furniture. Catering to an intellectual crowd, it offers excellently prepared food, with an interesting menu that draws inspiration from Asia, the Middle East, and international vegetarian cuisine. Perhaps start with the Russian borscht or the falafel with hummus and pita, followed by grilled fish, spaghetti with broccoli-and-gorgonzola sauce, or one of the daily specials. One of the most popular dishes is the Orient-Express, an assortment of Middle Eastern vegetarian food, including hummus, falafel, tabbouleh, eggplant salad, and pita.

T.G.I. Fridays, Karl-Liebknecht-Strasse 5. ☎ **2382 79 60.**

> **Cuisine:** AMERICAN. **S-Bahn:** Alexanderplatz or Hackescher Markt. **Bus:** 100 to Spandauer Strasse.
> **Prices:** Appetizers and soups 8–17 DM ($4.70–$10); main courses 17–34 DM ($10–$20.05). AE, DC, MC, V.
> **Open:** Daily noon–midnight.

Americans should feel instantly at home in this well-known chain, opened in 1994 just a stone's throw from Museumsinsel. In summer there's outdoor dining beside the Spree River with a view of the Berliner Dom. This is one of the best places in Berlin for American bar food, cocktails (more than 400 mind-boggling concoctions), and a variety of American cuisine. Buffalo wings, potato skins, spinach-and-artichoke dip, nachos, black-bean soup, fajitas, Mexican pizza, fettucine Alfredo, baby-back ribs, filet mignon, blackened Cajun chicken, burgers, club sandwiches, and salads are just some of the choices on an extensive menu that's sure to attract the homesick in droves. There's even a children's menu.

★ **Zur Letzten Instanz,** Waisenstrasse 14–16. ☎ **242 55 28.**

> **Cuisine:** GERMAN. **U-Bahn:** Klosterstrasse or Alexanderplatz.
> $ **Prices:** main courses 13–20 DM ($7.65–$11.80). AE, V.
> **Open:** Daily noon–11pm.

Open since 1621, this tiny restaurant claims to be Berlin's oldest Gaststätte. Its rooms have plank floors, wainscoting, an old-fashioned Kachelofen (tiled heater), and a few antiques here and there. The menu offers Berlin specialties, including Boulette, Kohlroulade (stuffed cabbage rolls), Sülze, and Berliner Eisbein. For dessert there's Rote Grüze (cooked fruits in vanilla sauce). In summer, there are a few tables tucked into a tiny garden under spreading trees. You might have trouble finding this place—it's located about a five-minute walk behind the red-colored Rathaus (city hall).

Budget

Nordsee, Spandauer Strasse 4. ☎ **212 68 81.**

> **Cuisine:** SEAFOOD. **U-Bahn or S-Bahn:** Alexanderplatz.
> **Prices:** 6.50–13 DM ($3.85–$7.65). No credit cards.
> **Open:** Mon–Sat 10am–9pm, Sun 11am–7pm.

Part of a chain of casual seafood cafeterias, this Nordsee is larger than most, with a roomy dining area partitioned with "waves" of blue glass and a no-smoking section. Ordering is easy, since the menu is an illustrated lighted board behind the counter. Dishes include fish steaks, fish soup, paella, fried haddock, and herring. Nordsee is located on the corner of Spandauer Strasse and Karl-Liebknecht-Strasse, about halfway between Museumsinsel and Alexanderplatz.

IMPRESSIONS

> In the Berlin cafes and restaurants the busy time is from midnight on
> till three. Yet most of the people who frequent them are up again at
> seven. Either the Berliner has solved the great problem of modern
> life, how to do without sleep, or, with Carlyle, he must be looking
> forward to eternity.
> —Jerome K. Jerome, 1900
>
> Think of the man who first tried German sausage.
> —Jerome K. Jerome, 1889

Wienerwald, Rathausstrasse 5. ☎ 242 32 91.

Cuisine: CHICKEN/GERMAN. **S-Bahn and U-Bahn:** Alexanderplatz.
Prices: Soups and salads 4–14 DM ($2.35–$8.25); main courses 7–20
DM ($4.15–$11.80). AE, DC, MC, V.
Open: Daily 10am–midnight.

Wienerwald is a successful restaurant chain specializing in grilled
chicken, so it's not surprising that a branch has opened here just off
Alexanderplatz (look for it on the same side of square as the Rathaus,
next to the post office). Its menu includes a variety of chicken dishes,
with a quarter of a chicken accompanied by french fries or potato
salad costing only 7 DM ($4.15). There are also soups, a few
nonchicken dishes, and a salad bar.

Zum Nussbaum, Am Nussbaum 3, Nikolaiviertel.
☎ 0171 33 04182.

Cuisine: GERMAN. **S-Bahn and U-Bahn:** Alexanderplatz or Klos-
terstrasse.
Prices: 7–15 DM ($4.15–$8.85). No credit cards.
Open: Daily noon–10pm.

Located in the restored Nikolai Quarter just a few minutes' walk from
Alexanderplatz, this establishment was modeled after a bar dating
from 1507 that was destroyed in World War II. Pleasant and cozy,
with wood-paneled walls and tiny rooms common to medieval inns,
it offers a limited menu of German and Berlin specialties, including
Würste; Boulette; lentil stew; Berliner Eisbein with Sauerkraut and
puréed peas; Sülze with fried potatoes; Kasseler with potato salad;
and Rote Grütze, a North German dessert consisting of cooked fruits
with vanilla sauce. In warm weather you can sit at the couple of tables
outside under a nut tree (*Nussbaum*, by the way, means "nut tree").

4   Dahlem

Moderate

Alter Krug Dahlem, Königin-Luise-Strasse 52. ☎ 832 50 89.

Cuisine: GERMAN. **U-Bahn:** Dahlem-Dorf.
Prices: Appetizers and soups 9.50–$25 DM ($5.60–$14.75); main
courses 26–60 DM ($15.35–$35.40). AE, DC, MC, V.
Open: Mon–Wed and Fri–Sat noon–midnight, Sun noon–10pm.

This pleasant German restaurant occupies a 200-year-old building and is decorated in typical Teutonic fashion, with a low, open-beamed ceiling, ceramic-tile heater in the middle of the dining hall, cheerful yellow tablecloths, and candles on each table. In summer there's outdoor seating in the backyard garden. The English menu includes such favorites as boiled eel (a Berlin specialty), trout, salmon, veal Schnitzel, beef Stroganoff, pork chops, and lamb cutlets. The huge salads are meals in themselves; there's also a daily three-course meal for 43 DM ($25.35). Since the restaurant also serves as a retailer of wines from all over Germany, it keeps a large stock on hand and can recommend wines to accompany each dish. If you're interested in a specific wine from a specific region—Baden, Württemberg, Franken, Mosel, Saar, Rheingau, or Rheinhessen—you might strike it lucky here.

The restaurant is convenient if you're visiting the many museums in Dahlem. To reach the restaurant, turn left out of the U-Bahn station instead of right as you do for the museums.

Inexpensive

Luise, Königin-Luise Strasse 40. ☎ **832 84 87.**
   Cuisine: GERMAN/INTERNATIONAL. **U-Bahn:** Dahlem-Dorf.
   Prices: 10–20 DM ($5.90–$11.80). No credit cards.
   Open: Mon–Sat 10am–midnight, Sun and holidays 9:30am–midnight.

Although people living in Dahlem come here primarily to drink and socialize, Luise is also a good place for a snack or reasonably priced meal, especially in summer when it boasts a great beer garden (indoor dining tends to be a bit smoky, since every other German seems to smoke). Luise is so popular it's crowded even on a weekday afternoon—don't any of these people work? The menu lists spaghetti, soups, chili con carne, chicken, Schnitzel, roast beef, eggplant casserole, tortellini in gorgonzola sauce, and daily specials. A half a dozen choices of breakfast are served until 2pm. The drinking menu is substantial, including wines, grog, champagne, Schnaps, liqueur, brandy, and long drinks (mixed drinks). I'm fond of the Weissbier, a wheat beer. To reach this popular watering hole, turn right out of the Dahlem-Dorf U-Bahn station, cross the street, and almost immediately to your right you'll see the large baroque-style building and its beer garden.

5   Near Schloss Charlottenburg

Inexpensive

★ **Luisen-Bräu,** Luisenplatz 1. ☎ **341 93 88.**
   Cuisine: GERMAN. **Bus:** 109 from Bahnhof Zoologischer Garten or Kurfürstendamm to Schloss Charlottenburg.
   Prices: 9–20 DM ($5.30–$11.80). No credit cards.
   Open: Daily 11am–1am.

What better place to round off a day of museum sightseeing than at a brewery—this one conveniently located southeast of Schloss Charlottenburg, at the corner of Spandauer Damm. Nice, cheerful, and rustic, it has large windows and paneled walls, with the primary decoration provided by stainless-steel tanks of beer brewing at one end of the room. Customers sit at long wooden tables, and since you're expected to sit wherever there's an empty seat, the close contact with strangers makes it easy to strike up conversations, especially after the downing of a few beers. A small fifth-of-a-liter glass of the brew costs 2.70 DM ($1.60) (beers are served in such small glasses to keep them fresh). As for the food, it's served buffet style, with the price of meats dependent on the weight of the slice you order, just as in a butcher shop. Slices of Schweinebraten, Kasseler Rippenspeer, Leberkäs, Boulette, and Schweinshaxen are priced in 100-gram increments. There are also stews and salads, but if all you want is a beer, that's perfectly acceptable in a brewery. In summer there's outdoor seating.

6   Kreuzberg

Moderate

Abricot, Hasenheide 48. ☎ **693 11 50.**

> **Cuisine:** FRENCH. **Reservations:** Recommended. **U-Bahn:** Südstern.
> **Prices:** Appetizers and soups 8–19 DM ($4.70–$11.20); main courses 21–40 DM ($12.40–$23.60); fixed-price meal 75 DM ($44.25). AE, MC.
> **Open:** Dinner Wed–Mon 7pm–1am.

This upscale French restaurant is proof that Kreuzberg is no longer the playground of students. Attracting the well-heeled hip, Abricot occupies an older building that has been transformed into Berlin's version of the 1990s, with hi-tech lighting, abstract artwork, bouquets of flowers, starched white tablecloths, and apricot-colored walls. Professional service and imaginative seasonal cuisine combine to make this a favorite Kreuzberg establishment.

The menu changes often, but examples of past dishes are breast of duck in an orange-ginger sauce, roulade of rabbit with green pepper salad, and saddle of veal in sage and lemon sauce with carrots and crispy kohlrabi. There's also a fixed-price five-course meal. A fun place for a splurge. There's outdoor dining in summer.

Hasenburg, Fichtestrasse 1. ☎ **691 91 39.**

> **Cuisine:** GERMAN/CONTINENTAL. **Reservations:** Required. **U-Bahn:** Südstern.
> **Prices:** Appetizers 8–17 DM ($4.70–$10); main courses 24–28 DM ($14.15–$16.50); fixed-price meal 50 DM ($29.50). No credit cards.
> **Open:** Dinner daily noon–11:30pm in summer, 6pm–11:30pm in winter.

This favorite among Berlin's stylish yuppie class is sparingly decorated with modern soft lighting and wainscoting. Serving what can best be described as German cuisine influenced by French and

Italian kitchens, it offers good food served by an earnest and enthusiastic staff, who aren't afraid to advise against a dish when it's a bit off that night—which rarely happens anyway. An employee claims that he's never seen a more spotless kitchen and that the harmonious relationship between the kitchen and serving staff is reflected in the food and atmosphere. There's outdoor dining in fine weather under chestnut trees, but loud street traffic and the occasional sirens of ambulances delivering patients to a nearby hospital detract from the dining experience. If you're going to pay the price of a meal here, you might as well soak in the indoor ambience.

The limited menu changes weekly depending on what's in season, offering such main courses as Tafelspitz, Wiener Schnitzel, Sauerbraten in red wine sauce, and salmon. A three-course fixed-price meal is also offered nightly.

Tartuffel, Körterstrasse 15. ☎ **693 74 80.**

Cuisine: GERMAN/POTATOES. **U-Bahn:** Südstern.

Prices: Soups and appetizers 9–20 DM ($5.30–$11.80); main courses 20–30 DM ($11.80–$17.70); fixed-price meal 38–50 DM ($22.40–$29.50). No credit cards.

Open: Dinner only, Tues–Sat 6pm–midnight, Sun 5pm–midnight.

Is it any surprise you'd find a restaurant in Germany devoted to the potato? The Prussians valued the spud since the 18th century, when they fought the so-called Kartoffelkrieg (Potato War) against the Austrians. Pleasantly decorated with the ubiquitous abstract art, white tablecloths, and fresh flowers so beloved by Berlin's trendy restaurants, the Tartuffel (its name means potato in old German) offers a variety of potato and vegetarian dishes, including potato gratin with seafood and cheese, potatoes gratin with various seasonal vegetables, and for real potato lovers, the Tartuffelteller, a sampler of various potato dishes. There are also daily specials accompanied by potato dishes. Fixed-price meals, including a vegetarian menu, are also available. In summer there's outdoor dining.

Inexpensive

Grossbeerenkeller, Grossbeerenkeller 90. ☎ **251 30 64.**

Cuisine: GERMAN. **Reservations:** Recommended if dining after 7pm.

U-Bahn: Möckernbrücke.

Prices: 14–30 DM ($8.25–$17.70). No credit cards.

Open: Mon–Fri 4pm–2am, Sat 6pm–2am. **Closed:** Holidays.

There used to be hundreds of places like this in Berlin before World War II—simple, smoky bars peopled by the famous, the infamous, stars, artists, and politicians. Most of these bars were destroyed in the war, but Grossbeerenkeller survived and is now more than a century old, evident in its aged wooden ceiling and walls, which are hardly visible because of the photos of theater personalities who have been here. Theater-goers still stop in for a late-night meal, dining on the good home-style cooking for which this basement establishment is famous: simple and inexpensive dishes such as Berliner Wurst salad with grilled potatoes, Leberkäs, and Bauernfrühstück, as well as

Schnitzel, Rumpsteak, fish, and Sülze. Portions are hearty; forget your diet here.

Budget

 Henne, Leuschnerdamm 25. ☎ 614 77 30.

Cuisine: CHICKEN. **Reservations:** Strongly recommended. **U-Bahn:** Moritzplatz. **Bus:** 129 to Oranienplatz.

Prices: Salads 3.50 DM ($2.05); half a chicken 10 DM ($5.90). No credit cards.

Open: Dinner only, Wed–Sun 7pm–midnight.

One of the things that used to make Henne unique was its location smack beside the Wall. But even though the Wall is history, the restaurant is no less popular, for it turns out what is probably Berlin's best grilled chicken (*Henne* means hen), with deliciously crispy skin. In fact, that's the only thing served, barring a platter of sausages for nonpoultry eaters and side orders of potato salad and Kraut salad. The beer's good, too, especially the dark Klosterschwarzbier, and the ambience is even better. The place is packed with everyone from students to professionals in business suits. The restaurant itself looks ancient, with brown spotted walls, a clock that runs a few hours late, antlers everywhere, an elaborate wooden bar, and against one wall, small wooden barrels that used to hold grog, raspberry juice, and other unlikely concoctions. The whole place reminds me of some long-neglected hunting lodge. Incidentally, behind the bar hangs a photo of John F. Kennedy, who was invited to Henne during his Berlin trip. He didn't eat here, but he did send a letter of apology.

7   Elsewhere in Berlin

Very Expensive

Rockendorf's Restaurant, Düsterhauptstrasse 1.
☎ 402 30 99.

Cuisine: FRENCH. **Reservations:** Required. **S-Bahn:** Waidmannslust.

Prices: Fixed-price lunch 120–175 DM ($70.80–$103.25); fixed-price dinner 175–220 DM ($103.25–$129.80). AE, DC, MC, V.

Open: Lunch Tues–Sat noon–2pm; dinner Tues–Sat 7pm–midnight.

Rockendorf's is reputedly the best and most expensive restaurant in all of Berlin. Proof that this could well be true lies in the parking lot—it's jam-packed with Mercedeses, Porsches, and Jaguars. Occupying the first floor of a restored Jugendstil villa, the restaurant can be entered only after ringing the front-door bell, whereupon diners are ushered upstairs. Plush yet understated, this is where Berlin's top echelon have their business luncheons or romantic evenings. The service, of course, is the best that money can buy.

The kitchen is under the direction of the restaurant's namesake, chef Siegfried Rockendorf. He offers only complete meals, which range from three to six courses at lunch; there are both a six-course menu and a nine-course menu at dinner. Rockendorf has such an unblemished record that diners are comfortable leaving everything to him. A handwritten bill of fare (in German) changes every day, with an emphasis on the seasons, including wild game in winter. Lunch may start off with asparagus with truffles, followed in succession by flounder in curry butter with wild rice; rack of lamb with thyme, artichokes, and tomatoes; and a Grand Marnier parfait and petits fours. Dinner is even more elaborate and may include the likes of pigeon breast with Périgord truffles; deer with cranberries and purée of brussels sprouts; or lobster lasagne with mussels in cognac sauce. Rockendorf's is a 10-minute taxi ride from the city center.

Moderate

 Zitadelle, Am Juliusturm. ☎ 334 21 06.

> **Cuisine:** GERMAN. **Reservations:** Recommended, especially on weekends. **U-Bahn:** Zitadelle.
> **Prices:** Main courses 20–40 DM ($11.80–$23.60); fixed-price meal 72.50 DM ($42.75). AE, DC, MC, V.
> **Open:** A la carte Sat–Sun 11am–11pm; banquets daily 7–11pm.

This restaurant is the best reason for coming to Spandau. The idea behind the place is to imitate as closely as possible the eating style of the Middle Ages—made easy by the fact that the restaurant actually lies within the Spandauer Zitadelle. Guests are requested to use only a special knife and their fingers (they didn't have forks back in medieval times). With brick vaulted ceilings, stone walls, wooden tables, and an open fireplace, this fortress restaurant offers an à la carte menu on weekends, with typical German fare such as pork cutlet or trout, but the real fun is in the evenings, when there's a medieval banquet with ballad singing and special entertainment. The fixed-price meal includes a welcoming drink served in a bull's horn, bread, appetizer, a main course such as Spiessbraten, and several other dishes. Highly recommended.

8   Specialty Dining

Hotel Dining

Au Lac, in the Hotel Seehof Berlin, Lietzensee Ufer 11. ☎ 32 00 20.

> **Cuisine:** CONTINENTAL. **Reservations:** Recommended, especially in summer. **Bus:** 149.
> **Prices:** Appetizers and soups 12–22 DM ($7.10–$13); main courses 35–43 DM ($20.65–$25.35); fixed-price dinner 75 DM ($44.25); fixed-price lunch 40 DM ($23.60). AE, DC, MC, V.
> **Open:** Lunch daily noon–3pm; dinner daily 6–11:30pm.

What a great place for a meal on a fine summer's day! There are few finer places than this in the city to enjoy a meal outdoors—on a terrace overlooking a lake lined with willow trees, with swans, seagulls, and joggers adding to the idyllic scenery. The menu changes often, but always includes plenty of fish selections and meat dishes that may range from rack of lamb to rabbit. A fixed-price lunch and a four-course dinner are also offered.

Belle Epoque, in the Savoy Hotel, Fasanenstrasse 9–10. ☎ **31 10 30.**
    Cuisine: FRENCH. **Reservations:** Recommended. **U-Bahn:** Bahnhof
    Zoologischer Garten or Kurfürstendamm.
    Prices: Appetizers and soups 9.50–23 DM 10–23 DM ($5.90–$13.55);
    main courses 25–40 DM ($14.75–$23.60). AE, DC, MC, V.
    Open: Daily noon–11:30pm.

Light, airy, and elegant, with crystal chandeliers hanging from the
high ceilings, the Belle Epoque looks turn of the century but is actually new. Piano music serenades diners in the evenings, making it a
popular place for dinner before or after attending one of the many
theaters in the area. The cuisine is light and healthful, with a menu
that changes daily and emphasizes the seasons. You might opt for a
salad with mushrooms, avocados, and grapefruit or an appetizer of
pike pâté with broccoli and salmon. Main courses might include
tender roast chicken, prepared with mushrooms and steamed chicory
and covered with flaky pastry; breaded veal with fresh herbs, zucchini,
and spinach noodles; lamb cutlet with basil sauce, spinach, and corn-
meal pancakes; grilled salmon with asparagus, morels, hollandaise,
and potatoes; fried sole with marinated salmon and capers; or breast
of duck in orange sauce with morello cherries, Kenya beans, and
potato pancakes. Leave room for dessert, which might be fresh fruit
flambé with black-currant sorbet or marinated figs over gooseberry
mousse with black-currant ice cream.

Berliner Stube, in the Steigenberger Hotel, Los-Angeles-Platz 1.
    ☎ **210 80.**
    Cuisine: GERMAN. **Reservations:** Not required. **U-Bahn:** Kurfür-
    stendamm.
    Prices: Appetizers and soups 7.50–25 DM ($4.40–$14.75); main courses
    14–40 DM ($8.25–$23.60). AE, DC, MC, V.
    Open: Lunch daily noon–3pm; dinner daily 6–11:30pm.

Designed to resemble an old-style Berliner pub, this rustic eatery
specializes in typical German home-cooked meals. The English menu
makes ordering easy, with selections ranging from smoked eel and
roasted herring to lamb stew, Königsberger Klopse (meatballs in a
caper sauce), knuckle of pork, and steak. There are several fish choices,
from poached halibut to roasted salmon steak. You may wish to take
advantage of the special lunch, which changes daily and offers a complete meal for less than 25 DM ($14.75).

Harlekin, in the Grand Hotel Esplanade, Lützowufer 15. ☎ **26 10 11.**
    Cuisine: FRENCH. **Reservations:** Recommended. **U-Bahn:** Nollen-
    dorfplatz.
    Prices: Appetizers and soups 20–33 DM ($11.80–$19.45); main courses
    43–55 DM ($25.35–$32.45); fixed-price dinner 100–155 DM ($59–
    $91.45); fixed-price lunch 90 DM ($53.10). AE, DC, MC, V.
    Open: Lunch Mon–Fri noon–3pm; dinner Mon–Sat 6pm–midnight.

Harlekin is considered by many to be the city's top hotel restaurant.
Named after the Lüpertz sculpture "Harlekin" that stands at the
restaurant's entryway, it features an open kitchen and tables widely

placed for intimacy, each with starched white tablecloths, candles, and flowers. Next door is Harry's New York Bar—some may find the noise that infiltrates distracting, others may find it exhilarating. In any case, the food won't disappoint. The à la carte menu changes weekly, with past dishes ranging from rack of lamb with an herb crust to orange roughy served with caviar. Four-course fixed-price meals are available for lunch or dinner; dinner also offers a seven-course meal.

Kempinski Grill & Hummer Bar, in the Bristol Hotel Kempinski, Kurfürstendamm 27. ☎ **8843 4-792.**

> **Cuisine:** LOBSTER. **Reservations:** Required. **U-Bahn:** Uhlandstrasse.
> **Prices:** Appetizers and soups 14–50 DM ($8.25–$29.50); main courses 50–63 DM ($29.50–$37.15). AE, DC, MC, V.
> **Open:** Daily noon–11:30pm.

Long an old standby, the Kempinski Grill & Hummer Bar gives pleasure with both its superb service and its fine cuisine. A small and intimate restaurant, with seating for only 45, plus a small bar, it boasts an open copper grill where diners can observe the chefs at work. The menu features lobster, available as an appetizer, a bisque with ravioli, or an entree. For those with large appetites, there are a steak served with half a lobster and an all-you-can-eat lobster meal for 140 DM ($82.60). Other choices on the limited menu include goose-liver terrine, Thai risotto with crayfish, caviar, oysters, fish, lamb, and venison.

⭐ **Le Grand Silhouette,** in the Grand Hotel, Friedrichstrasse 158–164. ☎ **232 70.**

> **Cuisine:** FRENCH. **Reservations:** Required. **U-Bahn:** Französische Strasse. **S-Bahn:** Friedrichstrasse.
> **Prices:** Appetizers 23–30 DM ($13.55–$17.70); main courses 40–50 DM ($23.60–$29.50). AE, DC, MC, V.
> **Open:** Dinner only, Mon–Sat 6pm–1am.

Ever since the Grand Hotel opened in 1987, Le Grand Silhouette has reigned as one of the undisputed champions of fine cuisine in eastern Berlin and was once considered one of the top restaurants in eastern Europe. Situated on the hotel's bright and airy top floor, it has Jugendstil decor from the turn of the century. Guests usually begin their culinary journey with a predinner cocktail at the adjoining bar, where they can look over the menu and make their choices. Then it's on to one of the widely spaced tables in a bi-level dining area. Note how each table has a different place setting. Plates range from hand-painted one-of-a-kind items to those with gilded etchings; even the napkins are different, from their color and style to the way they're arranged. Common to each table, however, are orchids, a reoccurring motif throughout the hotel. From 9pm, a small band plays gentle, listenable tunes, and there's also a small dance floor.

From the changing English menu, diners might choose from such hors d'oeuvres as smoked fish, Baltic salmon, and iced tenderloin of beef. Entrees might include calves' sweetbreads; fried duck liver;

scallops in champagne on a bed of spinach; halibut filet in a cress cream; and lamb, veal, steak, and pheasant breast in a morel cream with truffles. Desserts include various mousses and soufflés, and the extensive wine list encompasses 300 world vintages. If you don't see something on the menu, chances are it can be made for you. The staff is very accommodating—the manager assured me the restaurant stays open until the last guest is ready to leave, even if that means staying open through the night.

Park Restaurant, in the Steigenberger Hotel, Los-Angeles-Platz 1.
☎ 210 80.

Cuisine: INTERNATIONAL. **Reservations:** Recommended, especially on Fridays. **U-Bahn:** Kurfürstendamm.
Prices: Appetizers and soups 12–30 DM ($7.10–$17.70); main courses 34–50 DM ($20.05–$29.50). AE, DC, MC, V.
Open: Dinner only, Tues–Sat 6pm–midnight.

The Steigenberger's premier restaurant, the spacious and modern Park features international food, with an emphasis on low-cholesterol, healthy dishes made with Asian-influenced ingredients and topped with light sauces. Fresh fish is always available. The popular Saturday "Wine and Dine" is a five-course fixed-price dinner for 99 DM ($58.40), which even includes the cost of the wine.

Dining with a View

Panorama 37, in the Forum Hotel Berlin, Alexanderplatz.
☎ 23 89-0.

Cuisine: CONTINENTAL. **Reservations:** Recommended. **S- or U-Bahn:** Alexanderplatz.
Prices: Appetizers and soups 8–23 DM ($4.70–$13.55); main courses 30–40 DM ($17.70–$23.60); fixed-price lunch 20 DM ($11.80), fixed-price dinner 50 DM ($29.50). AE, DC, MC, V.
Open: Daily noon–midnight.

Thirty-seven floors up and almost in the exact center of eastern Berlin, this restaurant is a great place from which to watch the day fade and the night take over. For the best view, reserve a window table facing the Television Tower. The dinner menu includes steaks, seafood, changing specials, and good desserts, as well as a reasonably priced four-course fixed-price meal. Lunch is even more economical, with a limited menu offering light dishes ranging from tortellini to chicken breast and salmon, plus a two-course fixed-price lunch. The bar, also on the 37th floor, is a romantic spot to top off a night on the town. For high-rollers, there's also a casino.

Dining Clusters

As mentioned at the beginning of this chapter, the city's greatest concentration of restaurants centers around the Ku'damm, but nowhere are they more numerous than in the nearby **Europa-Center.** Easy to spot because of the Mercedes-Benz star that crowns its roof, this huge complex contains a number of German and international eateries—Japanese, Swiss, French, fast food. **Mövenpick,** a coffee-house on the ground floor, spills over onto Breitscheidplatz with tables and colored umbrellas.

In eastern Berlin, **Die Berliner Markthalle,** a new shopping complex on Karl-Liebknecht-Strasse across from Alexanderplatz, offers a variety of dining possibilities, including a Chinese restaurant, a McDonald's, a cafe, and a bar. **Ihre Frisch-Backstübe** on the ground floor offers sandwiches, Würste, salads, and desserts, while **Alexander Bräu** is a microbrewery on the first floor with outdoor seating and a menu of Berliner specialties, including Boulette, Würste, Kasselerbraten, Berliner Eisbein, and Schweinshaxe. Restaurants vary in their hours but are open daily.

Fast Food & *Imbisse*

An *Imbiss* is a food stall or a tiny hole-in-the-wall where take-out food is available or customers eat standing up at chest-high counters. There are several such places near Bahnhof Zoo, up and down the Ku'damm, and on Alexanderplatz, where sausages, Boulette, Turkish specialties like dönerkebab, or cans of beer are sold for about 2.50 DM to 5 DM ($1.45 to $2.95). Many sell side dishes to accompany them, including french fries and potato salad. There are also Imbisse in the Tiergarten park, and at Berlin's many markets. During my last visit to the weekend market on Strasse des 17. Juni, for example, I found stalls selling everything from Turkish pizzas to sausages, chili con carne, and hamburgers. Check the shopping chapter for more information on markets.

In addition, several inexpensive locales described above in the restaurant section serve take-out food or are actually Imbisse. These include **Asia-Quick** (Chinese), **Einhorn** (vegetarian), **Ihre Frisch-Backstübe** and **Joseph Langer** (German), **Karavan** (Turkish), **Nordsee** (fish), **Orient** (Middle Eastern), **Piccola Taormina Tavola Calda** (Italian), and **Rogacki** (German).

Breakfast & Sunday Brunch

Many Berlin hotels and pensions include breakfast in their rates. However, in case yours doesn't or you're hungry again by lunchtime, you might want to take advantage of what has become a Berlin tradition, the Sunday brunch. Not surprisingly, the most elaborate brunches are those served at Berlin's best hotels. Some establishments even provide entertainment, usually Dixieland jazz (called *Frühschoppen*).

For breakfast throughout the week, there are also many cafes that serve a variety of breakfasts, from simple continental to elaborate German-style breakfasts complete with Muesli (a cereal), yogurt, fruit, breads, cheeses, Wurst, a soft-boiled egg, juice, and coffee.

In addition to the suggestions here, the coffeehouses in the section that follows also serve breakfast throughout the week.

Café Bleibtreu, Bleibtreustrasse 45. ☎ 881 47 56.

Cuisine: BREAKFAST/SNACKS. **S-Bahn:** Savignyplatz.

Prices: Coffee from 2.80 DM ($1.65), breakfast 7–11 DM ($4.15–$6.50). No credit cards.

Open: Breakfast only, Mon–Fri 9:30am–2pm, Sat–Sun 9:30am–3pm.

This pleasant cafe/bar—with outdoor seating in summer—is popular with a 30ish crowd for breakfast, which ranges from the light Französisches Frühstück (French breakfast) consisting of two croissants and marmalade to the more substantial Frühstück Bleibtreu, which includes ham, Wurst, cheese, honey, one egg, fruit, and orange juice. It's a few minutes' walk north of the Ku'damm.

★ **Eierschale,** Rankestrasse 1. ☎ 882 53 05.

Cuisine: BUFFET BREAKFAST. **U-Bahn:** Kurfürstendamm.

Prices: Fixed-price brunch 11.90 DM ($7). AE, MC, DC, V.

Open: Breakfast only, daily 8am–2pm.

Right off the Ku'damm, across from the Gedächtniskirche, this popular music house offers a daily breakfast brunch that includes breads, croissants, marmalade, Würste, cheeses, eggs (soft-boiled, scrambled, or fried), ham, salad, and cereal. On Sundays it's especially nice, with jazz bands playing from 10am through much of the day, but get there early to get a seat.

Henry's Treff, in the Opernpalais, Unter den Linden 5.
☎ 200 22 69.

Cuisine: BUFFET BRUNCH. **Bus:** 100 to Staatsoper. **S-Bahn:** Friedrichstrasse.

Prices: Fixed-price brunch 39 DM ($23).

Open: Brunch only, Sun 11am–2pm.

A classy cocktail bar in the famous Opernpalais in Berlin-Mitte, Henry's offers a leisurely Sunday brunch accompanied by a jazz band. In the same building is the Operncafé, which offers a breakfast buffet daily from 8:30am to midnight.

Kempinski Eck, in the Bristol Hotel Kempinski, Kurfürstendamm 27.
☎ 88 43 40.

Cuisine: BUFFET BRUNCH. **U-Bahn:** Uhlandstrasse.

Prices: Fixed-price brunch 44 DM ($25.95) for adults, 22 DM ($13) for children. AE, DC, MC, V.

Open: Brunch only, Sun 11am–2pm.

The Kempinski Eck, located in the first-class Bristol Kempinski Hotel on the corner of the Ku'damm and Fasanstrasse, is a favorite spot for people-watching, especially in summer, when there's outdoor sidewalk seating. The lavish buffet spread has everything from breads and sausages to eggs, ham, fruit, and desserts. A civilized and dignified way to start a Sunday.

L.A. Café, in the Hotel Inter-Continental Berlin, Budapester Strasse 2.
☎ 26 02-0.

Cuisine: BRUNCH. **S-Bahn and U-Bahn:** Bahnhof Zoologischer Garten.

Prices: Fixed-price brunch 45 DM ($26.55) for adults, 22.50 DM ($13.25) for children. AE, DC, MC, V.
Open: Brunch only, Sun 11:30am–3pm.

This breezy California-style cafe in the Inter-Continental offers a Sunday buffet brunch complete with a glass of champagne and a live jazz band.

Schwarzes Café, Kantstrasse 148. ☎ 313 80 38.

Cuisine: BREAKFAST. **S-Bahn:** Savignyplatz. **U-Bahn:** Uhlandstrasse.
Prices: Coffee from 3 DM ($1.75); breakfast 7–16 DM ($4.15–$9.45). No credit cards.
Open: Wed–Mon 24 hours, Tues 3am–5pm.

Located just east of Savignyplatz, this unconventional cafe is popular with a hip, younger crowd; breakfasts are a specialty (more than a dozen choices) and are available anytime—from the simple continental to scrambled eggs with all the trimmings.

Shell, Knesebeckstrasse 22. ☎ 312 83 10.

Cuisine: BREAKFAST. **S-Bahn:** Savignyplatz.
Prices: Breakfast 5–40 DM ($2.95–$23.60). V.
Open: Breakfast only, Mon–Fri 10am–2pm, Sat–Sun 10am–3pm.

Just north of Savignyplatz, Shell occupies what was once a corner gas station and features a curved facade with huge windows that let in the sunshine. Popular with the many young people who live in the area, it offers a variety of breakfasts, from a simple continental with bread, marmalade, and butter to a champagne breakfast with salmon and caviar. An American breakfast with fried eggs, bacon, yogurt with fruit or cornflakes, freshly squeezed orange juice, marmalade, and bread is also available.

Café Sidney, Winterfeldstrasse 40. ☎ 216 52 53.

Cuisine: BREAKFAST. **U-Bahn:** Nollendorfplatz.
Prices: 6.50–15 DM ($3.85–$8.85). No credit cards.
Open: Breakfast only, daily 9am–4am.

This modern and breezy cafe/bar stands on a square called Winterfeldplatz, famous for its Saturday morning market, making this a good place to have Saturday breakfast. It's also a good place for breakfast in the middle of the night.

Yorckschlösschen, Yorckstrasse 15. ☎ 215 80 70.

Cuisine: BREAKFAST. **Bus:** 119 from Kurfürstendamm to Grossbeerenstrasse. **U-Bahn:** Mehringdamm.
Prices: 4.50–20 DM ($2.65–$11.80). No credit cards.
Open: Breakfast only, daily 9am–3pm.

This is one of Berlin's most popular places to be on Sunday, when live Dixieland jazz serenades a largely young clientele from 2 to 6pm. Located in Kreuzberg, it's a typical student hangout, with a wooden plank floor and posters adorning the walls. There's also an outdoor beer garden. Get there early, get a table and order breakfast, and then hang around for the music to start. Continental breakfast, scrambled eggs, and fried eggs are among the breakfast options. Incidentally, from October to March there's free live "Blues & Boogie Night" on Wednesday from 4pm to 1am.

Coffeehouses

The afternoon coffee break is a national custom. Germans not only drink coffee but also put away large portions of cakes and pastries. Here are some of the best places to indulge.

If you're on a budget go to one of the chains that sell both the brew and the beans for an inexpensive cup of coffee. **Tschibo** is one such chain, offering a cup of coffee or espresso for 1.95 DM ($1.15). You can drink it standing up at one of the chest-high tables. Two convenient locations are at 11 Kurfürstendamm, across from the Gedächtniskirche, and at Wilmersdorfer Strasse 117. They're open Monday through Friday from 9am to 6:30pm (to 8:30pm on Thursday) and Saturday from 9am to 2pm (to 6pm the first Saturday of the month).

Einstein, Kurfürstenstrasse 58. ☎ **261 50 96.**

U-Bahn: Nollendorfplatz.
Prices: Espresso 4 DM ($2.35); large coffee with milk 5.30 DM ($3.10); cocktails and long drinks from 12 DM ($7.10) AE, DC, V.
Open: Daily 10am–2am.

Einstein probably wouldn't mind lending his name to this student cafe, located in a beautiful high-ceilinged town house dating from the 1920s, with waiters in black suits and bow ties. Henny Porten, one of Germany's first silent film stars, lived here. Popular with Berlin's younger generation, it's a good place for either coffee or alcoholic drinks, and breakfast is served until 2pm. In summer there's seating for as many as 180 persons outside. Einstein is on Kurfürstenstrasse (not to be confused with the Ku'damm), north of Nollendorfplatz.

Café Im Literaturhaus, Fasanenstrasse 23. ☎ **882 54 14.**

U-Bahn: Uhlandstrasse.
Prices: Coffee from 3.80 DM ($2.25). No credit cards.
Open: Daily 9:30am–1am.

Just off the Ku'damm in a neighborhood with restored turn-of-the-century villas, art galleries, and the Käthe-Kollwitz-Museum (next door), you'll find this refined oasis—a cafe above a bookstore. In summer you can sit outside amidst the greenery of a garden. Breakfast is served until 1pm to a decidedly artsy crowd; also available are salads and snacks, plus such desserts as Apfelstrudel with vanilla sauce, rice pudding with kiwi purée, and Rote Grütze.

★ **Café Kranzler,** Kurfürstendamm 18–19. ☎ **882 69 11.**

U-Bahn: Kurfürstendamm.
Prices: Coffee from 3.80 DM ($2.25). AE, DC, MC, V.
Open: Daily 8am–midnight.

There used to be many cafes in Berlin, but most were destroyed during World War II, taking with them a way of life that has all but vanished in today's more hectic world. One of the few to have survived the ravages of the war is Café Kranzler, one of Berlin's most famous coffeehouses. Founded in 1825 and formerly on Unter den Linden, it's now in a modern building occupying a prime spot on the Ku'damm and is one of the city's premier people-watching spots—especially in summer, when it becomes a sidewalk cafe. In winter Café Kranzler still makes a nice place to sit because of the huge floor-to-ceiling windows. In addition to breakfasts and snacks, it offers cakes and tortes, including Sachertorte.

Leysieffer, Kurfürstendamm 218. ☎ **882 78 20.**
U-Bahn: Uhlandstrasse or Kurfürstendamm.
Prices: Coffee from 4.50 DM ($2.65); cakes 5–7 DM ($2.95–$4.15). AE, DC, MC, V.
Open: Mon–Sat 9am–7pm, Sun and holidays 10am–7pm.

Almost across the street from Café Kranzler is this small cafe in what once served as the Chinese embassy. The ground floor is a shop selling bonbons, chocolates, cakes, and marmalades, while the coffee shop upstairs resembles an art gallery, with a black-and-white tile floor, an ornate stucco ceiling, and pictures on the wall by the owner's sister. The place is best known for its cakes, including an exotic fruit cake and a butter cake with almonds. Some people rave about its Rote Grütze, cooked fruits with vanilla sauce, a specialty of northern Germany. Breakfast is served until noon. The miniaturesize balcony has room for only a lucky few, right above the Ku'damm.

★ **Café Möhring,** Kurfürstendamm 213. ☎ **881 20 75.**
U-Bahn: Uhlandstrasse.
Prices: Pot of coffee 7.50 DM ($4.40). AE, V.
Open: Daily 8am–midnight.

When Café Möhring first opened here on the Ku'damm back in 1898, it was out in the countryside. Now, of course, it sits on some of the most expensive property in Berlin. (It was rebuilt after a fire burned it to the ground in 1973.) In addition to cakes and coffees, including the spiked variety, it offers daily specials, from soups and salads to main courses.

★ **Operncafé,** in the Opernpalais, Unter den Linden 5.
☎ **200 22 69.**
S-Bahn: Friedrichstrasse. **Bus:** 100 to Staatsoper.
Prices: Coffee from 3.80 DM ($2.25); tortes from 5 DM ($2.95). AE, MC, V.
Open: Daily 8:30am–midnight.

Located on one of Berlin's most famous boulevards is one of its most famous coffeehouses, the Operncafé. It occupies part of a palace originally built in 1733, destroyed during World War II, then painstakingly and lovingly restored and now called Opernpalais. Elegant with chandeliers and a panoramic mural of Berlin architecture, it offers a grand breakfast buffet for 16.50 DM ($9.75) until noon, as well as 25 different tortes made fresh daily. It's especially nice to sit on the outdoor terrace underneath the trees of this pretty square in the heart of eastern Berlin.

Late-Night Dining

If hunger strikes after midnight, there are a number of restaurants open to 1 or 2am or later, mostly in the inexpensive and budget price range. The following places, described above in detail, are all within walking distance of the Ku'damm. Remember that opening hours listed in this book are the hours for which food is served, ending with the last order (many establishments, especially those with bars, remain open an hour or so after the last order). Remember, too, to check the nightlife chapter, since many bars serve food and are open to the wee hours.

Expensive restaurants serving food past midnight include **Fioretto** (Italian) and **Paris Bar** (French), both open to 1am. Moderately priced restaurants near the Ku'damm with late hours include **Florian** (continental), open to 1am, and **Fofi's Estiatorio** (Greek), open to 12:30am.

If you're searching for an inexpensive restaurant, try **Ciao Ciao** (Italian), open to 2am on Sunday through Thursday and to 3am on Friday and Saturday; **Grung Thai** (Thai), open to 3am; **San Marino** (Italian), open to 1am; and **Taverna Plaka** (Greek), open to 1am. Budget restaurants open late are **Asia-Quick** (Chinese), open to 3am; **Athener Grill** (Greek/Italian), open to 4am during the week and to 5am on weekends; **Jimmy's Diner** (American/Mexican), open to 4am during the week and to 6am on Friday and Saturday nights; **Karavan** (Turkish), open to 1am; **Orient** (Middle Eastern), open to 4am; and **Piccola Taormina Tavola Calda** (Italian), open to 2am on weekdays and to 3am on Friday and Saturday.

Picnic Fare & Where to Eat It

All department stores have large food departments with counters serving prepared meats, salads, and take-out food. Two of the largest are **KaDeWe** (Kaufhaus des Westens), on Wittenbergplatz (☎ **21 210**), with a huge food department on the sixth floor; and **Wertheim,** 231 Kurfürstendamm (☎ **88 20 61**), with a food section in the basement. You can buy everything from cheese, bread, fruit, and wine to Leberkäs, grilled chicken, and casseroles. Both food departments are open Monday through Friday from 9am to 6:30pm (to 8:30pm Thursday) and Saturday from 9am to 2pm (to 6pm the first Saturday of each month in winter, 4pm in summer). In addition, restaurants listed above under "Fast Food and *Imbisse*" sell take-out foods that may be perfect for an afternoon picnic.

And where to eat your goodies? The largest and most convenient green space in the center of Berlin is the Tiergarten, a park located just northwest of Bahnhof Zoo. It stretches all the way to the Brandenburger Tor, with ponds, woods, meadows, and trails throughout.

6

What to See & Do in Berlin

IT WOULD BE WORTH COMING TO BERLIN FOR ITS MUSEUMS ALONE, SO impressive and diverse are they. From Egyptian art treasures to contemporary art, from musical instruments to traditional costumes and furniture, Berlin offers something for everyone. I can't imagine being bored here even for a minute.

Rather, the problem is just the opposite: There are so many choices they may seem bewildering—compounded by the fact that Berlin's museum treasures were divided between East and West after World War II. Both East and West Berlin therefore set about developing and expanding their own Egyptian museums, Islamic art museums, European art museums, and history museums, to name only a few. All these still exist today, and it is not easy to rank them, particularly since so many have at least a few items that catapult them into the must-see category. Perhaps the city will consider merging some of its collections, once the more pressing problems posed by reunification have been addressed.

But even though Berlin has an awesome number of museums, don't despair. The city is surprisingly compact, making it an easy place to explore. What's more, most of the major museums and attractions are clustered in four distinct parts of the city, all conveniently reached by an efficient public transportation system and easily seen in a few days.

Of Berlin's four major museum centers, Museumsinsel in Berlin-Mitte is the oldest and best known. This island in the middle of the Spree River is so laden with treasures in the Pergamon Museum I'm surprised it isn't sinking. Not to be outdone is Dahlem, which boasts the largest collection of museums in Berlin—including the famous Gemäldegalerie (Picture Gallery) and museums on non-European art. Charlottenburg is home of Schloss Charlottenburg (Charlottenburg Palace) and museums specializing in the antiquities, including the Ägyptisches Museum (Egyptian Museum) with the bust of Nefertiti. Finally, Berlin's newest museum district is in the Tiergarten; still under construction, this region will eventually be the city's center for European art. Though not as important as the museum centers above, Kreuzberg also has some unique and valuable museums.

Covering Berlin geographically will save you not only time but also money. Most of the museum clusters—including most of those in Dahlem, on Museumsinsel, in Charlottenburg, and in the Tiergarten—offer their own combination ticket (called a *Sammelkarte*), allowing entrance to several museums in the same geographic area at a reduced rate.

Suggested Itineraries

To help you get the most out of your visit, here are some suggested itineraries to guide you to the most important attractions. (Remember, however, that many museums are closed on Monday.) Since the dining, sightseeing, and nightlife chapters are all arranged according to geographic locations, it should be no problem to tailor these itineraries to your own choices in restaurants, attractions, and after-dark entertainment. Have fun!

IF YOU HAVE 1 DAY

Day 1   Berlin's most famous treasures are the Pergamon Altar and the bust of Nefertiti. If you wish to see both, head first thing in the morning to the Ägyptisches Museum (closed on Friday) in Charlottenburg, where Berlin's most beautiful woman holds court. Across the street is Schloss Charlottenburg, Berlin's most beautiful baroque palace, where you should visit the Knobelsdorff Flügel and the Schinkel Pavilion for a look at how Prussian royalty lived. At the very least, take a short stroll through the lovely gardens behind the palace. For lunch, head to the nearby Luisen-Bräu for a beer and typical German meal.

By early afternoon head for the Brandenburger Tor (Brandenburg Gate) (bus no. 100 from Bahnhof Zoo), built in the 1780s as the grand finishing touch to Berlin's most famous boulevard, Unter den Linden. After Berlin became a divided city, the gate (as well as the boulevard) ended up under East Berlin's jurisdiction and was inaccessible to West Berliners, making it a poignant symbol of Germany's division. After the November 1989 revolution in East Berlin and the subsequent fall of the Wall, it was here that many Berliners gathered to rejoice. Today visitors continue to seek out the Brandenburger Tor, which still crowns the start of Unter den Linden. Take a stroll down this thoroughfare, stopping off for a coffee at the celebrated Operncafé, located in the Opernpalais.

By 4pm at the latest, you should be in the Pergamon Museum in Museumsinsel, with its incredible Pergamon Altar, Market Gate of Miletus, and Babylonian Processional Street leading to the Gate of Ishtar. Round out your eastern Berlin experience with a trip to the Museum Haus am Checkpoint Charlie (open to 10pm), which was established in 1961 with the sole purpose of documenting the Berlin Wall and the many attempts of East Berliners to escape to the West. Today it's the best place in the city to gain an understanding of what Berlin was like during the decades of division.

Finish off the day with a leisurely evening stroll along the Ku'damm, Berlin's showcase avenue with its many shops and restaurants. Relax over coffee at one of the many coffeehouses or order a drink at one of the numerous bars near the Ku'damm; if it's summer, try to get a seat outdoors. And then start planning your next trip to Berlin.

IF YOU HAVE 2 DAYS

Day 1   Devote your entire morning to Dahlem, first visiting the Gemäldegalerie with its masterpieces from the 13th to the 18th century, including works by Dürer, Brueghel, Botticelli, Raphael, Rubens, and Rembrandt. Add to it one or two of the other museums that most interest you. The Museum für Deutsche Volkskunde (Museum of German Ethnology) has an excellent display of ethnic and historical items once in common use, including simple peasant furniture and household items. There are also fine museums of Asian art and one of the world's largest general ethnological museums.

In the afternoon, head for Charlottenburg, where your first stop should be Schloss Charlottenburg (Charlottenburg Palace) and its surrounding garden. At the palace itself, visit the Knobelsdorff-Flügel (New Wing) and the Schinkel Pavilion for a look at how Prussian royalty lived. Across the street is the Ägyptisches Museum (Egyptian Museum), famous for its bust of Queen Nefertiti. Other museums here include the Antiken Museum (Museum of Greek and Roman Antiquities), the Museum für Vor- und Frühgeschichte (Museum of Pre- and Early History), and the wonderful Bröhan Museum with its art deco and Jugendstil collection. Just southeast of the palace is the Luisen-Bräu, a good stop for a brew or meal. Finish the evening with a stroll down the Ku'damm.

Day 2   Go to eastern Berlin. Start with a stroll down Unter den Linden and a look at the Brandenburger Tor, then visit the outstanding Pergamon Museum on Museumsinsel (Museum Island). If you have time, add the Alte Nationalgalerie (National Gallery) or the Bode Museum. Finish the afternoon with a walk to Alexanderplatz, which was once considered the heart of East Germany's capital, and the nearby Nikolaiviertel (Nikolai Quarter), a small neighborhood of restored buildings housing several pubs and restaurants.

At the end of the day, head for the Museum Haus am Checkpoint Charlie. In the evening, try to attend a performance at the Deutsche Oper, Komische Oper, or the Philharmonie.

IF YOU HAVE 3 DAYS

Days 1–2   Spend Days 1 and 2 as outlined above under "If You Have 2 Days."

Day 3   Head for the Tiergarten museum complex (south of the Tiergarten park), a newly developed center for European art, where you'll find the Neue Nationalgalerie (New National Gallery), which houses German and European artists of the 19th and 20th centuries. Nearby are the Kunstgewerbe Museum (Museum of Applied Arts), with its collections dating from the Middle Ages to the present day, the Kupferstich-kabinett (Collection of Prints and Drawings), and the Musikinstrumenten Museum (Museum of Musical Instruments).

Spend the rest of the day according to your own special interests: the Babelsberg Studio if you're interested in the history of German films; the Käthe-Kollwitz-Museum (near the Ku'damm) with its powerful drawings by one of Berlin's best-known artists; the Bauhaus-Archiv and the Hansaviertel (Hansa Quarter) for architectural buffs; the Ku'damm and Wilmersdorfer Strasse for shopping. In the evening, enjoy a rock, jazz, or blues concert at one of the city's many live-music houses.

Days 1–3   Spend Days 1–3 as outlined above. In addition, if you're in Berlin on a Saturday or Sunday, be sure to schedule in a trip to the flea market held every weekend on Strasse des 17. Juni near the Tiergarten park. It offers antiques, curios, and junk, as well as arts and crafts from Berlin's enterprising young artists.

Day 4   Pamper yourself with a day of relaxation. Take an excursion to Wannsee or Havel, where you can swim or take a pleasure boat and spend a relaxing day. Alternatives include one of the suggested walking tours in the next chapter, heading for the Spreewald and a boat ride, or visiting those museums you haven't yet had time for.

Day 5   Head for Potsdam with its Sanssouci palace and park.

1   The Top Attractions

Since most of the top attractions are also located in important museum centers with other worthwhile museums nearby, be sure to read the next section, "More Attractions," to plan your day's itinerary. Under the same roof as the Gemäldegalerie in Dahlem, for example, are no fewer than five other museums, each important in its own right and included in the single admission price to the Gemäldegalerie.

In Berlin-Mitte (Eastern Berlin)

★ **Pergamon Museum,** Kupfergraben, Museumsinsel. ☎ 203 55-0.

Named after its most treasured possession, the Pergamon Altar, this is essentially a museum of architecture, the first of its kind when it opened in 1930. Its collection of Greek and Roman antiquities ranks among the world's best, and it also contains Near Eastern and Asian art, Islamic art, and German folk art. Along with the Gemäldegalerie in Dahlem and the Ägyptisches Museum in Charlottenburg, it is one of Berlin's most visited museums.

The **Pergamon Altar,** a huge and magnificent Hellenistic structure dating from 160–180 B.C., occupies a hall of its own directly behind the museum's main entryway. Coming from a town that now belongs to Turkey, it was dedicated to Zeus and Athena. A 7-foot frieze along the base of the altar depicts the struggle of the Greek gods against the giants (Zeus and Athena are portrayed in the eastern frieze, across from the steps).

In an adjoining room is the Roman Architecture Hall, where you'll find another one of the museum's major treasures, the **Market Gate of Miletus.** Erected around A.D. 120, this two-story Roman gate provided access to a public market but was also large enough to contain a few shops as well. Entering the next room, you'll come upon the museum's third architectural gem, the dazzling **Babylonian Processional Street,** which leads to the **Gate of Ishtar.** Originally

Did You Know . . . ?

- By the year 1700, nearly one Berliner in five was of French extraction.

- In the 1920s the city boasted 35 theaters, several opera houses, more than 20 concert halls, and as many as 150 daily and weekly newspapers.

- Founded in the early 1840s, Berlin's Tiergarten zoo housed 10,000 animals in 1939; only 91 animals survived the war.

- From 1949 until the Wall went up in 1961, approximately 3 million East Germans fled their country.

- Thirty percent of western Berlin is forests, rivers, and lakes, and there are 485 miles of hiking trails and biking paths.

- Berlin is closer to Poland (only 60 miles away) than it is to any city in former West Germany.

- Berlin claims to have more students, dogs, (200,000) and local rock groups (1,000) than any other city in Europe.

- The world's first radio reporter was heard over the airwaves of Berlin.

990 feet long and twice as wide as reconstructed here, the street was used for religious processionals during the reign of Nebuchadnezzar II (605–562 B.C.); it is bordered by walls decorated with lions in stride, against a striking blue background. The gate itself is of blue and ochre tiles, decorated with fanciful bulls and dragons.

Upstairs are the collections of Asian and Islamic art, including Chinese pottery from the Stone Age to the beginning of this century, as well as significant pieces of Chinese sculpture. The Japanese department contains ceramics and porcelain, lacquerware, and woodblock prints by one of Japan's foremost artists, Hokusai (1760–1849). The highlight of the Islamic department is the Facade from Mschatta, a desert palace begun in the 8th century but never completed. Note the intricate designs carved in its walls, not unlike the designs of an elaborate carpet. Carpets, too, are a part of the museum's collection, many from the 13th, 14th, and 15th centuries.

Note that the museum is entered via a bridge off a lane called Kupfergraben, behind and to the left of Das Alte Museum.

Admission: 4 DM ($2.35) adults, 2 DM ($1.20) children; free Sun and holidays.

Open: Daily 9am–5pm (on Mon and Tues open only for those sections of the museum containing the Pergamon Altar, the Market Gate of Miletus, and the Gate of Ishtar). *Note:* At press time, it looked like all of the Pergamon will be closed on Monday; check with the tourist office. **S-Bahn:** Hackeschar Markt. or Friedrichstrasse. **Bus:** 100 to Deutsche Staatsoper.

In Dahlem

★ **Gemäldegalerie (Picture Gallery),** Arnimallee 23–27.
☎ **830 1-1.**

Based on the royal collections and added to through the years, the Gemäldegalerie is considered by many to be Berlin's top art museum. It offers a comprehensive survey of European painting from the 13th to the 18th century, with more than 1,500 works in its possession. Only half of these are now on display—a shortcoming that will be remedied when the gallery moves into new and larger quarters in the Tiergarten precinct.

The museum's holdings are arranged historically and systematically, by schools and by periods. Included are works by German, Flemish, Dutch, Netherlandish, Italian, French, English, and Spanish artists, including important works by Botticelli, Raphael, Dürer, Cranach, Holbein, Titian, El Greco, Brueghel, Rubens, Vermeer, Velázquez, Gainsborough, Goya, and Murillo. The Rubens collection is outstanding, but the crowning glory of the museum is probably its 20 or so paintings by Rembrandt, one of the world's largest holdings by this master. Look for his self-portrait, and, one of my favorites, his portrait of Hendrickje Stoffels, his common-law wife (the intimacy of their relationship is reflected in her gaze at the painter). The famous and striking *Man with the Golden Helmet* is no longer attributed to Rembrandt.

Other notable paintings include Botticelli's *Venus,* Dürer's portrait of a Nürnberg patrician, and Hans Holbein's portrait of the merchant Georg Gisze. Brueghel the Elder's *The Netherlands Proverbs* enacts more than a hundred adages and idioms. Lucas Cranach's *The Fountain of Youth* depicts old women being led to the fountain, swimming through it, and then emerging young and beautiful. Note that apparently only women need the bath—men in the painting regain their youth through relations with younger women.

Since the museum is large, you will probably want to concentrate on your particular areas of interest. The ground floor is devoted to German, Netherlandish, and Italian art from the 13th through the 16th century, as well as to French and English paintings of the 18th century. The first floor is where you'll find French, Flemish, and Dutch 17th-century paintings, Spanish works of art, and Italian paintings of the baroque and rococo periods. Pick up a map of the museum, as well as a pamphlet in English. If you get hungry, there's a good restaurant in the museum, with outdoor seating.

Admission: 4 DM ($2.35) adults, 2 DM ($1.20) children and students; free Sun and holidays.

Open: Tues–Fri 9am–5pm, Sat–Sun 10am–5pm. **Closed:** Jan 1; Tues after Easter and after Whitsunday; May 1; and Dec 24, 25, and 31. **U-Bahn:** Dahlem-Dorf.

In Charlottenburg

★ **Schloss Charlottenburg (Charlottenburg Palace),** Spandauer Damm. ☎ **32 09 11.**

Schloss Charlottenburg, now considered Berlin's most beautiful baroque building, started out as something far less grand. Constructed in the 1690s as a small residence for Sophie Charlotte, wife of the future Friedrich I, it was later greatly expanded into a palace fit for kings. Indeed, it served as the summer residence of almost all Prussian kings from Friedrich I to Friedrich Wilhelm IV, and today it contains objects spanning the periods from the baroque to Biedermeier.

The first thing that catches your eye as you approach the front of the palace is the equestrian statue of the Great Elector standing in the forecourt. Considered a treasure of baroque art, it was cast in one piece to a design by Andreas Schlüter in 1700. While being moved to a safe haven during World War II, it accidentally sank to the bottom of Tegel Harbor, where it remained until the early 1950s. It found a new home here in 1952.

The central section of the palace, topped with a dome and a clock, takes in the **Historical Apartments,** which served as the private living quarters of Sophie Charlotte and her husband. Containing rich furnishings, including a priceless Chinese porcelain cabinet and lacquered furniture, the apartments can be visited only on guided tours conducted solely in German (last tour at 4pm). You might want to check to see whether the influx of foreign visitors has prodded the officials into offering tours in English. Otherwise, unless you speak German, you're better off skipping the Historical Apartments and heading instead for the **Knobelsdorff-Flügel** (New Wing), located to the right as you face the apartments.

On the ground floor of the Knobelsdorff-Flügel are more royal living quarters, where visitors can wander at will through rooms charmingly decorated with furniture, paintings, and porcelain, in styles from the romantic and Biedermeier periods. Upstairs you'll find the Golden Gallery with its gold-and-green ornamentation—a ballroom considered one of the most impressive examples of German rococo—and the state dining hall. Be sure too to walk through the Galerie der Romantik, a collection of paintings from the German romantic period.

Next head for the **Schinkel Pavilion,** located at the far east end of the palace behind the Knobelsdorff-Flügel. A small and delightful summer house built in 1825 in the style of an Italian villa by Karl Friedrich Schinkel, one of Berlin's most respected architects, it has small and cozy rooms, each one differently decorated with sculptures, examples of applied arts, and paintings from the early 19th century. There are also drawings, sketches, and paintings by the amazing Schinkel, who was an accomplished artist in addition to being an architect.

As with most European palaces, a **park** stretches behind Schloss Charlottenburg. First laid out in 1697 in French style and transformed into an English garden in the first half of the 19th century, it was destroyed in World War II and subsequently restored to its baroque form. Besides the Schinkel Pavilion, it contains two other important structures. The **Mausoleum,** located at the west end of the park, holds the tombs of Queen Luise, Friedrich Wilhelm III, Kaiser Wilhelm I, and Kaiserin Augusta. It was built in 1810 according to the designs of Schinkel, and with its Doric columns resembles an ancient temple. The **Belvedere,** located at the far end of the park near the Spree River, is a former teahouse that now contains Berlin porcelain of the 18th and 19th centuries including some by KPM Berlin.

Admission: Combination ticket covering all the above, 8 DM ($4.70) adults, 3 DM ($1.75) students and children; for the Knobelsdorff-Flügel, 3 DM ($1.75) adults, 1.50 DM (90¢) students and children; for the Schinkel Pavilion or Belvedere, 2.50 DM ($1.45) adults, 1.50 DM (90¢) students and children; for the Mausoleum, 1 DM (60¢) adults, 50 pfennigs (30¢) students and children; Galerie der Romantik, 4 DM ($2.35) adults, 2 DM ($1.20) students and children.

Open: Tues–Fri 9am–5pm, Sat–Sun 10am–5pm. **Closed:** Mausoleum, Nov–Mar. **Bus:** 109, 110, or 145 to Charlottenburger Schloss. **U-Bahn:** Sophie-Charlotte-Platz or Richard-Wagner-Platz, then a 10-minute walk.

⭐ **Ägyptisches Museum (Egyptian Museum),** Schlossstrasse 70. ☎ **32 09 11.**

Just across the street from Schloss Charlottenburg is this collection illustrating Egyptian cultural history. Originally constructed in the 1850s as barracks for the royal bodyguards, the building now houses Berlin's most famous art object—**Queen Nefertiti** (called *Konigin Nofretete* in German). She's up on the first floor, in a dark room all to herself. Created more than 3,300 years ago and unearthed in 1912 by a team of German archeologists, the bust never left the sculptor's studio but, rather, served as a model for all further portraits of the queen.

In adjoining rooms are smaller likenesses of Nefertiti's husband, King Ahkenaton, and her daughter, Princess Meritaton. Look also for Queen Tiyi, Akhenaton's mother, remembered for her shrewdness in politics. Other items in this amazing museum include burial cult objects, a mummy, sarcophagi, a papyrus collection, tools used in everyday life, and the Kalabasha Gate.

Admission: 4 DM ($2.35) adults, 2 DM ($1.20) students and children; free Sun and holidays.

Open: Mon–Thurs 9am–5pm, Sat–Sun 10am–5pm. **Closed:** Jan 1; Maundy Thursday; May 1; and Dec 24, 25, and 31. **Bus:** 109, 110, or 145 to Charlottenburger Schloss. **U-Bahn:** Sophie-Charlotte-Platz or Richard-Wagner-Platz, then a 10-minute walk.

In Kreuzberg

⭐ **Museum Haus am Checkpoint Charlie,** Friedrichstrasse 44. ☎ **251 10 31.**

Since the Berlin Wall came down, a visit to this museum is more important than ever, especially if this is your first trip to Berlin. Popularly known as the Museum of the Wall, it was established soon after the Wall was erected in 1961, with the sole purpose of documenting the grisly events that were taking place because of Berlin's division. Located near what was once a major border check for foreigners entering East Berlin, Checkpoint Charlie, it manages to vividly convey what life was like during the grim decades of the Cold War through the use of photographs, films, newspaper clippings, and items used in successful and unsuccessful escape attempts (a hot-air balloon, cars with hidden compartments). The museum also documents nonviolent revolutions that have taken place throughout the world, with information on Mahatma Gandhi, Lech Walesa, and the peaceful 1989 revolution in East Germany.

The museum also has an outdoor exhibit a block farther north at former Checkpoint Charlie on the nearby corner of Zimmerstrasse and Friedrichstrasse, where a border control house, relics of the Cold War, and a part of the Wall remain.

Admission: 7.50 DM ($4.40) adults, 4.50 DM ($2.65) students.
Open: Daily 9am–10pm. **U-Bahn:** Kochstrasse.

2   More Attractions

Museums

IN DAHLEM

You can reach Dahlem in about 20 minutes from the city center by taking U-Bahn 1 to the Dahlem-Dorf station. From the station, signs point the way to the various museums, most of which are a five-minute walk away. The Gemäldegalerie (described above under "The Top Attractions") and museums for sculpture, ethnology, and East Asian, Islamic, and Indian art are all located in a huge sprawling complex with entrances on either Arnimallee or Lansstrasse. One admission price, 4 DM ($2.35) for adults and 2 DM ($1.20) for children, allows entry to all museums in this entire complex. Note that museums in Dahlem are closed on Monday.

Several of the Dahlem museums will eventually find new homes in the Tiergarten arts complex by the end of the 1990s. The Kupferstichkabinett (Museum of Prints and Drawings) has already reopened in Tiergarten. Next to move will be the Gemäldegalerie in 1997, followed by the Skulpturengalerie at the turn of the century. Thus, Tiergarten will be the new center for European art, while Dahlem will continue to house collections of non-European art.

⭐ **Skulpturengalerie (Sculpture Gallery),** Arnimallee 23–27. ☎ **830 11.**

This gallery contains approximately 1,200 works of European sculpture, dating from the early Christian and Byzantine periods to the end of the 18th century. Most notable are its works from the Italian Renaissance and German Gothic periods, including carvings by one of Germany's most famous artists, Tilman Riemenschneider. Extending along two floors, the gallery also displays wooden religious figurines, ivories, marble reliefs, and bronzes.

Frommer's Favorite Berlin Experiences

A Stroll Along the Ku'damm No trip to Berlin would be complete without a leisurely stroll down the Ku'damm, the city's showcase boulevard.

Cafe Life Cafes are where people meet friends, discuss the day's events, read the newspaper, or just sit at a sidewalk table and watch the never-ending parade.

A Picnic in the Tiergarten The Tiergarten in the heart of the city, home of the Berlin Zoo and Aquarium, is laced with hiking paths that skirt ponds and cut through meadows, a good place for a picnic or a leisurely walk.

Browsing the Market at Strasse des 17. Juni The best flea market in the city has a wide variety of antiques, curios, and junk, as well as handcrafted items such as jewelry and clothes. Food stalls sell sausages, drinks, and Turkish fast food, giving the market a festive atmosphere. Held Saturdays and Sundays only.

The Sixth-Floor Food Emporium of KaDeWe With 1,000 kinds of sausage, 500 sorts of bread, 1,500 types of cheese, and counters selling ready-to-eat dishes, this is a true culinary adventure that's not to be missed.

Museum Hopping Since most museums in Berlin are located in clusters and offer combination tickets at a discount, you can literally race from one museum to the next, if only to see the great masterpieces.

A Lazy Day at the Beach Europe's largest inland beach is at Wannsee, which boasts a children's playground, shops, and restaurants. A great place to while away a fine summer's day—and if you wish, you can swim au naturel.

An Evening with the Berlin Philharmonic Orchestra Don't miss the chance of hearing one of the world's great orchestras at the fabulous Philharmonic Hall.

Pub Crawling 'til Dawn There are no mandatory closing hours for bars in Berlin, which means you can celebrate all night long. And if you do stay out all night, there are cafe/bars ready to serve you breakfast in the wee hours.

A Sunday Jazz Brunch Sunday brunch is very much in vogue in Berlin, and there are a number of places that offer a tempting buffet of goodies. Even more popular are those that offer live jazz as well, such as the Eierschale and Yorckschlösschen.

Admission: Combination ticket 4 DM ($2.35) adults, 2 DM ($1.20) students and children; free Sun and holidays.

Open: Tues–Fri 9am–5pm, Sat–Sun 10am–5pm. **Closed:** Jan 1; Tues after Easter and after Whitsunday; May 1; and Dec 24, 25, and 31. **U-Bahn:** Dahlem-Dorf.

⭐ **Museum für Völkerkunde (Ethnological Museum),**
Lansstrasse 8. ☎ **830 11.**

One of the world's largest ethnological museums, this establishment contains half a million objects from around the world—ranging from everyday household objects to fine gold jewelry to spears and cult artifacts.

Particularly fascinating are the watercraft from the Pacific region, including life-size boats from Tonga, Samoa, the Marshall Islands, and Micronesia. There are also original dwellings and facades from the Pacific islands, including a men's clubhouse from Palau and a hut from New Guinea. Equally impressive is the museum's fine collection of pre-Columbian artifacts, especially its gold objects and Peruvian antiquities. Other departments center on Buddhist art in China, the nomadic cultures of Mongolia, shadow puppetry and the marionette theaters of Asia, folk music from around the world, ceremonial masks, and African sculpture.

Admission: Combination ticket 4 DM ($2.35) adults, 2 DM ($1.20) students and children; free Sun and holidays.

Open: Tues–Fri 9am–5pm, Sat–Sun 10am–5pm. **Closed:** Jan 1; Tues after Easter and after Whitsunday; May 1; and Dec 24, 25, and 31. **U-Bahn:** Dahlem-Dorf.

⭐ **Museum für Deutsche Volkskunde (Museum of German Ethnology),** Im Winkel 6–8. ☎ **839 01-01.**

Whereas the Museum für Völkerkunde (above) contains objects relating to people from around the world, this ethnological museum concentrates on items relating to the German-speaking people in central Europe, from the 16th century to the present day—with an emphasis on everyday rural folk culture before and during the early stages of the Industrial Revolution. Devoted to past generations of middle- and working-class Germans who were skilled in making almost everything they needed, it provides an interesting contrast to the extravagance of Schloss Charlottenburg and the lifestyle of Germany's ruling class.

On the ground floor is a wonderful collection of peasant furniture, including beds, chests, and cupboards. A display called "Furniture as Dowry" explains that items of furniture were one of the most important things in a young woman's dowry and were passed down from generation to generation as heirlooms. The clothing section is equally fascinating, with everything from shawls and bonnets to bridal gowns and hats. Other displays contain cooking, baking, and eating and drinking utensils, including those made of stoneware, porcelain, pewter, and glass.

The first floor is devoted to displays demonstrating various household tasks: turning flax into linen thread, knitting and crocheting, weaving, and lacemaking. Life today is certainly easier, but does that make it better? As you look at all these objects made lovingly by hand and compare them with their factory-produced counterparts, you may well question the price of progress. At any rate, this is a museum well worth a visit. Note that it is not connected to the other museums in

Dahlem and therefore is not included in the combination ticket price; follow the signs from the subway station.

Admission: 4 DM ($2.35) adults, 2 DM ($1.20) students and children; free Sun and holidays.

Open: Tues–Fri 9am–5pm, Sat–Sun 10am–5pm. **Closed:** Jan 1; Tues after Easter and after Whitsunday; May 1; and Dec 24, 25, and 31. **U-Bahn:** Dahlem-Dorf.

Museum für Indische Kunst (Museum of Indian Art),
Lansstrasse 8. ☎ 830 11.

Quite simply, this is the most significant collection of Indian art in Germany, its displays covering a period of almost 4,000 years and including items from not only India but Nepal, Tibet, Burma, Thailand, and Indonesia. Objects range from prehistoric terra-cotta and stone sculptures of Buddhist, Jainist, and Hindu divinities to finely crafted miniatures, ivories, and murals. Of special note is the **Turfan Collection** of famous 6th- to 10th-century frescoes depicting Buddhist legends. The museum is also famous for its art from the Buddhist cave-monasteries along what was once the legendary Silk Road in Central Asia. In addition, be on the lookout for the 9th-century stone sculpture of the god Siva and his wife, considered a masterpiece of Nepalese art.

Admission: Combination ticket 4 DM ($2.35) adults, 2 DM ($1.20) students and children; free Sun and holidays.

Open: Tues–Fri 9am–5pm, Sat–Sun 10am–5pm. **Closed:** Jan 1; Tues after Easter and after Whitsunday; May 1; and Dec 24, 25, and 31. **U-Bahn:** Dahlem-Dorf.

Museum für Islamische Kunst (Museum of Islamic Art),
Lansstrasse 8. ☎ 830 11.

All Islamic countries are represented in this important collection of carpets, sculptures, examples of Arabic script, pottery, glass, jewelry, miniatures, and other applied arts from the 8th to the 18th century. The museum begins with representative selections of the finest in Islamic art; subsequent rooms follow its chronological development through the ages. Highlights include a Koran parchment from the 9th century, enameled Syrian glassware, and Turkish carpets from the 16th and 17th centuries.

Admission: Combination ticket 4 DM ($2.35) adults, 2 DM ($1.20) students and children; free Sun and holidays.

Open: Tues–Fri 9am–5pm, Sat–Sun 10am–5pm. **Closed:** Jan 1; Tues after Easter and after Whitsunday; May 1; and Dec 24, 25, and 31. **U-Bahn:** Dahlem-Dorf.

Museum für Ostasiatische Kunst (Museum of Far Eastern Art), Lansstrasse 8. ☎ 830 11.

Chinese, Korean, and Japanese art from 3000 B.C. to the present is on display here, including woodcuts, paintings, bronzes, ceramics, lacquerware, and sculptures. The first of its kind in Germany when it was established in 1906, the museum offers a fine overview of Far Eastern decorative and religious art. Of note are a 17th-century lacquered Chinese imperial throne with mother-of-pearl inlays, a collection of Japanese woodblock prints, and Japanese and Chinese paintings and scrolls. Because the paintings and scrolls are fragile, displays change every three months and center on different themes. On one of my visits, for example, there was a special exhibition of 18th- and 19th-century woodblock prints depicting foreigners (who, despite their rounded eyes, still look rather Asian). Another special print exhibition was devoted to Japanese women during the four seasons.

Admission: Combination ticket 4 DM ($2.35) adults, 2 DM ($1.20) children and students; free Sun and holidays.

Open: Tues–Fri 9am–5pm, Sat–Sun 10am–5pm. **Closed:** Jan 1; Tues after Easter and after Whitsunday; May 1; and Dec 24, 25, and 31. **U-Bahn:** Dahlem-Dorf.

Brücke-Museum, Bussardsteig 9. ☎ **831 20 29.**

Located on a quiet dead-end street at the edge of the Grünewald is this small but important museum dedicated to members of Die Brücke (The Bridge), a group of artists established in Dresden in 1905 and credited with introducing expressionism to Germany. Works on display include Erich Heckel's *Man in His Younger Years (Mann in Jungen Jahren),* Emil Nolde's *Vacation Guests (Feriengäste),* Max Pechstein's *Fishing Boat (Fischerboot),* and Ernest Ludwig Kirchner's *Berlin Street Scene (Berliner Strassenszene).*

Admission: 4 DM ($2.35) adults, 2 DM ($1.20) students and children.

Open: Wed–Mon 11am–5pm. **U-Bahn:** Get off at Dahlem-Dorf, then about a 15-minute walk. **Bus:** 115.

IN BERLIN-MITTE (EASTERN BERLIN)

The first three museums described here (and Pergamon Museum under "The Top Attractions"), located in eastern Berlin on Museumsinsel (Museum Island), comprise the city's oldest museum complex. Construction began in the 1820s under the direction of Friedrich Wilhelm III, who wished to make available to the viewing public the art treasures that had been collected by the royal family. Through the next century, particularly under the guidance of museum director Wilhelm von Bode, there was a determined effort to rival the other great museums of Europe, especially those of Paris, London, Madrid, and Vienna. The many German archeologists sent into the field brought back important artifacts from Persia, Greece, and Egypt, and the museums developed outstanding collections.

After World War II, many works originally displayed here ended up in Dahlem, Charlottenburg, and the Tiergarten museum complex. However, Museumsinsel is still world-renowned for its ancient architectural and sculptural wonders, particularly the Pergamon Altar.

A *Sammelkarte,* or combination ticket, is available for several museums in Berlin-Mitte, costing 8 DM ($4.70) for adults and 4 DM ($2.35) for students and children. It allows entry to the Pergamon Museum, Bode Museum, Alte Nationalgalerie, and Otto-Nagel-Haus.

Note that at press time a discussion was underway that would change the opening hours for museums in Berlin-Mitte to coincide with the opening hours of most other museums in Berlin: that is, closed on Monday and open the rest of the week from 9am to 5pm. To avoid disappointment, contact the Berlin Tourist Information Office for exact hours or consult *Berlin Programm,* available at the tourist office or at magazine kiosks.

Bode Museum, Bodestrasse 1–3 (entrance on Monbijoubrücke), Museumsinsel. ☎ **203 55-0.**

Named after the former director responsible for bringing famous works of art to Museumsinsel, this is actually several museums housed in one. Here you'll find the very interesting **Egyptian Museum** with its **Papyrus Collection,** the **Early Christian and Byzantine Collection,** the **Sculpture Collection,** and the **Picture Gallery.**

On the ground floor you'll find the Egyptian Museum, considered one of the world's best with its lively presentation of the life and times of the Pharaohs. The Early Christian and Byzantine Collection gives an overview of early Christian art in Rome and the Byzantine Empire, and includes a valuable 6th-century mosaic from the Church of San Michele in Ravenna and a collection of icons. The Picture Gallery, many of whose masterpieces ended up in Dahlem following World War II, nevertheless has German and Netherlandish works from the 15th and 16th centuries; Dutch, Flemish, French, and English paintings from the 17th and 18th centuries; and Italian works. The Bode Museum also boasts a Coin Cabinet, its more than half a million coins, medallions, and seals making up one of the largest and most important such collections in the world.

Admission: 4 DM ($2.35) adults, 2 DM ($1.20) students and children; combination ticket 8 DM ($4.70) and 4 DM ($2.35), respectively. Free Sun and holidays.

Open: Wed–Sun 9am–5pm. **S-Bahn:** Hackescher Markt or Friedrichstrasse. **Bus:** 100 to Deutsche Staatsoper.

Alte Nationalgalerie (Old National Gallery), Bodestrasse, Museumsinsel. ☎ **203 55-307.**

Taking up where the Picture Gallery of the Bode Museum leaves off, the Corinthian-style Alte Nationalgalerie contains paintings and sculptures from the 19th and early 20th centuries, including classical, romantic, Biedermeier, impressionist, and expressionist works, mainly by German and French artists. Among them are a few works by Gottfried Schadow, Adolph von Menzel, Edgar Degas, Paul Cézanne, and Auguste Rodin. Of special note are the German expressionist and impressionist departments on the upper floor, with works by Max Liebermann, Max Slevogt, Ernst Ludwig Kirchner, Emil Nolde, and Oskar Kokoschka.

Admission: 4 DM ($2.35) adults, 2 DM ($1.20) students children; combination ticket 8 DM ($4.70) and 4 DM ($2.35), respectively. Free Sun and holidays.

Open: Wed–Sun 9am–5pm. **S-Bahn:** Hackescher Markt or Friedrichstrasse. **Bus:** 100 to Deutsche Staatsoper.

Altes Museum (Old Museum), Museumsinsel (entrance on Lustgarten). ☎ **203 55-0.**

Built according to plans by Karl Friedrich Schinkel and considered one of his greatest works, this museum was the first constructed on Museumsinsel—and is the first one you see if you approach the island from Unter den Linden. Easily recognized by its 18 Ionic columns, it offers changing exhibitions from the art of ancient times to modern art. Refer to *Berlin Programm* for current exhibitions.

Admission: Varies according to exhibit.

Open: Wed–Sun 9am–5pm. **S-Bahn:** Hackescher Markt or Friedrichstrasse. **Bus:** 100 to Deutsche Staatsoper.

Deutsches Historisches Museum (German Historical Museum), Unter den Linden 2. ☎ **215 02-0.**

This museum was originally built in the 17th century as an arsenal for the Prussian army and it's still considered a fine example of Baroque architecture. Before the Wall came down, it served as East Germany's principal museum of German history, with the expected socialist point of view. It now features changing exhibitions related to German history; plans for the future include the opening of a new permanent exhibition later in the decade with comprehensive displays of German history from ancient to present times. Contact the Berlin tourist office for updated information.

Admission: Varies according to exhibit.

Open: Thurs–Tues 10am–6pm. **S-Bahn:** Friedrichstrasse. **Bus:** 100 to Deutsche Staatsoper.

Märkisches Museum, Am Köllnischen Park 5. ☎ **270 05 14.**

Whereas the museum described above concerns itself with the history of Germany, this one concentrates on the cultural history of Berlin and is housed in an attractive fortress-like building from the turn of the century. Displays (unfortunately in German only) include prehistoric archeological finds, beginning with the Stone Age; models of the city around 1500, when it consisted of two villages called Berlin and Cölln, and of Berlin in 1750; and paintings, glassware, tin, porcelain (including KPM Berlin), wrought-iron furniture, and other arts and handcrafts produced through the ensuing centuries. There's also a special section dedicated to Berlin theater, with photographs and pictures of famous actors, actresses, and directors from the 18th to 20th centuries.

Admission: 3 DM ($1.75) adults, 1 DM (60¢) children and students.

Open: Tues–Sun 10am–6pm. **U-Bahn:** Märkisches Museum or Jannowitzbrücke.

Otto-Nagel-Haus, Märkisches Ufer 16–18. ☎ **279 14 02.**

Situated on the banks of a canal, this small museum features proletarian and antifascist artwork. Though there are some changing displays, it is primarily devoted to Otto Nagel and his contemporaries. In his paintings, the Berlin-born Nagel (1894–1967) realistically portrayed the city's working class of the 1920s and 1930s, with no

Eastern Berlin Sights

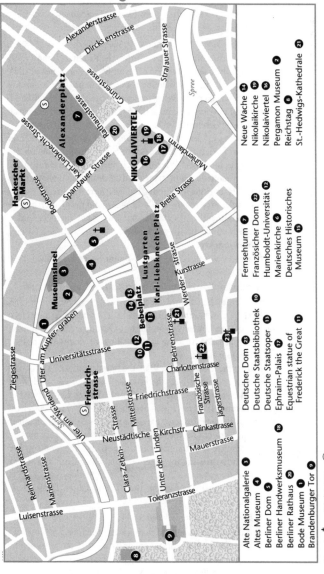

Neue Wache	**14**	Nikolaikirche	**19**
Nikolaiviertel	**16**	Pergamon Museum	**8**
Reichstag	**9**	St.-Hedwigs-Kathedrale	**21**

Fernsehturm	**7**	Humboldt-Universität	**12**
Französischer Dom	**22**	Marienkirche	**6**
		Deutsches Historisches Museum	**15**

Deutscher Dom	**23**	Ephraim-Palais	**17**
Deutsche Staatsbibliothek	**13**	Equestrian statue of Frederick the Great	**11**
Deutsche Staatsoper			

Alte Nationalgalerie	**3**	Berliner Handwerksmuseum	**18**
Altes Museum	**4**	Berliner Rathaus	**20**
Berliner Dom	**5**	Bode Museum	**1**
		Brandenburger Tor	**9**

Church ✝■   S-Bahn stop Ⓢ

attempt at glorification. Look, also, for sculptures by Käthe Kollwitz and Ernst Barlach. A very interesting museum.

Admission: 4 DM ($2.35) adults, 2 DM ($1.20) students and children; combination ticket 8 DM ($4.70) and 4 DM ($2.35), respectively; free Sun and holidays.

Open: Sun–Thurs 9am–5pm (with expected new hours to be Tues–Sun 9am–5pm). **S-Bahn:** Märkisches Museum.

Reichstag (Parliament), Platz der Republik. ☎ **39 77-0.**

Although technically in western Berlin, the Reichstag is most easily combined with a sightseeing trip to Berlin-Mitte. Completed in 1894, the German Parliament building is once again used for sessions of the German Parliament. When sessions are not being held, the building is open to visitors. Of most interest is the exhibition "Fragen an die Deutsche Geschichte" (Questions of German History), with displays relating to German history from 1800 to the present. Since displays are in German only, be sure to rent a cassette in English and headphones for 2 DM ($1.20) which will guide you through the exhibits in about 45 minutes. Included are displays and photographs on workers' uprisings, the industrial age, Bismarck's reign, World War I, Hitler's rise to power, World War II and the division of Germany, and the events of 1989 that opened the East German border. Entrance is on Reichstag's north side.

Admission: Free.

Open: Tues–Sun 10am–5pm. **S-Bahn:** Unter den Linden. **Bus:** 100 to Reichstag.

Brandenburger Tor (Brandenburg Gate), Unter den Linden.

One of Berlin's best-known structures, this gate was built from 1788 to 1791 by Carl Gotthard Langhans as the grand western entrance onto Unter den Linden. It is topped by a Quadriga created by Johann Gottfried Schadow that shows the goddess of victory in a chariot pulled by four steeds.

During the decades of the Wall, the Brandenburger Tor stood in a no-man's land, marking the boundary between East and West Berlin; it eventually became the symbol of a divided Germany. After the November 1989 revolution and the fall of the Wall, it was here that many Berliners gathered to rejoice and dance together on top of the Wall. Plans call for the restoration of Pariser Platz to its former glory, complete with fountains and flowers. For the moment, the square is a favorite site for street vendors selling Communist and Russian memorabilia.

S-Bahn: Unter den Linden. **Bus:** 100 to Unter den Linden/ Brandenburger Tor stop.

Berliner Dom, Lustgarten. ☎ **246 91 35.**

One of the most striking and dominating structures on Museumsinsel, the Berlin Cathedral was constructed at the turn of the century to serve as the court church of the Hohenzollerns. Severely damaged during World War II, it was finally reopened in 1994 after decades of restoration. Queen Sophie Charlotte and her husband, Friedrich I, the first Prussian king, are buried here, in tombs designed by Andreas Schlüter. The gilded wall altar was designed by Schinkel. Organ concerts are given Monday through Saturday at 2pm.

Admission: 3 DM ($1.75) for adults, 1.50 DM (90¢) students and children. Organ concerts 7–10 DM ($4.15–$5.90).

Open: Mon–Sat 9am–5pm, Sun 11:30am–5pm.

IN CHARLOTTENBURG

The first three museums described below are located near the corner of Schlossstrasse and Spandauer Damm. Charlottenburg's top two attractions, Schloss Charlottenburg and the Ägyptisches Museum are described above under "The Top Attractions." If you plan to visit several of these museums, consider purchasing a *Sammelkarte* (combination ticket) for 8 DM ($4.70) for adults and 4 DM ($2.35) for students and children, which allows entry to the Ägyptisches Museum, Antikenmuseum, Museum für Vor- und Frühgeschichte, and the Galerie der Romantik (located in Schloss Charlottenburg). In addition, Schloss Charlottenburg has its own combination ticket.

Other sights in Charlottenburg include the Kaiser-Wilhelm Gedächtniskirche (Kaiser Wilhelm Memorial Church) and the Käthe-Kollwitz-Museum, both located near the Ku'damm.

Antikenmuseum (Museum of Greek and Roman Antiquities). Schlossstrasse 1. ☎ 32 09 11.

Standing directly across from the Ägyptisches Museum and also originally designed as barracks, the Antikenmuseum contains Greek, Etruscan, and Roman pottery; ivory carvings; glassware; jewelry; wood and stone sarcophagi; and small statuettes in marble. Particularly outstanding are the Attic red-figure vases of the 5th century, with their depictions of everyday life in ancient Greece and the world of the gods. But the most impressive collections are in the basement Schatzkammer (Treasury), with its silver collection and its exquisite jewelry from about 2000 B.C. to late antiquity.

Admission: 4 DM ($2.35) adults, 2 DM ($1.20) children and students; combination ticket 8 DM ($4.70) and 4 DM ($2.35), respectively; free Sun and holidays.

Open: Mon–Thurs 9am–5pm, Sat–Sun 10am–5pm. **Closed:** Jan 1; Maundy Thursday; May 1; and Dec 24, 25, and 31. **Bus:** 109, 110, or 145 to Charlottenburger Schloss. **U-Bahn:** Sophie-Charlotte-Platz or Richard-Wagner-Platz, then a 10-minute walk.

Museum für Vor- und Frühgeschichte (Museum of Pre- and Early History). Spandauer Damm. ☎ 32 09 11.

This museum, in the west wing of Schloss Charlottenburg (to the left if you're facing the palace, outside the palace gate), is dedicated to the history of mankind from the Old Stone Age through the Bronze Age and late Iron Age, illustrated with objects from prehistoric Europe and the Near East. Arranged in chronological order, the displays start with Paleolithic cave paintings and idols and continue with sections devoted to the creation of written language; the beginning of agriculture; metalworking; Trojan antiquities; and items relating to the pre-Roman Iron Age and the early Germanic tribes. Also included are glass, pottery, jewelry, and coins of the Roman provinces, as well as archeological finds from the Spandau district of Berlin.

Spandau was first settled in the 7th century by Slavic people and remains Berlin's most extensively researched archeological site.

Admission: 4 DM ($2.35) adults, 2 DM ($1.20) students and children; combination ticket 8 DM ($4.70) and 4 DM ($2.35), respectively; free Sun and holidays.

Open: Mon–Thurs 9am–5pm, Sat–Sun 10am–5pm. **Closed:** Jan 1; Maundy Thursday; May 1; and Dec 24, 25, and 31. **Bus:** 109, 110, or 145 to Charlottenburger Schloss. **U-Bahn:** Sophie-Charlotte-Platz or Richard-Wagner-Platz, then a 10-minute walk.

⭐ **Bröhan Museum,** Schlossstrasse la. ☎ **321 40 29.**

Located right next to the Antikenmuseum, this privately owned museum—the only one in the Charlottenburg complex—is named after Professor Karl Bröhan, who started the collection housed here. He began gathering art nouveau (Jugendstil) and art deco pieces at a time when others thought they were worthless and were throwing them away. With approximately 1,600 objects dating from 1889 to 1939, including exquisite vases, glass, furniture, silver, sculptures, and paintings, the museum ranks as one of the finest of its kind in the world.

Pieces are beautifully arranged, with most rooms resembling period salons rather than museum galleries. Outstanding is the porcelain collection, including KPM Berlin, Meissen, and Royal Copenhagen, as well as the turn-of-the-century buffet created by Hector Guimard (1867–1942), who also designed the cast-iron entranceways of the Paris Métro. Also on display are glass by Emile Gallé, Bohemian iridescent glass, paintings by a group of artists known as the Berlin Secession, silver objects by Viennese artist Josef Hoffmann, and magnificent furniture crafted by Jacques-Emile Ruhlmann. In short, it's a joy to walk through the airy rooms filled with the graceful motifs of art nouveau and art deco. Make sure you don't miss it.

Admission: 6 DM ($3.55) adults, 3 DM ($1.75) students.

Open: Tues–Sun 10am–6pm (Thurs to 8pm). **Bus:** 109, 110, or 145 to Charlottenburger Schloss. **U-Bahn:** Sophie-Charlotte-Platz or Richard-Wagner-Platz, then a 10-minute walk.

⭐ **Käthe-Kollwitz-Museum,** Fasanenstrasse 24. ☎ **882 52 10.**

Just south of the Ku'damm, this small but significant museum displays the powerful, gripping drawings and sketches of Käthe Kollwitz (1867–1945). A Berliner, Kollwitz was a genius who captured the human emotions of her subjects, from the tenderness mothers feel toward their children to the despair and grief caused by poverty and oppression. The artist herself lost a son to war. Don't miss the opportunity to see her works, spread on four floors—their power will stay with you long afterward.

Admission: 6 DM ($3.55) adults, 3 DM ($1.75) students.

Open: Wed–Mon 11am–6pm. **U-Bahn:** Uhlandstrasse.

Kaiser-Wilhelm Gedächtniskirche (Kaiser Wilhelm Memorial Church), Breitscheidplatz. ☎ **24 50 23.**

Sights Around Charlottenburg

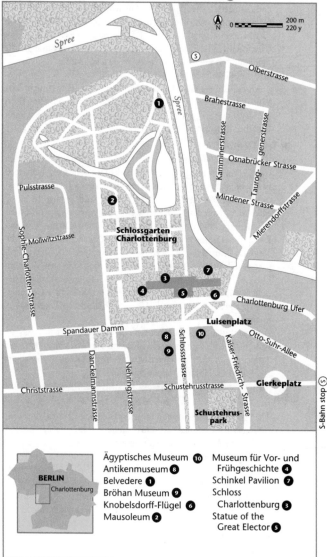

Ägyptisches Museum ⑩
Antikenmuseum ⑧
Belvedere ❶
Bröhan Museum ❾
Knobelsdorff-Flügel ❻
Mausoleum ❷

Museum für Vor- und
  Frühgeschichte ❹
Schinkel Pavilion ❼
Schloss
  Charlottenburg ❸
Statue of the
  Great Elector ❺

BERLIN
Charlottenburg

This church, which marks the beginning of the Ku'damm, would be difficult to overlook. In fact, almost half a century after the end of World War II, it comes as something of a surprise to see the skeletal ruins of a war-damaged steeple in the heart of modern Berlin. But lest we forget the horrors of war, the Gedächtniskirche was left as a bombed-out shell of its former self. The church dates from 1895, and today it contains a small museum with displays related to war and destruction. Beside it, in striking contrast, stands a newer, octagonal church with a hexagonal tower. Designed by Professor Egon Eiermann and completed in 1961, it's made of blue glass plates from Chartres. In the Berliner style of nicknaming everything in sight, the new church is known as the "powderbox and lipstick."

Admission: Free.

Open: Ruined church Tues–Sat 10am–4pm; new church daily 9am–7:30pm. Services held Sun and holidays 10am and 6pm; short services Mon–Fri 1pm, 5:30pm, and 6pm. Organ concerts Sat 6pm.

U-Bahn: Kürfurstendamm or Bahnhof Zoologischer Garten.

IN THE TIERGARTEN

Besides the following museums, the precinct known as the Tiergarten contains the city's largest and oldest park of the same name (described below in "Parks and Gardens"), the Hansaviertel (Hansa Quarter) north of the park, a zoo (described below), and an area stretching south of the park designated as the city's newest cultural center. This last, with the Philharmonie in the middle, is known as the "Cultural Forum" and is home of the Neue Nationalgalerie, the Kunstwerbe Museum (Museum of Applied Arts), the Kupferstichkabinett (Collection of Print and Drawings) and the Musikinstrumenten Museum. Once additional construction is completed throughout the next decade, it will also house two museums now in Dahlem: the Gemäldegaleries and Skulpturengalerie. Check with the Berlin Tourist Information Office for exact details.

A combination ticket (*Sammelkarte*) allowing entry to the Neue Nationalgalerie, Kunstgewerbe Museum, Kupferstichkabinett, and Musikinstrumenten Museum is available for 8 DM ($4.70) for adults and 4 DM ($2.35) for students and children.

⭐ **Neue Nationalgalerie (New National Gallery),**
Potsdamer Strasse 50. ☎ **266 26 62.**

The first museum to open in the Tiergarten cultural area, the Neue Nationalgalerie is called "new" to distinguish it from eastern Berlin's much older Alte Nationalgalerie on Museumsinsel. In fact, it owes its core collection to the latter, since it received more than 600 artworks from the older museum after World War II. A starkly modern building designed by architect Mies van der Rohe and built in the 1960s, it's set in a vast square surrounded by a sculpture garden. Featuring art of the 19th and 20th centuries, it shows changing exhibitions on the ground floor, while a lower floor houses the permanent collection.

Highlights of the permanent collection are works by Adolph von Menzel (1815–1905)—the world's largest collection of this Berlin artist—and works by Monet, Manet, Pissarro, Renoir, Beckmann, Corinth, Klee, Picasso, Kokoschka, Kirchner, and Dalí. With the galleries covering art from preimpressionism and realism to impressionism, expressionism, modern classicism, and surrealism, there's great variety in this small, bright, and airy museum—one of my Berlin favorites. If you aren't familiar with German artists of the past century, this is a good introduction.

Admission: Permanent collection 4 DM ($2.35) adults, 2 DM ($1.20) students and children; combination ticket 8 DM ($4.70) and 4 DM ($2.35), respectively; temporary exhibits average 4–8 DM ($2.35–$4.70); free Sun and holidays.

Open: Tues–Fri 9am–5pm, Sat–Sun 10am–5pm. **Closed:** Jan 1; Tues after Easter and after Whitsunday; May 1; Dec 24, 25, and 31. **U-Bahn:** Kurfürstenstrasse, then bus no. 148 or 248. **Bus:** 129 from the Ku'damm.

Kunstgewerbe Museum (Museum of Applied Arts),

Tiergartenstrasse 6. ☎ **266 29 11.**

A five-minute walk from the Neue Nationalgalerie and located next door to the Philharmonie, this modern red-brick museum is devoted to European applied arts from the early Middle Ages to the present day: glassware, porcelain, beer steins, tableware, measuring instruments, and more. Particularly outstanding is the collection of medieval goldsmiths' works, including the *Guelph Cross* and the *Domed Reliquary,* among the richest ecclesiastical treasures in any German museum; an 8th-century piece associated with Charlemagne; and the baptism bowl of Emperor Barbarossa. The *Lüneburg Town Hall Silver Plate,* another priceless treasure, consists of 32 vessels and implements in gold-plated silver. There are also displays of Venetian glass, early Meissen porcelain, and Jugendstil vases and other objects. The bottom floor is devoted to changing exhibits of contemporary crafts and product design, from typewriters to teapots and furniture.

Admission: 4 DM ($2.35) adults, 2 DM ($1.20) students and children; combination ticket 8 DM ($4.70) and 4 DM ($2.35), respectively; free Sunday and holidays.

Open: Tues–Fri 9am–5pm, Sat–Sun 10am–5pm. **Closed:** Jan 1; Tues after Easter and after Whitsunday; May 1; Dec 24, 25, and 31. **U-Bahn:** Kurfürstenstrasse, then bus no. 148 or 248. **Bus:** 129 from the Ku'damm.

Kupferstichkabinett—Sammlung der Zeichnungen und Druckgraphik (Collection of Prints and Drawings),

Matthäikirchplatz 8. ☎ **266 20 01.**

This museum, which originally was in Dahlem and is expected to reopen in the Tiergarten by 1995 (check with the tourist office to confirm), specializes in prints and drawings from the German masters, including important works by Albrecht Dürer.

Admission: 4 DM ($2.35) adults, 2 DM ($1.20) for students and children; combination ticket 8 DM ($4.70) and 4 DM ($2.35), respectively; free Sun and holidays.

Open: Tues–Fri 9am–5pm, Sat–Sun 10am–5pm. **Closed:** Jan 1; Tues after Easter and after Whitsunday; May 1; Dec 24, 25, and 31. **U-Bahn:** Kurfürstenstrasse, then bus no. 148 or 248. **Bus:** 129 from the Ku'damm.

Musikinstrumenten Museum (Museum of Musical Instruments), Tiergartenstrasse 1. ☎ **25 48 10.**

A small gray building in the shadow of the larger Philharmonie, the Musikinstrumenten Museum reopened in its new Tiergarten home in 1984. The collection, which originated in 1888, suffered greatly during World War II, with a loss of more than 3,000 pieces out of a 4,000 total. The past decades have seen so many new acquisitions, however, that the museum once again boasts a healthy collection of European musical instruments from the 16th century to the present day, with valuable pieces from the Renaissance and baroque periods. Included are spinets, clavichords, violins, trumpets, flutes, alpenhorns, harps, zithers, guitars, and the now-forgotten glass harmonica, for which Mozart and others wrote compositions.

Admission: 4 DM ($2.35) adults, 2 DM ($1.20) for students and children; combination ticket 8 DM ($4.70) and 4 DM ($2.35), respectively; free Sun and holidays.

Open: Tues–Fri 9am–5pm, Sat–Sun 10am–5pm. **Closed:** Jan 1; Tues after Easter and after Whitsunday; May 1; Dec 24, 25, and 31. **U-Bahn:** Kurfürstenstrasse, then bus no. 148 or 248. **Bus:** 129 from the Ku'damm.

IN KREUZBERG

Kreuzberg's most popular museum, **Museum Haus am Checkpoint Charlie,** is described above under "The Top Attractions." Unfortunately, no combination ticket is offered for Kreuzberg's museums.

Martin-Gropius-Bau, Stresemannstrasse 110. ☎ 254 86-0.

The Martin-Gropius-Bau, beautiful inside and out, was designed by architect Martin Gropius in 1881. It houses two museums: Berlinische Galerie and the Jewish department of the Berlin Museum. The **Berlinische Galerie,** the city's museum for modern art, photography, and architecture, features changing exhibitions and a permanent display, with an emphasis on art of the 20th century. Though most of its works are by contemporary Berlin artists, it also shows international art.

Admission: Permanent exhibition 8 DM ($4.70) adults, 4 DM ($2.35) children; temporary exhibitions cost extra.

Open: Tues–Sun 10am–8pm. **U-Bahn:** Kochstrasse. **S-Bahn:** Anhalter Bahnhof or Potsdamer Platz. **Bus:** 129 or 341.

Topographie des Terrors, Stresemannstrasse 110. ☎ 245 86-703.

Located beside the Martin-Gropius-Bau and easily overlooked, this low-slung building houses a museum documenting Hitler's reign of terror. Fittingly, it occupies what was once the site of Hitler's feared Gestapo and SS headquarters, where enemies of the state—Jews, Communists, Social Democrats, and members of the resistance movements—were held for questioning and torture by the Third Reich's secret police. Through photographs and explanations, the museum depicts Hitler's rise to power, the fate of Jews and gypsies sent to concentration camps, the rule of the Gestapo, and other grim statistics. Unfortunately, most of the explanations are in German only and do not go into the depth the subjects deserve. However, a booklet in English is available for a small fee. Scattered along a footpath on the expansive grounds of the museum, called the Prinz-Albrecht-Gelände, are photographs and explanations of buildings that used

Sights Around the Tiergarten

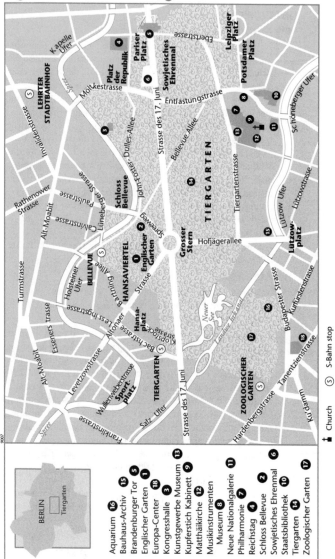

to exist in the immediate area during Hitler's regime. Incidentally, on Niederkirchnerstrasse, the street just north of the museum grounds, is a remnant of the Berlin Wall.

Admission: Free.

Open: Tues–Sun 10am–6pm. **U-Bahn:** Kochstrasse. **S-Bahn:** Anhalter Bahnhof or Potsdamer Platz. **Bus:** 129 or 341.

IN FRIEDRICHSHAIN

 East Side Gallery, Mühlenstrasse.

Formerly a part of East Berlin, Friedrichshain precinct borders what used to be West Berlin, its western boundary marked by the Spree River and the Wall. Although the western side of the Wall was often sprayed with graffiti and painted with murals, the eastern side was strictly off limits (to put it mildly) and was therefore always white and shiny. In a surprise move, eastern German authorities decided in 1990 to leave a kilometer-long section of the Wall standing along Mühlenstrasse and invited artists from around the world to decorate its blank eastern side with murals. Since there is hardly any of the Wall remaining today, this open-air gallery is bound to become a major tourist attraction. Look for my favorites: a Trabant (East German car) crashing through the Wall, and Brezhnev and Honecker kissing each other with the caption, "Will no one save me from this deadly love?"

Admission: Free.

Open: Daily 24 hours. **S-Bahn:** Hauptbahnhof. **U-Bahn:** Schlesisches Tor.

IN ORANIENBURG

Gedenkstätte und Museum Sachsenhausen (Memorial and Museum Sachsenhausen), Strasse der Nationen 22, Oranienburg. ☎ **03301/80 37 15.**

Twenty-one miles north of Berlin but easily reached via a 45-minute ride on the S-Bahn with a normal transportation ticket, Oranienburg is an important destination for those who wish to know more about Hitler's death camps. In operation from 1936 to 1945, Sachsenhausen was one of the most infamous concentration camps, housing 220,000 prisoners from 22 countries, 100,000 of whom died here. Since 1961 its grounds have served as a memorial, containing original barracks and other camp structures and two museums complete with photographs. Films are shown in German and French only, but pictures speak louder than words. This is a sobering experience that's not recommended for children under 12.

Admission: Free.

Open: Summer, Tues–Sun 8am–6pm; winter, Tues–Sun 8am–4:30pm. **S-Bahn:** Oranienburg, then a 20-minute walk or short taxi ride.

IN ZEHLENDORF

Museumsdorf Düppel, Clauertstrasse 11. ☎ **802 66 71.**

Open in summer only, this open-air reproduction of a medieval village features thatch-roofed houses and live demonstrations of woodworking, baking, weaving, and other household chores. Explanations are in German only, but coming here makes a pleasant trip in fine weather. Good for a family outing.

Admission: 3 DM ($1.75) adults, 1 DM (60¢) children.

Open: May to early Oct, Sun and holidays 10am–5pm (enter before 4pm), Thurs 3–7pm (enter by 6pm). **Bus:** 211 to Lindenthaler

Allee/Ecke Clauertstrasse; 118 or 115 to Potsdamer Chaussee/Ecke Lindenthaler Allee.

IN KÖPENICK

Besides the museum below, Köpenick, an important industrial town with a history stretching back to the 9th century, is an interesting place to visit. Even the Wall's demise hasn't brought much change to this working-class area.

Kunstgewerbemuseum (Museum of Applied Arts), Schloss Köpenick, Schloss Insel. ☎ **657 26 51.**

There's been a fortress on this island in the river ever since the 12th century. In the 16th century it was remodeled into a hunting lodge for Elector Joachim II, but in the mid-17th century it was once again changed, under the direction of a Dutch architect, into the baroque palace it is today. It was here that Friedrich II (Frederick the Great) was court-martialed in 1730, along with his friend Lieutenant von Katte, for trying to flee the country and kingly responsibilities.

In addition to the palace, the island contains a small garden, pleasant for a stroll. But of course the most important thing to do here is to visit the **Kunstgewerbemuseum** (Museum of Applied Arts), located in the palace itself. It contains glass, ceramics, jewelry, tapestries, furniture, and silver and gold objects, from the Middle Ages through the 20th century. What makes the contemporary collection particularly interesting is the presence of artists from East Berlin, Dresden, Leipzig, Erfurt, Weimar, and other cities formerly of East Germany, thus providing insight into the DDR art scene during the Wall's existence. Another highlight of the palace, which still has its baroque stucco ceilings, is the **Wappensaal** (Coat of Arms Hall), the most ornate room in Schloss Köpenick and site of Friedrich II's court-martial; above the fireplace is the coat of arms of the Prussian Brandenburg State.

Admission: 4 DM ($2.35) adults, 2 DM ($1.20) students and children; free Sun and holidays.

Open: Wed–Sun 9am–5pm. **Directions:** S-Bahn to Köpenick, then tram no. 60, 61, 62, or 68 to Schlossinsel; or S-Bahn to Spindlersfeld, then a 15-minute walk.

Panoramas

Fernsehturm (Television Tower), Alexanderplatz, Berlin-Mitte. ☎ **242 33 33.**

From the time the Fernsehturm was completed in 1969 until the fall of the Wall 20 years later, this towering structure in eastern Berlin was popular for the view it afforded of West Berlin far in the distance, especially on clear days when there's a 24-mile visibility (an update of the day's visibility is posted on the outside door). Elevators whisk visitors to the 670-feet-high observation platform in 35 seconds. More than 1,200 feet tall, the tower is Berlin's tallest edifice and contains the revolving Tele-Café, which makes a complete turn every hour. Come for a cup of coffee on a clear day and enjoy the stunning views.

Admission: 5 DM ($2.95) adults, 2.50 DM ($1.45) children.

Open: Observation platform, daily 9am–11:30pm; Tele-Café, daily 9am–10:45pm. **Closed:** until 1pm second and fourth Tues of every month. **S-Bahn or U-Bahn:** Alexanderplatz.

Rathaus Schöneberg, John-F.-Kennedy-Platz, Schöneberg.

☎ **7831.**

It is from the steps of Rathaus Schöneberg that John F. Kennedy gave his famous "Ich bin ein Berliner" speech (see "For Visiting Americans" under "Special-Interest Sightseeing" later in this chapter). Should you choose to climb the 230-foot-high bell tower, you'll be rewarded with a good view of Schöneberg precinct.

Admission: Free.

Open: Wed and Sun 10am–3:30pm. **U-Bahn:** Rathaus Schöneberg.

Siegessäule (Victory Column), Grosser Stern, Tiergarten.

☎ **391 29 61.**

Originally in front of the Reichstag but now located in the Tiergarten park in the middle of a traffic circle, the Siegessäule is Berlin's oldest observation tower. It was dedicated in 1873 to commemorate three victorious wars. More than 220 feet high, it's topped by a gilded goddess of victory, as well as a 157-foot-high observation platform, reached via 290 steps of a spiral staircase.

Admission: 1.50 DM (90¢) adults, 1 DM (60¢) children.

Open: Mon 1–5:30pm, Tues–Sun 9am–5:30pm. **Closed:** In frost or bad weather. **Bus:** 100 to Grosser Stern.

Parks & Gardens

Many visitors are surprised to learn that the city limits encompass a large area of woods and lakes. During the decades when West Berlin was surrounded by East Germany and the Wall, its green spaces and water—accounting for a full 30% of its total 190 square miles—served as an important emotional escape valve for urban dwellers in need of nature. The most popular destinations for a day's outing continue to be the Havel and Wannsee lakes. For more information on these destinations, see "Organized Tours" and "Sports and Recreation" later in this chapter.

The Tiergarten, from Bahnhof Zoo to Brandenburger Tor.

Berlin's most convenient park, as well as its largest, is the Tiergarten. Approximately 1.86 miles long and half a mile wide, it stretches east from Bahnhof Zoo all the way to the Brandenburger Tor. Originally used as a hunting reserve and then as the elector's private park, the Tiergarten was opened to the public at the end of the 19th century. Largely destroyed in World War II, it suffered further damage when Berliners used most of its trees for fuel during the long cold winters. Today trees have been replanted, and it's one of the most popular places in the city for picnics, jogging, sunbathing, and strolling. In addition to ponds, streams, a rose garden, and an English-style garden, it also contains the Zoologischer Garten (Berlin Zoo), located in the massive park's southwest corner, described below.

IMPRESSIONS

> *But the real heart of Berlin is a small damp*
> *black wood—the Tiergarten.*
> —Christopher Isherwood, *Goodbye to Berlin*, 1939

⭐ **Botanischer Garten (Botanical Garden),** Königin-Luise-Strasse 6–8, Dahlem. ☎ **83 00 60.**

Berlin's Botanischer Garten was laid out at the turn of the century and boasts 104 acres and 18,000 species of plants. Its 16 greenhouses contain plants from all continents and environments, from rain forests to deserts. Don't miss the Troperehaus, constructed in 1907 and one of the world's largest greenhouses. Outdoor beds are arranged geographically, so that visitors can wander through landscapes that resemble the Alps, Japan, the Himalayas, South Africa, North America, and other regions. There's also a garden of medicinal plants, as well as a garden for the visually handicapped, where visitors can smell and touch the plants. The small Botanisches Museum displays the history and usage of various plants, but only in German.

Admission: 4 DM ($2.35) adults, 2 DM ($1.20) students and children; Botanisches Museum, free.

Open: Botanischer Garten, Nov–Feb daily 9am–4pm, Mar and Oct daily 9am–5pm, April and Sept daily 9am–7pm, May–Aug daily 9am–8pm. Greenhouses, Nov–Feb daily 10am–3:15pm, Mar and Oct daily 9am–4:15pm, Apr–Sept daily 9am–5:15pm. Botanisches Museum, open Tues–Sun 10am–5pm. **S-Bahn:** Botanischer Garten.

Pfaueninsel and Schloss Pfaueninsel (Peacock Island), Havel Lake. ☎ **805 30 42.**

Pfaueninsel is the largest island in the Havel and has long been one of the most popular destinations for day-trippers from Berlin. A 185-acre nature reserve with many rare trees and birds, the island gets its name from a flock of 60 or so peacocks that has roamed freely since 1795. There used to be a ménagerie as well, including monkeys and bears, which in the mid-1800s formed the basis of the Berlin Zoo. Closed to cars, the island lends itself perfectly to strolls. It takes about an hour or two to walk around the island, though you'll probably want to make several stops along the way.

Most famous on the island is **Schloss Pfaueninsel,** almost directly in front of the ferry landing. It's a fake ruin built in the 1790s by Friedrich Wilhelm II for his mistress, the Countess Lichtenau. In contrast to his uncle, Frederick the Great, who spent much of his life waging wars and building empires, Friedrich Wilhelm II apparently preferred to spend his time building architectural fantasies—a much milder Prussian version of Bavaria's Ludwig II. The castle, later used by Friedrich Wilhelm III and Queen Luise as a summer residence, consists of two floors, with four rooms on each level. Originally constructed of wood, it has been reinforced with concrete. It contains a small museum with furnishings and artworks dating from 1795 to 1830, including valuable carpets and portraits of the former royal inhabitants.

As you walk around the island, note the many rare trees and shrubs that were planted here, including Weymouth and Arolla pines, sequoias, ginkgos, and cedars. Other items of interest include the **Schweizerhaus** (Swiss Cottage), designed by Karl Friedrich Schinkel in 1825; the **Kavaliershaus,** built in 1804 and renovated by Schinkel in 1826, when he added the facade of a late-Gothic patrician home from Danzig; and the **Meierei** (Dairy Farm), located on the north end of the island and also built in the style of a ruin.

Admission: Pfaueninsel, free; Schloss Pfaueninsel 3 DM ($1.75) adults, 1.50 DM (90¢) students and children.

Open: Pfaueninsel, summer daily 8am–8pm; winter daily 10am–4pm. Schloss Pfaueninsel, Apr–Oct Tues–Sun 10am–5pm. **Directions:** Bus No. 116 or 216 to Pfaueninsel, then by foot to Nikolskoer Weg, then ferry (2 DM [$1.20] one way).

A Zoo

 Zoologischer Garten (Berlin Zoo), Budapester Strasse 32 and Hardenbergplatz 8. ☎ **25 40 10.**

Founded in 1844 and located just a short walk from the Ku'damm or Bahnhof Zoo, the Berlin Zoo is Germany's oldest and one of Europe's best zoos, home to more than 14,000 animals of almost 2,000 species. Probably the best-known and most-beloved resident is BaoBao, the panda, but other popular animals include the elephants, giraffes, camels, kangaroos, antelopes, lions, tigers, and monkeys. There's also a birdhouse (Europe's largest) with 720 species.

The grounds of the zoo are beautifully designed, with ponds and streams and thatched cottages and timber-frame structures housing the animals. It's a great place to escape from the urban atmosphere, especially in fine weather. The adjacent **Aquarium,** built in 1913, has a collection of more than 6,000 fish, reptiles, and amphibians, including sea turtles, sharks, snakes, alligators, frogs, and spiders.

Admission: Combination ticket, allowing entrance to both the zoo and the aquarium, 15 DM ($8.85) adults, 12 DM ($7.10) students, 7.50 DM ($4.40) children. Tickets for zoo only 10 DM ($5.90) adults, 8 DM ($4.70) students, and 5 DM ($2.95) children.

Open: Summer, daily 9am–6:30pm; winter, daily 9am–5pm. **S-Bahn and U-Bahn:** Zoologischer Garten.

3 Cool for Kids

There are several attractions listed above that children would enjoy.

The Museum für Völkerkunde (Ethnological Museum) in Dahlem is one of the largest ethnological museums in the world, with a fascinating display of boats, canoes, masks, dwellings, weapons, clothing, and other fascinating items. Fun and educational. The **Museum Haus am Checkpoint Charlie** in Kreuzberg documents the decades of the Berlin Wall. On display are vehicles used in daring escapes, including cars with hidden compartments and a hot-air balloon. With its many photographs, it is one of the best places to show your child what Berlin during the Cold War was all about. **Museumsdorf Düppel,** in Zehlendorf, is a re-created open-air medieval village complete with thatch-roofed houses and live demonstrations of woodworking, baking, weaving, and other occupations.

At the **Zoologischer Garten and Aquarium,** no one can resist BaoBao the panda. There are monkeys, lions, elephants, and camels as well. The Berlin Zoo, founded in 1844, houses more than 14,000 animals of all kinds. Fun for the entire family, it's only minutes from the Ku'damm. At the **Botanischer Garten** you can show your child that cocoa grows on trees and that there are such things as insect-eating plants. The Botanical Garden, laid out at the turn of the century, also has a special area for the visually handicapped, who are encouraged to smell and touch the plants. Berlin's famous park, the **Tiergarten,** located right in the heart of the city, is another good spot for an outing.

A day at **Wannsee Beach** is always fun, and children can enjoy a playground here (complete with slides) as well as the swimming. An alternative is **BLUB,** Berlin's largest bathing paradise, a complex of indoor and outdoor pools, including a wave pool, a 396-foot super slide, a children's pool, and an outdoor heated pool open year round. See "Sports and Recreation" for full details.

Something older children might enjoy is the **Museum für Verkehr und Technik** (Museum for Transport and Technology), Trebbiner Strasse 9, in Kreuzberg (☎ **254 84 0**), near the U-Bahn stations Gleisdreieck and Möckernbrücke. The main building contains old model cars, trains, boats, and displays relating to the information age, from printing technology to computers, with most explanations unfortunately only in German. Of most interest to children from around the world, therefore, is probably the nearby Spectrum building, with four floors of hands-on displays, experiments, and models, including pulleys, pendulums, trick mirrors, optical illusions, electrical experiments, and more. This is a good place to spend a rainy day. It's open Tuesday to Friday from 9am to 5:30pm and Saturday and Sunday from 10am to 6pm; admission is 4 DM ($2.35) for adults and 2 DM ($1.20) for children and students.

Grips, Altonaer Strasse 22 (☎ **391 40 04**), near the Hansaplatz U-Bahn station, the undisputed champion of children's theater in Berlin, is famous throughout Germany, with shows that appeal to kids 7 and up. Its highly praised performances are designed for different age groups, including older children. If your child doesn't understand German, try to attend one of the productions meant for a young age group, where there's lots of action and the plot is easy to follow.

4   Special-Interest Sightseeing

FOR THE ARCHITECTURE LOVER   Because Berlin suffered such widespread destruction during World War II, the city is conspicuously devoid of the architectural gems that grace many other European cities. One notable exception is **Schloss Charlottenburg,** Berlin's most beautiful baroque structure, described above under "The Top Attractions."

In addition, some buildings remain that were designed by Karl Friedrich Schinkel (1781–1841), one of Berlin's best-known architects. Among his surviving works are the **Schinkel Pavilion** on the grounds of Schloss Charlottenburg, the **Altes Museum** on Museum Island, the Neue Wache on Unter den Linden, and the **Schlossbrücke** (also called the Marx-Engels-Brücke), which connects Unter den Linden and Karl-Liebknecht-Platz in eastern Berlin.

The bulk of Berlin's architecture, however, dates back only a few decades. The most famous modern buildings are those in the **Hansaviertel** (Hansa Quarter), which stretches along the northern border of the Tiergarten park. The quarter consists primarily of housing projects, from one-family dwellings to apartment buildings, along with two churches, a library, and a school. The Hansaviertel resulted from a 1957 international gathering of 48 leading architects (from more than 12 countries), who were asked to design a community for Berliners still homeless as a result of World War II. Famous architects who participated included Walter Gropius, Alvar Aalto, Pierre Vago, Oscar Niemeyer, and Werner Düttmann. For orientation, be sure to consult the outdoor map of the Hansaviertel, which lists each building and its architect; the closest subway station is Hansa station. Incidentally, Le Corbusier's design was of such proportions that it was built in the western end of the city near the Olympiastadion (Olympic Stadium). It's Berlin's largest housing project, with 530 apartments.

Another place of interest to architecture fans is the **Bauhaus-Archiv,** Klingelhöferstrasse 13–14 (☎ **261 16 18** or **254 00 233**). Located in a light, airy building designed by Walter Gropius, it is dedicated to preserving the ideals and artifacts of the Bauhaus school of design. The Bauhaus, founded by Gropius in Weimar in 1919 and disbanded in Berlin in 1933, revolutionized the teaching of architecture and industrial design through its emphasis on aesthetics.

The Bauhaus-Archiv contains a small museum, an extensive collection of documents, and a library. The museum's permanent collection includes architectural models, designs, paintings, drawings, and applied arts, including the work of Gropius, Hannes Meyer, Ludwig Mies van der Rohe, Marcel Breuer, and Ludwig Hilberseimer. Also shown are paintings and drawings by Herbert Bayer, Lyonel Feininger, Johannes Itten, Wassily Kandinsky, Paul Klee, Laszlo Moholy-Nagy, George Muche, and Oskar Schlemmer. Note, however, that items on permanent display are sometimes removed to make way for temporary special exhibitions.

The Bauhaus-Archiv, which can be reached by taking bus no. 100, 109, 129, or 341 to Lützowplatz, is open Wednesday through Monday from 10am to 5pm. Admission is 4 DM ($2.35) for adults and 2 DM ($1.20) for students. On Mondays, admission is free.

FOR FILM BUFFS   Home of Marlene Dietrich and the acclaimed Berlin International Film Festival held in February, Berlin also boasts **Babelsberg Studios,** located just south of the city near Potsdam. Formerly DEFA Studios, which produced such early classics as *Metropolis* and *The Blue Angel,* Babelsberg has been making serious efforts to attract world-class producers; German director Volker Schlöndorff is managing director of the studios. Open to the public daily from 9am to 5pm, the studio grounds include a theme park, cavernous halls housing one of the world's largest collections of film props (including models, masks, and creatures used in decades of filmmaking), movie sets (including one from the *Never-Ending Story III*), a stunt show, a special-effects display, and a Berlin street scene from the 1920s. Allow three hours for a tour of the grounds. Admission is 14 DM ($8.25) for adults, 10 DM ($5.90) for students, and 6 DM ($3.55) for children. To get there, take S-Bahn 3 or 7 to Griebnitzsee station, then bus no. 693 to Bahnhof Drewitz.

FOR VISITING AMERICANS   More than 100 streets, boulevards, and squares are named after Americans, a testament to the close ties Berlin has had through the years with the United States. Most famous of all is probably **John-F.-Kennedy-Platz,** the square in front of Rathaus Schöneberg. It was from here that Kennedy gave his famous "Ich bin ein Berliner" speech on June 26, 1963, just months before he was assassinated. **Rathaus Schöneberg** (☎ **7831**) remains of interest to Americans because of its huge Freedom Bell, modeled after the U.S. Liberty Bell and given to Berlin by the American people in 1950. Located in a tower (follow the signs that say *Zum Turm*), the tower and bell are open free to the public twice a week, on Wednesday and Sunday from 10am to 3:30pm. In the tower you'll also find display cases devoted to the history of the bell, including some of the 16 million signatures of Americans who pledged their support by signing the "Declaration of Freedom" (the bulk of the signatures are kept in a vault in the tower). At any rate, you have to climb a lot of steps to reach the tower, but the view from the top is grand. To reach Rathaus Schöneberg, take U-4 to the U-Bahn station of the same name, from which it's a minute's walk.

Other streets and places named after Americans include **Truman Plaza, Clayallee** (named in honor of Gen. Lucius Clay for his part in the Berlin Airlift of 1948–49), and the **John F. Kennedy School** (part of the Berlin school system but staffed by both American and German teachers).

5   Organized Tours

In light of the many changes taking place in Berlin because of reunification, tour companies have been redesigning their offerings. In particular, trips to the environs have increased greatly, so be sure to inquire for updated tour offerings and schedules.

BY BUS   With the aid of this book, you shouldn't have to spend money on a tour. However, you may wish to take one upon arrival in Berlin simply for orientation and for identifying the highlights. You can then return to the sights that interest you and enjoy them at leisure.

There are a number of tour companies in Berlin, with most of their buses departing from the Ku'damm area. Oldest and largest of these is **Severin + Kuhn,** Kurfürstendamm 216 (☎ **883 10 15**), which is open daily from 9am to 7pm. A three-hour tour of Berlin costs 39 DM ($23), while a four-hour evening nightclub tour costs 109 DM ($64.30), including two drinks.

If you're in Berlin for several days, you might want to take the Severin + Kuhn day trip to historic Potsdam, favored residency of Prussian royalty, where you'll visit Frederick the Great's rococo palace, Sanssouci, and its surrounding gardens. You'll also see Schloss Cecilienhof, former home of the crown prince and his family. It was here that the 1945 Potsdam Agreement was signed by the Allied Powers following World War II. The seven-hour tour costs 95 DM ($56.05), including lunch.

From May through September, Severin + Kuhn offers a 5-hour trip to the Spreewald, including a boat ride, for 54 DM ($31.85). Another tour worth considering is the 10-hour trip to Dresden for 99 DM ($58.40). For more information, contact Severin + Kuhn.

Other tour companies with similar tour offerings include **BVB,** whose buses depart from Kurfürstendamm 225 (☎ **8859 88-0**); **Berolina,** whose buses depart from the corner of the Kurfürstendamm and Meinekestrasse (☎ **882 20 91**); and **Berliner Bären Stadtrundfahrt (BBS),** with departures from the corner of the Ku'damm and Rankestrasse (☎ **213 40 77**).

BY BOAT   The Spree, a river that winds its way through the heart of Berlin, serves as a popular waterway for boat trips throughout the year. With departures at several places throughout Berlin, trips ranging from one to four hours are the most popular. One of the most convenient departure spots is at the Schlossbrücke in Berlin-Mitte (eastern Berlin) next to Museumsinsel. Operated by the **Berliner Wassertaxi Stadtrundfahrten** (☎ **972 61 24**), one-hour excursions through the historic heart of the city depart every half an hour in summer and every hour or so in winter, costing 9 DM ($5.30) for adults and 5 DM ($2.95) for students and children. For more information on boat trips and places of departure, contact the Berlin Tourist Information Office.

If you're in Berlin from April to the end of October, you can also climb aboard one of the many boats plying the waters of Havel and Wannsee Lakes. One of the most popular trips is from Wannsee (near the U-Bahn station) to Pfaueninsel and back, operated by **Stern and Kreisschiffahrt** (☎ **810 00 40**); the outfit also operates boats in eastside Berlin, including boat trips from Treptow to Müggelsee through Köpenick. Contact Stern and Kreisschiffahrt for exact dates and prices.

BY FOOT   If you're interested in Berlin's dark past—a subject all but ignored by other tour companies—you might wish to join one of the two guided walking tours offered in English by **Berlin Walks.** "Infamous Third Reich Sites"—offered Monday, Thursday, and Saturday at 11am—takes in the sites that once served as the nucleus of Hitler's regime, including the former location of Hitler's bunker, the headquarters of the Gestapo, Goebbels' propaganda ministry, and Speer's Reich Chancellery. "Where Was the Wall"—offered Tuesday, Friday, and Sunday at 11am—traces the former boundary of the Wall, tells of extraordinary escape attempts, shows some remaining sections of the Wall, and ends with the remarkable story of its collapse. The price of each tour, which lasts from 1½ to 2 hours, is 18 DM ($10.60) for adults and 12 DM ($7.10) for students; free for children under 15. For more information, call **211 66 63.**

6   Sports & Recreation

With approximately 6,000 sports grounds, 70 gyms, 60 indoor and outdoor public swimming pools, as well as numerous bowling alleys, tennis courts, and other facilities, Berlin offers a wide range of activities for the sports-minded visitor. If you'd rather watch than participate, check *Berlin Programm* for a day-by-day account of spectator events, from ice hockey and soccer to basketball and table tennis.

In summer both Berliners and visitors flock to **Wannsee,** site of Europe's largest lake beach. On a warm sunny day, as many as 20,000 people will take advantage of its facilities, which include a children's playground, slides, and a terrace with shops and restaurants. And if you wish you can rent one of those huge basketlike beach chairs common to northern Germany, which help shield against wind as well as sun. The beach—open May through September, daily from 7am to 8pm—costs 3.50 DM ($2.05) for adults and 2 DM ($1.20) for children. To reach it, take the S-Bahn to Nikolassee. Incidentally, don't be surprised to see topless bathing. Wannsee even has a section devoted to nude bathing.

If it's winter or you prefer swimming pools, you might try **BLUB,** Buschkrugallee 64, in Britz (☎ **606 60 60**). A huge bathing-entertainment leisure complex, it contains a pool with 3-foot-high artificial waves, a 396-foot-long water slide (Europe's longest), bathing grottoes complete with mist and music, saunas, steam baths, and a heated outdoor pool open year round. There's also a children's area, two restaurants, and a bar. Admission is 21 DM ($12.40) for adults, 18 DM ($10.60) for students, and 16 DM ($9.45) for children, with a four-hour limit. It's open daily from 10am to 11pm. The nearest U-Bahn station is Grenzallee.

If you really feel like splurging on the baths, you might wish to indulge in the hot baths and saunas of the **Thermen,** located in the Europa-Center but with its own entryway at Nürnberger Strasse 7 (☎ **261 60 32**). Open Monday through Saturday from 10am to midnight and Sunday from 10am to 9pm, it charges 27 DM ($15.95) for three hours, which includes use of a thermal swimming pool (with an outdoor rooftop lane), saunas, steam room, fitness room, TV room, table-tennis room, and a sunning terrace with 150 lounge chairs. For the ultimate, pamper yourself by buying a day ticket, which costs 32 DM ($18.90). Also available is a solarium, massage, and a restaurant. Bathing here is mixed, and in typical European style, visitors are required to go in the buff.

7

Strolling Around Berlin

Even though Berlin is a large city, most of its sights, shops, restaurants, and attractions are concentrated in specific neighborhoods, making the city easy to explore on foot.

From my experience, visitors usually prefer walking wherever possible, simply because it is sometimes easier than figuring out which bus to take and because it allows them to see some of the city en route. Natives, more likely to jump on the subway or bus, are often astounded at the great distances visitors are prepared to walk. How often have you been told by a native, "It's too far to walk," only to discover that it's actually only a 10- or 20-minute hike?

For a complete description of many of the sights and refueling stops mentioned in these tours, see Chapter 6 or Chapter 5, respectively.

Walking Tour 1
Along the Ku'damm

Start   The Europa-Center on Tauentzienstrasse.

Finish   Wittenbergplatz.

Time   Allow approximately three hours, not including stops along the way.

Best Times   Weekdays, when shops are open; or the first Saturday of the month, when shops stay open until 6pm in winter and 4pm in summer.

Worst Times   Tuesdays, when the Käthe-Kollwitz-Museum is closed, or Sundays, when all shops are closed.

The Kurfürstendamm is Berlin's most famous boulevard, home of the city's most expensive shops, hotels, restaurants, bars, and nightclubs. No visit to Berlin would be complete without at least one stroll down the Kurfürstendamm, affectionately called the Ku'damm by Berliners, who are also apt to complain about their beloved boulevard. It's too crowded with tourists, they say, and there are too many bad restaurants out to make a buck. But that doesn't stop them from coming here, especially when the weather's warm and they can sit at one of the outdoor cafés to watch the passing parade. And what a parade it is: tourists from around the world, street performers, shoppers, punks, bejeweled women. Never a dull moment on the Ku'damm.

By the way, the Ku'damm stretches $2^1/_2$ miles, but don't worry—we'll cover only the more important eastern half of it, with excursions into the most interesting side streets along the way, visiting department stores, boutiques, and several shops specializing in art deco. It's a loop stroll, ending up at nearby Wittenbergplatz, home of the largest department store on the continent, KaDeWe. Our tour begins at the:

1. **Europa-Center,** easy to spot from far away because of the Mercedes-Benz star at its top. The 22-story building contains offices, a hotel, more than 100 shops and

Walking Tour—Along the Ku'damm

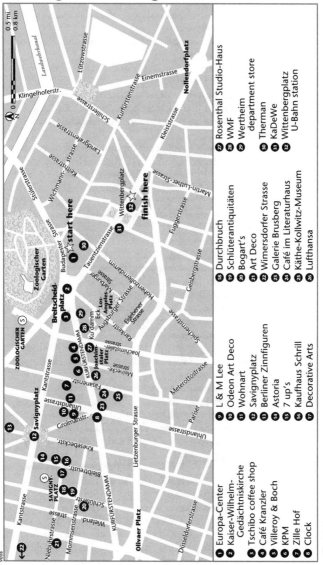

0.5 mi
0.8 km

① start here

Wittenbergplatz
finish here

Ⓢ Zoologischer Garten

Ⓢ ZOOLOGISCHER GARTEN

Ⓢ SAVIGNY-PLATZ

① Europa-Center
② Kaiser-Wilhelm-Gedächtniskirche
③ Tschibo coffee shop
④ Café Kranzler
⑤ Villeroy & Boch
⑥ KPM
⑦ Zille Hof
⑧ Clock

⑨ L & M Lee
⑩ Odeon Art Deco
⑪ Wohnart
⑫ Savignyplatz
⑬ Berliner Zinnfiguren
⑭ Astoria
⑮ 7 up's
⑯ Kaufhaus Schrill
⑰ Decorative Arts

⑱ Durchbruch
⑲ Schlüterantiquitäten
⑳ Bogart's
㉑ Art Deco
㉒ Wimersdorfer Strasse
㉓ Galerie Brusberg
㉔ Café im Literaturhaus
㉕ Käthe-Kollwitz-Museum
㉖ Lufthansa

㉗ Rosenthal Studio-Haus
㉘ WMF
㉙ Wertheim department store
㉚ Therman
㉛ KaDeWe
㉜ Wittenbergplatz U-Bahn station

Ⓢ S-Bahn stop

restaurants, a movie theater, cabarets, and a casino. In the main atrium on the ground floor is a strange-looking contraption measuring 42 feet high. It's a clock, showing the time by way of colored water passing through pipes, and is known as the Fliessenden Uhr (the "Running Clock"; get it?). Be sure to stop off at the Berlin tourist office, located in the Europa-Center but with its own separate entryway on Budapester Strasse, for maps and sightseeing brochures.

Just west of the Europa-Center is a structure that would be hard to miss: it's the:

2. **Kaiser-Wilhelm-Gedächtniskirche** on Breitscheidplatz. This ruined church looks quite out of place beside the modern high-rises that surround it. Left as a reminder of World War II, it marks the beginning of the Ku'damm.

West of the Gedächtniskirche on Breitscheidplatz is the:

3. **Tschibo coffee shop,** a popular chain where you can drink a cup of coffee for 1.95 DM ($1.15), standing up at one of the chest-high counters. Walking past Tschibo along the north side of the Ku'damm, you'll soon come to:

4. **Café Kranzler,** Ku'damm 18, one of Berlin's most famous coffee shops and a favored spot for people-watching at its sidewalk tables.

Just beyond Kranzler is:

5. **Villeroy & Boch,** Ku'damm 20, a porcelain shop with fun and exuberant contemporary patterns.

Farther down is the much more serious:

6. **KPM,** Ku'damm 26a, a shop that deals in the exquisite porcelain of the Königliche Porzellan-Manufaktur, one of Berlin's most famous products with a history dating back more than 200 years.

The next intersection is Fasanenstrasse, and if you turn right here and walk past the Bristol Kempinksi Hotel, within a minute you'll come to:

7. **Zille Hof,** Fasanenstrasse 14, a jumble of junk stalls underneath the S-Bahn tracks on the left. Who knows, you might find a treasure here among the crowded and dusty shelves laden with plates, glasses, pots and pans, books, clothing, and odds and ends. If nothing else, its entryway is worth a photograph.

Back on the Ku'damm, continue heading west to the corner of Uhlandstrasse. Here, in the median that runs in the middle of the Ku'damm, you'll notice a futuristic-looking row of lights. Believe it or not, it's a:

8. **Clock,** and here's how it works. Every light of the top row represents five hours; the lights beneath it each represent one hour; the third row stands for five minutes; and the bottom-row lights each represent one minute. If you count them all together, they'll tell you the exact time. Thus, if you had two lights on the top row, followed by one light in the next row, three lights on the third, and then two, it would be 11:17am. If you still have difficulty, consider the fact that the Berliners think this a child's game.

Refueling Stops

One of my favorite restaurants on the Ku'damm for a reasonably priced, diverse, and quick meal is **Restaurant Marché Mövenpick,** Ku'damm 14–15, a cafeteria that imitates the neighborhood market with stands offering salads, soups, pasta, daily specials, cakes, coffee, and desserts. **Café Kranzler,** Ku'damm 18, a famous coffeehouse with outdoor tables, is a favorite spot for people-watching. No less popular is **Kempinski Eck,** also with outdoor seating, located in the classy Bristol Hotel Kempinski on the corner of Fasanstrasse and Ku'damm.

Take a right onto Uhlandstrasse heading north, where immediately to your left is the first of many antiques stores on this tour (for full information on these stores, see Chapter 8):

9. **L & M Lee,** Ku'damm 32, but with an entrance on Uhlandstrasse. The store offers glassware, porcelain, silver, jewelry, lamps, and decorative objects from the Biedermeier to art deco periods.

Next to L & M Lee is:

10. **Odeon Art Deco,** Uhlandstrasse 20–25, an expensive but beautiful shop selling mint-condition lamps, mirrors, cocktail shakers, furniture, and other treasured art deco objects. Across the street is:

11. **Wohnart,** Uhlandstrasse 179–180, which displays beautifully designed contemporary furniture, lamps, cabinets, tea kettles, and other items for the home.

Return to the Ku'damm and continue walking west one more block to Knesebeckstrasse, where you should turn right. Within a five-minute walk you'll find yourself on:

12. **Savignyplatz,** a grassy square lined with restaurants, bars, and turn-of-the-century apartment buildings. This is where you'll find some of Berlin's interesting nightlife, including trendy bars and restaurants, so you might want to return here after dark.

North of Savignyplatz is the very special:

13. **Berliner Zinnfiguren,** Knesebeckstrasse 88, a small family-owned operation that has been producing and selling handcrafted pewter figurines since 1934. Of the approximately 10,000 figures for sale, the most popular are characters of Berlin, including the Potsdamer Soldat (Potsdam soldier), the Blumenfrau (flower vendor), and Frederick the Great playing a flute. They make great and inexpensive souvenirs of Berlin.

Refueling Stops

On the north end of Savignyplatz at Knesebeckstrasse 22, **Shell** is popular with young residents of the area, particularly for its international dishes, including light meals and vegetarian selections. Nearby is **San Marino,** Savignyplatz 12, an Italian pizzeria with outdoor seating in the square. If all you want is a drink, try **Zwiebelfisch,** Savignyplatz 7–8, open from noon to 6am, or **Cour Carrée,** Savignyplatz 5, recommended for its outdoor seating in the shade of spreading vines.

After your refreshments, begin from Savignyplatz's southwest corner, where you'll find the overhead tracks of the S-Bahn. Beneath the arches of the tracks are a few interesting shops, bars, and restaurants, including a boutique devoted to lamps. At the end of the passage is Bleibtreustrasse, home to a few interesting and trendy shops (see Chapter 8 for full information). You'll reach the first of these by making a right at Bleibtreustrasse, where you'll find:

14. Astoria, Bleibtreustrasse 50, which sells top-quality art deco statues, jewelry, mirrors, and some furniture and reproductions.

Retrace your steps and head south on Bleibtreustrasse, where you'll soon see on your left:

15. 7 up's, Bleibtreustrasse 48, a fun women's clothing store specializing in the creations of young Berlin designers working on commission.

Adjacent to this store is:

16. Kaufhaus Schrill, Bleibtreustrasse 46, a wacky store that sells costume jewelry, hundreds—if not thousands—of unusual ties, and clothing. There are two parts to this store, with separate entrances side by side.

Across the street, at the corner of Bleibtreustrasse and Niebuhrstrasse, is:

17. Decorative Arts, a shop that specializes mainly in glass and furniture from the Jugendstil period to the 1930s, including Thonet furniture and Gallé, Lutz, and Murano glass.

Walk west on Niebuhrstrasse for one block to Schlüterstrasse, where on the corner to your left is:

18. Durchbruch, Schlüterstrasse 54, which sells women's clothing of unusual and original German design, usually one-of-a-kind items, as well as imported French fashions.

Next door is:

19. Schlüterantiquitäten, Schlüterstrasse 53, which deals in 19th-century German antiques, including furniture and paintings.

Across the street and farther south is:

20. Bogart's, Schlüterstrasse 34, which specializes in Jugendstil and art deco lamps, chairs, tables, and desks.

Two short blocks farther west on Niebuhrstrasse brings you to Leibnizstrasse, where on the corner you'll find:

21. **Art Deco,** Leibnizstrasse 64, which sells beautifully crafted furniture, lamps, jewelry, and more, all in perfect condition.

Head north on Leibnizstrasse one block to Kantstrasse, make a left, and walk about five minutes west until you reach:

22. **Wilmersdorfer Strasse.** This is Berlin's main pedestrian shopping lane, where in quick succession you'll find such large department stores as Karstadt and Hertie. There are also a number of smaller shops and boutiques, as well as several restaurants. If you're tired or decide to spend the rest of the day shopping, you can return to your hotel by taking the subway from Wilmersdorfer Strasse station. Otherwise, head back down to the Ku'damm.

Refueling Stops

For a quick standup meal, try **Joseph Langer,** Wilmersdorfer Strasse 118, a butcher shop that also sells simple meals and Würste. Across the street is **Nordsee,** Wilmersdorfer Strasse 58, a fast-food fish restaurant. If you prefer a slightly more relaxed environment, head to **Udagawa Japan Imbiss,** Kantstrasse 118, an informal, reasonably priced Japanese restaurant serving everything from teriyaki to stews and tempura. Another good choice is **Athener Grill,** Ku'damm 156, near Adenauerplatz. This cafeteria sells both Greek and Italian food, from moussaka to pizza; next door is **Ciao Ciao,** an Italian restaurant with outdoor seating. A popular watering hole in the area is **New York,** Olivaer Platz 15, where Berlin's trendy youth gather.

Walking back in the direction of the Gedächtniskirche, this time on the south side of the Ku'damm, you'll again pass a number of shops. This, after all, is Berlin's classiest shopping street. Note the many freestanding display cases along the sidewalk, advertising the wares of nearby shops. If it were evening, you'd notice wares of a different sort being offered, since the Ku'damm has long been a favored spot for the ladies of the night (prostitution, by the way, is legal in Germany).

After a 10-minute walk on the Ku'damm, you'll reach:

23. **Galerie Brusberg,** located near Uhlandstrasse at Ku'damm 213. The gallery, up on the first floor, represents such famous names as Salvador Dalí, Bernhard Dörries, Max Ernst, Joan Miró, and Pablo Picasso, as well as lesser-known artists. Entry is free, so it's worth a spin through to see the latest exhibit.

One block past the gallery is Fasanstrasse, where you should turn right. This is a wonderful street that's lined with turn-of-the-century villas embellished with graceful, ornate facades. On your right you'll see:

24. **Café im Literaturhaus,** Fasanstrasse 24. On the ground floor is an interesting bookstore specializing in biographies of writers and artists and novels in German; upstairs is a wonderful coffeeshop. Just past this building is one of my favorite Berlin museums, the:

25. **Käthe-Kollwitz-Museum,** Fasanstrasse. A Berliner, Kollwitz was a genius in capturing human emotions in her powerful portraits of the people around her. She certainly deserves more worldwide recognition for her works.

Return to the Ku'damm and make a right, passing the offices of:

26. **Lufthansa,** Ku'damm 220, where you can confirm a flight if you're booked on that German airline.

Nearby is:

27. **Rosenthal Studio-Haus,** Ku'damm 226, which sells porcelain, Boda crystal, Rosenthal porcelain, and kitchenware. Ordinary and not-so-ordinary cookware and tableware are featured at:

28. **WMF,** Ku'damm 229, a well-known chain throughout Germany. Next door is:

29. **Wertheim department store,** Ku'damm 231, convenient for stocking up on sundry items, film, or a souvenir of Berlin.

Refueling Stops

In the **basement of Wertheim department store,** next to the food department, is an informal cafeteria with various counters devoted to different foods, from salads and stews to chicken and beer. If you need caffeine, retrace your steps to **Café im Literaturhaus,** Fasanstrasse 23, a refined oasis where you can linger over a cup of coffee in its outside garden or, in winter, in its greenhouse. Another coffeehouse is **Leysieffer,** Ku'damm 218, popular for its chocolates and its upstairs cafe, where you can indulge in a slice of fabulous cake or another dessert. For something a bit stronger than coffee, you might try Berlin's **Hard Rock Café,** located just off the Ku'damm at Meinekestrasse 21. Quieter and more reasonably priced is **Eierschale,** Rankestrasse 1, around the corner from Wertheim. It's a popular bar with live jazz in the evenings.

Where the Ku'damm ends, Tauentzienstrasse runs from the Europa-Center to Wittenbergplatz. At the start of Tauentzienstrasse, right beside the Europa-Center, is Nürnbergstrasse, where at no. 7 is the entrance to:

30. Thermen, a deluxe bathing spa with a thermal pool, saunas, a steam room, and more. In European style, visitors are required to make the rounds au naturel. Back on Tauentzienstrasse and heading away from the Europa-Center, you'll pass one clothing boutique after the other. Prices are cheap and the styles young and fun, and since most are open-fronted shops it may be difficult to resist giving the sales racks a once-over. If you don't succumb, however, within minutes you'll find yourself at Wittenbergplatz, home of:

31. Kaufhaus des Westens, popularly called **KaDeWe.** It's the star of this walk, and not to be missed is its huge food department up on the sixth floor. It makes American grocery stores look like dime stores, so complete and lavish are its shelves of gourmet foods. There are more than 1,000 kinds of sausages alone. A true culinary adventure.

Finally, on Wittenbergplatz is the:

32. Wittenbergplatz U-Bahn station, one of Berlin's most beautiful stations, with art nouveau grillwork and oak ticket booths. In the station you'll find an odd electromechanical scale, one of 55 such mechanical treasures dating from the 1920s still in operation in Berlin's subways. It's on Bahnsteig (platform) I, down the escalator (you need a valid subway ticket to enter the platform). After all the German food you've been enjoying you might not want to do this, but by inserting a 10-pfennig coin and stepping onto the weighing platform, you'll receive a card printed with your weight in kilos and the date.

Final Refueling Stops

The **KaDeWe's food emporium** on the sixth floor is also a good place to eat. Spread throughout are separate counters with stools, each specializing in a different food or drink. Choose from counters selling salads, pastas, potato dishes, grilled chicken, wines, and much more. If you wish, you can order take-out and eat your goodies on one of the benches on Wittenbergplatz. Another good place for take-out food, especially if you're vegetarian, is **Einhorn,** Wittenbergplatz 5–6, located at the opposite end of the square from KaDeWe. A natural foods shop, it also offers daily specials ranging from vegetarian lasagne or spinach casserole to vegetarian moussaka.

For finer dining, head for Ming's Garden, Tauentzienstrasse 16, an upscale Chinese restaurant across from the Europa-Center with an entrance on Marburger Strasse. For a variety of food, try the Europa-Center's **Mövenpick,** which is divided into sections selling pizza, salads, German food, and drinks.

Walking Tour 2
Tiergarten Park

Start   Bahnhof Zoo.

Finish   Reichstag building.

Time   Allow approximately two hours, not including stops along the way.

Best Times   Saturdays and Sundays, when the market on Strasse des 17. Juni takes place.

Worst Times   There are no bad days for this tour, unless the weather's bad.

Take this stroll when you're tired of museums and want to spend the day outdoors. It takes you through the Tiergarten park all the way to the Brandenburger Tor (Brandenburg Gate), with several interesting stops along the way. If you really want to make an outing of it, pack a picnic lunch. There aren't many possibilities for refreshment on this walk.

Across from Bahnhof Zoo, Berlin's main train station, and the square from which buses depart is the main entrance to the:

1. **Zoologischer Garten,** Hardenbergplatz 8. Opened in 1844, this is Germany's oldest zoo and is beautifully designed, with ponds, streams, willows and lofty trees, and thatched cottages and timber-frame structures housing animals. Altogether, the zoo is home to more than 14,000 animals—and to think this oasis exists right in the city center.

   Leave the zoo from the same door you entered, turning right on Hardenbergplatz and walking north parallel to the zoo and main tracks. Actually, you can see some of the zoo's occupants from here, including the rhino, elephants, camels, and domestic animals in the children's petting zoo. Soon you'll leave the zoo and tracks behind you as you enter the grounds of the:

2. **Tiergarten,** Berlin's largest park, stretching approximately 1.9 miles from Bahnhof Zoo all the way to the Branden-burger Tor. Originally the private hunting grounds of Prussian royalty, it was heavily damaged during World War II and suffered further damage in the cold winters that followed when Berliners chopped down its trees for fuel. Today the ponds, wide grassy meadows, and wooded areas look like they've been here forever.

   Keep heading north, walking over a bridge spanning a canal and passing a pond that will appear on your right. Approximately 10 minutes after leaving the grounds of the zoo, you'll come to a wide, busy thoroughfare, Strasse des 17. Juni. If it's a weekend, turn left and head straight for the:

3. **Grosser Berliner Trödelmarkt mit Kunstmarkt,** the flea market near Tiergarten station (you can see the market from the station's platform) on Strasse des 17. Juni. This is one of my favorite places to shop in all of Berlin, not only because of all the antiques but also because of the crafts section, where young people sell jewelry, drawings, clothing, and other things they've made. I've picked up some great gifts here for friends back home. The crafts section is separated from the antiques stalls by a bridge and a large stone gate—don't miss it.

Refueling Stops

There are a number of **food stalls** (called *Imbisse*) mixed in with the antiques at the market on Strasse des 17. Juni, where you can eat everything from sausage and french fries to Turkish pizza and beer. If you'd rather sit down (exhausted from all that shopping), backtrack under the elevated platform of the S-Bahn station, where on the east side you'll find a small white building called the **Berlin Pavilion** on Strasse des 17. Juni. There's a small cafe and restaurant here, with tables outside in summer. Another good thing to know is that there are toilet facilities.

If you take this tour on a weekday when there's no market, head east on Strasse des 17. Juni (east is easy—simply walk in the direction of that huge column rising from the middle of the street in the distance). Almost immediately to your left, past the Berlin Pavilion, is a street called Klopstock. Turn left on Klopstock, where you'll soon find yourself in the midst of the:

4. **Hansaviertel (Hansa Quarter).** This area was developed in the late 1950s during a competition in which 48 architects from more than 12 countries participated—with each architect designing one building in his own style. Most are apartments, since Berlin was still suffering from a housing crunch after World War II. At any rate, on your right as you walk north on Klopstock you'll see a map of the area, keyed to the various buildings and their designers. Building 22 by Alvar Aalto, by the way, won the competition. A blue, green, and white apartment house, it will be to your right as you continue walking north on Klopstock.

Within minutes after passing the Aalto building, you'll reach Hansaplatz. Take a right onto Altonaer Strasse, which brings you back to Strasse des 17. Juni, where you'll see that column again. Within a few minutes you will find yourself back on Strasse des 17. Juni, at a huge roundabout called:

5. **Grosser Stern** ("Great Star," because of the many roads leading away from it). Note the beautiful gas lamps

surrounding the Grosser Stern. Berlin still has 40,000 gas lamps, as well as 100 full-time employees whose job it is to clean them and make sure they're still burning. In the middle of the traffic circle is a huge column, called the:

6. **Siegessäule (Victory Column).** Erected in the 1870s, it commemorates three victorious wars—against Denmark in 1864, against Austria in 1866, and against France in 1870–71. More than 220 feet high, it's topped by a gilded goddess of victory. In good weather, visitors can climb the 290 steps of a spiral staircase to an observation platform 157 feet high, from where they are rewarded with views of the city.

From the Grosser Stern and its Siegessäule, continue walking east on Strasse des 17. Juni in the direction of the Brandenburger Tor, which you can see far in the distance. Rather than walk along the boulevard, I suggest you enter the park at your right and take one of the paths there to the gate. You might even wish to stop somewhere here for a picnic.

As you walk through the park, you might be able to glimpse a couple of buildings through the trees on your left (depending how leafy the trees are). First is the:

7. **Kongresshalle,** built in 1957 by American Hugh A. Stubbins as part of the Hansaviertel architectural competition (and rebuilt in 1980 when part of the roof caved in). Berliners have nicknamed it the "Pregnant Oyster" because of its form. Beside the Kongresshalle is a:

8. **Carillon.** Europe's largest, it's more than 130 feet tall and contains 68 bells that have a range of $5^1/2$ octaves. The carillon is played twice daily, at noon and 6pm, for five minutes.

If you don't stop along the way, it takes about 20 minutes to walk from the Siegessäule to the Brandenburger Tor. Just before reaching the gate, you'll see the:

9. **Sowjetisches Ehrenmal (Soviet Memorial)** to your left on Strasse des 17. Juni. Constructed of marble from Hitler's chancellery, it was erected after World War II as a memorial to the 20,000 Soviet soldiers who lost their lives in the war.

And here we are at the:

10. **Brandenburger Tor.** Built by Carl Gotthard Langhans from 1788 to 1791 as the west entrance onto Under den Linden, it is topped by the famous Quadriga created by Johann Gottfried Schadow and consisting of the goddess of peace in a chariot pulled by four steeds; the Quadriga was severely damaged in World War II but has since been restored. After the Wall went up in 1961, the Brandenburger Tor became inaccessible from West Berlin, making it a symbol of a divided Berlin. After the November

Walking Tour—Tiergarten Park

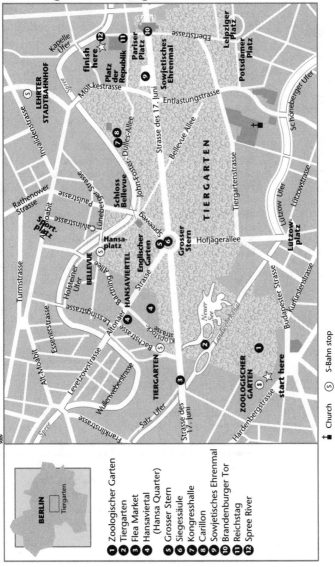

BERLIN
Tiergarten

1. Zoologischer Garten
2. Tiergarten
3. Flea Market
4. Hansaviertel (Hansa Quarter)
5. Grosser Stern
6. Siegessäule
7. Kongresshalle
8. Carillon
9. Sowjetisches Ehrenmal
10. Brandenburger Tor
11. Reichstag
12. Spree River

† Church   Ⓢ S-Bahn stop

1989 revolution, it was here that many Berliners, from both
East and West, gathered to rejoice and dance together on
top of the Wall. I myself witnessed part of the celebration
in the months that followed, as people from around the
world chiseled at the Wall for a piece of history. At the end
of February 1990, the East German government began
tearing down the Wall in anticipation of a united Germany.

Finally, for the first time in decades, people could pass freely from Strasse des 17. Juni past the Brandenburger Tor to Unter den Linden in East Berlin. Today the Brandenburger Tor continues to attract a steady stream of visitors to Berlin, as well as vendors from former eastern European countries selling souvenir pieces of the Wall, Russian watches, dolls, postcards, helmets, and military insignia.

To the left of the Brandenburger Tor is a large, solemn-looking building, the:

11. **Reichstag (Parliament).** Completed in 1894 in neo-Renaissance style to serve the needs of Bismarck's united Germany, the building had its darkest hour on the night of February 17, 1933, when a mysterious fire broke out. The Nazi government blamed the German Communist Party for setting the flame and used the incident as an excuse to arrest Communist party members and other enemies of the Nazis and to abolish such basic democratic rights as freedom of the press. Damaged in World War II, the Reichstag was restored with the exception of its dome. Since 1971, part of it has been used for an exhibition called "Fragen an die deutsche Geschichte" (Questions Concerning German History), with displays relating to German history from 1800 to the Cold War. Earphones with a cassette recording in English are available for rent to guide visitors through the displays. Note that the Reichstag is closed to the public when the German parliament is in session. The German parliament had its first joint session here (both East and West) on October 4, 1990, after more than four decades of separation.

Behind the northeast corner of the Reichstag is the:

12. **Spree River.** It once formed part of the border between the two Berlins. East German soldiers, armed with guns and binoculars, used to keep watch from a guard tower here, a sight that always caused me anxiety even though I was on the lucky side of the Wall. There is a row of white crosses here in remembrance of the people who lost their lives as they attempted to flee to the West.

At the south end of the Reichstag is a bus stop; bus 100 goes back to Bahnhof Zoo or Alexanderplatz.

Final Refueling Stops

There are several possibilities for a light meal or snack in the **Reichstag** building, all near the north entryway. The Cafeteria serves one-pot stews (Eintöpfe), Gulaschsuppe, Wurst, coffee, beer, and soft drinks. The Café-Stube is a self-service café offering coffee, tortes, and other desserts, while the Restaurant is for sit-down waitress service and features German food.

Walking Tour 3
Berlin-Mitte (Eastern Berlin)

Start   Friedrichstrasse S-Bahn Station.

Finish   Nikolaiviertel.

Time   Allow approximately two hours, not including stops along the way.

Best Times   Weekdays, when museums aren't as crowded, or Sunday, when they're free.

Worst Times   Mondays and Tuesdays, when some museums are closed.

This stroll brings you through what used to be the heart of old Berlin before World War II, later serving as East Germany's capital. From the historic boulevard Unter den Linden, you'll pass Museumsinsel (Museum Island), home of some of Berlin's great museums, and end your tour at the Nikolaiviertel (Nikolai Quarter), a restored neighborhood of restaurants and pubs.

The tour starts after you exit from the Friedrichstrasse S-Bahn station, where to the east underneath the arches of the elevated train tracks on Georgenstrasse is the:

1. **Berliner Antik- und Flohmarkt (Berlin Antique and Flea Market).** Here about 60 vendors sell everything from glassware and lamps to porcelain, jewelry, clothing, books, pocketwatches, canes, toys, and odds and ends. Prices aren't cheap, but it's fun walking through; the market is open Wednesday through Monday from 11am to 6pm. Here, too, is the:

2. **Heinrich-Zille-Museum,** featuring drawings and personal items of one of Berlin's most well known and beloved graphic artists and caricaturists. A chronicler of turn-of-the-century Berlin, Zille is particularly known for his sketches of the poor and working class, who he depicted with compassionate humor.

   After visiting the market, walk south on Friedrichstrasse a couple of minutes until you come to:

3. **Unter den Linden,** once Berlin's most fashionable and liveliest boulevard. Its history stretches back several centuries, when the Elector passed this way on his journey to the Tiergarten to hunt. By 1675 it was a paved road, and in the centuries that followed it served as the lifeline of old Berlin. In fact, prior to World War II, Berlin's busiest intersection was right here at Friedrichstrasse and Unter den Linden, and on a corner of the intersection was the famous Café Kranzler (now on the Ku'damm). Today, after decades of amputation by the Wall at the Brandenburger Tor, Unter den Linden is once again a lively and crowded thoroughfare—indeed, you risk your life trying to cross it (hopefully, more crosswalks will be constructed). To the

west is a view of Brandenburger Tor, topped by the Quadriga; Unter den Linden stretches $7/10$ of a mile, from Brandenburger Tor to the Schlossbrücke.

Take a left onto Unter den Linden, shaded with lime trees (Unter den Linden means "under the lime trees"), and walk one block east to Charlottenstrasse, where you should take a right. After three short blocks you'll find yourself at the historic:

4. **Gendarmenmarkt,** once considered one of Berlin's most attractive squares and formerly the site of the city's main market. Totally destroyed during World War II, it has been painstakingly restored and features three neoclassical buildings. Most important is the Schauspielhaus, designed by Karl Friedrich Schinkel in 1821 and now a concert house flanked by the German and French cathedrals.

   Return to Unter den Linden via Charlottenstrasse and turn right; you'll immediately pass the neobaroque:

5. **Deutsche Staatsbibliothek** (National Library; formerly Prussian State Library), containing over 5 million volumes, and the neoclassical:

6. **Humboldt-Universität** (Humboldt University), where Hegel, Marx, and the Brothers Grimm taught. In the median in front of the university is an:

7. **Equestrian statue of Frederick the Great.** Just past the statue, to your right, is a square called:

8. **Bebelplatz,** dominated by St.-Hedwigs-Kathedrale. On May 10, 1933, the Nazis staged on this square a massive burning of books deemed offensive to the regime, including works by Thomas Mann, Sigmund Freud, and Albert Einstein. At the east end of Bebelplatz is the:

9. **Staatsoper Unter den Linden,** designed by Georg Wenzeslaus von Knobelsdorff in the 1740s and rebuilt after the war. Today it serves as a venue for opera, ballet, and concerts. Next on Unter den Linden, to your left, is the:

10. **Neue Wache (New Guardhouse).** Easy to spot with its columns resembling those of a Greek temple, it was built from 1816 to 1818 according to plans designed by architect Karl Friedrich Schinkel. In 1931 it became a memorial to German soldiers killed in World War II; in 1960 it became a memorial to victims of fascism and militarism, with an eternal flame burning for the Unknown Soldier and Unknown Resistance Fighter. Its purpose was changed once again in 1993, when it became Germany's primary memorial for all victims of war and totalitarianism. The eternal flame lit by the East German communists was extinguished forever, and in its place is a life-sized version of Käthe Kollwitz's sculpture *Mother with Dead Son.*

    Beside the Neue Wache is the:

Walking Tour—Eastern Berlin

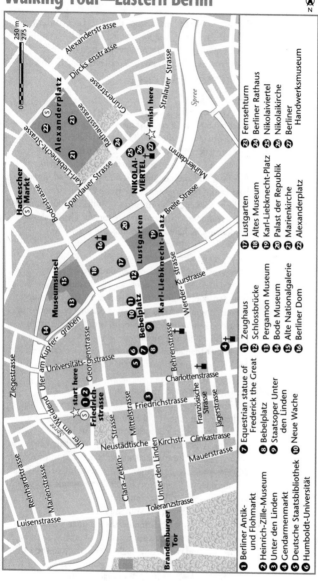

⊛ N

1 Berliner Antik- und Flohmarkt
2 Heinrich-Zille-Museum
3 Unter den Linden
4 Gendarmenmarkt
5 Deutsche Staatsbibliothek
6 Humboldt-Universität

7 Equestrian statue of Frederick the Great
8 Bebelplatz
9 Staatsoper Unter den Linden
10 Neue Wache

11 Zeughaus
12 Schlossbrücke
13 Pergamon Museum
14 Bode Museum
15 Alte Nationalgalerie
16 Berliner Dom

17 Lustgarten
18 Altes Museum
19 Karl-Liebknecht-Platz
20 Palast der Republik
21 Marienkirche
22 Alexanderplatz

23 Fernsehturm
24 Berliner Rathaus
25 Nikolaiviertel
26 Nikolaikirche
27 Berliner Handwerksmuseum

✝ Church   Ⓢ S-Bahn stop

11. **Zeughaus (Arsenal),** Unter den Linden 2. Built in the
    17th century as an arsenal for the Prussian army, it—
    together with the Charlottenburg Palace—is considered a
    pinnacle of baroque construction in Berlin. Of special note
    are the 22 sculpted masks of dying warriors by Andreas

Schlüter above the windows of the inner courtyard. After World War II, the Zeughaus served as East Berlin's Museum of German History, presenting a decidedly socialist view. Today it holds special changing exhibitions relating to German history.

A Refueling Stop

The **Opernpalais,** Unter den Linden 5, is one of Berlin's most famous eating establishments. Occupying part of a palace originally built in 1733 and faithfully restored after its destruction in World War II, it features several restaurants, including an expensive dining hall up on the first floor and a restaurant specializing in seafood in the basement. On the ground floor is the Operncafé, a coffeehouse famous for its tortes—it offers indoor dining as well as outdoor seating in a pretty square. There's also an outdoor *Imbiss* here serving drinks and snacks.

Unter den Linden terminates at:

12. Schlossbrücke (Palace Bridge), designed by Schinkel. Its eight statues, also by Schinkel, are goddesses and warriors from Greek mythology. At the eastern base of the bridge, to the left, is one of several companies offering one-hour sightseeing tours of Berlin by boat, with boats departing every half an hour in summer.

Rather than crossing Schlossbrücke, however, take a left on Am Zeughaus and walk to the second bridge. This is the entrance to the:

13. Pergamon Museum, the most important and famous museum on Museumsinsel, developed through the 19th and early 20th centuries as a museum complex meant to rival those of other European capitals. The Pergamon Museum is its crowning achievement. Essentially a museum of architectural wonders, it's named after its most prized treasure, the Pergamon Altar, dating from 160 to 180 B.C. It also contains Asian, Near Eastern, and Islamic art, as well as German folk art. Don't miss it.

Beside the Pergamon Museum is the:

14. Bode Museum, which contains the Egyptian Museum, the Early Christian and Byzantine Collection, the Sculpture Collection, and the Picture Gallery with art from the 14th to the 18th century. Behind the Pergamon is the:

15. Alte Nationalgalerie (Old National Gallery), which features art from the 19th and 20th centuries.

From the Nationalgalerie, walk south on Museumsinsel in the direction of the huge church. That's the:

16. Berliner Dom (Berlin Cathedral), erected at the turn of the century in Italian Renaissance style to serve as the court church of the Hohenzollerns. After decades of restoration following massive World War II destruction, it reopened in 1994 and contains the tombs of Queen Sophie Charlotte and her husband, Friedrich I, both designed by Andreas Schlüter. The cathedral faces a tree-lined square called the:

17. Lustgarten (Pleasure Garden), once the site of the royal botanical garden but paved by the Nazis for parades and rallies. Also facing the Lustgarten is the:

18. Altes Museum (Old Museum), which stages changing exhibitions devoted to art and objects of ancient times. Built from plans by Schinkel, it features 18 Ionic columns and resembles a Greek temple. Incidentally, behind the Altes Museum is the Neues Museum (New Museum), which has supposedly been "under restoration" for decades but has shown little signs of change. East Berliners have always joked that at the present rate of progress, restoration wouldn't be complete until well into the 21st century—if at all. Now that Berlin is united, maybe money for restoration will be made available at last.

Refueling Stops

The area around Museumsinsel used to be a culinary wasteland, but that has slowly changed thanks to the progress of capitalism. Just a minute's walk west of the Pergamon Museum is **Lucky Strike,** Georgenstrasse 5, underneath the arches of the elevated S-Bahn tracks. American-owned and decorated like an American diner, it features American food ranging from burgers, sandwiches, and gumbo for lunch to red snapper, barbecue spareribs, steaks, and stewed rabbit for dinner. On the opposite end of Museumsinsel, behind the Berliner Dom across the Spree River, is the popular **T.G.I. Fridays,** Karl-Liebknecht-Strasse 5, an American chain serving a wide variety of American favorites, including potato skins, Mexican pizza, fettucine Alfredo, baby-back ribs, blackened chicken, burgers, sandwiches, and salads. A plus is the outdoor dining in summer—or perhaps it's the 400 or so cocktails offered by the restaurant's bar.

Opposite the Lustgarten is the:

19. Karl-Liebknecht-Platz (formerly Marx-Engels-Platz), a huge square lined with drab socialist architecture. The most conspicuous building here is the:

20. Palast der Republik (Palace of the Republic), once popular in East Berlin for its various concert halls and restaurants. Insulated with asbestos, it is now closed, its future undecided. It occupies the former site of Berlin's royal palace, once the largest baroque structure north of the Alps. Although what remained after World War II could have been salvaged, the Politbüro dynamited it in 1950 as a symbol of "Prussian imperialism."

With the Lustgarten on your left and the Palast der Republik on your right, walk past the Berliner Dom, cross the Spree River, and continue down Karl-Liebknecht-Strasse. After crossing Spandauer Strasse, you'll see a small brick church on your right, looking rather out of place with the huge Fernsehturm (Television Tower) behind it. This is the:

21. **Marienkirche (Church of St. Mary),** the second-oldest church in Berlin. First constructed in the 13th century and then added to through the centuries, it's noted for its marble baroque pulpit by Andreas Schlüter. Note, too, its *Dance of Death* mural in its tower hall at the back of the church; painted in the 15th century, the mural was subsequently covered up and wasn't rediscovered until 1860. The church is open Monday through Thursday from 10am to noon and 1 to 4pm and Saturday from noon to 4pm.

Behind the church sprawls:

22. **Alexanderplatz.** Named after Czar Alexander I, it served as an oxen market and a military exercise field in Berlin's early days, later becoming the center of East Berlin during the decades of Communist rule. Future plans call for the construction of a huge office-and-shopping complex, complete with 40-story skyscrapers. In the meantime, its landmark building is the:

23. **Fernsehturm,** a 1,200-foot-high tower containing an observation platform and a revolving restaurant. Before the Wall fell, of course, this was one of the few opportunities East Germans had for a glimpse of the West. But even a reunited Germany has not dimmed its popularity—the views from here are stupendous. If you're tired, you can take the S-Bahn from Alexanderplatz to Bahnhof Zoo and beyond.

A Refueling Stop

The **Tele-Café,** a revolving cafe 650 feet above ground in the Fernsehturm, is a great—though slightly expensive—place for a snack. Making a complete turn every hour, it offers unparalleled views of Berlin and a limited menu of coffee, cakes, ice cream, beer, wine, and warm and cold dishes.

At the southwestern end of Alexanderplatz, on the corner of Rathausstrasse and Spandauer Strasse, is an imposing red-brick building topped with a tower. This is the:

24. **Berliner Rathaus (City Hall),** which served as the seat of Berlin's municipal administration after its construction in the 1860s. Since reunification, it has become the home of the entire Berlin central government. Because of its red color, it is also called the Rote Rathaus (Red City Hall). Note the frieze around the entire building—it's a stone chronicle of the history of Berlin.

Walk past the Rathaus heading east, cross Spandauer Strasse, and to your left you'll see a small side street leading to church spires. This is the beginning of the:

25. Nikolaiviertel (Nikolai Quarter), a re-created neighborhood of Berlin as it was centuries ago. In the center is the:

26. Nikolaikirche (St. Nicholas's Church), regarded as Berlin's oldest church even though it was destroyed during World War II and was largely rebuilt. Its history dates back to 1230, but the style of the church changed several times in the following centuries. The buildings you see around the church are all new, but many were built according to plans of earlier buildings that existed elsewhere.

Facing the church, walk around it to the right and you'll see several shops selling handcrafted items. Take the first right (behind the church), which brings you to a busy street called Mühlendamm. Here, at Mühlendamm 5, you'll find the:

27. Berliner Handwerksmuseum (Berlin Crafts Museum), a tiny museum that features changing exhibitions of items produced in Berlin in the past, from pottery to hats and jewelry. It's open Tuesday through Friday from 9am to 5pm, Saturday from 9am to 6pm, and Sunday from 10am to 5pm.

Since the Nikolaiviertel is small and consists largely of apartment houses and bars, explore it at your leisure, stopping off for a beer or meal at one of the places below.

Final Refueling Stops

Among the best-known Gaststätten in the Nikolaiviertel are **Zum Nussbaum,** Am Nussbaum 3, modeled after a 16th-century pub, and **GeorgBrau,** Spree Ufer 4, a microbrewery beside the Spree River with outdoor seating. For more substantial dining, head for **Reinhard's,** Poststrasse 28, an American-style bistro featuring an international menu popular with Berlin's business set.

8

Berlin Shopping

Sʜᴏᴘᴘɪɴɢ ʜᴀꜱ ᴀʟᴡᴀʏꜱ ʙᴇᴇɴ ᴀɴ ɪɴᴛᴇɢʀᴀʟ ᴘᴀʀᴛ ᴏꜰ ᴛʜᴇ Bᴇʀʟɪɴ ꜱᴄᴇɴᴇ. After all, the city's most famous and liveliest boulevard, the Ku'damm, is also its main shopping street. Add to that a myriad of markets, department stores, specialty shops, art galleries, and antiques shops, and it soon becomes clear that Berlin has just about everything anyone could possibly want. In fact, there's a saying that if it exists, it's available in Berlin. Just one trip through the KaDeWe department store made a believer of me.

1   The Shopping Scene

In case you haven't noticed, Germany is not a shopper's paradise in terms of cut-rate bargains. You won't find overwhelmingly cheaper prices here for German-made goods, primarily because the dollar is not as strong as it once was. In addition, Germany is one of the more expensive countries of Europe, far more expensive than countries to the south.

However, you will find a greater variety of European goods here than you would back home, including clothing, kitchenware, antiques, and artwork. Only you can judge whether your purchase is a true bargain, especially if it's a one-of-a-kind print or an antique. If you do plan on making a major purchase, be sure to comparison-shop before leaving home. It may not be worth it to buy that German comforter and pay the expense of shipping it home, only to find you've saved all of $5 for your efforts.

MAIN SHOPPING STREETS   Berlin and the **Kurfürstendamm** are synonymous. Two and a half miles long, the Kurfürstendamm, called Ku'damm by the locals, is the city's showcase—quite literally. Up and down its sidewalks you'll see freestanding display cases containing goods from the surrounding stores, just a little something to whet your appetite. There are boutiques and shops here selling clothing, accessories, porcelain, kitchenware, eyeglasses, and art. But don't neglect the side streets, since they're a virtual treasure trove of antiques shops, bookstores, and more clothing stores and art galleries. The area north of the Ku'damm along **Bleibtreustrasse, Schlüterstrasse,** and **Leibnizstrasse,** for example, has several stores specializing in art deco. **Tauentzienstrasse** is good for inexpensive and fun fashions.

The other big name in shopping streets is **Wilmersdorfer Strasse,** a pedestrians-only lane lined with department stores, boutiques, and restaurants. This is where the locals come to shop, both for essentials and such nonessential essentials as yet another skirt. Since there is a large concentration of stores here, you can cover a lot of ground in a short amount of time—simply take the U-Bahn to Wilmersdorfer Strasse.

HOURS, TAXES & SHIPPING   Most shops and businesses are open Monday through Friday from 9 or 10am to 6 or 6:30pm and Saturday from 9am to 2pm. On the first Saturday of the month (called *langer Samstag*), shops remain open until 6pm in winter (October through March) and 4pm in summer (April through September). In addition, some shops remain open longer on Thursday, until 8:30pm. Note, however, that some of the smaller establishments, especially art galleries and antiques shops, are open only in the afternoons. Be sure to check individual listings, therefore, to avoid disappointment.

If you purchase more than 60 DM ($35.40) worth of goods from any one store, you or not a resident of an EU (European Union) country, and you're taking your purchases out of the country, you're entitled to a recovery of the value-added tax (VAT), in German, *Mehrwertsteuer,* which is 15% in Germany. Note, however, that you will not receive the total 15% refund. Rather, depending on the item you purchase, you will receive a refund of 6% to 10% of the purchase price. If you've purchased an object of considerable worth, even that can add up to a saving (note that items purchased may not be used before departure). When shopping, look for shops with the Tax-Free sticker.

In any case, the procedure for obtaining the VAT refund is the same. All department stores and most major shops will issue a Tax-Free Cheque at the time of your purchase. Simply fill in the reverse side of the cheque and, upon leaving Germany, present the Tax-Free Cheque, the receipt from the store, and the purchased goods to the German Customs official, who will stamp your cheque. If you're leaving Germany from Berlin's Tegel Airport, you can receive your cash refund immediately at the Berliner Bank counter in the Main Hall. In Frankfurt, you can receive an immediate refund at the International Departure Hall B Transit. Remember to show your purchases to the Customs officials before checking your luggage, unless you are hand-carrying your purchase. If you're leaving Germany by train, ask the Customs official who comes into your train to stamp your cheque.

You may wish to ship your purchases home, especially if you've gone overboard and can no longer carry everything with a reasonable semblance of dignity. Most shops used to dealing with tourists will ship your purchases home, which may be the easiest route to take. Your Tax-Free Cheque will indicate that the goods have already left the country; in some cases, you may even receive an immediate refund of the VAT at the store.

If you wish to send home a package yourself, you can do so at all major post offices. All you have to do is show up with your goods, since post offices sell boxes complete with string and tape. Boxes come in five sizes and range in price from 2.90 DM ($1.70) to 5.50 DM ($3.25). If you're sending a purchase for which you are entitled to a VAT refund, be sure to have an official at the post office stamp your Tax-Free Cheque (which you can then later present at the airport for an immediate refund).

Shopping Along the Ku'damm

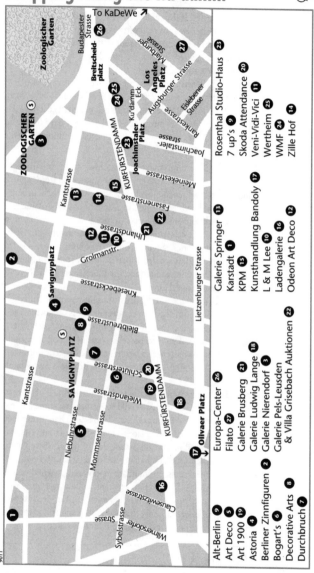

Alt-Berlin	⑨
Art Deco	⑤
Art 1900	⑲
Astoria	⑪
Berliner Zinnfiguren	②
Bogart's	⑥
Decorative Arts	⑧
Durchbruch	⑦
Europa-Center	㉖
Filato	㉗
Galerie Brusberg	㉑
Galerie Ludwig Lange	⑱
Galerie Nierendorf	③
Galerie Pels-Leusden & Villa Grisebach Auktionen	㉒
Galerie Springer	⑬
Karstadt	①
KPM	⑮
Kunsthandlung Bandoly	⑰
L & M Lee	⑩
Ladengalerie	⑯
Odeon Art Deco	⑫
Rosenthal Studio-Haus	㉓
7 up's	⑨
Skoda Attendance	⑳
Veni-Vidi-Vici	⑪
Wertheim	㉕
WMF	㉔
Zille Hof	⑭
S-Bahn stop	Ⓢ

Keep in mind, however, that there is a limit to the duty-free goods you can bring back with you to the United States. If you're sending a package, it will automatically go to customs upon arrival in the United States. If the total value of goods acquired abroad is less than $50, the package is sent on to the post office and is delivered to you by your mail carrier. If the value is more than $50, the amount you owe will be collected by your mail carrier upon delivery of your package. Note that it is illegal to mail liquor to the United States. Bringing meat into the United States is also prohibited—which is a shame, considering all that wonderful German sausage.

As for hand-carried items, you are allowed to bring back free of duty $400 worth of personal and household goods obtained abroad. Anything above this $400 personal exemption is charged a flat 10% on the next $1,000. That means the most you will have to pay on purchases valued at $1,400 (your $400 personal exemption plus the next $1,000) is only $100.

BEST BUYS   If souvenirs make your heart beat faster, you'll delight in Berlin's stuffed toy bears (the city mascot), porcelain freedom bells (fashioned after the Freedom Bell hanging in Rathaus Schöneberg), and ashtrays and bowls picturing the Brandenburger Tor. Sidewalk vendors sell such souvenirs as pieces of the Wall (some enclosed in acrylic or plastic), East German and Russian military insignia, hats, watches, and accessories ranging from hair ribbons and jewelry to toys. You'll find vendors wherever there's a steady stream of tourists, including the Ku'damm and around the Brandenburger Tor.

If kitsch doesn't appeal to you, Germany is also known for kitchen gadgets and cutlery, beautiful linens, those luxuriously fluffy *Federbetten* (literally feather beds, or down comforters), binoculars and telescopes, cameras, and toys (including model trains, tin soldiers, and building blocks). If you like porcelain, brands to look for include Rosenthal, antique Meissen, and Berlin's own Königliche Porzellan-Manufaktur—assuming, of course, that you have a Swiss bank account.

Another good purchase in Berlin is original artwork. There are so many galleries in the city that you could easily spend an entire lifetime making the rounds of changing exhibits. If you don't have the money for a major purchase, a good place to look for handmade arts and crafts is the weekend market on Strasse des 17. Juni, where young Berliners hawk their wares, including jewelry, sketches, and clothing.

Finally, antiques are also in abundant supply, as shown in the city's several flea markets and many antiques shops. Following a worldwide trend, shops dealing in art nouveau (Jugendstil) and art deco are also on the rise, appropriate for a city that was in the vanguard of the arts at the turn of the century and in the decades that followed.

2   Shopping A to Z

In addition to the specialty stores listed, the best source for most needs is a large department store (see "Department Stores and Malls," below).

Antiques

The best place to search for antiques and curios is at one of Berlin's several **flea markets.** Not only is the atmosphere festive, but the range

---

Frommer's Smart Shopper

Value-Conscious Shoppers Should Take Advantage of the Following:

1. Berlin's many department stores, which can often offer merchandise at prices cheaper than those of the smaller boutiques.

2. A return of the value-added tax (VAT) on goods totaling more than 60 DM ($35.40) purchased in any one store.

3. Open-fronted clothing boutiques on Tauentzienstrasse, the Ku'damm, and Wilmersdorfer Strasse, offering cheap and fun fashions.

4. Berlin's many galleries dealing in local, German, and international art.

5. The city's many flea markets, which are fun entertainment even if you don't buy anything, though it would be hard to resist the bargains ranging from antiques and curios to handcrafted items.

Questions to Ask If You're on a Budget

1. Does the store offer a VAT refund? You can receive a refund of up to 10% on goods purchased in Germany that you're taking out of the country.

2. How much does it cost to ship a package back home? Mail service is expensive in Germany; you may be much better off carrying your purchases home instead of shipping them.

3. Can you get it cheaper elsewhere? Ask yourself whether it's worthwhile shopping around. If you're at a market, try bargaining: some vendors are willing to lower their prices.

4. Is the item cheaper in Germany than back home? Do a little homework before beginning your trip, especially in regard to major purchases.

---

of goods offered by the vendors is usually much more extensive than that offered by a single store. My favorite flea market is the **Grosser Berliner Trödelmarkt mit Kunstmarkt** held every Saturday and Sunday on Strasse des 17. Juni, where vendors sell porcelain, coffee grinders, glassware, brass, door knockers, lamps, clothing, and a seemingly endless supply of junk, as well as handmade arts and crafts. An indoor market, the **Berliner Antik- und Flohmarkt** can be found at the Friedrichstrasse S-Bahn station and is open six days a week. Check under "Markets," below, for more information.

Otherwise, most of the stores below specialize in decorative objects from the turn of the century through the 1930s, a period that has enjoyed a resurgence in popularity the past few years. The shops here are all located on or near the Ku'damm or Bleibtreustrasse.

Alt-Berlin, Bleibtreustrasse 48. ☎ **881 67 56.**

In contrast to most other antiques shops around the Ku'damm (which specialize in Jugendstil and art deco objets d'art), this one deals in antiques mainly from the 1800s and is packed with glassware, porcelain, toys, candelabras, light fixtures, vases, toys, and an assortment of odds and ends. **Open:** Mon–Fri 2–6pm, Sat 10am–2pm. **S-Bahn:** Savignyplatz.

Art Deco, Leibnizstrasse 64. ☎ **323 1711.**

This shop sells beautifully crafted art deco furniture, lamps, and accessories, including a good selection of mirrors, all in mint condition. The collection includes pieces from throughout Europe, all manufactured between 1920 and 1940. **Open:** Mon–Fri 11am–1pm and 2–6:30pm, Sat 11am–2pm. **S-Bahn:** Savignyplatz. **U-Bahn:** Wilmersdorfer Strasse.

★ **Art 1900**, Kurfürstendamm 53. ☎ **881 56 27.**

This ranks as one of the finest and most exclusive of Berlin's shops dealing in original Jugendstil and art deco pieces. The craftsmanship of its furniture, statues, glass, and porcelain is exquisite, with correspondingly high prices. If money is no object, you'll definitely want to stop by here. Art 1900 is located near the corner of Schlüterstrasse. **Open:** Mon–Fri 10am–6:30pm, Sat 10am–2pm (open to 6pm first Sat of the month in winter, 4pm in summer). **U-Bahn:** Uhlandstrasse or Adenauerplatz.

Astoria, Bleibtreustrasse 50. ☎ **312 83 04.**

Near the corner of Bleibtreustrasse and Kantstrasse, this art deco shop offers a beautiful selection of statues, jewelry, and some furniture, including mirrors, lamps, tables, and dressers. If the originals are too expensive but you like the sleek art deco look, you might be interested in some of the shop's replicas, which make up about 10% of the inventory. **Open:** Mon–Fri 1–6:30pm, Sat 11am–2pm. **S-Bahn:** Savignyplatz.

Bogart's, Schlüterstrasse 34. ☎ **882 24 42.**

Taking its name from actor Humphrey Bogart, this shop specializes in Jugendstil and art deco furniture, including lamps, chairs, tables, and desks. **Open:** Mon–Fri 2–6:30pm, Sat 11am–2pm. **S-Bahn:** Savignyplatz.

Decorative Arts, Niebuhrstrasse 1. ☎ **882 73 73.**

A small shop on the corner of Niebuhrstrasse and Bleibtreustrasse, Decorative Arts specializes in items from the Jugendstil period through the 1930s, including Thonet furniture and Gallé, Lutz, and Murano glass. **Open:** Mon–Fri 3–6:30pm, Sat 10:30am–2pm. **S-Bahn:** Savignyplatz.

Harmel's, Damaschkestrasse 24. ☎ **324 22 92.**

Located off the western end of the Ku'damm near Lehninerplatz, this antiques store is the place to shop for non-German European antiques. Almost everything in the shop—from lamps and jewelry to silver—is imported from other European countries, including

Belgian glass and British furniture. Although most items stem from the Victorian era, art nouveau and art deco items are also in stock. **Open:** Mon–Fri 3–6:30pm, Sat 11am–2pm. **U-Bahn:** Adenauerplatz. **Bus:** 119, 129, or 219.

L & M Lee, Kurfürstendamm 32. ☎ **881 73 33.**

Entrance to this shop is on Uhlandstrasse, where you'll find an assortment of antiques ranging from the Biedermeier to art deco periods (from about 1820 to 1920). Included are glassware, porcelain, silver, jewelry, lamps, and decorative objects. **Open:** Mon–Fri 10am–6pm, Sat 10am–2pm (to 4pm first Sat of the month). **U-Bahn:** Uhlandstrasse.

Odeon Art Deco, Uhlandstrasse 20–25. ☎ **883 60 21.**

Just north of the Ku'damm, this small shop carries well-made art deco lamps, mirrors, free-standing cocktail bars, jewelry, cocktail shakers, furniture, and other accessories, all in great condition. **Open:** Mon–Fri 1–6:30pm, Sat 11am–2pm. **U-Bahn:** Uhlandstrasse.

20th Century Box, Damaschkestrasse 24. ☎ **324 21 66.**

Antiques in a wide price range, including those from the Jugendstil and art deco periods, are for sale here, ranging from furniture and mirrors to accessories. **Open:** Mon–Fri 3–6:30pm, Sat 11am–2pm. **U-Bahn:** Adenauerplatz.

Zille Hof, Fasanenstrasse 14. ☎ **313 43 33** or **881 95 09.**

It's hard to believe this quirky place exists near the exclusive Bristol Hotel Kempinski just off the Ku'damm—it looks like an abandoned junkyard. Occupying a little courtyard that spreads beside and under the elevated tracks of the S-Bahn, Zille Hof is a good place to browse through glasses, plates, rusted pots and pans, furniture, dusty books, postcards, clothing, and piles on piles of junk. If nothing else, this place is worth a photograph. **Open:** Mon–Fri 8:30am–5:30pm, Sat 8:30am–1pm. **U-Bahn:** Uhlandstrasse.

ART GALLERIES

There are so many art galleries in Berlin that it almost amounts to an epidemic—albeit a very nice one. One pamphlet lists more than 175 galleries; the city magazine *zitty* lists about 125. In any case, there are far too many to mention here. The ones below, all within easy walking distance of the Ku'damm, offer a varied assortment of contemporary art.

Galerie Brusberg, Kurfürstendamm 213. ☎ **882 76 82.**

Located on the second floor of a turn-of-the-century patrician home, this well-known gallery exhibits the works of Dalí, Ernst, Miró, Picasso, and Bernhard Dörries, as well as lesser-known artists of considerable talent. These include East Berlin painters who continued to express themselves when their city was under Communist rule. The gallery is light and airy, with enough space to properly display the paintings and sculptures. With its museumlike quality, Galerie Brusberg is definitely worth a stop. **Open:** Tues–Fri 10am–6:30pm, Sat 10am–2pm. **U-Bahn:** Uhlandstrasse.

Ladengalerie, Kurfürstendamm 64. ☎ **881 42 14.**

This one-room gallery specializes in one-person shows by contemporary German artists. One exhibition, for example, was Sarah Schumann's "Travels in the DDR." The displays are always interesting, making it worth a spin through. **Open:** Mon–Fri 10am–6:30pm, Sat 10am–2pm (to 6pm first Sat of the month in winter, 4pm in summer). **U-Bahn:** Adenauerplatz.

Galerie Ludwig Lange, Wielandstrasse 26. ☎ **881 29 26.**

On the ground floor of an ornate turn-of-the-century building, this beautiful gallery emphasizes German sculpture, including the works of Berliner Waldemar Grizmek. There is even a charming sculpture garden in the back, not to be missed. **Open:** Tues–Fri 11am–6pm, Sat 10am–2pm. **U-Bahn:** Adenauerplatz.

Galerie Nierendorf, Hardenbergstrasse 19. ☎ **785 60 60.**

Throughout its 70-year history, this gallery has specialized in the works of German Expressionist artists and German artists of the 1920s. **Open:** Tues–Fri 11am–5pm. **S-Bahn and U-Bahn:** Bahnhof Zoologischer Garten.

Galerie Pels-Leusden and Villa Grisebach Auktionen,
Fasanenstrasse 25. ☎ **885 91 50.**

Built a century ago as the home of architect Hans Grisebach, the beautiful Villa Grisebach has been restored and now serves as a gallery of contemporary art. (It stands next to the Käthe-Kollwitz-Museum.) Twice a year, in June and November, it also serves as the stage for the Villa Grisebach Auction, a sale of international painting, graphic art, and sculpture from the 19th and 20th centuries. Former auctions have dealt with works by Adolph von Menzel, Franz Marc, Erich Heckel, Paul Klee, Emil Nolde, Georg Kolbe, Jean Dubuffet, and Christo, drawing art dealers from around the world. **Open:** Mon–Fri 10am–6:30pm, Sat 10am–2pm. **U-Bahn:** Uhlandstrasse.

Galerie Springer, Fasanenstrasse 13. ☎ **31 70 63.**

Near the elevated tracks of the S-Bahn, Galerie Springer has none of the highbrow look of most other galleries, yet it has long remained on the crest of Berlin's artistic wave by recognizing young local talents and then sending them on to fame. Exhibitions range from avant-garde paintings to photography. Henry Miller's watercolors were for sale on one of my recent visits. **Open:** Mon–Fri 10am–7pm, Sat 11am–2pm. **U-Bahn:** Uhlandstrasse.

Crafts

If you're looking for handmade arts and crafts, the best place to look is the **weekend market** held on **Strasse des 17. Juni,** just west of the Tiergarten S-Bahn station open from 9am to 4pm. Many young entrepreneurs and artisans set up shop here, selling sketches, jewelry, batik clothing, and other items they've made themselves. In addition, check with the Berlin tourist office to see whether any special crafts fairs are being held.

Department Stores & Malls

IN THE EUROPA-CENTER AREA

Europa-Center, Tauentzienstrasse and Budapester Strasse.

Across the square from the Gedächtniskirche and easy to spot with the Mercedes-Benz star atop its roof, this is Berlin's largest indoor shopping center. In addition to its tourist information office, casino, hotel, thermal spa, and office space, it boasts approximately 70 shops on its first three floors, offering everything from records and cassettes to clothing, shoes, and accessories. A good place to explore on a cold or rainy day. There are also plenty of cafes, restaurants, and bars where you can stop for refreshment. **Open:** Shops, Mon–Fri 10am–6pm, Sat 10am–2pm (to 6pm first Sat of the month in winter, 4pm in summer); Europa-Center itself stays open to 3am. **U-Bahn:** Kurfürstendamm or Bahnhof Zoologischer Garten.

 **KaDeWe**, Wittenbergplatz. ☎ **21210.**

Quite simply, the largest department store on the European continent. Officially known as Kaufhaus des Westens (which means "department store of the West") but popularly referred to as KaDeWe, it's just a five-minute walk from the Ku'damm and the Gedächtniskirche. It occupies 51,600 square yards of selling space, has an inventory of 250,000 items, and employs a staff of 3,000. In addition to shopping its seven floors, customers can not only eat and buy theater tickets but also have their shoes repaired, their marriages and vacations planned, their hair done, their dogs shampooed, their money exchanged, their purchases wrapped and shipped abroad, their pictures taken, and—if necessary after all that—first aid administered.

The many departments sell almost everything, and many leading designers have their own boutiques here. Especially good departments include those devoted to fabrics, linen and bedding (you'll ooh and ah over those goosedown comforters and all the colorful designer sheets that go with them), and glass and porcelain. Souvenirs are sold on the fourth floor, including beer steins and ashtrays stamped with the motif of Berlin, the bear.

But by far the biggest attraction is the amazing sixth-floor food emporium. There are 1,000 sorts of sausage, 500 kinds of bread, 1,500 types of cheese, and gourmet items from around the world. There are exotic teas, coffees, liquors, wines, jams, sweets, vegetables, fruits, spices, canned goods, and fresh seafood, including eels, lobster, and fish still swimming around in tanks. Throughout the sixth floor you'll find various sit-down counters where you can dine on everything from soup to seafood.

You could easily get lost and spend the rest of your days in the store—but there are certainly worse fates in life. **Open:** Mon–Wed and Fri 9am–6:30pm, Thurs 9am–8:30pm, Sat 9am–2pm (to 6pm first Sat of the month in winter, 4pm in summer). **U-Bahn:** Wittenbergplatz.

Wertheim, Kurfürstendamm 231. ☎ **88 20 61.**

Conveniently situated at the eastern end of the Ku'damm, across from the Gedächtniskirche, Wertheim is good for basic needs such as shampoo, film, or picnic supplies. It also has fine clothing, porcelain, and housewares departments. **Open:** Mon–Wed and Fri 9am–6:30pm, Thurs 9am–8:30pm, Sat 9am–2pm (to 6pm first Sat of the month in winter, 4pm in summer). **U-Bahn:** Kurfürstendamm.

ON WILMERSDORFER STRASSE

Hertie, Wilmersdorfer Strasse 118–119. ☎ **311 050.**

Hertie department store, together with Quelle across the street, is a good medium-price store, serving the basic needs of families. Stop here for those traveling necessities. **Open:** Mon–Wed and Fri 9am–6:30pm, Thurs 9am–8:30pm, Sat 9am–2pm (to 6pm first Sat of the month in winter, 4pm in summer). **U-Bahn:** Wilmersdorfer Strasse.

Karstadt, Wilmersdorfer Strasse 109–111. ☎ **31 891.**

At the corner of Kantstrasse and Wilmersdorfer Strasse, this large department store is one of a chain that can be found all over Germany (and slightly more upscale than competing chains). A good place to look for clothing and accessories. **Open:** Mon–Wed and Fri 9am–6:30pm, Thurs 9am–8:30pm, Sat 9am–2pm (to 6pm first Sat of the month in winter, 4pm in summer). **U-Bahn:** Wilmersdorfer Strasse.

Quelle, Wilmersdorfer Strasse 50. ☎ **320 05 211** or **320 050.**

The last of the three big department stores on Wilmersdorfer Strasse, with much the same merchandise and comparable prices, Quelle is a good place to stock up on film. There's a good cafeteria on the second floor. **Open:** Mon–Wed and Fri 9am–6:30pm, Thurs 9am–8:30pm, Sat 9am–2pm (to 6pm first Sat of the month in winter, 4pm in summer). **U-Bahn:** Wilmersdorfer Strasse.

IN BERLIN-MITTE (EASTERN BERLIN)

Kaufhof, Alexanderplatz. ☎ **21 64 000.**

Occupying the former East German Centrum department store this western German chain offers everything from toys and cassettes to household items, clothing, and food. A good place to stock up on necessities in eastern Berlin. **Open:** Mon–Wed and Fri 9am–6:30pm, Thurs 9am–8:30pm, Sat 9am–2pm (to 6pm first Sat of the month in winter, 4pm in summer). **U- and S-Bahn:** Alexanderplatz.

Fashions

The best places to check for clothing and accessories are the many department stores listed above, where there are various departments for men, women, children, and teenagers. In addition, there are many boutiques in the Europa-Center, as well as open-fronted shops along the Ku'damm, Tauentzienstrasse, and Wilmersdorfer Strasse selling young, fun fashions at inexpensive prices.

The following shops are just a few of the more specialized boutiques selling Berlin-designed avant-garde fashions.

Durchbruch, Schlüterstrasse 54. ☎ 881 55 68.

Durchbruch means "breakthrough," a timely name for a shop in Berlin. But the shop, the logo for which is a brick wall sliced in half, preceded the crumbling of the Wall by about six years; thus, "breakthrough" could also apply to its influence on Berlin's fashion scene. For this is where those in the know come for women's clothing of unusual and original German design, usually one-of-a-kind items, as well as some imported French and Japanese fashions.

Local names to look for include Fiona Bennett, who creates outrageous and ingenious headgear, and Lisa D., a well-known Berlin designer whose explosive creativity includes clothing pulled together with silk strings. If you don't want to show up at the next cocktail party wearing the same thing as everyone else, try Durchbruch, located north of the Ku'damm. **Open:** Mon–Wed and Fri 11am–6:30pm, Thurs 11am–8:30pm, Sat 10am–2pm (to 6pm first Sat of the month in winter, 4pm in summer). **S-Bahn:** Savignyplatz.

Filato, Nürnberger Strasse 24a. ☎ 24 54 77.

Filato is the label of two Berlin designers, Andrea Schuricht and Jutta Meierling, who use only natural materials in their line of casual and dressy womenswear. The unusual cuts and unexpected twists of their fashions appeal to young professional women who desire well-tailored clothes but who don't want to look too conservative. The shop, which sells other labels besides Filato, is found one block south of Tauentzienstrasse and the Europa-Center. **Open:** Mon–Fri 11am–6pm, Sat 10am–2pm (to 6pm first Sat of the month in winter, 4pm in summer). **U-Bahn:** Augsburger Strasse.

7 up's, Bleibtreustrasse 48. ☎ 883 51 08.

This fun clothing store specializes in the creations of young Berlin designers working on commission. The inventory is very mixed and includes clothing, belts, shoes, and other accessories for women. **Open:** Mon–Wed and Fri 10:30am–6:30pm, Thurs 10:30am–8:30pm, Sat 10:30am–2pm (to 6pm first Sat of the month in winter, 4pm in summer). **S-Bahn:** Savignyplatz.

Skoda Attendance, Kurfürstendamm 50. ☎ 885 10 09.

Self-taught Claudia Skoda is one of Berlin's most successful designers, with women's fashions sold at designer shops throughout Germany and in Paris, London, and Tokyo. Using a unique technique of knitting and weaving and incorporating stretch materials to create unusual fabrics, Skoda describes her style as "progressively feminine." **Open:** Mon–Fri 11am–6pm, Sat 11am–2pm. **U-Bahn:** Uhlandstrasse.

Veni-Vidi-Vici, Uhlandstrasse 20. ☎ 885 49 90.

Berliner Sabine Cordey, an up-and-coming young designer of menswear, began her career by cutting up old suits and coats and redesigning them in the style of the 1980s. She became so successful that she now imports material from Italy and employs a small team of seamstresses to realize her ideas. Her clothing, which combines the classic with a touch of the avant-garde, is appropriate for all ages, from bankers to pony-tailed artistic types. Since clothing here is custom-made, make sure you have time for fittings. **Open:** Mon–Wed and Fri 10:30am–6:30pm, Thurs 10:30am–8:30pm, Sat 10am–2pm (to 6pm first Sat of the month in winter, 4pm in summer). **U-Bahn:** Uhlandstrasse.

FOOD

Almost all department stores in Germany have food departments, usually in their basements. In Berlin the ultimate in food emporiums is the sixth floor of the **KaDeWe department store** on Wittenbergplatz, with an incredible stockpile of gourmet foods (see "Department Stores and Malls," above). If it's to be found anywhere in Berlin, KaDeWe is the place.

If your tastes run toward natural foods, across the square from KaDeWe is a small shop called **Einhorn,** Wittenbergplatz 5–6 (☎ 218 63 47). In addition to ready-made vegetarian dishes, the place also sells Muesli, breads, organic fruits and vegetables, nuts, and more. It's open Monday through Friday from 10am to 6pm and Saturday from 10am to 2pm. A second Einhorn is located at Mommsenstrasse 2 (☎ 881 42 41), a minute's walk north of the Ku'damm, with the same hours.

Gifts & Souvenirs

The largest selection of gifts and souvenirs can be found in Berlin's department stores, particularly **KaDeWe** and **Wertheim,** which are used to a steady flow of tourist traffic. Other places to look for unique gifts include the **weekend crafts market on Strasse des 17. Juni,** where young entrepreneurs sell their own creations; **Harry Lehmann,** see "Perfume" below, which has been selling perfume almost 70 years; and **Rosenthal Studio-Haus** and **WMF,** described below under "Kitchenwares."

Berlin-Grafik, Schlossstrasse 60. ☎ 342 85 44.

Located near Schloss Charlottenburg, this tiny shop sells original drawings and reproductions, many of famous Berlin architecture. Engravings of Berlin begin at 20 DM ($11.80). **Open:** Mon–Fri 11am–6pm, Sat 11am–2pm (to 6pm first Sat of the month in winter, 4pm in summer). **Bus:** 110, 145.

Berliner Zinnfiguren, Knesebeckstrasse 88. ☎ 31 08 02.

Located just north of Savignyplatz, this small family-owned shop has been producing and selling handcrafted pewter figurines since 1934. Approximately 10,000 various figures are for sale, including more than 1,000 animals alone. Some are collectors items; others are appropriate as toys. Most popular are characters of Berlin, including the Potsdamer Soldat (soldier), the Blumenfrau (Flower Vendor), and Frederick the Great playing the flute. Flat, unpainted figures begin at only 1.50 DM (95¢), a great souvenir of Berlin. **Open:** Mon–Fri 10am–noon and 1–6 pm, Sat 10am–1pm. **S-Bahn:** Savignyplatz.

Gipsformerei der Staatlichen Museen Berlin, Sophie-Charlotten-Strasse 17–18. ☎ **321 70 11.**

If you're shopping for the person who has everything or looking for something unique to Berlin, this is the store for you. Where else can you buy a genuine fake bust of Nefertiti or reproductions of Egyptian, Roman, and Asian statues, the originals of which have homes in Berlin's many museums? This is the city's official plaster-casting workshop, established more than 150 years ago to supply institutions around the world with museum-quality copies of Berlin's treasures. Thousands of plaster casts have been produced through the decades, with copies available at the workshop's store or from one of its catalogues. Egyptian, Greek, Roman, Asian, Indian, African, and South American reproduced artworks are represented, though most of the workshop's reproductions are statues from the Middle Ages, the Renaissance, and the 19th century. Indeed, if you see it in one of Berlin's state museums, it's probably available here. The bust of Nefertiti costs almost 1,500 DM ($885), but plaster copies of carved Egyptian gems and Babylonian trinkets are priced under 50 DM ($29.50). It's located near Schloss Charlottenburg, just north of Spandauer Damm. **Open:** Mon–Fri 9am–4pm (Wed to 6pm). **Bus:** 110 or 145. **S-Bahn:** Westend.

Kunsthandlung Bandoly, Brandenburgische Strasse 27. ☎ **881 49 10.**

This gallery deals in reproductions of famous paintings, small etchings of Berlin, and copperplate prints depicting the city's old architecture. Small etchings of such sights as the Brandenburger Tor are available for as little as 13 DM ($7.65), making this a good place to purchase a souvenir of Berlin. **Open:** Mon–Fri 10am–1pm and 3–6pm, Sat 10am–1pm. **U-Bahn:** Adenauerplatz.

Wertheim, Kurfürstendamm 231. ☎ **88 20 61.**

This department store, right on the Ku'damm across from the Gedächtniskirche, features a souvenir shop on the ground floor with its own sidewalk entrance. Berlin bears, T-shirts, post-cards, glasses, mugs, and many other souvenirs with Berlin motifs are for sale. **Open:** Mon–Wed and Fri 9am–6:30pm, Thurs 9am–8:30pm, Sat 9am–2pm (to 6pm first Sat of the month in winter, 4pm in summer). **U-Bahn:** Kurfürstendamm.

Kitchenware

Rosenthal Studio-Haus, Kurfürstendamm 226. ☎ **881 7051.**

This smart-looking shop sells a wide range of decorative and functional items for the home, including Rosenthal porcelain, Boda glass, tableware, and chrome kitchenware. Prices are high, but if you're looking for a wedding gift, this is a good place to start. **Open:** Mon–Wed and Fri 9:30am–6:30pm, Thurs 9:30am–8:30pm, Sat 9:30am–2pm (to 6pm first Sat of the month in winter, 4pm in summer). **U-Bahn:** Kurfürstendamm.

WMF, Kurfürstendamm 229. ☎ **882 39 41.**

As many people know, the Germans make some of the best and most sought-after kitchen gadgets around. WMF, a chain found all over Germany, specializes in both tableware and cookingware, from chrome eggcups to pots and pans—sleek, functional, and sturdy. But WMF also has all those useful gadgets, from bottle stoppers to hardboiled-egg slicers. **Open:** Mon–Wed and Fri 9:30am–6:30pm, Thurs 9:30am–8:30pm, Sat 9am–2pm (to 6pm first Sat of the month in winter, 4pm in summer). **U-Bahn:** Kurfürstendamm.

Markets

Some of Berlin's best buys can be found at its many markets. One is indoor and held almost daily; others are outdoor and open only one or two days a week. Below are some of the best.

Berliner Antik- und Flohmarkt (Berlin Antique and Flea Market), Friedrichstrasse S-Bahn station, Georgenstrasse, Berlin-Mitte. ☎ **208 26 45.**

Flea markets located at train or subway stations are not a new concept in Berlin. In 1892 the Franziskaner flea market opened under the tracks of Friedrichstrasse station. After the division of Berlin, Die Nolle in western Berlin opened on an abandoned platform at Nollendorfplatz station. When reunification called Nollendorfplatz station back into service, many of the vendors there moved to this newest station flea market, located at the Friedrichstrasse S-Bahn station in former East Berlin, underneath the arches of the elevated tracks. Altogether, about 100 vendors sell antiques and curios here, including second-hand books, jewelry, lamps, dolls, silver, porcelain, glass, brass, and odds and ends. **Open:** Wed–Mon 11am–6pm. **S-Bahn:** Friedrichstrasse.

★ Grosser Berliner Trödelmarkt mit Kunstmarkt (Market on Strasse des 17. Juni), Strasse des 17. Juni. ☎ **322 81 99.**

My favorite market, this one I never miss when I'm in Berlin. Stretching just west of the Tiergarten S-Bahn station, this weekend market offers a staggering variety of antiques, including silverware, books, china, glass, jewelry, used CDs, LPs, clothing, kitchenware—and junk. Don't miss the second half of the market (past the stone portal and on the other side of the bridge), which features such original arts and crafts as funky and ethnic jewelry, clothing, hats, sketches, and innovative artwork. It's a good place to hunt for gifts, and prices are very reasonable. Don't miss it. **Open:** Sat and Sun 9am–4pm. **S-Bahn:** Tiergarten.

Berliner Kunst & Nostalgiemarkt (Berlin Art and Nostalgia Market), Am Zeughaus and Kupfergraben. ☎ **922 86 36** or **282 23 23.**

The market on Strasse des 17. Juni is bigger and better than this newcomer to the weekly market scene, but if you're visiting the many museums on Museumsinsel in Berlin-Mitte on a weekend you might take a spin through its outdoor stalls. Located near the entryway to the Pergamon Museum, it begins from Am Zeughaus just west of Museumsinsel off Unter den Linden and stretches north on Kupfergraben past the elevated S-Bahn tracks. Used books, records, CDs, artwork, clothing, jewelry, hats, antiques, and odds and ends are for sale. **Open:** Sat and Sun 11am–5pm. **S-Bahn:** Friedrichstrasse. **Bus:** 100.

Weihnachtsmarkt, Breitscheidplatz and from Nürnberger Strasse to Joachimstaler Strasse.

Every December from the beginning of the month to Christmas Eve, there's a traditional Christmas market in the inner city. It radiates out from the Gedächtniskirche on Breitscheidplatz to Wittenbergplatz, particularly on Nürnberger Strasse and Joachimstaler Strasse. Colorful stalls sell those wonderful German Christmas ornaments, as well as candies, cookies, sausages, and other goodies, including Glühwein (spiced mulled wine). (Incidentally, there are other Christmas markets in Berlin—for example, in Spandau's Altstadt, known for its traditional ambience and handmade decorations, and on Karl-Liebknecht-Platz in eastern Berlin, complete with a fun fair.) **Open:** Dec 1–24 daily 11am–9pm. **U-Bahn:** Kurfürstendamm, Bahnhof Zoologischer Garten, or Wittenbergplatz.

Winterfeldplatz Market, Winterfeldplatz, Schöneberg.

Berlin's largest weekly market selling fruits, vegetables, meat, eggs, bread, cheese, flowers, clothing, jewelry, and accessories is just a five-minute walk south of Nollendorfplatz. This is where Berliners come to do their shopping, especially on Saturday, whether it's for cabbage, olives, basil, mozzarella, or flowers. And of course, they also come to meet their friends and exchange the latest gossip. After making their purchases, many of the younger shoppers retire to Slumberland or Café Sidney, two bars on Winterfeldplatz. **Open:** Wed and Sat dawn–1pm. **U-Bahn:** Nollendorfplatz.

Perfume

For the big names in perfume from around the world, head for the ground floor of **KaDeWe** (see "Department Stores and Malls," above).

However, if you're looking for a scent unique to Berlin or an inexpensive and unusual gift, try **Harry Lehmann,** Kantstrasse 106 (☎ 324 35 82). This tiny family-owned shop has been selling its own concoctions since 1926, with approximately 50 scents now available (made from flowers, leaves, and grasses). They are sold by weight, starting at 3.50 DM ($2.05) for 10 grams. You can either bring your own perfume bottle or purchase one of the inexpensive vials available, a concept begun by Harry Lehmann, who decided it was a shame that pretty bottles had to be discarded when the perfume ran out. In addition to its scents, the shop—now in its third generation of owners—also sells Kölnisch Wasser and other colognes, as well as after-shave lotion for men. Don't be put off by the fake flowers; they're just one of the idiosyncrasies of this charming little establishment. It's found just a stone's throw west of the Wilmersdorfer Strasse pedestrian lane. It's open Monday through Friday from 9am to 6:30pm and Saturday from 9am to 2pm (to 6pm the first Saturday of the month in winter, 4pm in summer). Take the U-Bahn to Wilmersdorfer Strasse.

Porcelain

KPM, Kurfürstendamm 26a. ☎ **881 18 02.**

The Königliche Porzellan-Manufaktur (KPM) is a Berlin tradition stretching back more than 225 years. In 1763 Frederick the Great acquired a preexisting porcelain company, renamed it the Königliche Porzellan-Manufaktur, and gave it royal-purveyor status. Since then, monarchs and heads of state from around the world have owned KPM porcelain, including Catherine II of Russia; Louis XVI of France; and Elizabeth II, Princess Diana, and Margaret Thatcher of the United Kingdom. Although the firm's official name was changed in 1918 to Staatliche Porzellan-Manufaktur, its pieces are still identified with the KPM mark and everyone simply calls it KPM.

KPM today makes table settings, vases, baskets, figurines, and art pieces. All decorations and floral designs are hand-painted. The most popular items with tourists include reproductions of the Freedom Bell in Rathaus Schöneberg, white statues of the Berlin bear, and Christmas plates issued each year.

Although not as centrally located, the main shop of KPM is at Wegelystrasse 1 (☎ **39 00 90**). **Open:** Ku'damm branch, Mon–Fri 9:30am–6:30pm, Sat 9am–2pm (to 6pm first Sat of the month in winter, 4pm in summer); main shop, Mon–Fri 9am–6pm, Sat 9am–2pm (to 6pm first Sat of the month in winter, 4pm in summer). **U-Bahn for Ku'damm branch:** Uhlandstrasse. **S-Bahn for main shop:** Tiergarten.

9

Berlin Nights

ASIDE FROM THE DIVERSITY AND QUALITY OF ITS MUSEUMS, THE ONE THING that sets Berlin apart from all other German cities is its nightlife. When the streets of Munich and Hamburg are being rolled up at 1am, the Berliners are just getting started. The city never sleeps, simply because it doesn't have to. There are no closing hours for nightclubs, discos, and bars, so a few establishments stay open round the clock, while others call it quits at 3am or as late as 6am.

Little wonder that Berlin enjoys a popularity among Europe's younger generation of travelers comparable to that of Copenhagen or Amsterdam. One native Berliner once told me, "The reason everyone comes to Berlin is its nightlife." But the action starts late—you'll never see anything if you're in bed by 11pm. I suspect that more than a few travelers have remained unaware of the city's nighttime transformation, perhaps blissfully so. There's something to be said for early curfews.

On the other hand, it would be hard to remain completely unaware of Berlin's darker nighttime side, because there are signs of it everywhere and the city doesn't hide it. Everything exists side by side—the tawdry beside the sophisticated. One single street near the Ku'damm may contain a first-class hotel, a strip joint and peep show, an Italian pizzeria, a pornography shop, and a restaurant serving French haute cuisine. The Ku'damm itself, by day Berlin's most popular shopping street, is by night the domain of dolled-up prostitutes; they are as much an accepted part of the boulevard as the display cases. It's this diversity that makes the city interesting. It's this tolerance that has made the city what it is today.

But you don't have to be a night owl to enjoy evenings in Berlin. There are cabarets, wine cellars, live-music houses, and gambling casinos. More refined tastes can indulge in opera, chamber music, two world-renowned orchestras, and classical and contemporary theater.

To find out what's going on in the traditional performing arts, pick up a copy of *Checkpoint Berlin* or *Berlin Programm*. Both give a day-by-day account of events in all the city's opera houses, theaters, and concert halls. Rock concerts, experimental theater, and avant-garde happenings are also covered in the city magazines *tip* and *zitty*.

If you don't mind paying a commission and don't want to bother going to the venue's own box office, convenient ticket outlets can be found at **Centrum,** Meinekestrasse 25 (☎ 882 76 11); the **Europa-Center,** Tauentzienstrasse 9 (☎ 261 70 51); the **KaDeWe department store,** Wittenbergplatz (☎ 24 80 36); and the **Wertheim department store,** Kurfürstendamm 231 (☎ 882 25 00).

You'll save money, however, by buying your ticket directly from the theater or concert hall during box-office hours or an hour before the performance begins. Some theaters give students discounts for unused tickets on the night of the performance. And for those who don't mind the waiting until the day of a performance to see whether they can get tickets, the Deutsche Oper Berlin (see below) offers "last-minute tickets," unsold tickets available for about 50% off the regular price.

1 The Performing Arts

Classical Music

★ **Philharmonie,** Mattäikirchstrasse 1, Tiergarten. ☎ 25 48 80 or 254 88-132.

Without a doubt, this is Berlin's most famous concert hall, in part because it's the home of the world-renowned **Berlin Philharmonic Orchestra.** Situated on the southern edge of the Tiergarten district in an area known as the Cultural Forum, the Philharmonie was designed by architect Hans Scharoun in 1963. It's an asymmetrical structure with a tentlike roof. The main auditorium seats more than 2,200, with conductor and orchestra placed at the very center and no concert-goer more than 100 feet from the podium. The acoustics are said to be nearly perfect.

The Berlin Philharmonic Orchestra, founded in 1882, has been led by some of the world's greatest conductors. It gained acclaim under the baton of the late Herbert von Karajan, acclaim that now continues unabated for his successor, Claudio Abbado. Leading guest conductors and soloists regularly join the Berlin Philharmonic, including such notables as Sir Yehudi Menuhin, Zubin Mehta, Christoph von Dohnányi, Sir Georg Solti, Daniel Barenboim, and Seiji Ozawa.

The Philharmonic performs approximately 100 times in Berlin during its August-through-June season, attracting more than 220,000 people annually. Each year it also performs 20 to 30 concerts worldwide. Because the orchestra is so popular, tickets often sell out two months in advance. If you're able to procure one, consider yourself very lucky.

Major Concert & Performance Halls

Deutschlandhalle, Messedamm 26. ☎ 3 03 81.

Deutsche Oper Berlin, Bismarckstrasse 35, Charlottenburg. ☎ 34 381 or 341 02 49.

Internationales Congress-Centrum (ICC), Am Messedamm. ☎ 30 38-0 or 30 38-44 44.

Metropol, Nollendorfplatz 5. ☎ 216 41 22.

Philharmonie, Mattäikirchstrasse 1, Tiergartten. ☎ 25 48 80 or 254 88-132.

Quasimodo, Kantstrasse 12a. ☎ 312 80 86.

Schauspielhaus Berlin, Gendarmenmarkt, Berlin-Mitte. ☎ 20 90-21 56 or 20 90-21 57.

Staatsoper Unter den Linden, Unter der Linden 7, Berlin-Mitte. ☎ 200 47 62.

Waldbühne, Ruhleben, Charlottenburg. ☎ 852 40 80.

The Philharmonie is also the venue of the **Radio Symphony Orchestra, Berlin Symphonic Orchestra,** guest orchestras, and ensembles. The famous **Berlin Jazz Festival** also takes place here. In addition to the main hall, there's also a smaller **Kammermusiksaal** (Chamber Music Hall).

Open: Box office Mon–Fri 3:30–6pm, Sat–Sun and holidays 11am–2pm. **Bus:** 129, 148, or 248.

Prices: 12–100 DM ($7.10–$59) for Philharmonic Orchestra.

Schauspielhaus Berlin, Gendarmenmarkt, Berlin-Mitte.

☎ **20 90-21 57** (information), **20 90-21 56** (tickets).

Located on the historic Gendarmenmarkt square in eastern Berlin, this concert hall—designed by Schinkel and built from 1819 to 1821—features concerts by both the Radio Symphony Orchestra, the Berlin Symphonic Orchestra, and guest orchestras and ensembles. It has both a large music hall and a chamber-music hall.

Open: Box office Tues–Sat 2–6pm. **U-Bahn:** Französische Strasse or Stadtmitte. **Bus:** 100.

Prices: 10–80 DM ($5.90–$47.20).

Opera, Operetta & Ballet

Deutsche Oper Berlin, Bismarckstrasse 35 Charlottenburg.

☎ **34 381** (information), **341 02 49** (tickets).

Whereas most of Europe's opera houses are grand and ornate edifices dating from another era, the Deutsche Oper Berlin was rebuilt after World War II in an intentionally plain and modern style, made even plainer by the stark street-side wall designed to shut out traffic noise. Seating 1,900, it features performances of opera almost every night, except when there's ballet. The Deutsche Oper Berlin attained worldwide success in the 1920s under such great conductors as Richard Strauss, Bruno Walter, Leo Blech, Wilhelm Furtwängler, Erich Kleiber, and Otto Klemperer.

Open: Box office Mon–Sat 11am–7pm, Sun 10am–2pm; performances daily at 7, 7:30, or 8pm. **U-Bahn:** Deutsche Oper. **Bus:** 101.

Prices: 15–135 DM ($8.85–$79.65); student reductions of 50% available on unsold tickets 30 minutes before performances; last-minute tickets 50% reduction on day of performance.

Komische Oper, Behrenstrasse 55, Berlin-Mitte. ☎ **229 26 03** (information), **229 25 55** (tickets).

Although Komische Oper translates as "comic theater," this innovative opera company serves as an alternative to the grander, more mainstream productions of Berlin's two other opera houses, above. Referring to itself as Berlin's "music theater," it presents a varied program of opera, operetta, and ballet, with productions ranging from Mozart's *The Marriage of Figaro* to Sergei Prokofiev's ballet *Romeo and Juliet.*

Open: Box office (located at Unter den Linden 41) Mon–Sat noon–5:30pm, Sun 1–4:30pm; performances usually at 7 or 8pm. **S-Bahn:** Unter den Linden. **U-Bahn:** Französische Strasse.

Prices: Opera and ballet 8–70 DM ($4.70–$41.30).

Staatsoper Unter den Linden, Unter den Linden 7, Berlin-Mitte.
☎ 200 47 62.

Located on the famous Unter den Linden, the Staatsoper (State Opera) has long been one of Berlin's premier opera houses. Although the present building dates only from the 1950s, its facade faithfully copies that of the preexisting structure, first erected in the 1740s by Knobelsdorff and renovated in 1927. The schedule features opera, ballet, and concerts.

Open: Box office Mon–Sat noon–6pm, Sun and holidays 2–6pm; performances most evenings at 7 or 7:30pm. **Bus:** 100. **U-Bahn:** Französische Strasse. **S-Bahn:** Friedrichstrasse.

Prices: 6–150 DM ($3.55–$88.50).

Theater

With a long tradition behind it, Berlin has played a leading role in the history and development of the German theater. Hauptmann, Ibsen, Strindberg, and Brecht have all left their mark on Berlin's stages, as have such well-known directors as Max Reinhardt, Erwin Piscator, and Gustaf Gründgens.

Unfortunately, several theaters were forced to close following reunification, but a few remain. You'll be at a disadvantage if you don't speak German, but if you do, you're in for a treat.

★ **Berliner Ensemble**, Am Bertolt-Brecht-Platz, Berlin-Mitte.
☎ 282 31 60.

Bertolt Brecht and Helene Weigel founded this remarkable theater in 1945, and it has been staging Brecht's work ever since. Even when the Wall cut off the Berliner Ensemble from Western eyes, it maintained a reputation in West Germany as one of the best places in the world to see Brecht. It also features works by guest playwrights.

Open: Box office Mon–Sat 11am–6pm, Sun 3–6pm; performances usually at 7:30pm. **S-Bahn and U-Bahn:** Friedrichstrasse.

Prices: 30 DM ($17.70).

Schaubühne am Lehniner Platz, Kurfüurstendamm 153, Wilmersdorf. ☎ 89 00 23.

One of the Berlin's leading venues for experimental drama, located toward the eastern end of the Ku'damm near Lehniner Platz, it occupies what used to be a former theater. Although the original 1920s facade has been preserved, the inside has the latest in modern theatrical technology, including three stages where plays can be given simultaneously.

Open: Box office Mon–Sat 11am–6:30pm, Sun and holidays 3–6:30pm; performances usually Tues–Sun 7:30 or 8pm. **U-Bahn:** Adenauerplatz. **Bus:** 119, 129, or 219.

Prices: 15–50 DM ($8.85–$29.50).

Theater des Westens, Kantstrasse 12, Charlottenburg.
☎ 882 28 88.

Built in 1896 and occupying a prime spot near the Ku'damm and Bahnhof Zoo, this is the place to go for operettas, musicals, and popular productions.

Open: Box office Mon–Sat 10am–6pm; performances usually Tues–Sun at 8pm. **U-Bahn and S-Bahn:** Bahnhof Zoologischer Garten.

Prices: 15–70 DM ($8.85–$41.30).

2 The Club & Music Scene

Cabaret

As Liza Minnelli sang, "Life is a cabaret, old chum," and nowhere is that more true than in Berlin. Granted, the old days of stinging political satires are long gone, which in any case required an excellent command of the German language to understand. Some nightclubs do offer political commentary, but mostly you'll find music and dance, including transvestite shows, or variety shows.

Chez Nous, Marburger Strasse 14. ☎ **213 18 10.**

The transvestite show put on here has been titillating Berliners and visitors for more than 30 years with its elaborate costumes, singing, dancing, and parodies. A Berlin institution, with two shows Monday through Saturday at 8:30 and 11pm (at 6 and 8:30pm Sundays), it's located just a minute's walk from the Europa-Center. **U-Bahn:** Kurfürstendamm or Augsburger station.

Admission: 15 DM ($8.85), plus an obligatory drink minimum of 30 DM ($17.70) Sun–Thurs, 35 DM ($20.65) Fri–Sat; long drinks average 25 DM ($14.75).

Die Stachelschweine, in the basement of the Europa-Center, Tauentzienstrasse and Budapester Strasse. ☎ **261 47 95.**

This is one of Berlin's old-timers, a cabaret with more than 40 years under its belt. Its name means "porcupine," and it carries on the pre-Nazi tradition of political commentary—which means you have to understand German to appreciate it.

Tickets sell out quickly, so come here immediately upon arrival in Berlin to procure a ticket. The box office is open Monday through Friday from 10:30am to 12:30pm. Performances are held Monday through Saturday, usually at 7:30pm. **U-Bahn:** Bahnhof Zoologischer Garten or Kurfürstendamm.

Admission: 22–40 DM ($13–$23.60).

Wintergarten, Potsdamer Strasse 96, Tiergarten. ☎ **262 70 70** or **261 60 60.**

One of the biggest names prior to World War II, Wintergarten reopened its doors in 1992, now occupying a renovated art deco building in the Tiergarten. It stages nightly variety shows in the grand old tradition, complete with magic shows, acrobatics, circus acts, parodies, and revues. There are shows nightly at 8:30, plus a Sunday

IMPRESSIONS

He said that in Berlin, if you wanted to make a scandal in the theater, you had to have a mother committing incest with two sons; one wasn't enough.

—Arnold Bennett, quoting Rudolf Kommer, 1925

matinee at 3:30pm. **U-Bahn:** Kurfüstenstrasse. **Bus:** 129, 148, 248, or 341.

   Admission: Sun–Thurs 39–57 DM ($23–$33.65), Fri–Sat 49–69 DM ($28.90–$40.70).

Rock Concerts & Other Shows

If you buy tickets to one of Berlin's premier rock concerts, you'll probably be heading toward one of these major concert halls. For local bands and live music houses that offer nightly entertainment, refer to the section that follows, "Live Music Houses." Also check *Checkpoint Berlin* for the latest concert information.

Deutschlandhalle, Messedamm 26. ☎ **3 03 81.**

With 14,000 seats, the Deutschlandhalle is Berlin's largest arena. The place is used for occasional rock concerts—the B52's, Aerosmith, James Brown, and Tears for Fears have played here—as well as for conventions, horse shows, and other events with mass attendance. It's located on the grounds of the city's largest conference and convention center, the Internationales Congress-Centrum (ICC).

   Open: Box office Mon–Fri noon–6pm, Sat 10am–2pm. **U-Bahn:** Kaiserdamm. **S-Bahn:** Westkreuz. **Bus:** 219 or 149.

Internationales Congress-Centrum (ICC), Am Messedamm. ☎ **30 38-0** or **30 38-44 44.**

The massive ICC, right next to the Funkturm (Radio Tower), opened in 1979. Besides some 80 lecture halls and meeting rooms, it boasts two main halls (one seating 2,000, the other 5,000) used for both conferences and concerts. Past performers here have included Johnny Cash, Harry Belafonte, Falco, and Laurie Anderson.

   Open: Box office Mon–Fri noon–6pm, Sat 10am–2pm. **Bus:** 104, 105, 110, 149, or 219.

Metropol, Nollendorfplatz 5. ☎ **216 41 22.**

A disco on weekends, the Metropol offers some of the best music around during its weekday-evening concerts. Though the space is too small to accommodate the big names, you can catch your favorite lesser-known artists here before they do make it big; Paul Young, David Sanborn, Ziggy Marley, and Johnny Clegg and Savuka have played here. A smaller, separate stage called Loft provides a more intimate setting for concerts ranging from punk rock to rhythm and blues.

   Open: Box office Mon–Fri 11am–3pm and 3:30–6pm. **U-Bahn:** Nollendorfplatz.

Tempodrom, Tiergarten. ☎ **394 40 45.**

Tempodrom is a huge tent right in the middle of the city, erected in an effort to provide alternative performances at a permanent site. The programs include circus shows, theater, music, and revues. Consult *Checkpoint Berlin, tip, zitty,* or *Berlin Programm* for current attractions. The tent is located near the Kongresshalle at the north end of the Tiergarten, not far from the Reichstag building.

   Open: Performances May to October. **Bus:** 100 to Kongresshalle stop.

Waldbühne, Ruhleben, Charlottenburg. ☎ 852 40 80.

Beautifully situated in a wooded ravine near the Olympiastadion (Olympic Stadium), the Waldbühne is Germany's largest open-air arena. It's Berlin's best-loved spot for rock, pop, and folklore concerts held in summer. Although such performers as Joe Cocker, Tina Turner, and Prince are usually featured, the Berlin Philharmonic Orchestra has been known to give concerts here as well. Be sure to pack a picnic and a warm blanket and bring along raingear just in case.

Open: Performances May to October. **U-Bahn:** Ruhleben, then a 20-minute walk through a park; or Olympiastadion.

Live Music Houses

A-Trane, Bleibtreustrasse 1, Charlottenburg. ☎ 313 25 50.

Located on the corner of Bleibtreustrasse and Pestalozzistrasse not far from Savignyplatz, this small but classy venue offers live jazz, featuring both local and international talents, on Tuesday through Saturday evenings in an intimate setting. A half-liter of beer starts at 6 DM ($3.55).

Open: Tues–Sat at 9pm; music begins at 10pm. **S-Bahn:** Savignyplatz.

Admission: Usually 15 DM ($8.85), more for big names. Student discounts available.

Eierschale, Rankestrasse 1, Charlottenburg. ☎ 882 53 05.

Conveniently situated just off the Ku'Damm across the street from the Gedächtniskirche, this popular music house/bar offers live music nightly beginning at 8:30 or 9pm, primarily traditional jazz and blues. With outdoor sidewalk seating in the summer, it's also a good place to come for breakfast, especially on Sunday, when there's live music all day long. It charges 4.90 DM ($2.90) for a beer when there isn't a band and 6.30 DM ($3.70) when there is.

Open: Sun–Thurs 8pm–2am, Fri–Sat 8pm–4am. **U-Bahn:** Kurfürstendamm.

Admission: 4 DM ($2.35) when there's live music, which goes toward the first drink.

Ewige Lampe, Niebuhrstrasse 11a (entrance on Leibnizstrasse), Charlottenburg. ☎ 324 39 18.

This small and popular jazz bar features bands primarily from the United States, Germany, and Holland and can get pretty crowded. Either buy your ticket in advance or get there early. A large beer costs 6 DM ($3.55); a glass of wine starts at 7.50 DM ($4.40).

Open: Wed–Sun 8pm–2am; music begins at 9pm. **S-Bahn:** Savignyplatz.

Admission: 10 ($5.90), more for big names.

Loft, Nollendorfplatz 5, Schöneberg. ☎ 216 10 20.

Located in the massive art deco building that also houses the Metropol disco/concert hall, the Loft serves as a smaller arena for everything from punk rock and experimental music to rhythm and blues, with concerts held two to four times a week. Musicians come from around the world, including many bands from the United States and the

United Kingdom. If there's an opening act as well, the band is likely to be one of Berlin's own. **U-Bahn:** Nollendorfplatz.

Admission: 15–20 DM ($8.85–$11.80), depending on the group.

Quasimodo, Kantstrasse 12a. ☎ **312 80 86.**

Situated in the basement of a small building dwarfed by the adjacent Theater des Westens, Quasimodo features contemporary jazz and rock groups and is ranked as one of the best places in town to hear live music. Check *Checkpoint Berlin, tip,* or *zitty* for concert information.

Open: Nightly at 9pm; performances begin around 10pm. Upstairs cafe, nightly at 5pm. **U-Bahn:** Bahnhof Zoologischer Garten.

Admission: 10–25 DM ($5.90–$14.75), depending on the band.

Dance Clubs & Discos

Big Eden, Kurfürstendamm 202, Charlottenburg. ☎ **882 61 20.**

Right on the Ku'damm, Big Eden has been around seemingly forever. Opened in 1968, the disco proudly displays photographs of celebrities who have passed through its doors in the years that followed, including Klaus Kinski, Roman Polanski, Telly Savalas, and a very young-looking Paul McCartney. Those days when the Big Eden was the hottest thing in town have long gone, but it still attracts young visitors of every nationality. Teenagers crowd the dance floor until midnight; after they catch the last subway home, an older generation of revelers in their 20s through 40s takes over. In addition to a large dance floor, the place also has pool tables and video games. It maintains a strict front-door policy: No one admitted who even looks drunk. Note that drink prices are rather stiff, with beer starting at around 8 DM ($4.70) after 10pm. Before 10pm, a beer is only 5 DM ($2.95).

Open: Sun–Thurs 8pm–4am, Fri–Sat 8pm–7am. **U-Bahn:** Uhlandstrasse.

Admission: Sun–Thurs free; Fri–Sat 9 DM ($5.30), which includes a ticket good for 2 DM ($1.20) worth of drinks; Unaccompanied women admitted free.

Café Keese, Bismarckstrasse 108 ☎ **312 91 11.**

This place is a Berlin institution, and a unique one at that. For in contrast to most dance halls, it's the women who ask the men to dance here (except for the hourly "Men's Choice," when the green light goes on). Seating 700, the place is popular with the middle-aged set, though some of the curious include visitors in their 30s and 40s. If the place looks like it's straight out of the 1960s, that's because it is. It opened in 1966, a sister to one that's been in operation in Hamburg since 1948, and both claim that in the past 40-some years more than 95,000 couples have met on their dance floors and married. Who knows, maybe this will be your lucky night. No jeans or tennis shoes are allowed; most men are in coats and ties, and women are dressed up. Café Keese features a live band most evenings. If you're over 30, you'll probably get a kick out of this place, about a 15-minute walk north of the Ku'Damm. A beer here costs 8 DM ($4.70).

Open: Mon–Thurs 8pm–3am, Fri–Sat 8pm–4am, Sun 4pm–1am. **U-Bahn:** Ernst-Reuter-Platz.

Admission: Free, but there's an obligatory minimum drink charge of 8 DM ($4.70) Sun–Thurs, 16 DM ($9.45) Fri–Sat.

⭐ **Clärchen's Ballhaus,** Auguststrasse 24–25, Berlin-Mitte. ☎ 282 92 95.

In prewar Berlin, neighborhood dance halls were as common as the neighborhood pub, a place for couples to dance away their cares. Miraculously, this one still survives, straight out of the pages of history. Founded in 1913 by Clärchen and presently run by her grandson, this modest and casual dance hall is popular with middle and older generations, both married and single. A live band serenades those on the dance floor, and on Wednesdays it's the women who do the asking.

Open: Tues–Wed and Fri–Sat 7:30pm until management decides to close. **S-Bahn:** Oranienburger Strasse. **U-Bahn:** Rosenthaler Platz.

Admission: Tues 4.60 DM ($2.70); Wed and Fri–Sat 6.40 DM ($3.75).

Far Out, Kurfürstendamm 156, Charlottenburg. ☎ 3200 07 10.

Catering to a slightly older and more sophisticated crowd than Big Eden (see above), this disco is modern, spacious, clean, and laid-back, featuring rock from the 1970s and '80s. If you want to see it at its roaring best, don't even think about showing up before midnight. It's located toward the western end of the Ku'damm, on the side street between Ciao Ciao restaurant and the Schaubühne am Lehniner Platz theater. Beer starts at 5 DM ($2.95).

Open: Tues–Thurs and Sun 10pm–4am, Fri–Sat 10pm–6am. **U-Bahn:** Adenauerplatz.

Admission: Tues–Thurs and Sun 5 DM ($2.95); Fri–Sat 10 DM ($5.90).

First, Joachimstaler Strasse 26, Charlottenburg. ☎ 882 26 86.

The name says it all—First considers itself number one in Berlin as the disco for the city's well-heeled yuppie and business crowd. The music ranges from pop and disco tunes to jazz and swing. A small place not far from the Ku'Damm, it has a long drink menu and even accepts credit cards.

Open: Wed–Sun 11pm–5am. **U-Bahn:** Kurfürstendamm. **Admission:** Free.

Metropol, Nollendorfplatz 5. ☎ 216 41 22.

Housed in a colossal, striking art deco building converted from a former theater, for several years now the Metropol has managed to remain on top as one of the most popular and innovative establishments on the Berlin scene, due in part to the many diversions it offers (including a laser show). On weekends it's strictly a disco with three dance floors and eight bars; during the week it features live concerts with bands from around the world. In addition, a separate and smaller arena called the Loft presents live concerts two to four times a week. The disco crowd tends to be people in their 20s.

Open: Disco, Fri–Sat 9pm–6am; concert box office, Mon–Fri 11am–3pm and 3:30–6pm. **U-Bahn:** Nollendorfplatz.
Admission: Disco cover charge 10 DM ($5.90).

3   The Bar Scene

Before setting out for one of Berlin's many bars, there are a couple of things you should know. First of all, absolutely the worst thing you can do in a German *Kneipe*, or bar, is to sit at a table marked *Stammtisch*—it's reserved for privileged regulars. In addition, it's considered bad manners to drink without raising your glass to your fellow drinkers (the clinking was thought to scare away bad spirits in medieval times). Unless otherwise stated, there is no cover charge or admission to the following bars. *Prost!*

Pubs & Bars

ON OR NEAR THE KU'DAMM

Aschinger, Kurfürstendamm 26. ☎ 882 55 58.

A microbrewery, this basement establishment is one of the most civilized places on the Ku'damm to go for a beer. Sporting vaulted cellar rooms, dark-wood paneling, and subdued lighting, it offers a full range of self-made brews—from a light, thirst-quenching Pilsner to a dark, heavy Bock beer. In summer there's sidewalk seating. For those with appetites, there's even an *Imbiss*-style counter with an array of German food, including various Würste, Boulette, Leberkäse, pork dishes, and daily specials. A fifth-liter of beer—served in such small mugs to keep the beer as fresh as possible—is 2.80 DM ($1.65).

Open: Sun–Thurs 11am–1am, Friday–Sat 11am–2am. **U-Bahn:** Kurfürstendamm.

Ax Bax, Leibnizstrasse 34. ☎ 313 85 94.

For a 30-something Berliner out on the town, Ax Bax is likely to be on the agenda. Everyone who's anyone puts in an appearance at this popular watering hole, including writers and personalities in the film industry, and the average age of customers here is a comfortable 35 to 40. Founded by a transplant from Vienna, this combination restaurant/bar offers a changing buffet of Viennese specialties, which may include a meat-and-vegetable strudel, Viennese salad, or marinated beef. Early in the evening people come to eat; after 10pm they come for the more serious business of drinking, though food is served until a late 1am. It's located a few minutes' walk west of Savignyplatz, off Kantstrasse.

Open: Daily 6pm–1am. **S-Bahn:** Savignyplatz.

IMPRESSIONS

> *Public courtesans are more numerous here than in any town in Europe. . . . They appear openly at windows in the day time, beckon to passengers as they walk in the . . . streets, and ply for employment in any way they please, without disturbance from the magistrate.*
> —John Moore, 1779

Café Bleibtreu, Bleibtreustrasse 45. ☎ 881 47 56.

This is one of my favorite cafés, day or night. I like the atmosphere, the clientele, and the background music. One of the first so-called cafe/bars to open in 1972, it has a warm, pleasant feel to it, with plants, ceiling fans, and large front windows. A half-liter of beer costs 4.90 DM ($2.90). This place is popular with a 30-ish crowd and serves breakfast until 2pm.

Open: Sun–Thurs 9:30am–1am, Fri–Sat 9:30am–2:30am. **S-Bahn:** Savignyplatz.

Cour Carrée, Savignyplatz 5. ☎ 312 52 38.

There's nothing special about this place except that it occupies a prime spot on Savignyplatz and offers outdoor seating beneath a canopy of spreading vines. Come in the summertime, and watch the world go by. A food menu lists French and international dishes.

Open: Daily noon–2am. **S-Bahn:** Savignyplatz.

Dicke Wirtin, Carmerstrasse 9. ☎ 312 49 52.

The days when this was the hottest bar around have long passed, but it still has a faithful and devoted clientele. I've never been here in the wee hours of the night, but judging from the serious beer drinkers who are already here by early evening, things can only get rowdier. Named after the rather large barmaid who used to run the place, it's an old-style German pub and is known for its stews costing 4.50 DM ($2.65) a bowl. A half-liter of beer is a very reasonable 4.20 DM ($2.45). It's located just off Savignyplatz.

Open: Daily noon–4am. **S-Bahn:** Savignyplatz.

Diener, Grolmanstrasse 47. ☎ 881 53 29.

This is a typical German *Kneipe,* or bar, except for the fact that it's been here for decades and is named after a former champion boxer named Franz Diener. Filling the walls are photographs of famous people who have dropped in, including theater and film stars. Otherwise it's an unpretentious-looking place, the service is friendly, and it serves German soups and snacks.

Open: Daily 6pm–1am. **S-Bahn and U-Bahn:** Savignyplatz and Uhlandstrasse.

Extra Dry, Pariser Strasse 3. ☎ 885 22 06.

This cafe *for women only* is certainly one of the best of its kind in Berlin. Clean, modern, and nicely furnished, it maintains a strict policy against alcoholic drinks, offering instead milkshakes, fruit cocktails, and such light snacks as quiche, soups, and sandwiches. It serves as a meeting place for various women's groups, including those involving battered women and women who have been drug-dependent and need a clean environment in which to socialize. It's also a good place for women traveling alone or tired of the usual bar scene— somewhere to simply sit and write letters if that's what you feel like doing. It's located within a 15-minute walk south of the Ku'damm or one stop by subway.

Open: Tues–Thurs noon–11pm, Fri noon–midnight, Sat 11am–midnight, Sun 11am–11pm. **U-Bahn:** Spichernstrasse.

Hard Rock Café, Meinekestrasse 21. ☎ 884 62-0.

You know Berlin is in when a Hard Rock Café moves to town. Opened in 1992, this world-wide chain features the usual rock 'n' roll memorabilia, T-shirts for sale, hamburgers, and beer, which costs 4.90 DM ($2.90) a half-liter. It's located just south of the Ku'damm.

Open: Daily noon–1am. **U-Bahn:** Uhland or Kurfürstendamm.

Ku'dorf, Joachimstaler Strasse 15. ☎ 883 66 66.

Located in a basement, the Ku'Dorf is a sprawling underground "village" that consists of several "lanes" lined with one tiny bar after another. In fact, there are 18 bars here, each decorated in a different theme, so customers simply walk around until they find one that fits their fancy. At one end of the village is a disco. Note, however, that every single person in the Ku'Dorf is likely to be a tourist, perhaps because the place is so conveniently located, and it was packed during my last visit. If you want to be among Berliners, go someplace else. A half-liter of beer is the same everywhere, 7.50 DM ($4.40) and there's an admission charge of 5 DM ($2.95).

Open: Tues–Thurs 8pm–1am, Fri–Saturday 8pm–5am. **U-Bahn:** Kurfürstendamm.

New York, Olivaer Platz 15. ☎ 883 62 58.

Casual yet trendy, this is one of the "in" places for people in their 20s and 30s. Even in the middle of the day people hang out here, read the newspaper, eat American food, and shoot pool, making it a good place to go if you're in search of a drink in the afternoon. Resembling a cafe by day, after midnight it looks more like a bar; breakfast is served from 2am on Friday and Saturday. It's located on a square south of the Ku'Damm near Adenauerplatz.

Open: Sun–Thurs 9:30am–2am, Fri–Sat 9:30am–4am. **U-Bahn:** Adenauerplatz.

Schwarzes Café, Kantstrasse 148. ☎ 313 80 38.

This cafe's trademark is its unconventionality, with some of the strangest hours in town. *Schwarz* means "black," and true to its name, its front room is painted black. If you find black rooms depressing, head upstairs to a more bright and cheerful surrounding, where only the furniture is black. Breakfasts are a specialty, available anytime and ranging from 8.50 DM ($5) for a continental to 15.50 DM ($9.15) for the works. Schwarzes also has a large selection of coffees, including concoctions with alcohol and ice cream.

Open: Wed–Mon 24 hrs, Tues 5:30pm–3am. **S-Bahn and U-Bahn:** Savignyplatz and Uhlandstrasse.

Times Bar, in the Savoy Hotel, Fasanenstrasse 9–10. ☎ 31 10 30.

A great place for a quiet drink, this hotel bar is also convenient if you're visiting the nearby Theater des Westens. A small wood-paneled room, it offers a selection of international newspapers for its customers to leisurely peruse, including the *Financial Times, English Times, International Herald Tribune,* and *USA Today.*

Open: Daily 5pm–1am. **U-Bahn:** Bahnhof Zoologischer Garten or Kurfürstendamm.

Wirtshaus Wuppke, Schlüterstrasse 21. ☎ **313 81 62.**

This is a plain and unrefined worker's neighborhood pub, and although most people come just to drink, there are daily specials written on a blackboard, including hearty stews and salads. For entertainment, there's a pinball machine. The owner, Harold, speaks English.

Open: Summer, daily 9am–3am; winter, daily noon–3am.
S-Bahn: Savignyplatz.

Wirtshaus Zum Löwen, Hardenbergstrasse 29. ☎ **262 10 20.**

This beer hall recalls those in Munich and even serves Bavarian beer, Löwenbräu. There's outdoor seating in summer, but even in winter you can drink inside and still pretend you're in a beer garden—the interior is ingeniously constructed to resemble a tree-filled Bavarian plaza. As with most beer halls, hearty platters of German food are also available, and there's live music beginning at 7pm. A half-liter of beer costs 5.90 DM ($3.45) during the day and 6.90 DM ($4.05) at night. It's located northwest of the Gedächtniskirche, in the direction of Bahnhof Zoo.

Open: Summer, Sun–Thurs 10am–midnight, Fri–Sat 10am–2am; Winter, Sun–Thurs 11am–midnight, Fri–Sat 11am–2am.
U-Bahn: Kurfürstendamm or Bahnhof Zoologischer Garten.

Zillemarkt, Bleibtreustrasse 48a. ☎ **881 70 40.**

On the same street as Café Bleibtreu, this pleasant and airy establishment is named after an antiques-and-curios market that used to take place here. The building goes back to the turn of the century and features a brick-and-cement floor, grillwork, and plants. In summer, there's a garden out back with outdoor seating. It serves breakfast until a late 4pm.

Open: daily 9am–1am. **S-Bahn:** Savignyplatz.

Zwiebelfisch, Savignyplatz 7–8. ☎ **312 73 63.**

An oldtimer, the Zwiebelfisch has been around for more than 20 years and still enjoys great popularity. Because it stays open later than the other bars in the area, this is where everyone ends up. It can be at its most crowded at 4am.

Open: Daily noon–6am. **S-Bahn:** Savignyplatz.

Near Wilmersdorfer Strasse

Wilhelm Hoeck, Wilmersdorfer Strasse 149. ☎ **341 31 10.**

If you find yourself on Wilmersdorfer Strasse after a hard day's shopping, reward yourself with a drink here. You'll find two doors at this address. The door on the left leads to a simple family-style restaurant; the one on the right leads to the bar, which has been around since 1892. The decor features old wooden beer barrels against one wall, as well as long-ago photographs that illustrate the history of the place. If you're hungry, a menu offers home-cooked dishes "from Grandmother's kitchen," including Kasseler Braten (smoked pork chops) with cabbage and potatoes, Schnitzel with vegetables and potatoes, and fried liver with apples, onions, and potatoes; most platters are priced between 9 and 15 DM ($5.30 and $8.85). A half-liter of beer is 4.50 DM ($2.65).

Open: Mon–Sat 8am–midnight. **U-Bahn:** Bismarckstrasse.

Near Nollendorfplatz

Bar Am Lützowplatz, Lützowplatz 7. ☎ **262 68 07.**

This is one of Berlin's most unique settings for a bar—it's long and narrow like a tunnel, stretching back more than 150 feet and featuring a 50-foot-long bar and minimalist lighting. Designed by architect Jurgen Sawade, who also did the nearby Hotel Grand Esplanade, this upscale bar attracts a well-groomed business set, including those who wish to be seen, and can be so crowded it's hard to get a foot in the door, especially during the 5–9pm happy hour when drinks are half price.

Open: Daily 3pm–5am (from 5pm in winter). **U-Bahn:** Nollendorfplatz. **Bus:** 100, 119, or 129.

Harry's New York Bar, in the Hotel Grand Esplanade, Lützowufer 15. ☎ **26 10 11** or 254 78 821.

Harry's New York Bar first opened in Paris in 1911 and gained fame as the favorite watering hole of F. Scott Fitzgerald, Ernest Hemingway, and Gertrude Stein. Berlin's rendition is as popular as its Paris namesake and offers a varied cocktail and spirits menu. Very sophisticated with its red-leather sofas and incredibly long bar (emphasized by slick back lighting), it attracts visiting business professionals from around the world. There's live piano jazz music every night except Sunday after 8pm, and everything is under the watchful eyes of all the U.S. presidents, whose portraits line one entire wall.

Open: Daily noon–1am or later, often to 3am. **U-Bahn:** Nollendorfplatz. **Bus:** 100, 119, 192.

Café Sidney, Winterfeldstrasse 40. ☎ **216 52 53.**

This modern and breezy cafe/bar stands on a square called Winterfeldplatz, famous for its morning market on Wednesdays and Saturdays. Breakfast is always available, and there are two pool tables.

Open: Daily 9am–4am. **U-Bahn:** Nollendorfplatz.

Slumberland, Winterfeldplatz. ☎ **216 53 49.**

Everyone seems to drop by here after visiting the Saturday market on Winterfeldplatz. But Slumberland is at its most crowded in the very late hours, after other bars have closed down. It plays African, soul, jazz, Caribbean, reggae, and calypso music, and even has a real sand floor—along with fake banana trees and palms—to set the mood.

Open: Sun–Fri 8pm–4am, Sat 11am–6pm and 9pm–5am. **U-Bahn:** Nollendorfplatz.

Café Swing, Nollendorfplatz 3–4. ☎ **216 61 37.**

Popular with a young and slightly radical crowd, the Swing is about as informal and casual as you can get. A bit run-down, it offers outdoor seating in summer, and on Saturday evenings there's free live music from 1am.

Open: Daily 10:30am–4am. **U-Bahn:** Nollendorfplatz.

In Kreuzberg

Café Fontane, Fontanepromenade 1. ☎ **691 33 45.**

This modern and trendy bar features split-level seating, palm trees, a billiard table, a large window facade, and an outdoor terrace. It's a great place from which to watch the sun set over the treetops of the park across the street. It's also a good place for breakfast (served anytime) in fine weather.

Open: Sun–Thurs 9am–4am, Fri–Sat 9am–5am. **U-Bahn:** Südstern.

Leydicke, Mansteinstrasse 4. ☎ **216 29 73.**

Opened in 1877, this is one of Berlin's oldest drinking institutions, evident from its antique bar and shelves, wainscot, and ceiling. It even makes and sells its own wines and liqueurs, produced from fruit brought in from western Germany. Wine by the glass starts at 6 DM ($3.55).

Open: Mon–Fri 5pm–midnight, Sat 2pm–midnight, Sun 6pm–midnight. **S-Bahn and U-Bahn:** Yorckstrasse. **Bus:** 119 from the Ku'damm to Mansteinstrasse stop.

Madonna, Wiener Strasse 22. ☎ **611 69 43.**

Though Oranienburger Strasse in Berlin-Mitte has stolen the spotlight for outrageousness, Kreuzberg has long been a center of Berlin's avant-garde and alternative nightlift scene. Madonna is one of its standbys, familiar to anyone in the know about Berlin's bar scene. Although singer Madonna may first come to mind, its namesake is actually the other Madonna, present in several religious statues decorating the place, along with fake stained-glass windows. If you want to look like everyone else here, wear denim or leather.

Open: Sun–Thursday 11am–3am, Friday–Saturday 11am–4am. **U-Bahn:** Görlitzer Bahnhof. **Bus:** 129.

Rampenlicht, Körtestrasse 33. ☎ **692 13 01.**

Housed in an older building typical of Kreuzberg, Rampenlicht has an artsy, sophisticated atmosphere, with black wainscoting, black chairs, and the sparse decoration only of plants. In summer there's outdoor seating on the sidewalk. Breakfast is served until 4pm.

Open: Daily 9am–2am. **U-Bahn:** Südstern.

Café Wunderbar, Körtestrasse 38. ☎ **692 11 20.**

This is the most casual watering hole in the Südstern area of bars. It's simple and pleasant with blue-and-yellow walls, a window facade with a view of a towering church, sidewalk tables, a pool table, and a collection of German newspapers and magazines.

Open: Daily 11am–3am. **U-Bahn:** Südstern.

In Berlin-Mitte (Eastern Berlin)

Eastern Berlin is changing rapidly, with more and more restaurants, bars, and entertainment facilities opening daily. You may, therefore, wish to do a little scouting on your own, since new bars will probably spring up after this book's press time.

Bar am Pfauenauge, in the Grand Hotel, Friedrichstrasse 158–164. ☎ 232 70.

This elegant bar is probably the most sophisticated in all eastern Berlin. Located up on the first floor of the Grand Hotel, it can be reached via a magnificent sweeping staircase. There's live music in the evenings.

Open: Daily 3pm–3am. **U-Bahn:** Französische Strasse. **S-Bahn and U-Bahn:** Friedrichstrasse.

Georg Brau, Spreeufer 4. ☎ 242 42 44 or 242 34 15.

Located on the banks of the Spree in the heart of the renovated Nikolai Quarter not far from Alexanderplatz, this microbrewery features spacious indoor seating, but even better are the outdoor tables right beside the river. A great place for a beer on a fine summer's day (especially on Saturday and Sunday from 10am to 1pm, when there's live music and half-price beer), it serves its brew only in small fifth-liter glasses to keep it at its freshest, priced at 2.80 DM ($1.65). If that's too much of a bother, you can order the one-meter-long Georg-Pils, a long board with 12 small glasses of beer for 28 DM ($16.50). A limited menu lists such Berlin specialties as Kasslerbraten, Grillhaxen, Boulette, Sülze, and Eisbein, all served with side dishes.

Open: Summer, daily 10am–midnight; winter, Mon–Fri noon–midnight, Sat–Sunday 10am–midnight. **U-Bahn:** Alexanderplatz or Klosterstrasse.

Silberstein, Oranienburger Strasse 27. ☎ 28 12 095.

This is the trendiest, hippest, and most sophisticated bar on Oranienburger Strasse, located in the shadows of the newly renovated synagogue. It's decorated in minimalist style, with a bare floor, modern art on the walls, and high-backed chairs that are artsy but slightly uncomfortable. If you like them, though, you can buy them—everything in the bar is for sale, including the tables and artwork. And don't be surprised by the enterprise you see on Oranienburger Strasse itself—it's a popular strip for prostitutes.

Open: Mon–Friday 4pm–4am, Sat–Sunday noon–4am. **S-Bahn:** Oranienburger Strasse.

Tacheles, Oranienburger Strasse 53–54. ☎ 282 31 30.

This place is so alternative that for several years it didn't have a telephone or a sign outside its door and didn't seem likely to make it through another year. No wonder: The building itself is a bombed-out department store, still missing glass in its windows and lacking heat and famous for its extraordinary state of disrepair. In 1990 it was taken over by squatting artists who have slowly transformed it into studio/gallery/living space. On the ground floor is a cafe, while

IMPRESSIONS

A student at twenty takes easily to anything, even to Berlin.
—Henry Addams, 1906

in the basement is a disco open only on weekends. There's also a small cinema on a top floor and art openings. A bizarre place, straight out of *Star Wars*. A half-liter of beer starts at 4.40 DM ($2.60); admission to the disco is 5 to 10 DM ($2.95 to $5.90).

Open: Bar, daily 10am–5am; disco, 11pm–5am. **S-Bahn:** Oranienburger Strasse.

T.G.I. Fridays, Karl-Liebknecht-Strasse 5. ☎ 2382 79 60.

Germany, great for beer, wine, and spirits, has always been a disaster when it comes to well-made cocktails. Hopefully, the 1994 debut of this popular American chain is a taste of things to come. It offers more than 400 mindboggling concoctions, as well as an eclectic mix of American cuisine ranging from potato skins and burgers to fajitas and blackened Cajun chicken. Even better, it's conveniently located just a stone's throw from Museumsinsel, on the banks of the Spree River, with outdoor seating.

Open: Daily noon–midnight. **S-Bahn:** Alexanderplatz or Hackescher Markt. **Bus:** 100 to Spandauer Strasse.

Zum Nussbaum, Propstrasse. ☎ 0171 33 04182.

A reconstruction of a famous inn built in 1571 but destroyed during World War II, Zum Nussbaum is a tiny, pleasant, and cozy place in the Nikolai Quarter, with wood-paneled walls and minuscule rooms. There are a few tables outside, where you have a view of the Nikolaikirche (St. Nicholas's Church), after which the quarter was named.

Open: Daily noon–2am. **U-Bahn:** Alexanderplatz or Klosterstrasse.

Gay & Lesbian Bars

Andreas Kneipe, Ansbacher Strasse 29. ☎ 218 32 57.

This well-known gay bar has been here more than a quarter of a century, popular for both its location just off Wittenbergplatz and its laid-back atmosphere where almost anyone—including women and straight couples—can feel comfortable among the mixed clientele.

Open: Daily 11am–4am. **U-Bahn:** Wittenbergplatz.

Hafen, Motzstrasse 19. ☎ 214 11 18 or 211 41 18.

This well-known hangout is simply decorated with plastic flowers at the bar, a ship hanging from the ceiling (Hafen translates as "harbor"), candles, and a red light burning softly in the back of the small one-room bar. At its best late at night.

Open: Daily 9pm to whenever the bartender decides to close. **U-Bahn:** Nollendorfplatz.

Tom's Bar, at the corner of Motzstrasse and Eisenacher Strasse. ☎ 213 45 20.

Around the corner from Hafen (see above), this bar attracts men from their 20s to 40s. Pictures of men adorn the walls, a glass display case advertising a leather shop sits against one wall, and pornographic films are shown on a large screen in the back room. In the basement is a "contact" room.

Open: Daily 10pm–6am. **U-Bahn:** Nollendorfplatz.

Beer Gardens

Loretta's Garden, Lietzenburgerstrasse 89. ☎ **882 33 54.**

Situated just a short walk south of the Ku'damm in the heart of the city, this huge beer garden seats about 6,000 people under a spread of trees. You fetch your own beer here, with half-liter mugs costing about 6.50 DM ($3.85). Stalls sell snacks and food ranging from barbecued chicken to sausages.

Open: Apr to late Sept, daily 10am–1am. **U-Bahn:** Uhlandstrasse.

Luise, Königin-Luise-Strasse 40. ☎ **832 84 87.**

Located in Dahlem not far from the area's many museums, Luise is a popular watering hole with several hundred seats outdoors. In addition to half-liter mugs of beer selling for 5.50 DM ($3.25), it also offers Weissbier, a wheat beer.

Open: In good weather, 10am–1am. **U-Bahn:** Dahlem-Dorf.

4 More Entertainment

Films

An escape to the movies costs about 10 DM ($5.90) in Berlin. On Wednesdays, however, many movie theaters offer discounted tickets for 7 DM ($4.15). You won't have any trouble finding a cinema showing the latest movies from Hollywood—except they're likely to be dubbed in German. Berlin's main cinematic attraction lies in its "Off-Ku'damm" cinemas, those specializing in film classics and in new releases by independent German and international filmmakers. Check *Checkpoint Berlin, tip,* or *zitty* for listings of current films. (*OF*) means that the film is in the original language; (*OmU*), that it's in the original language with German subtitles. The following are well-known cinemas.

Arsenal, Welserstrasse 25. ☎ **218 68 48.**

The original Off-Ku'damm cinema, since the 1970s it has been paving the way for alternative programming, retrospectives, series, and experimental and avant-garde films from around the world, usually in their original language. **U-Bahn:** Victoria-Luise-Platz.

Tickets: 10 DM ($5.90).

Kino Zeughaus, Deutsches Historisches Museum, Unter den Linden 2. ☎ **215 02-0.**

If you understand German, this theater in the German Historical Museum is the best place to see the German classics, retrospectives, and rarely shown films. Foreign films are also shown, usually in their original language. **Bus:** 100.

Tickets: 4 DM ($2.35) for matinees (free for those paying museum admission), 5 DM ($2.95) for evening shows.

Odeon, Hauptstrasse 116. ☎ **781 5667.**

This is the place to go if you want to see the latest Hollywood flick, since it specializes in recent English-language releases. **U-Bahn:** Innsbrucker Platz.

Tickets: 10 DM ($5.90).

Casinos

If you wish to try your luck at the gambling tables, head toward the Europa-Center on Budapester Strasse, where you'll find the **Spielbank Berlin** (☎ **250 08 90**). Since opening in 1975, it has witnessed an average of 1,000 guests a day, who come to play French and American roulette, blackjack, baccarat, and the one-arm bandits. Admission is 5 DM ($2.95), and a coat and tie are required of men in the winter. The Spielbank Berlin is open daily from 3pm to 3am, and the nearest U-Bahn stations are Kurfürstendamm and Bahnhof Zoologisher Garten, both just a couple of minutes away.

There's another casino located on the 37th floor of the **Forum Hotel Berlin** on Alexanderplatz in eastern Berlin. **Note:** Identification is required for entry into any German casino—bring your passport.

10

Easy Excursions from Berlin

IF TIME ALLOWS FOR ONLY ONE EXCURSION OUTSIDE BERLIN, HEAD STRAIGHT for Potsdam and Frederick the Great's palace of Sanssouci. In summertime, another great destination is the Spreewald, where you can hike or take a boat trip through a unique landscape of waterways.

1 Potsdam

15 miles SW of Berlin

GETTING THERE   You can catch the S-Bahn 3 or 7 at several major stations in central Berlin—including Alexanderplatz, Bahnhof Zoologischer Garten, and Charlottenburg—and ride it all the way to Potsdam Stadt station for the price of a normal single ticket, which is 3.50 DM ($2.05). Since Potsdam is included in Greater Berlin's transportation network, 24-hour and weekly tickets are also valid throughout Potsdam.

From Potsdam Stadt station, it's a good 40- to 50-minute walk to Schloss Sanssouci; it isn't as bad as it sounds because you'll pass along Brandenburger Strasse, a pedestrian street running through Potsdam's quaint Altstadt (Old Town). An alternative is to board tram no. 91 or 96 from the bridge in front of the station and take it to Luisenplatz, from which the palace is a 10-minute walk. In addition, bus no. A1 departs infrequently from Potsdam Stadt and travels to Schloss Sanssouci and Neues Palais, charging its own fare.

After visiting Schloss Sanssouci and Neues Palais, you can return to Potsdam Stadt by boarding bus no. 695 and taking it back to Luisenplatz, transferring there to tram no. 91 or 96. Alternatively, you can walk from Neues Palais to the Wildpark station in about eight minutes and take the local train to Potsdam Stadt.

ESSENTIALS • Information   To get visitor information, you should contact **Potsdam-Information,** Friedrich-Ebert-Strasse 5 (☎ **0331/21100**), located in the heart of the city about 10-minutes' walk from Potsdam Stadt station. It's open in summer Monday through Friday from 9am to 8pm and Saturday and Sunday from 9am to 6pm. In winter, hours are Monday through Friday from 10am to 6pm and Saturday and Sunday from 11am to 3pm.

For information on Schloss Sanssouci, including guided-tour schedules, you should call or drop by Sanssouci-Information (☎ **0331/969 41 85**), located in the palace and open daily from 9am to 5pm (to 4pm in winter).

Situated only 15 miles southwest of Berlin, Potsdam was once Germany's most important baroque town, serving both as a garrison and as the residence of Prussia's kings and royal families throughout the 18th and 19th centuries. It was from here that Frederick the Great built his empire. And to rule more ably, he built the delightful rococo Schloss Sanssouci, where he could escape on occasion to maintain his sanity. Although much of Potsdam was destroyed during World War II, his palace still stands, surrounded by a 750-acre estate containing several other magnificent structures, including

Potsdam

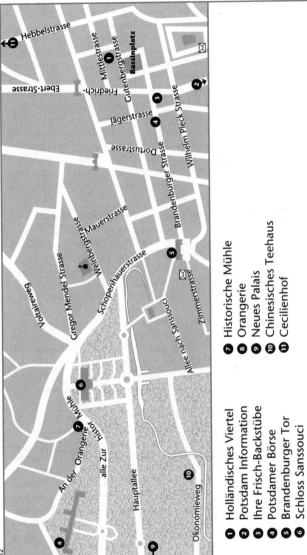

Legend:

1. Holländisches Viertel
2. Potsdam Information
3. Ihre Frisch-Backstübe
4. Potsdamer Börse
5. Brandenburger Tor
6. Schloss Sanssouci
7. Historische Mühle
8. Orangerie
9. Neues Palais
10. Chinesisches Teehaus
11. Cecilienhof

Church ✚   Post Office ⊠   Information ❶

Neues Palais. History enthusiasts will also want to visit Cecilienhof, site of the 1945 Potsdam Conference that sealed Germany's fate.

What to See & Do

The best way to see Potsdam is via your own two feet, so wear comfortable walking shoes. Start with a stroll through the **Holländisches Viertel** (Dutch Quarter), located about a 15-minute walk north of

Potsdam Stadt station, between Friedrich-Ebert-Strasse and Hebbelstrasse. The 134 homes of gabled brick, built in the mid-1700s for settlers from the Low Countries, represent the largest concentration of Dutch-style homes outside Holland; they are slowly being renovated. Nearby is **Brandenburger Strasse,** a quaint pedestrian shopping lane lined with shops and cafes housed in beautifully restored buildings with ornate facades. It leads straight through the **Altstadt** (Old Town). At the western end of Brandenburger Strasse is Luisenplatz, where you'll find a large stone portal, Potsdam's own Brandenburger Tor. From here, Allee nach Sanssouci leads to the royal estate. This is the most dramatic way to approach Schloss Sanssouci, since your first view of it includes six grassy terraces with the palace perched on top. From Schloss Sanssouci, you can reach Neues Palais by walking through the wonderful surrounding park in approximately 20 minutes.

★ **Schloss Sanssouci and Park,** Zur historischen Mühle.
☎ **0331/96 94-190.**

Although Potsdam was first mentioned in documents in 993 and became the second residence of the Great Elector of Brandenburg in 1660, it was under Friedrich Wilhelm I that the city blossomed into a garrison town. Credited with building the great Prussian army, Friedrich Wilhelm I was succeeded by a rather reluctant son, Friedrich II, who first tried to shirk his responsibilities by fleeing to England with his friend Lieutenant von Kette. They were caught and tried as deserters, and Friedrich was forced to witness the beheading of his friend (some said lover) as punishment. Friedrich II thereafter conformed to his father's wishes, married, and became the third king of Prussia, more popularly known as Friedrich der Grosse (Frederick the Great). He doubled the size of the Prussian army and went on to make Prussia the greatest military power on the Continent.

It was Frederick the Great who built much of Sanssouci as we know it today, in part to satisfy his artistic and intellectual passions. For instead of being able to devote himself fully to literature and to issues of the Enlightenment, as he would have liked, Frederick became involved in one war after another, including the Silesian Wars and the Seven Years' War. He retreated to Sanssouci to meditate, pursue philosophy, and forget the worries of life; in fact, *sans souci* means "without worry." Among the guests who came to Sanssouci was Voltaire, the great French philosopher. He stayed in Potsdam for three years, during which time he and the king spent many an evening together.

Schloss Sanssouci (Sanssouci Palace), the summer residence of Frederick the Great, was designed by Georg von Knobelsdorff in the 1740s according to plans drawn up by the king himself. Although it looks comparatively modest and ordinary if approached from the main road and entrance, it is breathtaking viewed from the park on the other side. For the palace sits atop six grassy terraces, cut into the side of a hill like steps in a pyramid. The terraces were once vineyards and seem to overwhelm the much smaller one-story palace. It's only after you've climbed the staircases leading up through the terraces that the cheerful and airy palace finally reveals itself, like a surprise package.

Frederick the Great must have liked wine, because the motifs of grapes and wine are carried from the vineyards into the palace itself. Note the figures supporting the roof facing the vineyards—they look a bit tipsy, as though they've just indulged in the fruits of the vine. Inside are statues of Bacchus, god of wine, as well as pictures and reliefs of grapes, vines, and people enjoying themselves.

Yet Frederick led a rather austere life, preferring to sleep in a soldier's camp bed rather than a royal bed. Even the Festival Hall is modestly small, noted for its inlaid marble floor in the pattern of a vineyard. The Concert Room is exquisite—a stucco ceiling in the pattern of a spider web gives the illusion that the room is so light and airy, it's held together with fragile strands. In this room is also Frederick the Great's flute, preserved in a glass case. A devoted and enthusiastic musician and patron of the arts, the Prussian king even found the time to compose 120 flute compositions.

The Voltaire Room boasts hand-carved wooden reliefs of birds, flowers, and fruit painted in bright yellows, blues, reds, and other colors, as well as a chandelier with delicate porcelain and brass flowers.

Schloss Sanssouci is open only for guided tours, which are conducted exclusively in German (hopefully this will change someday). Since the tours fill up quickly, especially on weekends and during the summer, try to get here before noon on a weekday. Tours leave every 20 minutes and last 40 minutes. If you can't get into the palace, don't despair; I personally think the exterior, viewed from the back below the vineyard terraces, is the most important thing to see. If you're worried about getting into the palace, however, and wish to have a tour in English, you're better off joining an organized sightseeing tour from Berlin (see "Organized Tours" in Chapter 6 for a list of companies offering trips to Potsdam). The disadvantage of the tours, however, is that they don't allow you time to explore Potsdam on your own. An alternative would be to join an organized tour and then remain in Potsdam, finding your own way back to Berlin.

Be sure to walk through the grounds of **Sanssouci Park.** It's huge, containing a wide range of gardens, ponds, streams, and statues of Greek and mythological figures. There are, for example, the Dutch, Sicilian, and Nordic gardens, as well as the Östlicher Lustgarten (Eastern Pleasure Garden) and Westlicher Lustgarden (Western Pleasure Garden). In the Östlicher Lustgarten you'll find the **Bildergalerie** (Picture Gallery), built between 1755 and 1763 to house Frederick the Great's collection. It still contains works by Italian Renaissance, Dutch, and Flemish old masters.

The **Orangerie,** located in the Westlicher Lustgarten and reached via pathways through the Sicilian and Nordic gardens, was built in Italian Renaissance style to house tropical plants, later being turned into rather elaborate guest accommodations. Here, too, is the Chinesisches Teehaus (Chinese Teahouse), constructed in the shape of a clover and featuring gilded statues of mandarins.

Admission: 8 DM ($4.70) adults; 4 DM ($2.35) students, children, and senior citizens. Sanssouci Park grounds are free.

Open: Apr–Sept, daily 9am–5pm; Oct, Feb, Mar, daily 9am–4pm; Nov–Jan, daily 9am–3pm. **Closed:** First and third Mon of every month. **Bus:** A1 or 695.

Neues Palais, Sanssouci Park. ☎ 0331/97 31 43.

The largest building in Sanssouci Park, Neues Palais is about a 20- to 30-minute walk west of Schloss Sanssouci. It was built 20 years after Schloss Sanssouci as a show of Prussian strength following the devastation of the Seven Years' War and served as a summer residence of the royal family. In fact, Wilhelm II, Germany's last kaiser, used it as his summer residence right until 1918, his last year in power. In contrast to the light-hearted architectural charms of Schloss Sanssouci, Neues Palais is grave and solemn. It contains a marbled and grandiose festival hall, royal apartments, and a charming theater (which, unfortunately, is not open to the public except during concerts). Look for the most famous painting in Neues Palais—Franz Krüger's *Parade Unter den Linden* from 1837.

If you find yourself waiting for the start of a tour or you're in need of refreshment, try the Schloss Cafe in Neues Palais (closed Mondays and Tuesdays in winter). A coffee shop, it is located in the former living quarters of a marquis and features a rococo room with murals, chandeliers, and gilded woodwork.

From October through May, Neues Palais can be viewed only on guided tours, conducted in German and lasting approximately one hour. From May to September, the palace can be viewed either by guided tour or by walking through on your own.

Admission: Without guided tour, 6 DM ($3.55) adults, 3 DM ($1.75) students, children, and senior citizens; with guided tour, 8 DM ($4.70) and 4 DM ($2.35), respectively.

Open: Apr–Sept, daily 9am–5pm; Oct, Feb, and Mar, daily 9am–4pm; Nov–Jan, daily 9am–3pm. **Closed:** Second and fourth Mon of every month. **Bus:** A1 or 695.

Cecilienhof, Neuer Garten. ☎ 03733/0331/96 94-245.

The Neuer Garten (New Garden) was laid out at the end of the 18th century, alongside Lake Heiligensee. It's the home of Cecilienhof, Potsdam's newest palace, which resembles an English country lodge more than a German palace. It was built between 1913 and 1916 in mock-Tudor style by Kaiser Wilhelm II and served as a royal residence of the last German crown prince and his wife, Cecilie, until the end of World War II. Its 176 rooms now contain a museum, a hotel, and a restaurant. It also boasts 55 chimneys, each unique.

Cecilienhof gained everlasting fame in 1945 when it served as headquarters for the Potsdam Conference. It was here that Truman, Stalin, and Churchill (and later Atlee) met to discuss the disarmament and future of a divided Germany. There's a museum with explanations in English showing the conference room and the round table where the Big Three sat. The table, by the way, was made in Moscow specifically for the conferences.

Admission: 4 DM ($2.35) adults; 3 DM ($1.75) students, children, and senior citizens.

Open: Daily 9am–5pm. **Closed:** Second and fourth Mon of every month. **Bus:** 695.

Where to Dine

MODERATE

Schlossrestaurant, in the Hotel Schloss Cecilienhof, Neuer Garten. ☎ 3705 108.

Cuisine: GERMAN. **Reservations:** Recommended weekends. **Bus:** 695.

Prices: Soups and appetizers 10–22 DM ($5.90–$13); main courses 27–43 DM ($15.95–$25.35). AE, DC, MC, V.

Open: Daily 11:30am–11pm.

Located in Cecilienhof, Potsdam's newest palace, built in the style of an English country lodge and site of the 1945 Potsdam Conference, this hotel restaurant is rather solemnly decorated, befitting the building's historic significance. A dark-paneled drawing room with red-upholstered chairs and red-velvet curtains pulled back to reveal a peaceful garden, it looks like it hasn't changed much through the decades—you can almost imagine Churchill sitting at one of the tables. Its limited menu, changing often, may offer such starters as a salad with asparagus or avocado or tomato soup with shrimp, with past entrees including salmon steak with Calvados, cauliflower, potatoes, and tomatoes; chicken breast filled with wild mushrooms and tomatoes and served with potato gratin and salad; and veal medallions in lemon-Port sauce served with tomato.

INEXPENSIVE

★ **Historische Mühle,** Zur Historischen Mühle. ☎ 231 10.

Cuisine: GERMAN. **Bus:** A1, 695.

Prices: Soups 2.50–5 DM ($1.45–2.95); main courses 10–20 DM ($5.90–$11.80). No credit cards.

Open: Apr–Oct, Tues–Sun 10am–6pm; Nov–Mar, Wed–Sun 10am–5pm.

A two-minute walk from Schloss Sanssouci, this place is my top choice for a meal in Potsdam. It's pleasantly situated in a forest of green near the Historic Mill. Start your meal with a bowl of Ukrainian Soljanka soup, followed by a main course of Schweinebraten with red cabbage and potatoes, Kasselbraten with Sauerkraut and potatoes, Hungarian Gulasch, Schnitzel with mushrooms and french fries, grilled chicken with vegetables and potatoes, Eisbein, or duck with red cabbage and potato dumpling. If the weather is warm, you may opt instead for a beer in the restaurant's large beer garden. An alternative is the Jagdhaus, an *Imbiss* on the grounds of the restaurant selling beer and Wurst, with outdoor seating.

Potsdamer Börse, Brandenburger Strasse 35–36. ☎ **225.**
Cuisine: GERMAN.
Prices: Soups and appetizers 5–14 DM ($2.95–$8.25); main courses 12–26 DM ($7.10–$15.35). AE, DC, MC, V.
Open: Daily 11am–10:30pm

Conveniently located a minute's walk from Potsdam's Bassinplatz bus center, in the heart of the Altstadt, this cozy family restaurant served as a distillery and wine merchant's shop in the 18th century and underwent renovation after reunification. Its menu includes the usual German fare, from Schnitzel to smoked pork and sausages. Adjoining the restaurant is the Marktklause, a German-style pub with even cheaper food and snacks, including Gulaschsuppe, Berliner Boulette, Wurst, and scrambled eggs.

BUDGET

Ihre Frisch-Backstübe, Brandenburger Strasse and Friedrich-Ebart Strasse. ☎ **48 21 15.**
Cuisine: SANDWICHES/SNACKS.
Prices: 3–6 DM ($1.75–$3.55). No credit cards.
Open: Mon–Fri 6:30am–6:30pm, Sat 6:30am–2pm, Sun 11am–2pm.

Located on Potsdam's main pedestrian lane, near Bassinplatz, this was one of the first West Berlin chains to move into Potsdam after reunification, and it has enjoyed a roaring success with both the locals and visitors. It's a bakery, offering freshly baked goods, sandwiches, baguettes, and daily specials ranging from pizza by the slice to noodle casseroles, all on display behind the cafeteria's glass case. There are chest-high tables where you can eat your goodies, or you can order take-out and eat at one of the benches on Brandenburger Strasse's pedestrian thoroughfare, where you can watch the parade of people pass by.

There's a smaller branch of Ihre Frisch-Backstübe about halfway down Brandenburger Strasse, in front of Horten department store. It's an outdoor *Imbiss* with the same hours.

---

2 The Spreewald

60 miles SE of Berlin

GETTING THERE • By Train   The most convenient gateway to the Spreewald is Lübbenau (Spreewald), which you can reach in about an hour by train from Berlin-Lichtenberg station. Trains depart every hour or so, with a round-trip ticket costing less than 30 DM ($17.70). If you don't want to hassle with trains, you can join an organized tour of the Spreewald, complete with boat ride (see "Organized Tours" in Chapter 6 for more information).

ESSENTIALS • Information   For information about the Spreewald and boat trips from Lübbenau, contact the **Lübbenau Spreewaldfremdenverkehrsverein** tourist information office at Ehm-Welk-Strasse 15, 03222 Lübbenau (☎ **03542/36 68**). Located in the center of Lübbenau, in summer it's open daily from 9am to 6pm; winter hours are Monday through Friday from 9am to 4pm.

• **Getting Around**   The best way to get around Lübbenau is via your own two feet; you can walk from the train station to the main boat harbor (Spreewald Hafen) in approximately 20 to 25 minutes. From the Lübbenau train station, walk straight out of the front exit of the station and continue walking straight on Poststrasse, a tree-lined street that leads into town in about 15 minutes. Poststrasse ends at the town's main square, where you'll find Lübbenau's tourist information office (look for the "i" sign). Stop at the tourist office for directions to the main harbor for boat rides. Otherwise, turn right onto Ehm-Welk-Strasse, passing the church and taking a right onto Dammstrasse, which leads to the Kahnabfahrstelle (boat departure place) and a footpath onward to Lehde. At the boat harbor, you'll find punts and boatmen to take you through the Spreewald.

Approximately 60 miles southeast of Berlin, the Spreewald forms one of middle Europe's most unique landscapes and is a nature reserve under to protection of UNESCO. This is where the Spree River spreads out into countless streams and ponds, a labyrinth of waterways through woodlands—a bayou. Little wonder that for decades it's been a lure for city dwellers, who come here for a ride in a hand-poled boat, the German version of the gondola.

Lübbenau first settled by Slavs in the 9th or 10th century and the starting point for most boat rides, lies in the upper Spreewald, which contains about 300 miles of tree-lined canals winding through a flat countryside of meadows. Almost none of the canals is open to motorized vehicles, with the result that even barges laden with vegetables bound for market are also hand-poled.

WHAT TO SEE & DO   The most popular thing to do in the Spreewald is to take a **boat ride** through this watery wonderland. If you understand German and get a gregarious gondolier, you'll probably be regaled with tales about the Spreewald and the people who live here. Most of the inhabitants of the Spreewald are Sorbs, an ethnic minority of swamp-dwelling Slavs who spoke their own language until World War II and are still proud of their traditions and culture. As you glide along the canals, you'll pass rounded haystacks as tall as houses, poplar, ash, and weeping willow trees, and log and brick farmhouses surrounded by neat gardens. Since boats are the only means of transportation through the Spreewald, there are fireboats instead of fire trucks, and even children are ferried to school by boat.

Boat trips are offered only in good weather, from April to the end of October, when boatmen gather at the landing in Lübbenau as early as 8:30am to wait for customers. If you wish to make a full day of it, try to arrive in Lübbenau by 10am. Boats can seat up to 20, but will leave for trips with as few as 8 on slow days. If there are fewer than 8, the price of the trip will be negotiated (prices are low to begin with, so the trip is still a bargain).

There are several routes, of varying lengths, from which to choose, with trips ranging from three to eight hours. One of the most popular is the three-hour trip to **Lehde,** a Venice-style village of thatched-roof brick houses along narrow roads, with roosters crowing, canals everywhere, and family boats pulled up beside homes picturesquely situated on small islands. If you wish, you can arrange for a one-hour stopover in Lehde, where you may wish to dine or perhaps visit Lehde's **Spreewald Freilandmuseum,** an open-air museum consisting of nine original farmsteads, buildings, furniture, and artifacts common to the people of the Spreewald region. The museum is open April to mid-October on Tuesday through Sunday from 9am to 5pm. Admission is 3 DM ($1.75) for adults, 2 DM ($1.20) for students and senior citizens, and 1 DM (60¢) for children.

The price for the three-hour boat ride to Lehde is 7.50 DM ($4.40) per adult and 4 DM per child. Other boat trips available include a 6¹/₂-hour trip to the village of **Leipe,** costing 13.50 DM ($7.95) for adults and 6 DM ($3.55) for children, and even an 8-hour trip through the **Spreewald** at 15.50 DM ($9.15) for adults and 6 DM ($3.55) for children. Remember: Get there early for an all-day trip; for the three-hour trip to Lehde, you should arrive at the boat harbor by 1 or 2pm at the latest.

In addition to taking one of the boat trips above, you can rent **paddleboats** if you want to strike out on your own. Two-seaters cost 3.50 DM ($2.05) per hour or 25 DM ($14.75) for the whole day.

If you'd rather stick to dry land or come in the off season, you can also **hike** through the Spreewald. True, many paths end abruptly at one of the hundreds of canals, but that shouldn't deter you. In fact, you can even hike to Lehde on your own, less than 1¹/₂ miles from Lübbenau. You'll find the pathway off Dammstrasse, just past the main boat harbor, beside the Café Zum Nussbaum (look for the small green sign that says LEHDE 2,0 KM). It's a mystical experience walking through this special bayou, as you pass small garden plots and the flora and fauna that make up the unique waterway.

Finally, if time permits, don't forget to visit Lübbenau's **Spreewald Museum** (☎ **2472**), a short walk from the boat harbor in the Schlosspark. Housed in a building dating from the mid-1700s, the museum's displays relate to the customs and traditions of the Sorbs and the history of the Spreewald, complete with various modes of transportation through the region; it's open daily from April to mid-October from 9am to 5pm. Admission is 3 DM ($1.75) for adults, 2 DM ($1.20) for students and senior citizens, and 1 DM (60¢) for children.

WHERE TO DINE   Your boatman will suggest cafes and restaurants in the villages you visit. In Lehde, for example, there's **Zum Fröhlichen Hecht,** which first opened in 1640 as the only inn in Lehde and was owned by the same family for many generations.

In Lübbenau, your best bet for a meal is **Zum Grünen Strand der Spree,** Dammstrasse 77 (☎ **2423**), next to the boat harbor with a large outdoor terrace. It was founded 100 years ago, and even at the turn of the century it was the leading inn beside the boat harbor. Its specialties are fish from the Spreewald, including carp, trout, and pike, prepared in a special Spreewald sauce. Other dishes include sausage with Sauerkraut and potatoes, pork medallions with curry sauce or hollandaise, and duck with red cabbage and potatoes. Entrees range from 8 DM ($4.70) to 22 DM ($13), and American Express, MasterCard, and Visa are accepted. It's open daily from 10am to 7pm.

Appendix

A Vocabulary

German is not a difficult language to learn, especially pronunciation. Unlike English or French, it contains no hidden surprises and everything is pronounced exactly as it's written—according, of course, to German rules. *Ei* is always pronounced as a long *i;* thus, *nein* (which means "no") is pronounced *nine*. A *w* is pronounced *v;* a *v* is pronounced as *f.* As for those two dots over vowels (called an umlaut or a diaresis), they signal a slight change in pronunciation.

Phrases

ENGLISH	GERMAN	PRONUNCIATION
Hello	Guten Tag	goo-ten tahk
Goodbye	Auf Wiedersehen	owf vee-der-zay-en
How are you?	Wie geht es Ihnen?	vee gayt ess ee-nen
Very well	Sehr gut	zayr goot
Please	Bitte	bit-tuh
Thank you	Danke schön	dahn-keh shern
Excuse me	Verzeihung	fehrt-sahy-oong
You're welcome	Bitte Gern geschehen	gehrn geshai'en bit-tuh
Yes	Ja	yah
No	Nein	nine
Mr./Mrs.	Herr/Frau	hehr/vrow
I don't understand	Ich verstehe nicht	eesh fer-steh-he nisht
I understand	Ich verstehe	eesh fer-steh-he
Where is . . . ?	Wo ist . . . ?	voh eest
the main train station	der Hauptbahnhof	deyr howpt-bahn-hohf
a hotel	ein Hotel	eye-n hotel
a restaurant	ein Restaurant	eye-n res-tow-rahng
the toilet	die Toilette	dee twah-let-tah
a bank	ein Bank	eye-n bahnk
a post office	ein Postamt	eye-n postahmt
the bus stop	die Bus haltestelle	dee bus haltestelle

English	German	Pronunciation
the tourist information office	das Verkehr-samt	dass fehr-kerr-samt
To the right	Nach rechts	nakh reshts
To the left	Nach links	nakh leenks
Straight ahead	Geradeaus	geh-rah-deh-ous
Ladies/Gentlemen	Damen/Herren	dahmen/hehren
How much does it cost?	Wieviel kostet es?	vee-feel kah-stet ess
Expensive	Teuer	toyer
Cheap	Billig	bil-lich
The check, please	Die Rechnung, bitte	dee rekh-noong, bit-tuh
I would like . . .	Ich möchte . . .	ikh mersh-ta
stamps	Briefmarken	breef-mahr-ken
to eat	essen	ess-en
a room	ein Zimmer	ain tzim-mer
for one night	für eine Nacht	feer ai-neh nakht
Breakfast	Frühstück	frew-stewk
Lunch	Mittagessen	mi-tahg-gess-en
Dinner	Abendessen	ah-bend-ess-en
Free (vacant)/ occupied	Frei/besetzt	Frahy/besets
When?	Wann?	vahn
Yesterday	Gestern	geh-stern
Today	Heute	hoy-tuh
Tomorrow	Morgen	more-gen
Sunday	Sonntag	zohn-tahk
Monday	Montag	mon-tahk
Tuesday	Dienstag	deen-stahk
Wednesday	Mittwoch	mitt-voch
Thursday	Donnerstag	donner-stahk
Friday	Freitag	frahy-tahk
Saturday	Samstag	zahmz-tahk

Numbers

0	Null (nool)	17	Siebzehn (zeeb-tzayn)
1	Eins (aintz)	18	Achtzehn (akh-tzayn)
2	Zwei (tzvai)	19	Neunzehn (noyn-tzayn)
3	Drei (dry)	20	Zwanzig (tzvahn-tzik)
4	Vier (feer)	25	Fünf-und-zwanzig
5	Fünf (fewnf)	30	Dreissig (dry-sik)
6	Sechs (zex)	40	Vierzig (feer-tzik)
7	Sieben (zee-ben)	50	Fünfzig (fewnf-tzik)
8	Acht (ahkht)	60	Sechzig (zex-tzik)
9	Neun (noyn)	70	Siebzig (zeeb-tzik)
10	Zehn (tzeyn)	80	Achtzig (akht-tzik)
11	Elf (ellf)	90	Neunzig (noyn-tzik)
12	Zwölf (tzvuhlf)	100	Hundert (hoon-dert)
13	Dreizehn (dry-tzayn)	101	Hunderteins (hoon-dert-ahyns)
14	Vierzehn (feer-tzayn)	200	Zweihundert (tzvai-hoon-dert)
15	Fünfzehn (fewnf-tzayn)	1,000	Ein tausend (ahyn-tau-zent)
16	Sechszehn (zex-tzayn)		

B Menu Savvy

CONDIMENTS & TABLE ITEMS

Brot Bread
Brötchen Rolls
Butter Butter
Eis Ice
Essig Vinegar
Pfeffer Pepper
Salz Salt
Senf Mustard
Zitrone Lemon
Zucker Sugar

SOUPS

Erbsensuppe Pea soup
Gemüsesuppe Vegetable soup
Gulaschsuppe Spicy Hungarian beef soup
Hühnerbrühe Chicken soup
Kartoffelsuppe Potato soup
Leberknödelsuppe Beef-liver dumpling soup
Linsensuppe Lentil soup
Nudelsuppe Noodle soup
Ochsenschwanzsuppe Oxtail soup
Schildkrötensuppe Turtle soup

SALADS

Gemischter Salat Mixed salad
Gurkensalat Cucumber salad
Kopfsalat/Grünsalat Lettuce salad
Tomatensalat Tomato salad

SANDWICHES

Käsebrot Cheese sandwich
Schinkenbrot Ham sandwich
Wurstbrot Sausage sandwich

EGGS

Bauernfrühstück "Farmer Breakfast" Scrambled eggs
    with ham or sausage, onion, and potatoes
Eier in Schale Boiled eggs
Mit Speck With bacon
Rühreier Scrambled eggs
Spiegeleier Fried eggs
Verlorene Eier Poached eggs
Soleier Pickled eggs

VEGETABLES & SIDE DISHES

Artischocken Artichokes
Blumenkohl Cauliflower
Bohnen Beans

Bratkartoffeln Fried potatoes
Erbsen Peas
Grüne Bohnen Green beans
Gurken Cucumbers
Karotten Carrots
Kartoffeln Potatoes
Kartoffelsalat Potato salad
Knödel Dumplings
Kohl Cabbage
Reis Rice
Rote Rüben Red beets
Rotkraut Red cabbage
Salat Lettuce
Salzkartoffeln Boiled potatoes
Sauerkraut Sauerkraut
Spargel Asparagus
Spinat Spinach
Tomaten Tomatoes

MEATS

Aufschnitt Cold cuts
Bockwurst Berlin sausage
Boulette Cold meatball
Brathuhn Roast chicken
Bratwurst Grilled sausage
Eisbein Pig's knuckle
Ente Duck
Gans Goose
Gefüllte Kalbsbrust Stuffed breast of veal
Hammel Mutton
Hirn Brains
Kalb Veal
Kaltes Geflügel Cold poultry
Kassler Rippchen/Rippenspeer Pork chops
Lamm Lamb
Leber Liver
Leberkäs German meatloaf
Nieren Kidneys
Ragout Stew
Rinderbraten Roast beef
Rindfleisch Beef
Sauerbraten Marinated beef
Schinken Ham
Schlachteplatte Platter of blood sausage, liverwurst, kidneys, and boiled pork
Schweinebraten/Schweinsbraten Roast pork
Schweinshaxen Grilled knuckle of pork
Spanferkel Suckling pig
Sülze Jellied meat
Tafelspitz Boiled beef with vegetables

Taube Pigeon
Truthahn Turkey
Weiner Schnitzel Veal cutlet
Wurst (plural Würste) Sausage

FISH

Aal Eel
Brathering Grilled herring
Forelle Trout
Hecht Pike
Karpfen Carp
Krebs Crawfish
Lachs Salmon
Makrele Mackerel
Schellfisch Haddock
Seezunge Sole

DESSERTS

Blatterteiggebäck Puff pastry
Bratapfel Baked apple
Eis Ice cream
Käse Cheese
Kompott Stewed fruit
Obstkuchen Fruit tart
Obstsalat Fruit salad
Pfannkuchen Sugared pancakes
Pflaumenkompott Stewed plums
Rote Grütze Cooked fruits with vanilla sauce
Teegebäck Tea cakes
Torten Pastries

FRUITS

Ananas Pineapple
Apfel Apple
Apfelsinen Oranges
Bananen Bananas
Birnen Pears
Erdbeeren Strawberries
Kirschen Cherries
Pfirsiche Peaches
Weintrauben Grapes
Zitronen Lemons

BEVERAGES

Bier Beer
Berliner Weisse Draft wheat beer with a shot of raspberry or green woodruff syrup
Bier vom Fass Draft beer
Bock Bier Dark and rich beer
Ein Dunkles A dark beer
Ein Helles A light beer
Pils Light and bitter beer

Milch Milk
Saft Juice
Apfelsaft Apple juice
Sahne Cream
Schokolade Chocolate
Eine Tasse Kaffee A cup of coffee
Eine Tasse Tee A cup of tea
Tomatensaft Tomato juice
Wasser Water
Wein Wine
Sekt Champagne
Rotwein Red wine
Weisswein White wine
Weinbrand Brandy

Glossary of Terms

Altstadt old town (traditional part of town or city)
Apotheke pharmacy
Art deco stylized art and architecture in the 1920s and 1930s
Art nouveau highly decorative form of art, objects, and interior
   design with twining, flowing motifs, late 19th and early 20th
   centuries; *also see* Jurgendstil
Bahn railway, train
Bahnhof railway station
Hauptbahnhof main railway station
Stadtbahn (S-Bahn) commuter railway
Untergrundbahn (U-Bahn) subway, city underground
   system
Baroque ornate, decorated style of architecture in the 18th
   century, characterized by use of elaborate ornamentation and
   gilding. Also applied to art of the same period
Bauhaus style of functional design for architecture and objects,
   originating in early 20th century in Germany
Biedermeier solid, bourgeois style of furniture design and
   interior decoration in the middle 19th century
Der Blaue Reiter group of nonfigurative painters, founded in
   Munich in 1911 by Franz Marc and Wassily Kandinsky
Die Brücke group of avant-garde expressionist painters
   originating in Dresden around 1905
Burg fortified castle
Dom cathedral
Drogerie shop selling cosmetics and sundries
Expressionism style of painting in early 20th-century Germany
   characterized by strong use of form and color
Gothic medieval architectural-style characterized by arches,
   soaring spaces, and ribbed vaulting, lasting into the 16th
   century; also applied to painting of the period
Jugendstil German form of art nouveau

Kaufhaus department store
Kirche church
Kneipe bar, mostly for drinking
Konditorei cafe for coffee and pastries
Kunst art
Oper opera/opera house
Rathaus town or city hall
Schauspielhaus theater for plays
Schloss palace, castle
Secession modernist movement in German art that strongly
    disavowed expressionism
Stadt town, city
Tor gateway
Turm tower
Verkehrsamt tourist office
Zitadelle fortress

 The Metric System

LENGTH

1 millimeter (mm)	=	.04 inches (*or* less than $^1/_{16}$ in.)
1 centimeter (cm)	=	.39 inches (*or* just under $^1/_2$ in.)
1 meter (m)	=	39 inches (*or* about 1.1 yards)
1 kilometer (km)	=	.62 miles (*or* about $^2/_3$ of a mile)

To convert kilometers to miles, multiply the number of kilometers by .62. Also use to convert kilometers per hour (kmph) to miles per hour (m.p.h.)

To convert miles to kilometers, multiply the number of miles by 1.61. Also use to convert speeds from m.p.h. to kmph.

CAPACITY

1 liter (l)	=	33.92 fluid ounces	=	2.1 pints
	=	1.06 quarts	=	.26 U.S. gallons
1 Imperial gallon	=	1.2 U.S. gallons		

To convert liters to U.S. gallons, multiply the number of liters by .26.

To convert U.S. gallons to liters, multiply the number of gallons by 3.79.

To convert Imperial gallons to U.S. gallons, multiply the number of Imperial gallons by 1.2.

To convert U.S. gallons to Imperial gallons, multiply the number of U.S. gallons by .83.

WEIGHT

1 gram (g)	=	.035 ounces (or about a paperclip's weight)
1 kilogram (kg)	=	35.2 ounces
	=	2.2 pounds
1 metric ton	=	2,205 pounds = 1.1 short ton

To convert kilograms to pounds, multiply the number of kilograms by 2.2.

To convert pounds to kilograms, multiply the pounds by .45.

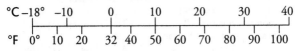

TEMPERATURE

To convert degrees Celsius to degrees Fahrenheit, multiply °C by 9, divide by 5, and add 32 (example: 20°C × 9/5 + 32 = 68°F).

To convert degrees Fahrenheit to degrees Celsius, subtract 32 from °F, multiply by 5, then divide by 9 (example: 85°F − 32 × 9/5 = 29.4°C).

Index

Now Save Money On All Your Travels By Joining FROMMER'S™ TRAVEL BOOK CLUB The World's Best Travel Guides At Membership Prices!

Frommer's Travel Book Club is your ticket to successful travel! Open up a world of travel information and simplify your travel planning when you join ranks with thousands of value-conscious travelers who are members of the *Frommer's Travel Book Club*. Join today and you'll be entitled to all the privileges that come from belonging to the club that offers you travel guides for less to more than 100 destinations worldwide. **Annual membership is only $25.00 (U.S.) or $35.00 (Canada/Foreign).**

The Advantages of Membership:

1. Your choice of **three free** books (any **two** *Frommer's Comprehensive Guides, Frommer's $-A-Day Guides, Frommer's Walking Tours* or *Frommer's Family Guides*—plus **one** *Frommer's City Guide, Frommer's City $-A-Day Guide* or *Frommer's Touring Guide*).
2. Your own subscription to the **TRIPS & TRAVEL** quarterly newsletter.
3. You're entitled to a **30% discount** on your order of any additional books offered by the club.
4. You're offered (at a small additional fee) our **Domestic Trip-Routing Kits.**

Our **Trips & Travel** quarterly newsletter offers practical information on the best buys in travel, the "hottest" vacation spots, the latest travel trends, world-class events and much, much more.

Our **Domestic Trip-Routing Kits** are available for any North American destination. We'll send you a detailed map highlighting the best route to take to your destination—you can request direct or scenic routes.

Here's all you have to do to join:

Send in your membership fee of $25.00 ($35.00 Canada/Foreign) with your name and address on the form below along with your selections as part of your membership package to the address listed below. Remember to check off your three free books.

If you would like to order additional books, please select the books you would like and send a check for the total amount (please add sales tax in the states noted below), plus $2.00 per book for shipping and handling ($3.00 Canada/Foreign) to the address listed below.

FROMMER'S TRAVEL BOOK CLUB
P.O. Box 473
Mt. Morris, IL 61054-0473.
(815) 734-1104

[ ] **YES!** I want to take advantage of this opportunity to join Frommer's Travel Book Club.

[ ] My check is enclosed. Dollar amount enclosed   *

(all payments in U.S. funds only)

Name _____

Address _____

City _____ State _____ Zip _____

All orders must be prepaid.

To ensure that all orders are processed efficiently, please apply sales tax in the following areas: CA, CT, FL, IL, IN, NJ, NY, PA, TN, WA and CANADA.

*With membership, shipping & handling will be paid by Frommer's Travel Book Club for the three free books you select as part of your membership. Please add $2.00 per book for shipping & handling for any additional books purchased ($3.00 Canada/Foreign).

Allow 4-6 weeks for delivery. Prices of books, membership fee, and publication dates are subject to change without notice. Orders are subject to acceptance and availability.

Please send me the books checked below:

FROMMER'S COMPREHENSIVE GUIDES

(Guides listing facilities from budget to deluxe,
with emphasis on the medium-priced)

	Retail Price	Code		Retail Price	Code
☐ Acapulco/Ixtapa/Taxco, 2nd Edition	$13.95	C157	☐ Jamaica/Barbados, 2nd Edition	$15.00	C149
☐ Alaska '94-'95	$17.00	C131	☐ Japan '94-'95	$19.00	C144
☐ Arizona '95 (Avail. 3/95)	$14.95	C166	☐ Maui, 1st Edition	$13.95	C153
☐ Australia '94-'95	$18.00	C147	☐ Nepal, 2nd Edition	$18.00	C126
☐ Austria, 6th Edition	$16.95	C162	☐ New England '95	$16.95	C165
☐ Bahamas '94-'95	$17.00	C121	☐ New Mexico, 3rd Edition (Avail. 3/95)	$14.95	C167
☐ Belgium/Holland/ Luxembourg '93-'94	$18.00	C106	☐ New York State, 4th Edition	$19.00	C133
☐ Bermuda '94-'95	$15.00	C122	☐ Northwest, 5th Edition	$17.00	C140
☐ Brazil, 3rd Edition	$20.00	C111	☐ Portugal '94-'95	$17.00	C141
☐ California '95	$16.95	C164	☐ Puerto Rico '95-'96	$14.00	C151
☐ Canada '94-'95	$19.00	C145	☐ Puerto Vallarta/ Manzanillo/ Guadalajara '94-'95	$14.00	C028
☐ Caribbean '95	$18.00	C148			
☐ Carolinas/Georgia, 2nd Edition	$17.00	C128	☐ Scandinavia, 16th Edition (Avail. 3/95)	$19.95	C169
☐ Colorado, 2nd Edition	$16.00	C143	☐ Scotland '94-'95	$17.00	C146
☐ Costa Rica '95	$13.95	C161	☐ South Pacific '94-'95	$20.00	C138
☐ Cruises '95-'96	$19.00	C150	☐ Spain, 16th Edition	$16.95	C163
☐ Delaware/Maryland '94-'95	$15.00	C136	☐ Switzerland/ Liechtenstein '94-'95	$19.00	C139
☐ England '95	$17.95	C159	☐ Thailand, 2nd Edition	$17.95	C154
☐ Florida '95	$18.00	C152	☐ U.S.A., 4th Edition	$18.95	C156
☐ France '94-'95	$20.00	C132	☐ Virgin Islands '94-'95	$13.00	C127
☐ Germany '95	$18.95	C158	☐ Virginia '94-'95	$14.00	C142
☐ Ireland, 1st Edition (Avail. 3/95)	$16.95	C168	☐ Yucatan, 2nd Edition	$13.95	C155
☐ Italy '95	$18.95	C160			

FROMMER'S $-A-DAY GUIDES

(Guides to low-cost tourist accommodations and facilities)

	Retail Price	Code		Retail Price	Code
☐ Australia on $45 '95-'96	$18.00	D122	☐ Israel on $45, 15th Edition	$16.95	D130
☐ Costa Rica/Guatemala/ Belize on $35, 3rd Edition	$15.95	D126	☐ Mexico on $45 '95	$16.95	D125
			☐ New York on $70 '94-'95	$16.00	D121
☐ Eastern Europe on $30, 5th Edition	$16.95	D129	☐ New Zealand on $45 '93-'94	$18.00	D103
☐ England on $60 '95	$17.95	D128			
☐ Europe on $50 '95	$17.95	D127	☐ South America on $40, 16th Edition	$18.95	D123
☐ Greece on $45 '93-'94	$19.00	D100			
☐ Hawaii on $75 '95	$16.95	D124	☐ Washington, D.C. on $50 '94-'95	$17.00	D120
☐ Ireland on $45 '94-'95	$17.00	D118			

FROMMER'S CITY $-A-DAY GUIDES

	Retail Price	Code		Retail Price	Code
☐ Berlin on $40 '94-'95	$12.00	D111	☐ Madrid on $50 '94-'95	$13.00	D119
☐ London on $45 '94-'95	$12.00	D114	☐ Paris on $45 '94-'95	$12.00	D117

FROMMER'S FAMILY GUIDES

	Retail Price	Code		Retail Price	Code
☐ California with Kids	$18.00	F100	☐ San Francisco with Kids	$17.00	F104
☐ Los Angeles with Kids	$17.00	F103	☐ Washington, D.C. with Kids	$17.00	F102
☐ New York City with Kids	$18.00	F101			

FROMMER'S CITY GUIDES

(Pocket-size guides to sightseeing and tourist
accommodations and facilities in all price ranges)

	Retail Price	Code		Retail Price	Code
☐ Amsterdam '93-'94	$13.00	S110	☐ Nashville/Memphis, 1st Edition	$13.00	S141
☐ Athens, 10th Edition (Avail. 3/95)	$12.95	S174	☐ New Orleans '95	$12.95	S148
☐ Atlanta '95	$12.95	S161	☐ New York '95	$12.95	S152
☐ Atlantic City/Cape May, 5th Edition	$13.00	S130	☐ Orlando '95	$13.00	S145
☐ Bangkok, 2nd Edition	$12.95	S147	☐ Paris '95	$12.95	S150
☐ Barcelona '93-'94	$13.00	S115	☐ Philadelphia, 8th Edition	$12.95	S167
☐ Berlin, 3rd Edition	$12.95	S162	☐ Prague '94-'95	$13.00	S143
☐ Boston '95	$12.95	S160	☐ Rome, 10th Edition	$12.95	S168
☐ Budapest, 1st Edition	$13.00	S139	☐ San Diego '95	$12.95	S158
☐ Chicago '95	$12.95	S169	☐ San Francisco '95	$12.95	S155
☐ Denver/Boulder/Colorado Springs, 3rd Edition	$12.95	S154	☐ Santa Fe/Taos/ Albuquerque '95	$12.95	S172
☐ Dublin, 2nd Edition	$12.95	S157	☐ Seattle/Portland '94-'95	$13.00	S137
☐ Hong Kong '94-'95	$13.00	S140	☐ St. Louis/Kansas City, 2nd Edition	$13.00	S127
☐ Honolulu/Oahu '95	$12.95	S151	☐ Sydney, 4th Edition	$12.95	S171
☐ Las Vegas '95	$12.95	S163	☐ Tampa/St. Petersburg, 3rd Edition	$13.00	S146
☐ London '95	$12.95	S156	☐ Tokyo '94-'95	$13.00	S144
☐ Los Angeles '95	$12.95	S164	☐ Toronto '95 (Avail. 3/95)	$12.95	S173
☐ Madrid/Costa del Sol, 2nd Edition	$12.95	S165	☐ Vancouver/Victoria '94-'95	$13.00	S142
☐ Mexico City, 1st Edition	$12.95	S170	☐ Washington, D.C. '95	$12.95	S153
☐ Miami '95-'96	$12.95	S149			
☐ Minneapolis/St. Paul, 4th Edition	$12.95	S159			
☐ Montreal/ Quebec City '95	$11.95	S166			

SPECIAL EDITIONS

	Retail Price	Code		Retail Price	Code
☐ Bed & Breakfast Southwest	$16.00	P100	☐ National Park Guide, 29th Edition	$17.00	P106
☐ Bed & Breakfast Great American Cities	$16.00	P104	☐ Where to Stay U.S.A., 11th Edition	$15.00	P102
☐ Caribbean Hideaways	$16.00	P103			

FROMMER'S WALKING TOURS

(With routes and detailed maps, these companion guides
point out the places and pleasures that make a city unique)

	Retail Price	Code		Retail Price	Code
☐ Berlin	$12.00	W100	☐ New York	$12.00	W102
☐ Chicago	$12.00	W107	☐ Paris	$12.00	W103
☐ England's Favorite Cities	$12.00	W108	☐ San Francisco	$12.00	W104
☐ London	$12.00	W101	☐ Washington, D.C.	$12.00	W105
☐ Montreal/Quebec City	$12.00	W106			

FROMMER'S TOURING GUIDES

(Color-illustrated guides that include walking tours,
cultural and historic sites, and practical information)

	Retail Price	Code		Retail Price	Code
☐ Amsterdam	$11.00	T001	☐ New York	$11.00	T008
☐ Barcelona	$14.00	T015	☐ Rome	$11.00	T010
☐ Brazil	$11.00	T003	☐ Scotland	$10.00	T011
☐ Hong Kong/Singapore/ Macau	$11.00	T006	☐ Sicily	$15.00	T017
			☐ Tokyo	$15.00	T016
☐ Kenya	$14.00	T018	☐ Turkey	$11.00	T013
☐ London	$13.00	T007	☐ Venice	$ 9.00	T014

Please note: If the availability of a book is several months away, we may have back issues of guides to that particular destination. Call customer service at (815) 734-1104.